MONSON
Free Library and Reading Room
ASSOCIATION

NO.   60484

RULES AND REGULATIONS

Assessed fines shall be paid by every person keeping Library materials beyond the specified time.

Every person who borrows Library materials shall be responsible for all loss or damage to same while they are out in his name.

All library materials shall be returned to the Library on the call of the Librarian or Directors.

General Laws of Mass., Chap. 266, Sec. 99

Whoever willfully and maliciously or wantonly and without cause writes upon, injures, defaces, tears or destroys a book, plate, picture, engraving or statute belonging to a law, town, city or other public library shall be punished by a fine of not less than five nor more than fifty dollars, or by imprisonment in the jail not exceeding six months.

CHELSEA HOUSE PUBLISHERS

Modern Critical Views

HENRY ADAMS
EDWARD ALBEE
A. R. AMMONS
MATTHEW ARNOLD
JOHN ASHBERY
W. H. AUDEN
JANE AUSTEN
JAMES BALDWIN
CHARLES BAUDELAIRE
SAMUEL BECKETT
SAUL BELLOW
THE BIBLE
ELIZABETH BISHOP
WILLIAM BLAKE
JORGE LUIS BORGES
ELIZABETH BOWEN
BERTOLT BRECHT
THE BRONTËS
ROBERT BROWNING
ANTHONY BURGESS
GEORGE GORDON, LORD BYRON
THOMAS CARLYLE
LEWIS CARROLL
WILLA CATHER
CERVANTES
GEOFFREY CHAUCER
KATE CHOPIN
SAMUEL TAYLOR COLERIDGE
JOSEPH CONRAD
CONTEMPORARY POETS
HART CRANE
STEPHEN CRANE
DANTE
CHARLES DICKENS
EMILY DICKINSON
JOHN DONNE & THE
  17th-CENTURY POETS
ELIZABETHAN DRAMATISTS
THEODORE DREISER
JOHN DRYDEN
GEORGE ELIOT
T. S. ELIOT
RALPH ELLISON
RALPH WALDO EMERSON
WILLIAM FAULKNER
HENRY FIELDING
F. SCOTT FITZGERALD
GUSTAVE FLAUBERT
E. M. FORSTER
SIGMUND FREUD
ROBERT FROST

ROBERT GRAVES
GRAHAM GREENE
THOMAS HARDY
NATHANIEL HAWTHORNE
WILLIAM HAZLITT
SEAMUS HEANEY
ERNEST HEMINGWAY
GEOFFREY HILL
FRIEDRICH HÖLDERLIN
HOMER
GERARD MANLEY HOPKINS
WILLIAM DEAN HOWELLS
ZORA NEALE HURSTON
HENRY JAMES
SAMUEL JOHNSON
BEN JONSON
JAMES JOYCE
FRANZ KAFKA
JOHN KEATS
RUDYARD KIPLING
D. H. LAWRENCE
JOHN LE CARRÉ
URSULA K. LE GUIN
DORIS LESSING
SINCLAIR LEWIS
ROBERT LOWELL
NORMAN MAILER
BERNARD MALAMUD
THOMAS MANN
CHRISTOPHER MARLOWE
CARSON MCCULLERS
HERMAN MELVILLE
JAMES MERRILL
ARTHUR MILLER
JOHN MILTON
EUGENIO MONTALE
MARIANNE MOORE
IRIS MURDOCH
VLADIMIR NABOKOV
JOYCE CAROL OATES
SEAN O'CASEY
FLANNERY O'CONNOR
EUGENE O'NEILL
GEORGE ORWELL
CYNTHIA OZICK
WALTER PATER
WALKER PERCY
HAROLD PINTER
PLATO
EDGAR ALLAN POE

POETS OF SENSIBILITY &
  THE SUBLIME
ALEXANDER POPE
KATHERINE ANNE PORTER
EZRA POUND
PRE-RAPHAELITE POETS
MARCEL PROUST
THOMAS PYNCHON
ARTHUR RIMBAUD
THEODORE ROETHKE
PHILIP ROTH
JOHN RUSKIN
J. D. SALINGER
GERSHOM SCHOLEM
WILLIAM SHAKESPEARE (3 vols.)
  HISTORIES & POEMS
  COMEDIES
  TRAGEDIES
GEORGE BERNARD SHAW
MARY WOLLSTONECRAFT SHELLEY
PERCY BYSSHE SHELLEY
EDMUND SPENSER
GERTRUDE STEIN
JOHN STEINBECK
LAURENCE STERNE
WALLACE STEVENS
TOM STOPPARD
JONATHAN SWIFT
ALFRED LORD TENNYSON
WILLIAM MAKEPEACE THACKERAY
HENRY DAVID THOREAU
LEO TOLSTOI
ANTHONY TROLLOPE
MARK TWAIN
JOHN UPDIKE
GORE VIDAL
VIRGIL
ROBERT PENN WARREN
EVELYN WAUGH
EUDORA WELTY
NATHANAEL WEST
EDITH WHARTON
WALT WHITMAN
OSCAR WILDE
TENNESSEE WILLIAMS
WILLIAM CARLOS WILLIAMS
THOMAS WOLFE
VIRGINIA WOOLF
WILLIAM WORDSWORTH
RICHARD WRIGHT
WILLIAM BUTLER YEATS

Further titles in preparation.

Modern Critical Views

HART CRANE

Modern Critical Views

HART CRANE

Edited with an introduction by

Harold Bloom

Sterling Professor of the Humanities
Yale University

1986
CHELSEA HOUSE PUBLISHERS
New York
New Haven   Philadelphia

60484

THE COVER:
Hart Crane, who loved Brooklyn Bridge, and conceived his epic of America in its image, is shown against the background of what he called its "harp and altar, of the fury fused." It was for him the great Whitmanian trope for poetic crossing, for the visionary point of transition between the American past and the uncertain national future.—H.B.

PROJECT EDITORS: Emily Bestler, James Uebbing
ASSOCIATE EDITOR: Maria Behan
EDITORIAL COORDINATOR: Karyn Gullen Browne
EDITORIAL STAFF: Laura Ludwig, Linda Grossman, Peter Childers
DESIGN: Susan Lusk

Cover illustration by Robin Peterson

Printed and bound in the United States of America

Library of Congress Cataloging in Publication Data

Hart Crane.
　　(Modern critical views)
　　Bibliography: p.
　　Includes index.
　　1. Crane, Hart, 1899–1932—Criticism and interpreta-
tion—Addresses, essays, lectures.　I. Bloom, Harold.
II. Series.
PS3505.R272Z675　1986　　811'.52　　85–7907
ISBN 0–87754–654–1

Chelsea House Publishers
Harold Steinberg, Chairman and Publisher
Susan Lusk, Vice President
A Division of Chelsea House Educational Communications, Inc.
133 Christopher Street, New York, NY 10014

Contents

Editor's Note

This volume gathers together a representative selection of the best criticism devoted to the poetry of Hart Crane. After my "Introduction," the essays are arranged in the chronological order of publication, from R. P. Blackmur's essay of 1935 to Lee Edelman's analysis of "Voyages," first published in this volume a half-century later. Blackmur's New Critical exegesis is printed here as the best instance of that school's judgment of Crane as a distinguished failure, a judgment that can be traced also in the writings on Crane by Allen Tate and Yvor Winters.

A juster approach is evidenced by Marius Bewley's careful reading of "The Broken Tower," and is carried on by Harvey Gross in his study of Crane's metric, and by Alan Trachtenberg in his analysis of the Brooklyn Bridge as Crane's prime symbol. The new view of *The Bridge* taken by Thomas A. Vogler is High Romantic, and is consonant with the major studies on Crane by Joseph Riddel, R. W. B. Lewis and Sherman Paul, all of whom relate Crane to the American Romantic tradition.

A more dialectical criticism is inaugurated by John T. Irwin's reading of Crane's tropes in a Freudian context, which can be contrasted with my antithetical reading of Crane's gnosis in the "Introduction." The essays by Donald Pease, Allen Grossman and Lee Edelman reflect in very different ways the influence of current advanced modes of criticism upon the reading of Crane.

Introduction

O Thou steeled Cognizance whose leap commits
The agile precincts of the lark's return. . . .

I remember reading these lines when I was ten years old, crouched over Crane's book in a Bronx library. They, and much else in the book, cathected me onto poetry, a conversion or investment fairly typical of many in my generation. I still have the volume of Crane that I persuaded my older sister to give me on my twelfth birthday, the first book I ever owned. Among my friends there are a few others who owned Crane before any other book. Growing up in the thirties, we were found by Crane's poetry, and though other poets followed (I went from Crane to Blake) the strength of first love still hovers whenever they, or I, read Crane.

The Marlovian rhetoric swept us in, but as with Marlowe himself the rhetoric was also a psychology and a knowing, rather than a knowledge, a knowing that precisely can be called a Gnosis, transcending the episte-mology of tropes. What the Australian poet Alec Hope, echoing Tambur-laine, perceptively called "The Argument of Arms" is as much Crane's knowing and language as it was Marlowe's. "Know ye not the argument of arms?" Tamburlaine calls out to his protesting generals before he stabs his own son to death for cowardice. As Hope expounds it, "the argument of arms" is poetic warfare, the agonistic interplay of the Sublime mode:

> There is no middle way and no compromise in such a world. Beauty is the rival of beauty as force of force, and only the supreme and perfect survives. Defeat, like victory, is total, absolute, final.

This is indeed Marlowe's knowing, and it would be pointless for a humanist critic to complain that such a vision is human-all-too-human. *Power* is the central poetic concept in Marlowe as it will be in Milton, and as it came to be in the American Milton, Emerson (a prose Milton, granted), and in Crane as a kind of American Marlowe. Hope rightly points to Hazlitt on *Coriolanus* as the proper theorist of the union of the Argument of Arms and the Argument of Poetry. Hazlitt also would not gain the approval of the natural supernaturalist kind of critical humanist:

> The principle of poetry is a very anti-leveling principle. It aims at effect,

it exists by contrast. It admits of no medium. It is everything by excess. It rises above the ordinary standard of sufferings and crimes.

But Crane is a prophet of American Orphism, of the Emersonian and Whitmanian Native Strain in our national literature. His poetic of power is therefore best caught by the American theorist proper:

> . . . though Fate is immense, so is Power, which is the other fact in the dual world, immense. If Fate follows and limits Power, Power attends and antagonizes Fate. We must respect Fate as natural history. For who and what is this criticism that pries into the matter? Man is not order of nature, sack and sack, belly and members, link in a chain, nor any ignominious baggage; but a stupendous antagonism, a dragging together of the poles of the Universe. . . .

This might be Melville, meditating upon his own Ahab, but of course it is the uncanny Sage of Concord, satirized by Melville as Plotinus Plinlimmon and as Confidence Man; yet the satire was uneasy. Crane is not very easy to satirize either, and like Shelley, with whom his affinities were deep, Crane goes on burying his critical undertakers. Whitman and Dickinson, Frost and Stevens all had time enough, but Crane, perhaps more gifted than any of them, was finished at an age when they had begun weakly or not at all. A Gnosis of man as a stupendous antagonism, Orphic and Promethean, needs time to work itself through, but time, reviled by all Gnostics with a particular vehemence, had its literal triumph over Crane. As with Shelley and Keats, we have a truncated canon, and yet, as with them, what we have is overwhelming. And what it overwhelms, amidst much else, is any privileging of understanding as an epistemological event, prior to being the catastrophe creation of an aesthetic and spiritual value.

I am concerned here with Crane's "religion" *as a poet* (not as a man, since that seems an inchoate mixture of a Christian Science background, an immersion in Ouspensky, and an all but Catholic yearning). But by poetic "religion" I mean American Orphism, the Emersonian or national religion of our poetry, which Crane inherited, quite directly, from his prime precursor Whitman. True precursors are always composite and imaginary, the son's changeling-fantasy of the father that his own poetry reinvents, and there is usually a near-contemporary agon, as well as a struggle with the fathering force of the past. The older contemporary antagonist and shaper for Crane was certainly Eliot, whose anti-Romantic polemic provoked in Crane an answering fury of High Romanticism, absurdly undervalued by Crane's critical contemporaries, but returning to its mainstream status in the generation that receives the recent abundance of poetic maturation in Ashbery, Merrill, Ammons, Hollander and others.

The governing deities of American Orphism, as of the ancient sort, are Eros or Phanes, Dionysus or Bacchus, and Ananke, the Necessity who appears as the maternal ocean in Whitman and Crane most overtly, but clearly and obsessively enough in Stevens also. Not so clear, though just as obsessive, must be our judgment upon Melville's representations of an Orphic Ananke in the great shroud of the sea. Melville's "that man should be a thing for immortal souls to sieve through!" is the apt epigraph of a crucial chapter on Greek Shamanism in E. R. Dodds's great book *The Greeks and the Irrational*. Dodds traced to Scythia the new Orphic religious pattern that credited man with an occult self of divine origin. This self was not the *psyche*, but the daemon; as Dodds says, "the function of the daemon is to be the carrier of man's potential divinity and actual guilt." Crane's daemon or occult self, like Whitman's, is the actual hero and victim of his own poetry. Crane as American Orpheus is an inevitable image, exploited already by writers as diverse as Yvor Winters in his elegy for Crane and Tennessee Williams in *Suddenly Last Summer*. The best of the Orphic hymns to Crane is the astonishing poem *Fish Food* of John Brooks Wheelwright, except that Crane wrote his own best Orphic elegy in "Atlantis," his close equivalent of Shelley's *Adonais*. But I narrow my subject here of Crane's "Orphism" down to its visionary epistemology or Gnosis. Crane's Eros, his Dionysus, above all his Whitmanian Ananke, remain to be explored, but in these remarks I concern myself only with Crane as "daemon," a potential divinity knowing simultaneously its achievement and its guilt.

The assumption of that daemon, or what the poets of Sensibility called "the incarnation of the Poetic Character," is the inner plot of many of the lyrics in *White Buildings*. The *kenosis* or ebbing-away of the daemon is the plot of the *Voyages* sequence, where the other Orphic deities reduce Crane to a "derelict and blinded guest" of his own vision, and where the "ocean rivers" churn up the Orphic heritage as a "splintered garland for the seer." Certainly the most ambitious of the daemonic incarnations is the sequence *For the Marriage of Faustus and Helen*, which is Crane at his most triumphantly Marlovian, but so much else is at play there that I turn to two lesser but perfect hymns of Orphic incarnation, *Repose of Rivers* and *Passage*.

Crane is a great master of transumptive allusion, of achieving poetic closure by a final trope that reverses or sometimes even transcends both his own lyric's dominant figurations and the poetic tradition's previous exploitations of these images. So, *Repose of Rivers* concludes:

> . . . There, beyond the dykes

> I heard wind flaking sapphire, like this summer,
> And willows could not hold more steady sound.

The poem's opening stanza gives a more complex version of that "steady sound" because the synaesthetic seeing/hearing of "that seething, steady leveling of the marshes" is both an irony and an oxymoron:

> The willows carried a slow sound,
> A sarabande the wind mowed on the mead.
> I could never remember
> That seething, steady leveling of the marshes
> Till age had brought me to the sea.

Crane is recalling his version of a Primal Scene of Instruction, a moment renewing itself discontinuously at scattered intervals, yet always for him a moment relating the inevitability of sexual orientation to the assumption of his poethood. The slow-and-steady dance of the wind on the marshes became a repressed memory until "age" as maturation brought the poet to the sea, central image of necessity in his poetry, and a wounding synecdoche here for an acceptance of one's particular fate as a poet. The repressed reveals itself as a grotesque sublimity, with the second stanza alluding to Melville's imagery in his story *The Encantadas:*

> Flags, weeds. And remembrance of steep alcoves
> Where cypresses shared the noon's
> Tyranny; they drew me into hades almost.
> And mammoth turtles climbing sulphur dreams
> Yielded, while sun-silt rippled them
> Asunder . . .

The seething, steady leveling of the mammoth turtles, their infernal love-death, is a kind of sarabande also. In climbing one another they climb dreams of self-immolation, where "yielded" means at once surrender to death and to one another. The terrible slowness of their love-making yields the frightening trope: "sun-silt rippled them / Asunder," where "asunder" is both the post-coition parting and the individual turtle death. Crane and D. H. Lawrence had in common as poets only their mutual devotion to Whitman, and it is instructive to contrast this stanza of *Repose of Rivers* with the Tortoise-series of Lawrence in *Birds, Beasts, and Flowers.* Lawrence's tortoises are crucified *into* sex, like Lawrence himself. Crane's Melvillean turtles are crucified *by* sex. But Crane tells a different story about himself: crucified *into* poetry and *by* poetry. The turtles are drawn into a sexual hades; Crane is *almost* drawn, with the phrase "hades almost" playing against "steep alcoves." Embowered by steep alcoves of cypresses, intensifying the dominant noon sun, Crane nearly yields to the sexual phantasmagoria of "flags, weeds," and the sound play alcoves/almost intensifies the narrowness of the escape from a primary sexuality, presumably an incestuous heterosexuality. This is the highly oblique burden of the extraordinary third stanza:

> How much I would have bartered! the black gorge
> And all the singular nestings in the hills
> Where beavers learn stitch and tooth.
> The pond I entered once and quickly fled—
> I remember now its singing willow rim.

What he would have bartered, indeed did barter, was nature for poetry. Where the second stanza was a *kenosis*, an emptying-out, of the Orphic self, this stanza is fresh influx, and what returns from repression is poetic apperception: "I remember now its singing willow rim," a line that reverberates greatly against the first and last lines of the entire poem. The surrendered Sublime here is a progressive triad of entities: the Wordsworthian Abyss of birth of "the black gorge"; "the singular nestings," instructive of work and of aggression; most memorably the pond, rimmed by singing willows, whose entrance actually marks the momentary daring of the representation of Oedipal trespass, or perhaps for Crane one should say "Orphic trespass."

If everything heretofore in *Repose of Rivers* has been bartered for the antithetical gift of Orpheus, what remains is to represent the actual passage into sexuality, and after that the poetic maturation that follows homosexual self-acceptance. Whether the vision here is of an actual city, or of a New Orleans of the mind, as at the end of the "River" section of *The Bridge*, the balance of pleasure and of pain is left ambiguous:

> And finally, in that memory all things nurse;
> After the city that I finally passed
> With scalding unguents spread and smoking darts
> The monsoon cut across the delta
> At gulf gates . . . There, beyond the dykes
>
> I heard wind flaking sapphire, like this summer,
> And willows could not hold more steady sound.

The third line of the stanza refers both to the pathos of the city and to Crane's own sexual initiation. But since "all things nurse" this memory, the emphasis must be upon breakthrough, upon the contrast between monsoon and the long-obliterated memory of sarabande-wind. "Like this summer," the fictive moment of the lyric's composition, the monsoon of final sexual alignment gave the gift of an achieved poethood, to hear wind synaesthetically, flaking sapphire, breaking up yet also distributing the Shelleyan azure of vision. In such a context, the final line massively gathers an Orphic confidence.

Yet every close reader of Crane learns to listen to the wind for evidences of *sparagmos*, of the Orphic breakup, as prevalent in Crane's winds as in Shelley's, or in Whitman's. I turn to *Passage*, *White Buildings*'s particular poem of Orphic disincarnation, where the rite of passage, the movement back to unfindable and fictive origins, is celebrated more memorably in the opening quatrain than anywhere else even in Crane, who is clearly the great modern poet of *thresholds*, in the sense definitively expounded in Angus Fletcher's forthcoming book of that title.

> Where the cedar leaf divides the sky
> I heard the sea.
> In sapphire arenas of the hills
> I was promised an improved infancy.

The Fletcherian *threshold* is a daemonic crossing or textual "image of voice," to use Wordsworth's crucial term. Such a chiasmus tends to hover where tropes collide in an epistemological wilderness. Is there a more outrageously American, Emersonian concept and phrase than "an improved infancy"? Crane presumably was not aware that *Passage* centered itself so directly at the Wordsworthian heart of the crisis poem, in direct competition with *Tintern Abbey* and the *Intimations of Immortality* ode. But the American version as established in the *Seadrift* poems of Whitman was model enough. Crane, inland far though he finds himself, hears the sea. The soft inland murmur promised Wordsworth so improved an infancy that it became an actual intimation of a more-than-poetic immortality. But for Whitman the secret of the murmuring he envied had to be listened for at the water-line. Crane quests for the same emblem that rewarded *Repose of Rivers*, but here the wind does not flake sapphire in the arenas of these inland hills, where the agon with the daemon, Whitman's dusky demon and brother, is to take place.

In Whitman's great elegy of Orphic disincarnation, *As I Ebb'd with the Ocean of Life*, the daemon comes to the poet in the shape of a sardonic phantom, "the real Me," and confronts Whitman, who may hold his book, *Leaves of Grass*, in hand, since the phantom is able to point to it:

> But that before all my arrogant poems the real Me stands yet untouch'd,
>   untold, altogether unreach'd,
> Withdrawn far, mocking me with mock-congratulatory signs and bows,
> With peals of distant ironical laughter at every word I have written,
> Pointing in silence to these songs, and then to the sand beneath.
> I perceive I have never really understood any thing, not a single object,
>   and that no man ever can,
> Nature here in sight of the sea taking advantage of me to dart upon
>   me and sting me,
> Because I have dared to open my mouth to sing at all.

In Crane's *Passage* the sulking poet, denied his promise, abandons memory in a ravine, and tries to identify himself with the wind; but it dies, and he is turned back and around to confront his mocking daemon:

> Touching an opening laurel, I found
> A thief beneath, my stolen book in hand.

It is deliberately ambiguous whether the real Me has stolen the book, or whether the book of Hart Crane itself is stolen property. Unlike the abashed Whitman, Crane is aggressive, and his phantom is lost in wonderment:

> "Why are you back here—smiling an iron coffin?"
> "To argue with the laurel," I replied:
> "Am justified in transience, fleeing
> Under the constant wonder of your eyes—."

But nature here, suddenly in sight of the sea, does take advantage of Crane to dart upon him and sting him, because he has dared to open his mouth to sing at all:

> He closed the book. And from the Ptolemies
> Sand troughed us in a glittering abyss.
> A serpent swam a vertex to the sun
> —On unpaced beaches learned its tongue and drummed.
> What fountains did I hear? what icy speeches?
> Memory, committed to the page, had broke.

The Ptolemies, alluded to here as though they were a galaxy rather than a dynasty, help establish the pyramid image for the serpent who touches its apex in the sun. The glittering abyss belongs both to time and the sun, and the serpent, drumming its tongue upon the beach where no Whitmanian bard paces, is weirdly prophetic of the imagery of Stevens's *The Auroras of Autumn*. The penultimate line glances obliquely at Coleridge's *Kubla Khan*, and the poem ends appropriately with the broken enchantment of memory, broken in the act of writing the poem. It is as though, point for point, *Passage* had undone *Repose of Rivers*.

The Bridge can be read as the same pattern of Orphic incarnation/disincarnation, with every Sublime or daemonic vision subsequently undone by an ebbing-out of poethood. That reading, though traditional, seems to me a weak misreading, inadequate to *The Bridge*'s strong misreadings of its precursors. Nietzsche and Pater, both of whom Crane had pondered, taught a subtler *askesis*, and *The Bridge* advances upon *White Buildings* (except for *Voyages*), by mounting a powerful scheme of transumption, of what Nietzsche called the poetic will's revenge against time and particularly against time's proclamation of belatedness: "It was." Crane shrewdly wrote, in 1918: "one may envy Nietzsche a little; think of being so elusive,—so mercurial, as to be first swallowed whole, then coughed up, and still remain a mystery!" But veteran readers of Crane learn to observe something like that when confronted by the majesty of *The Bridge* at its finest, as here in the final quatrains of the "Proem":

> Again the traffic lights that skim thy swift
> Unfractioned idiom, immaculate sigh of stars,
> Beading thy path—condense eternity:
> And we have seen night lifted in thine arms.
>
> Under thy shadow by the piers I waited;
> Only in darkness is thy shadow clear.
> The City's fiery parcels all undone,
> Already snow submerges an iron year . . .
>
> O Sleepless as the river under thee,
> Vaulting the sea, the prairies' dreaming sod,
> Unto us lowliest sometime sweep, descend
> And of the curveship lend a myth to God.

Crane in *White Buildings* is wholly Orphic, in that his concern is his relation, as poet, *to* his own vision, rather than *with* the content of poetic vision, to utilize a general distinction inaugurated by Northrop Frye, following after Ruskin. The peculiar power of *The Bridge* at its strongest, is that Crane succeeds in becoming what Pater and Nietzsche urged the future poet to be: an ascetic of the spirit, which is an accurate definition of a purified Gnosis. Directly before these three final quatrains of "To Brooklyn Bridge," Crane had saluted the bridge first as Orphic emblem, both harp and altar, but then as the threshold of the full triad of the Orphic destiny: Dionysus or prophet's pledge, Ananke or prayer of pariah, and Eros, the lover's cry. It is after the range of relations to his own vision has been acknowledged and accepted that a stronger Crane achieves the Gnosis of those three last quatrains. There the poet remains present, but only as a knowing Abyss, contemplating the content of that knowing, which is a fullness or presence he can invoke but scarcely share. He sees "night lifted in thine arms"; he waits, for a shadow to clarify in darkness; he knows, yet what he knows is a vaulting, a sweep, a descent, above all a curveship, a realization of an angle of vision not yet his own.

This peculiarly effective stance has a precursor in Shelley's visionary skepticism, particularly in his final phase of *Adonais* and *The Triumph of Life*. Crane's achievement of this stance is the still-unexplored origin of *The Bridge*, but the textual evolution of "Atlantis," the first section of the visionary epic to be composed, is the probable area that should be considered. Lacking space here, I point instead to the achieved stance of *Voyages VI* as the earliest full instance of Crane's mature Orphism, after which I will conclude with a reading of "Atlantis" and a brief glance at Crane's testament, *The Broken Tower.*

The governing deities of the *Voyages* sequence are Eros and Ananke, or Emil Oppfer and the Caribbean as Whitmanian fierce old mother moaning for her castaways. But the Orphic Dionysus, rent apart by Titanic forces, dominates the sixth lyric, which like Stevens's *The Paltry Nude Starts upon a Spring Journey* partly derives from Pater's description of Botticelli's Venus in *The Renaissance.* Pater's sado-masochistic maternal love-goddess, with her eyes smiling "unsearchable repose," becomes Crane's overtly destructive muse, whose seer is no longer at home in his own vision:

> My eyes pressed black against the prow,
> —Thy derelict and blinded guest
>
> Waiting, afire, what name, unspoke,
> I cannot claim: let thy waves rear
>
> More savage than the death of kings,
> Some splintered garland for the seer.

The unspoken, unclaimed name is that of Orpheus, in his terrible final phase of "floating singer." Crane's highly deliberate echo of Shakespeare's Richard II at his most self-destructively masochistic is assimilated to the poetic equivalent, which is the splintering of the garland of laurel. Yet the final stanza returns to the central image of poetic incarnation in Crane, *Repose of Rivers* and its "hushed willows":

> The imaged Word, it is, that holds
> Hushed willows anchored in its glow.
> It is the unbetrayable reply
> Whose accent no farewell can know.

This is the achieved and curiously firm balance of a visionary skepticism, or the Orphic stance of *The Bridge.* It can be contrasted to Lawrence again, in the "Orphic farewell" of *Medlars and Sorb Apples* in *Birds, Beasts and Flowers.* For Lawrence, Orphic assurance is the solipsism of an "intoxication of perfect loneliness." Crane crosses that intoxication by transuming his own and tradition's trope of the hushed willows as signifying an end to solitary mourning, and a renewal of poetic divination. *Voyages VI* turns its "imaged Word" against Eliot's neo-orthodox Word, or Christ, and Whitman's Word out of the Sea, or death, death that is the

Oedipal merging back into the mother. Crane ends upon "know" because knowledge, and not faith, is his religious mode, a Gnosis that is more fully developed in *The Bridge*.

The dozen octaves of the final version of "Atlantis" show Crane in his mastery of the traditional Sublime, and are wholly comparable to the final seventeen stanzas of Shelley's *Adonais*. Crane's absolute music, like Plato's, "is then the knowledge of that which relates to love in harmony and system," but Crane's love is rather more like Shelley's desperate and skeptical outleaping than it is like Diotima's vision. For six stanzas, Crane drives upward, in a hyperbolic arc whose burden is agonistic, struggling to break beyond every achieved Sublime in the language. This agon belongs to the Sublime, and perhaps in America it *is* the Sublime. But such an agon requires particular contestants, and "Atlantis" finds them in *The Waste Land* and, yet more repressedly, in Whitman's *Crossing Brooklyn Ferry*, the great addition to the second, 1856, *Leaves of Grass*, and Thoreau's favorite poem by Whitman.

Much of Crane's struggle with Eliot was revised out of the final "Atlantis," but only as overt textual traces; the deep inwardness of the battle is recoverable. Two modes of phantasmagoria clash:

> Through the bound cable strands, the arching path
> Upward, veering with light, the flight of strings,—
> Taut miles of shuttling moonlight syncopate
> The whispered rush, telepathy of wires.
> Up the index of night, granite and steel—
> Transparent meshes—fleckless the gleaming staves—
> Sibylline voices flicker, waveringly stream
> As though a god were issue of the strings. . . .

> A woman drew her long black hair out tight
> And fiddled whisper music on those strings
> And bats with baby faces in the violet light
> Whistled, and beat their wings
> And crawled head downward down a blackened wall
> And upside down in air were towers
> Tolling reminiscent bells, that kept the hours
> And voices singing out of empty cisterns and exhausted wells.

The latter hallucination might be called an amalgam of *Dracula* and the Gospels, as rendered in the high style of Tennyson's *Idylls of the King*, and obviously is in no sense a source or cause of Crane's transcendental opening octave. Nevertheless, no clearer contrast could be afforded, for Crane's lines answer Eliot's, in every meaning of "answer." "Music is then the knowledge of that which relates to love in harmony and system," and one knowledge answers another in these competing and marvelous musics of poetry, and of visionary history. Crane's bridge is to Atlantis, in fulfillment of the Platonic quest of Crane's Columbus. Eliot's bridge is to the Inferno, in fulfillment of the neo-Christian condemnation of Romantic, Transcendentalist, Gnostic quest. Crane's Sibylline voices stream upward; his night-illuminated bridge becomes a transparent musical score, until Orpheus is born out of the flight of strings. Eliot's Sibyl wishes to die; her counterpart plays a vampiric score upon her own hair, until instead of an Orphic birth upwards we have an impotent triumph of time.

This contrast, and others equally sharp, constitute the context of Crane's aspiration in "Atlantis." But this aspiration, which is for knowledge, in the particular sense of Gnosis, yields to Eliot, as it must, much of the world of things-as-they-are. The closing images of "The Tunnel," the section of *The Bridge* preceding "Atlantis," combine *The Waste Land*'s accounts of loss with Whitman's darker visions of those losses in *Crossing Brooklyn Ferry*:

> And this thy harbor, O my City, I have driven under,
> Tossed from the coil of ticking towers. . . . Tomorrow,
> And to be. . . . Here by the River that is East—
> Here at the waters' edge the hands drop memory;
> Shadowless in that abyss they unaccounting lie.
> How far away the star has pooled the sea—
> Or shall the hands be drawn away, to die?
>
> Kiss of our agony Thou gatherest,
>   O Hand of Fire
>   gatherest—

Emerson's was a Gnosis without Gnosticism; Crane's religion, at its darkest, shades from Orphism into Gnosticism, in a negative transcendence even of the Whitman who proclaimed: "It is not upon you alone the dark patches fall,/The dark threw its patches upon me also." The negative transcendence of "Atlantis" surmounts the world, history and even precursors as knowing, in their rival ways, as Eliot and Whitman. Crane condenses the upward intensities of his first six octaves by a deliberate recall of his own Columbus triumphantly but delusively chanting: "I bring you back Cathay!" But Crane's Columbus invoked the Demiurge under Emily Dickinson's name for him, "Inquisitor! incognizable Word/Of Eden." This beautiful pathos of defeat, in "Ave Maria," was consonant with Whitman's *Prayer of Columbus*, where the battered, wrecked old mariner denied all knowledge: "I know not even my own word past or present." Crane's American burden, in the second half of "Atlantis," is to start again where

Dickinson and Whitman ended, and where Eliot had sought to show no fresh start was possible. Knowledge in precisely the Gnostic sense—a knowing that knows the knower and is, *in itself*, the form of salvation— becomes Crane's formidable hymn addressed directly to itself, to poem and to bridge, until they become momentarily "—One Song, one Bridge of Fire!" But is this persuasively different from the "Hand of Fire" that gathers the kiss of our agony?

The dialectic of Gnosticism is a triad of negation, evasion and extrava- gance. Lurianic Kabbalah renders these as contraction, breaking-of-the- vessels and restitution. Fate, freedom, power is the Emersonian or American equivalent. All of these triads translate aesthetically into a dialectic of limitation, substitution and representation, as I have shown in several critical books starting with *A Map of Misreading*. Crane's negation or limitation, his contraction into Fate, is scarcely different from Eliot's, but then such rival negative theologies as Valentinian Gnosticism and Johannine Christianity are difficult to distinguish in their accounts of how to express divinity. Gnostic evasion, like Crane's notorious freedom and range in troping, is clearly more inventive than authorized Christian modes of substitution, just as Gnostic extravagance, again like Crane's hyperbolical Sublime, easily surpasses orthodox expressions of power.

Crane's elaborate evasiveness is crucial in the seventh stanza of "Atlan- tis," where the upward movement of the tropology has ended, and a westward lateral sweep of vision is substituted, with the bridge no longer confronted and addressed, but seen now as binding the continent:

> We left the haven hanging in the night—
> Sheened harbor lanterns backward fled the keel.
> Pacific here at time's end, bearing corn,—
> Eyes stammer through the pangs of dust and steel.
> And still the circular, indubitable frieze
> Of heaven's meditation, yoking wave
> To kneeling wave, one song devoutly binds—
> The vernal strophe chimes from deathless strings!

The third line implies not merely a circuit of the earth, but an achieved peace at the end of days, a millennial harvest. When the bridge returns in this stanza's last four lines, it has become heaven's own meditation, the known knowing the human knower. And such a knowing leads Crane on to the single most central stanza of his life and work:

> O Thou steeled Cognizance whose leap commits
> The agile precincts of the lark's return;
> Within whose lariat sweep encinctured sing
> In single chrysalis the many twain,—

Of stars Thou art the stitch and stallion glow
And like an organ, Thou, with sound of doom—
Sight, sound and flesh Thou leadest from time's realm
As love strikes clear direction for the helm.

Contrast the precise Shelleyan equivalent:

The One remains, the many change and pass;
Heaven's light forever shines, Earth's shadows fly;
Life, like a dome of many-colored glass,
Stains the white radiance of Eternity,
Until Death tramples it to fragments.—Die,
If thou wouldst be with that which thou dost seek!
Follow where all is fled!—Rome's azure sky,
Flowers, ruins, statues, music, words, are weak
The glory they transfuse with fitting truth to speak.

Superficially, the two stanzas are much at variance, with Crane's tone apparently triumphal, Shelley's apparently despairing. But the pragmatic or merely natural burden of both stanzas is quite suicidal. The bridge, as "steeled Cognizance," resolves the many into One, but this music of unity is a "sound of doom" for all flesh and its senses living in time's realm. Love's "clear direction," as in Shelley's climactic stanza, is towards death. But Shelley is very much involved in his own relation, as poet, to his own vision. Crane's role, as known to the bridge's knower, forsakes that relation, and a terrifyingly free concentration on the content of poetic vision is the reward. "Of stars Thou art the stitch and stallion glow" Marlowe himself would have envied, but since both terms of the trope, bridge and stars, exclude the human, Crane is impelled onwards to extraordinary achievements in hyperbole. When the bridge is "iridescently upborne / Through the bright drench and fabric of our veins," then the human price of Gnosticism begins to mount also. Crane insists that all this is "to our joy," but that joy is as dialectical as Shelley's despair. And Crane, supremely intelligent, counts the cost, foreknowing all criticism:

Migrations that must needs void memory,
Inventions that cobblestone the heart,—
Unspeakable Thou Bridge to Thee, O Love.
Thy pardon for this history, whitest Flower,
O Answerer of all,—Anemone,—
Now while thy petals spend the suns about us, hold—
(O Thou whose radiance doth inherit me)
Atlantis,—hold thy floating singer late!

Would it make a difference if this read: "Cathay,—hold thy floating singer late!" so that the prayer of pariah would belong to Columbus
and not to Orpheus? Yes, for the final stanza then would have the Orphic
strings leap and converge to a question clearly different:

> —One Song, one Bridge of Fire! Is it Atlantis,
> Now pity steeps the grass and rainbows ring
> The serpent with the eagle in the leaves . . . ?

Crane's revision of the Orphic stance of *White Buildings*, of lyrics
like *Repose of Rivers* and *Passage*, here allows him a difference that is a
triumph. His serpent and eagle are likelier to be Shelley's than Nietzsche's,
for they remain at strife *within* their border of covenant, the ring of
rainbows. Atlantis is urged to hold its Orpheus late, as a kind of newly
fused Platonic myth of reconcilement to a higher world of forms, a myth
of which Gnosticism was a direct heir. "Is it Cathay?," repeating the
noble delusion of Columbus, is not a question hinting defeat, but foreboding victory. Yet Orphic victories are dialectical, as Crane well knew.
Knowledge indeed is the kernel, for Crane astutely shows awareness of
what the greatest poets always know, which is that their figurations
intend the will's revenge against time's "it was," but actually achieve
the will's limits, in the bewilderments of the Abyss of troping and of
tropes.

The coda to Crane's poetry, and his life, is *The Broken Tower*, where
the transumption of the Orphic quest does allow a final triumph:

> And so it was I entered the broken world
> To trace the visionary company of love, its voice
> An instant in the wind (I know not wither hurled)
> But not for long to hold each desperate choice.

Crane mentions reading other books by Pater, but not the unfinished novel *Gaston de Latour*. Its first few chapters, at least, would
have fascinated him, and perhaps he did look into the opening pages,
where the young Gaston undergoes a ceremony bridging the spirit and
nature:

> Gaston alone, with all his mystic preoccupations, by the privilege of
> youth, seemed to belong to both, and link the visionary company about
> him to the external scene.

The "privilege of youth" was still Crane's when he died, and
The Broken Tower remains as one of those links. Such a link, finally,
is not to be judged as what Freud called "a false connection" or as another

irony to be ironically recognized, but rather as a noble synecdoche, self-mutilating perhaps as is a steeled Cognizance, but by its very turning against the self, endlessly reconstituting the American poetic self, the *pneuma* or spark of an American Gnosis.

R. P. BLACKMUR

New Thresholds, New Anatomies: Notes on a Text of Hart Crane

It is a striking and disheartening fact that the three most ambitious poems of our time should all have failed in similar ways: in composition, in independent objective existence, and in intelligibility of language. *The Waste Land*, the *Cantos*, and *The Bridge* all fail to hang together structurally in the sense that "Prufrock," "Envoi," and "Praise for an Urn"—lesser works in every other respect—do hang together. Each of the three poems requires of the reader that he supply from outside the poem, and with the help of clues only, the important, *controlling* part of what we may loosely call the meaning. And each again deliberately presents passages, lines, phrases, and single words which no amount of outside work can illumine. The fact is striking because, aside from other considerations of magnitude, relevance, and scope, these are not the faults we lay up typically against the great dead. The typical great poet is profoundly rational, integrating, and, excepting minor accidents of incapacity, a master of ultimate verbal clarity. Light, radiance, and wholeness remain the attributes of serious art. And the fact is disheartening because no time could have greater need than our own for rational art. No time certainly could surrender more than ours does daily, with drums beating, to fanatic politics and despotically construed emotions.

From *Language as Gesture*. Copyright © 1980 by Elizabeth Blackmur. Harcourt Brace Jovanovich.

But let us desert the disheartening for the merely striking aspect, and handle the matter, as we can, within the realm of poetry, taking up other matters only tacitly and by implication. Let us say provisionally that in their more important works Eliot, Pound, and Crane lack the ultimate, if mythical, quality of aseity, that quality of completeness, of independence, so great that it seems underived and an effect of pure creation. The absence of aseity may be approached variously in a given poet; but every approach to be instructive, even to find the target at all, must employ a rational mode and the right weapon. These notes intend to examine certain characteristic passages of Hart Crane's poems as modes of language and to determine how and to what degree the effects intended were attained. The rationale is that of poetic language; the weapons are analysis and comparison. But there are other matters which must be taken up first before the language itself can be approached at all familiarly.

Almost everyone who has written on Crane has found in him a central defect, either of imagination or execution, or both. Long ago, in his Preface to *White Buildings*, Allen Tate complained that for all his talent Crane had not found a suitable theme. Later, in his admirable review of *The Bridge*, Yvor Winters brought and substantiated the charge (by demonstrating the exceptions) that even when he had found a theme Crane could not entirely digest it and at crucial points simply was unable to express it in objective form. These charges hold; and all that is here said is only in explication of them from a third point of view.

Waldo Frank, in his Introduction to the *Collected Poems*, acting more as an apologist than a critic, proffers two explanations of Crane's incompleteness as a poet, to neither of which can I assent, but of which I think both should be borne in mind. Mr. Frank believes that Crane will be understood and found whole when our culture has been restored from revolutionary collectivism to a predominant interest in the person; when the value of expressing the personal in the terms of the cosmic shall again seem supreme. This hypothesis would seem untenable unless it is construed as relevant to the present examination; when it runs immediately into the hands of the obvious but useful statement that Crane was interested in persons rather than the class struggle. Mr. Frank's other explanation is that Crane's poetry was based upon the mystical perception of the "organic continuity between the self and a seemingly chaotic world." Crane "was too virile to deny the experience of continuity; he let the world pour in; and since his nuclear self was not disciplined to detachment from his nerves and passions, he lived exacerbated in a constant swing between ecstasy and exhaustion." I confess I do not understand "organic continuity" in this context, and all my efforts to do so are defeated by the subsequent word "detachment." Nor can I see how this particular concept of continuity can be very useful without the addition and control of a thorough supernaturalism. The control for mystic psychology is theology, and what is thereby controlled is the idiosyncrasy of insight, not the technique of poetry.

What Mr. Frank says not-rationally can be usefully retranslated to that plane on which skilled readers ordinarily read good poetry; which is a rational plane; which is, on analysis, the plane of competent technical appreciation. Such a translation, while committing grave injustice on Mr. Frank, comes nearer doing justice to Crane. It restores and brings home the strictures of Tate and Winters, and it brings judgment comparatively back to the minute particulars (Blake's phrase) which are alone apprehensible. To compose the nuclear self and the seemingly chaotic world is to find a suitable theme, and the inability so to compose rises as much from immaturity and indiscipline of the major poetic uses of language as from personal immaturity and indiscipline. Baudelaire only rarely reached the point of self-discipline and Whitman never; but Baudelaire's language is both disciplined and mature, and Whitman's sometimes so. *Les Fleurs du Mal* are a profound poetic ordering of a life disorderly, distraught, and deracinated, a life excruciated, in the semantic sense of that word, to the extreme. And Whitman, on his side, by a very different use of language, gave torrential expression to the romantic disorder of life in flux, whereas his private sensibility seems either to have been suitably well-ordered or to have felt no need of order.

Whitman and Baudelaire are not chosen with reference to Crane by accident but because they are suggestively apposite. The suggestion may be made, not as blank truth but for the light there is in it, that Crane had the sensibility typical of Baudelaire and so misunderstood himself that he attempted to write *The Bridge* as if he had the sensibility typical of Whitman. Whitman characteristically let himself go in words, in any words and by all means the handiest, until his impulse was used up. Baudelaire no less characteristically caught himself up in his words, recording, ordering, and binding together the implications and tacit meanings of his impulse until in his best poems the words he used are, as I. A. Richards would say, inexhaustible objects of meditation. Baudelaire aimed at control, Whitman at release. It is for these reasons that the influence of Whitman is an impediment to the *practice* (to be distinguished from the reading) of poetry, and that the influence of Baudelaire is re-animation itself. (It may be noted that Baudelaire had at his back a well-articulated version of the Catholic Church to control the moral aspect of his meanings, where Whitman had merely an inarticulate pantheism.)

To apply this dichotomy to Crane is not difficult if it is done tentatively, without requiring that it be too fruitful, and without requiring that it be final at all. The clue or nexus is found, aside from the poems themselves, in certain prose statements. Letters are suspect and especially letters addressed to a patron, since the aim is less conviction by argument than the persuasive dramatization of an attitude. It is therefore necessary in the following extract from a letter to Otto Kahn that the reader accomplish a reduction in the magnitude of terms.

Of the section of *The Bridge* called "The Dance" Crane wrote: "Here one is on the pure mythical and smoky soil at last! Not only do I describe the conflict between the two races in this dance—I also became identified with the Indian and his world before it is over, which is the only method possible of ever really possessing the Indian and his world as a cultural factor." Etc. I suggest that, confronted with the tight, tense, intensely personal lyric quatrains of the verse itself, verse compact with the deliberately inarticulate interfusion of the senses, Crane's statement of intention has only an *ipse dixit* pertinence; that taken otherwise, taken as a living index of substance, it only multiplies the actual confusion of the verse and impoverishes its achieved scope. Taken seriously, it puts an impossible burden on the reader: the burden of reading two poems at once, the one that appears and the "real" poem which does not appear except by an act of faith. This would be reading by legerdemain, which at the moment of achievement must always collapse, self-obfuscated.

Again, in the same letter, Crane wrote that, "The range of *The Bridge* has been called colossal by more than one critic who has seen the ms., and though I have found the subject to be vaster than I had at first realized, I am still highly confident of its final articulation into a continuous and eloquent span. . . . *The Aeneid* was not written in two years—nor in four, and in more than one sense I feel justified in comparing the historical and cultural scope of *The Bridge* to that great work. It is at least a symphony with an epic theme, and a work of considerable profundity and inspiration."

The question is whether this was wishful thinking of the vague order commonest in revery, convinced and sincere statement of intention, or an effect of the profound duplicity—a deception in the very will of things—in Crane's fundamental attitudes toward his work; or whether Crane merely misunderstood the logical import of the words he used. I incline to the notion of duplicity, since it is beneath and sanctions the other notions as well; the very duplicity by which the talents of a Baudelaire appear to their possessor disguised and disfigured in the themes of a Whitman, the same fundamental duplicity of human knowledge whereby an accustomed disorder seems the order most to be cherished, or whereby a religion which at its heart denies life enriches living. In the particular reference, if I am right, it is possible to believe that Crane labored to perfect both the strategy and the tactics of language so as to animate and maneuver his perceptions—and then fought the wrong war and against an enemy that displayed, to his weapons, no vulnerable target. He wrote in a language of which it was the virtue to accrete, modify, and interrelate moments of emotional vision—moments at which the sense of being gains its greatest access-moments at which, by the felt nature of knowledge, the revealed thing is its own meaning; and he attempted to apply his language, in his major effort, to a theme that required a sweeping, discrete, indicative, anecdotal language, a language in which, by force of movement, mere cataloguing can replace and often surpass representation. He used the private lyric to write the cultural epic; used the mode of intensive contemplation, which secures ends, to present the mind's actions, which have no ends. The confusion of tool and purpose not only led him astray in conceiving his themes; it obscured at crucial moments the exact character of the work he was actually doing. At any rate we find most impenetrable and ineluctable, in certain places, the very matters he had the genius to see and the technique to clarify: the matters which are the substance of rare and valid emotion. The confusion, that is, led him to content himself at times with the mere cataloguing statement, enough for him because he knew the rest, of what required completely objective embodiment.

Another, if ancillary, method of enforcing the same suggestion (of radical confusion) is to observe the disparity between Crane's announced purpose and the masters he studied. Poets commonly profit most where they can borrow most, from the poets with whom by instinct, education, and accident of contact, they are most nearly unanimous. Thus poetic character is early predicted. In Crane's case, the nature of the influences to which he submitted himself remained similar from the beginning to the end and were the dominant ones of his generation. It was the influence of what we may call, with little exaggeration, the school of tortured sensibility—a school of which we perhaps first became aware in Baudelaire's misapprehension of Poe, and later, in the hardly less misapprehending resurrection of Donne. Crane benefited, and was deformed by, this influence both directly and by an assortment of indirection; but he never surmounted it. He read the modern French poets who are the result of Baudelaire, but he did not read Racine of whom Baudelaire was himself a product. He read Wallace Stevens, whose strength and serenity may in some sense be assigned to the combined influence of the French moderns and, say, Plato; but he did not, at least affectively, read Plato. He read Eliot, and through and in terms of him, the chosen Elizabethans—though more in Donne and Webster than in Jonson and Middleton; but he did not, so to speak, read the Christianity from which Eliot derives his ultimate strength, and by which he is presently transforming himself. I use the word *read* in a strong sense; there is textual evidence of reading throughout the poems. The last influence Crane exhibited is no different in character and in the use to which he put it than the earliest: the poem called "The Hurricane" derives immediately from the metric of Hopkins but not ultimately from Hopkins' integrating sensibility. Thus Crane fitted himself for the exploitation of the peculiar, the unique, the agonized and the tortured perception, and he developed language-patterns for the essentially incoherent aspects of experience: the aspects in which experience assaults rather than informs the sensibility. Yet, granting his sensibility, with his avowed epic purpose he had done better had he gone to school to Milton and Racine, and, in modern times, to Hardy and Bridges—or even Masefield—for narrative sweep.

Crane had, in short, the wrong masters for his chosen fulfillment, or he used some of the right masters in the wrong way: leeching upon them, as a poet must, but taking the wrong nourishment, taking from them not what was hardest and most substantial—what made them great poets—but taking rather what was easiest, taking what was peculiar and idiosyncratic. That is what kills so many of Crane's poems, what must have made them impervious, once they were discharged, even to himself. It is perhaps, too, what killed Crane the man—because in a profound sense, to those who use it, poetry is the only means of putting a tolerable order upon the emotions. Crane's predicament—that his means defeated his ends—was not unusual, but his case was extreme. In more normal form it is the predicament of immaturity. Crane's mind was slow and massive, a cumulus of substance; it had, to use a word of his own, the synergical quality, and with time it might have worked together, clarified, and become its own meaning. But he hastened the process and did not survive to maturity.

Certainly there is a hasty immaturity in the short essay on Modern Poetry, reprinted as an appendix to the *Collected Poems*, an immaturity both in the intellectual terms employed and in the stress with which the attitude they rehearse is held. Most of the paper tilts at windmills, and the lance is too heavy for the wielding hand. In less than five pages there is deployed more confused thinking than is to be found in all his poems put together. Poetry is not, as Crane says it is, an architectural art—or not without a good deal of qualification; it is a linear art, an art of succession, and the only art it resembles formally is plain song. Nor can Stravinsky and the cubists be compared, as Crane compares them, in the quality of their abstractions with the abstractions of mathematical physics: the aims are disparate; expression and theoretic manipulation can never exist on the same plane. Nor can psychological analyses, in literature, be distinguished in motive and quality from dramatic analyses. Again, and finally, the use of the term *psychosis* as a laudatory epithet for the substance of Whitman, represents to me the uttermost misconstruction of the nature of poetry: a psychosis is a mental derangement not due to an organic lesion or neurosis. A theory of neurosis (as, say, Aiken has held it in *Blue Voyage*) is more tenable scientifically; but neither it seems to me has other than a stultifying critical use. Yet, despite the confusion and positive irrationality of Crane's language the general tendency is sound, the aspiration sane. He wanted to write good poetry and his archetype was Dante; that is enough. But in his prose thinking he had the wrong words for his thoughts, as in his poetry he had often the wrong themes for his words.

II

So far, if the points have been maintained at all, what I have written adds up to the suggestion that in reading Hart Crane we must make allowances for him—not historical allowances as we do for Shakespeare, religious allowances as for Dante and Milton, or philisophical as for Goethe and Lucretius—but fundamental allowances whereby we agree to supply or overlook what does not appear in the poems, and whereby we agree to forgive or guess blindly at those parts of the poems which are unintelligible. In this Crane is not an uncommon case, though the particular allowances may perhaps be unique. There are some poets where everything is allowed for the sake of isolated effects. Sedley is perhaps the supreme example in English; there is nothing in him but two lines, but these are famous and will always be worth saving. Waller is the more normal example, or King, where two or three poems are the whole gist. Crane has both poems and passages; and in fact there is hardly a poem of his which has not something in it, and a very definite something, worth saving.

The nature of that saving quality, for it saves him no less than ourselves, Crane has himself most clearly expressed in a stanza from the poem called "Wine Menagerie."

> New thresholds, new anatomies! Wine talons
> Build freedom up about me and distill
> This competence—to travel in a tear
> Sparkling alone, within another's will.

I hope to show that this stanza illustrates almost inexhaustibly, to minds at all aware, both the substance and the aspiration of Crane's poetry, the character and value of his perceptions, and his method of handling words to control them. If we accept the stanza as a sort of declaration of policy and apply it as our own provisional policy to the sum of his work, although we limit its scope we shall deepen and articulate our appreciation —a process, that of appreciation, which amounts not to wringing a few figs from thistles but to expressing the wine itself.

Paraphrase does not greatly help. We can, for the meat of it, no more be concerned with the prose sense of the words than Crane evidently was. Crane habitually re-created his words from within, developing meaning to the point of idiom; and that habit is the constant and indubitable sign of talent. The meanings themselves are the idioms and have a twist and life of their own. It is only by ourselves meditating on and *using* these idioms—it is only by emulation—that we can master them and accede to their life.

Analysis, however, does help, and in two directions. It will by itself increase our intimacy with the words as they appear; and it will as the nexus among comparisons disclose that standard of achievement, inherent in this special use of poetic language, by which alone the value of the work may be judged. (Analysis, in these uses, does not cut deep, it does not cut at all: it merely distinguishes particulars; and the particulars must be re-seen in their proper focus before the labor benefits.)

Moving in the first direction, toward intimacy, we can say that Crane employed an extreme mode of free association; that operation among words where it is the product rather than the addition that counts. There was, for example, no logical or emotional connection between thresholds and anatomies until Crane verbally juxtaposed them and tied them together with the cohesive of his meter. Yet, so associated, they modify and act upon each other mutually and produce a fresh meaning of which the parts cannot be segregated. Some latent, unsuspected part of the cumulus of meaning in each word excited, so to speak, and affected a corresponding part in the others. It is the juxtaposition which is the agent of selection, and it is a combination of meter and the carried-over influence of the rest of the poem, plus the as yet undetermined expectations aroused, which is the agent of emphasis and identification. It should be noted that, so far as the poem is concerned, the words themselves contain and do not merely indicate the feelings which compose the meaning; the poet's job was to put the words together like bricks in a wall. In lesser poetry of the same order, and in poetry of different orders, words may only indicate or refer to or substitute for the feelings; then we have the poetry of vicarious statement, which takes the place of, often to the highest purpose, the actual complete presentation, such as we have here. Here there is nothing for the words to take the place of; they are their own life, and have an organic continuity, not with the poet's mind nor with the experience they represent, but with themselves. We see that thresholds open upon anatomies: upon things to be explored and understood and felt freshly as an adventure; and we see that the anatomies, what is to be explored, are known from a new vantage, and that the vantage is part of the anatomy. The separate meanings of the words fairly rush at each other; the right ones join and those irrelevant to the juncture are for the moment—the whole time of the poem—lost in limbo. Thus the association "New thresholds, new anatomies!" which at first inspection might seem specious or arbitrary (were we not used to reading poetry) not only does not produce a distortion but, the stress and strain being equal, turns out wholly natural and independently alive.

In the next phrase the association of the word "talons" with the context seems less significantly performed. So far as it refers back and expresses a seizing together, a clutching by a bird of prey, it is an excellent word well-chosen and spliced in. The further notion, suggested by the word "wine," of release, would also seem relevant. There is, too, an unidentifiable possibility—for Crane used words in very special senses indeed—of "talons" in the sense of cards left after the deal; and there is even, to push matters to the limit, a bare chance that some element of the etymon—ankle, heel—has been pressed into service. But the possibilities have among them none specially discriminated, and whichever you choose for use, the dead weight of the others must be provisionally carried along, which is what makes the phrase slightly fuzzy. And however you construe "wine talons" you cannot, without distorting what you have and allowing for the gap or lacuna of what you have not, make your construction fit either or both of the verbs which it governs. Talons neither build nor distill even when salvation by rhyme is in question. If Crane meant—as indeed he may have—that wines are distilled and become brandies or spirits, then he showed a poverty of technique in using the transitive instead of the intransitive form. Objection can be carried too far, when it renders itself nugatory. These remarks are meant as kind of exploration; and if we now make the allowance for the unidentified distortion and supply with good will the lacuna in the very heart of the middle phrases, the rest of the stanza becomes as plain and vivid as poetry of this order need ever be. To complete the whole association, the reader need only remember that Crane probably had in mind, and made new use of Blake's lines:

> For a Tear is an Intellectual Thing,
> And a Sigh is the Sword of an Angel King.

It is interesting to observe that Blake was talking against war and that his primary meaning was much the same as that expressed negatively in "Auguries of Innocence" by the following couplet:

> He who shall train the Horse to War
> Shall never pass the Polar Bar.

Crane ignored the primary meaning, and extracted and emphasized what was in Blake's image a latent or secondary meaning. Or possibly he combined—made a free association of—the intellectual tear with

> Every Tear from Every Eye
> Becomes a Babe in Eternity;

only substituting the more dramatic notion of will for intellect. What is important to note is that, whatever its origin, the meaning as Crane presents it is completely transformed and subjugated to the control of the "new thresholds, new anatomies!"

The stanza we have been considering is only arbitrarily separated from the whole poem—just as the poem itself ought to be read in the context of the whole *White Buildings* section. The point is, that for appreciation—and for denigration—all of Crane should be read thoroughly, at least once, with similar attention to detail. That is the way in which Crane worked. Later readings may be more liberated and more irresponsible—as some people read the Bible for what they call its poetry or a case history for its thrill; but they never get either the poetry or the thrill without a preliminary fundamental intimacy with the rational technique involved. Here it is a question of achieving some notion of a special poetic process. The principle of association which controls this stanza resembles the notion of wine as escape, release, father of insight and seed of metamorphosis, which controls the poem; and, in its turn, the notion of extra-logical, intoxicated metamorphosis of the senses controls and innervates Crane's whole sensibility.

To illustrate the uniformity of approach, a few examples are presented, some that succeed and some that fail. In "Lachrymae Christi" consider the line

> Thy Nazarene and tinder eyes.

(Note, from the title, that we are here again concerned with tears as the vehicle-image of insight, and that, in the end, Christ is identified with Dionysus.) Nazarene, the epithet for Christ, is here used as an adjective of quality in conjunction with the noun tinder also used as an adjective; an arrangement which will seem baffling only to those who underestimate the seriousness with which Crane remodeled words. The first three lines of the poem read:

> Whitely, while benzine
> Rinsings from the moon
> Dissolve all but the windows of the mills.

Benzine is a fluid, cleansing and solvent, has a characteristic tang and smart to it, and is here associated with the light of the moon, which, through the word "rinsings," is itself modified by it. It is, I think, the carried-over influence of benzine which gives startling aptness to Nazarene. It is, if I am correct for any reader but myself, an example of suspended association, or telekinesis; and it is, too, an example of syllabic interpenetration or internal punning as habitually practiced in the later prose of Joyce. The influence of one word on the other reminds us that Christ the Saviour cleanses and solves and has, too, the quality of light. "Tinder" is a simpler instance of how Crane could at once isolate a word and bind it in, impregnating it with new meaning. Tinder is used to kindle fire, powder, and light; a word incipient and bristling with the action proper to its being. The association is completed when it is remembered that tinder is very nearly a homonym for tender and, *in this setting*, puns upon it.

Immediately following, in the same poem, there is a parenthesis which I have not been able to penetrate with any certainty, though the possibilities are both fascinating and exciting. The important words in it do not possess the excluding, limiting power over themselves and their relations by which alone the precise, vital element in an ambiguity is secured. What Crane may have meant privately cannot be in question—his words may have represented for him a perfect tautology; we are concerned only with how the words act upon each other—or fail to act—so as to commit an appreciable meaning. I quote the first clause of the parenthesis.

> Let sphinxes from the ripe
> Borage of death have cleared my tongue
> Once and again . . .

It is syntax rather than grammar that is obscure. I take it that "let" is here a somewhat homemade adjective and that Crane is making a direct statement, so that the problem is to construe the right meanings of the right words in the right references; which will be an admirable exercise in exegesis, but an exercise only. The applicable senses of "let" are these: neglected or weary, permitted or prevented, hired, and let in the sense that blood is let. Sphinxes are inscrutable, have secrets, propound riddles to travelers and strangle those who cannot answer. "Borage" has at least three senses: something rough (sonantly suggestive of barrage and barrier), a blue-flowered, hairy-leaved plant, and a cordial made from the plant. The Shorter Oxford Dictionary quotes this jingle from Hooker: "I Borage always bring courage." One guess is that Crane meant something to the effect that if you meditate enough on death it has the same bracing and warming effect as drinking a cordial, so that the riddles of life (or death) are answered. But something very near the contrary may have been intended; or both. In any case a guess is ultimately worthless because, with the defective syntax, the words do not verify it. Crane had a profound feeling for the hearts of words, and how they beat and cohabited, but here they overtopped him; the meanings in the words themselves are superior to the use to which he put them. The operation of selective cross-pollination not only failed but was not even rightly attempted. The language remains in the condition of that which it was intended to express: in the flux of intoxicated sense; whereas the language of the other lines of this poem here examined—the language, not the sense—is disintoxicated and candid. The point is that the quality of Crane's success is also the quality of his failure, and the distinction is perhaps by the hair of accident.

In the part of The Bridge called "Virginia," and in scores of places elsewhere, there is a single vivid image, of no structural importance, but of great delight as ornament: it both fits the poem and has a startling separate beauty of its own, the phrase: "Peonies with pony manes." The freshness has nothing to do with accurate observation, of which it is devoid, but has its source in the arbitrary character of the association: it is created observation. Another example is contained in

> Down Wall, from girder into street noon leaks,
> A rip-tooth of the sky's acetylene;

which is no more forced than many of Crashaw's best images. It is, of course, the pyramiding associations of the word acetylene that create the observation: representing as it does an intolerable quality of light and a torch for cutting metal, and so on.

Similarly, again and again, both in important and in ornamental phrases, there are effects only half secured, words which are not the right words but only the nearest words. E.g.: "What eats the pattern with ubiquity. . . . Take this sheaf of dust upon your tongue . . . Preparing *penguin* flexions of the arms . . . [A tugboat] with one *galvanic* blare . . . I heard the *hush of lava wrestling* your arms." Etc. Not that the italicized words are wrong but that they fall short of the control and precision of impact necessary to vitalize them permanently.

There remains to consider the second help of analysis (the first was to promote intimacy with particulars), namely, to disclose the standard of Crane's achievement in terms of what he actually accomplished; an effort which at once involves comparison of Crane with rendered possibilities in the same realm of language taken from other poets. For Crane was not alone; stlye, like knowledge, of which it is the expressive grace, is a product of collaboration; and his standard, whether consciously or not, was outside himself, in verse written in accord with his own bent: which the following, if looked at with the right eye, will exemplify.

> Sunt lacrimae rerum et mentem mortalia tangunt.
> (—Vergil)

> Lo giorno se n'andava, e l'aer bruno
>   toglieva gli animai, che sono in terra,
>   dalle fatiche loro.
> (—Dante)

> A brittle glory shineth in his face;
> As brittle as the glory is the face.
> (—Shakespeare)

> Adieu donc, chants du cuivre et soupirs de la flûte!
> Plaisirs, ne tentez plus un coeur sombre et boudeur!
> Le Printemps adorable a perdu son odeur!
> (—Baudelaire)

> But Love has pitched his mansion in
> The place of excrement;
> For nothing can be sole or whole
> That has not been rent.
> (—Yeats)

> She dreams a little, and she feels the dark
> Encroachment of that old catastrophe,
> As a calm darkens among water-lights.
> (—Stevens)

The relevant context is assumed to be present, as we have been assuming it all along with Crane. Every quotation, except that from Yeats which is recent, should be well known. They bring to mind at once, on one side, the sustaining, glory-breeding power of magnificent form joined to great intellect. Before that impact Crane's magnitude shrinks. On the other side, the side of the particulars, he shrinks no less. The significant words in each selection, and so in the lines themselves, will bear and require understanding to the limit of analysis and limitless meditation. Here, as in Crane, words are associated by the poetic process so as to produce a new and living, an idiomatic, meaning, differing from and surpassing the separate factors involved. The difference—which is where Crane falls short of his standard—is this. Crane's effects remain tricks which can only be resorted to arbitrarily. The effects in the other poets—secured by more craft rather than less—become, immediately they are understood, permanent idioms which enrich the resources of language for all who have the talent to use them. It is perhaps the difference between the immediate unbalance of the assaulted, intoxicated sensibility and the final, no less exciting, clarity of the sane, mirroring sensibility.

It is said that Crane's inchoate heart and distorted intellect only witness the disease of his generation; but I have cited two poets, if not of his generation still his contemporaries, who escaped the contagion. It is the stigma of the first order of poets (a class which includes many minor names and deletes some of the best known) that they master so much of life as they represent. In Crane the poet succumbed with the man.

What judgment flows from these strictures need not impede the appreciation of Crane's insight, observation, and intense, if confused, vision, but ought rather to help determine it. Merely because Crane is imperfect in his kind is no reason to give him up; there is no plethora of perfection, and the imperfect beauty, like life, retains its fascination. And there is about him, too—such were his gifts for the hearts of words, such the vitality of his intelligence—the distraught but exciting splendor of a great failure.

MARIUS BEWLEY

Hart Crane's Last Poem

There is a literary superstition to the effect that the last work of a good artist is likely to show a deeper insight or wisdom, a last gathering of forces, as death comes on. There is enough corroborative evidence offered by the late work of artists who will immediately spring to mind to suggest that the legend is sometimes true. The manuscript of "The Broken Tower" is dated March 25, 1932. As Hart Crane's death occurred on April 27, it is almost certainly his last poem. Brom Weber wrote of it: "This poem is as personal as any poem could be; it is unquestionably one of Crane's most magnificent pieces." His judgment, if more enthusiastically expressed, echoes the general opinion. Unfortunately, its magnificence seems to have been blinding enough to have prevented anyone from looking very closely at it, for I am not aware that the poem has ever been commented on sufficiently to give more than the barest indication of its meaning. It is one of the most difficult poems Crane ever wrote, and the general response to it has been one of bafflement. Yet, paradoxically, it is one of the most logically organized and coherent among Crane's more difficult pieces, and the statement it makes is more central to Crane's life and his view of poetry than any other title in *The Collected Poems*. But its images come to life only when we realize that they are the sheerest verbal integument for a meaning that perfectly informs every word and metaphor in the ten quatrains. To understand that meaning verse by verse is to revive the piety that, at the end, a poet may have a deeper intuition of the meaning of his own creative effort and his life than he ever had before.

If "The Broken Tower" is a deeply personal poem, it is also an

From *Accent* (Spring 1959). Copyright © 1959 by Marius Bewley.

objective and deliberately thought out expression of Crane's literary faith in his last months, and it expresses what he had learned of his own limitations by writing *The Bridge*. But it expresses most of all the anguish of that discovery, and it is from this center of pain that the poetry germinates. There is a letter that Crane wrote to Allen Tate acknowledging the latter's review of *The Bridge* in which he says:

> So many true things have a way of coming out all the better without the strain to sum up the universe in one impressive little pellet. I admit that I don't answer the requirements. My vision of poetry is too personal to "answer the call." And if I ever write any more verse it will probably be at least as personal as the idiom of *White Buildings* whether anyone cares to look at it or not.

Crane's early recognition (which is recurrent in his *Letters*) that *The Bridge* failed is behind this statement to Tate, for we find no such modesty in the notorious letter to Otto Kahn of September 12, 1927, outlining the design of his epic. After its publication, Crane's physical and moral decline allowed him little opportunity for serious composition. We have only "The Broken Tower" that merits serious attention, and if it is magnificent, it is also a little anomalous.

The best external clue to the meaning of the poem is Leslie Simpson's letter to the *New English Weekly*, which Philip Horton quotes in his biography of Crane:

> I was with Hart Crane in Taxco, Mexico, the morning of January 27, this year, when he first conceived the idea of "The Broken Tower." The night before, being troubled with insomnia, he had risen before daybreak and walked down to the village square. It so happened that one of the innumerable Indian fiestas was to be celebrated that day, and Hart met the old Indian bellringer who was on his way down to the Church. He and Hart were old friends, and he brought Hart up into the tower with him to help ring the bells. As Hart was swinging the clapper of the great bell, half drunk with its mighty music, the swift tropical dawn broke over the mountains. The sublimity of the scene and the thunder of the bells woke in Hart one of those gusts of joy of which only he was capable. He came striding up the hill afterwards in a sort of frenzy, refused his breakfast, and paced up and down the porch impatiently waiting for me to finish my coffee. Then he seized my arm and bore me off to the plaza, where we sat in the shadow of the Church, Hart the while pouring out a magnificent cascade of words. It was a Hart Crane I had never known and an experience I shall never forget.

If the experience which began the chain of subjective associations was an intensely personal one, the final meaning which the reader should take from the poem is far more public than the imagery in which it is expressed, and which seems at first so inscrutably private, as if only meant for the eyes of initiated illuminati.

While "The Broken Tower" is self-contained as a poem, it will aid understanding if it is read with *The Bridge*, and particularly with "For the Marriage of Faustus and Helen," freshly in mind. In some ways "The Broken Tower" is a return on Crane's part, after the grandiose aspiration of *The Bridge*, to the more modest intention of the earlier sequence of three poems that composes "Faustus." In the earlier sequence Crane asserts that in the interaction between the abstract ideal and the degrading encroachments of the world that seek to destroy it, the life of the imagination is necessarily condemned to death. Part III ends:

> Distinctly praise the years, whose volatile
> Blamed bleeding hands extend and thresh the height
> The imagination spans beyond despair,
> Outpacing bargain, vocable, and prayer.

But if the imagination persists beyond despair, its final victory is not a complete triumph. "Faustus and Helen" has shown us the ideal of beauty, symbolized by the Helen of Part I, swaying to jazz tunes and exposed to modern lust in the skyscraper roof garden of Part II. Finally, in Part III, the imaginative life and the ideal world towards which it aspires seem utterly destroyed by the catastrophe of the First World War, which Crane unsuccessfully attempts to merge with images of the Trojan siege. But always Anchises escapes to the sea and founds a new city. The imaginative ideal cannot, perhaps, be achieved in a permanent form, but the transient intimations it gives us are all we have of life:

> A goose, tobacco and cologne—
> Three-winged and gold-shod prophecies of heaven,
> The lavish heart shall always have to leaven
> And spread with bells and voices, and atone
> The abating shadows of our conscript dust.

These lines are damaged a little poetically by the awkward obscurity of the opening trio of images, but they express an attitude basically more mature than the mystagogic, self-induced levitation that is attempted in the "Atlantis" section of *The Bridge*. The creative imagination struggles against odds in the world, but it carries an implicit promise with it that makes life endurable. When we look at a goose we are much aware of the part the duck plays in its ancestry, but it also has a good deal of the swan. The reference to tobacco as a prophecy of heaven is unfortunate because it merely suggests the daydreaming escape of the tobacco trance, while the introduction of cologne is too private a reference to deserve discussion. As human beings, we are conscripted to the dust; our spiritual and emotional stature lessens in secular shadow, but the word of the poet, ringing out like a bell, prevents the ultimate encroachment of despair.

It was to this attitude that Crane returned in "The Broken Tower," but he was able to express it in his last poem with far greater concision; and the ordeal of having composed *The Bridge*, in which he tried to transcend his "conscript dust" towards some vaguely conceived cosmic consciousness, gives this poem the weight of a felt, a suffered, experience. It is coherent and emotionally realized in a degree that "Faustus and Helen" is not, but a similarity of imagery indicates the relation between the two pieces.

The first four stanzas of "The Broken Tower" comprise a movement that may be considered as a unit:

> The bell-rope that gathers God at dawn
> Dispatches me as though I dropped down the knell
> Of a spent day—to wander the cathedral lawn
> From pit to crucifix, feel chill on steps from hell.
>
> Have you not heard, have you not seen that corps
> Of shadows in the tower, whose shoulders sway
> Antiphonal carillons launched before
> The stars are caught and hived in the sun's ray?
>
> The bells, I say, the bells break down their tower;
> And swing I know not where. Their tongues engrave
> Membrane through marrow, my long-scattered score
> Of broken intervals. . . . And I, their sexton slave!
>
> Oval encyclicals in canyons heaping
> The impasse high with choir. Banked voices slain!
> Pagodas, campaniles with reveilles outleaping—
> O terraced echoes prostrate on the plain!

In my last quotation from "Faustus and Helen" Crane gives us a hint of the meaning of the bells and the tower. And there is Leslie Simpson's letter. Bells had already been established in his consciousness as the poet's voice, carrying, as we gather from the "Faustus" passage cited and from Simpson's account of the genesis of the poem, an insistent religious connotation. Such a connotation would be agreeable to Crane as the disciple of Whitman, for whom the poet was prophet and priest. If this is the meaning of the bells, then the tower that supports them must necessarily be the poet's vision. Helen of Part I stood for such a faith or vision in the earlier poem. It adds little to the grace of one's reading at this point to suggest that the bell-rope of the first line is the creative impulse of the poet: but that is what it is. Just as the rope of a great bell tyrannically exacts the coordinated response of its ringer's whole body, so are the exactions of the creative impulse on the poet equally tyrannical. And as a church bell calls worshipers to prayer, and rings out divine praises, so the poet endeavors to celebrate his imaginative vision in song. But for the poet of imperfectly realized vision, poetic creation is as much of a struggle as bell-ringing is for the sexton who does not understand the life and rhythm of his bell. So, momentarily relinquishing his grasp, the poet wanders disconsolately between the hell of creative sterility and the heaven of imaginative fulfillment in his art.

In the second verse, the shadows in the tower of vision are the poet's imperfect efforts to create. They recall "The abating shadows of our conscript dust" in "Faustus and Helen," and they suggest the shades of the dead. The sun in Apollo, the god of poetry and music, who enters appropriately here after the dawn image of the poem's opening line. Although the god is not named in the poem, the reference to "that tribunal monarch of the air / Whose thigh embronzes earth" leaves us in no doubt. Moreover, the complex metaphorical development that so closely attends the unfolding argument makes the identification inevitable. The shadow-songs in the poet's tower have been created in darkness, not under the patronage of Apollo, and they are imperfect. In Part II of "Faustus and Helen" Crane spoke of "the siren of the springs of guilty song," and these songs, swaying their shoulders as if in dance, invoke the siren, not the god. They are the songs of lust and darkness that (to quote "Faustus" once more) lead only to

> . . . metallic paradises
> Where cuckoos clucked to finches
> Above the deft catastrophe of drums.

In one of Crane's most impressive metaphors they are contrasted with the light and sweetness that poetry is capable of achieving. In *The Bridge*, stars were employed as a symbol of vision on the point of realization. To take a single instance, one might cite the seventh verse of "The Dance." The protagonist, before leaving his canoe near the headwaters of the river up which he has made his excursion backward in time to achieve mystic identification with the Indian heritage of the past, sees the morning star fading into light. It is not necessary to believe that Crane realized his vision in "The Dance" to recognize the symbolic role the morning star is called upon to play. It is the herald of that mystical immersion in his vision that follows almost immediately in the ritual dance and death. In

"The Broken Tower" the stars that fade into the light of morning represent perfect poems that are totally assimilated in the vision they express. Their light is absorbed by the sun, the god of perfect poetry, and in one of his finest lines Crane implements the star imagery with a suggestion of bees returning laden with sweetness to a great Platonic hive of absolute song. Perhaps it is worth remarking that Crane speaks of them in the second verse in terms of a hypothetical future, and, in any case, as beyond his reach. His tower is still inhabited with shadows.

In the third verse Crane gives us the poet's grapple with meaning. The torturing urgency to express what may even be inexpressible sometimes comes near to destroying the vision altogether:

> The bells, I say, the bells break down their tower.

This had happened, or had come dangerously near to happening, in Crane's own case when he wrote *The Bridge*. But even among the fragments of a vision no longer intact, the creative urgency of the poet continues. The bells swing, surrealistically, even without a supporting faith. This constitutes agony for the poet, and recalls his earlier lines,

> There is the world dimensional for
> those untwisted by the love of things
> Irreconcilable . . .

The commonplace dimensional world of things is only for those who accept its conventional boundaries; it cannot be for the poet, even when his vision is broken. His poetry may be imperfect, but he must continue to make it.

But imperfect or not, there is a sanctity about poems. They are the poet's encyclicals. They are described as oval because, since the metaphor is that of bells, sound radiates outward from its source in circles; and because, since they attempt to embody the poet's vision of the ideal and perfect, they suggest the circle of perfection, yet are imperfectly circular in themselves. Life is an enclosed and low-lying place from which the poet cannot free himself, and by the walls of which his vision is cut off. In the first verse the poet had been "dropped down the knell of a spent day," just as in the "Proem" of *The Bridge* elevators had dropped him from the skyscraper tower of his vision into the city streets where cinemas invite humankind to the pursuit of appearance rather than reality. The poet who seeks an absolute, as Crane had done in *The Bridge*, becomes more than ever aware of the shadow-filled impasse of this "world dimensional." The struggle to escape from its denials towards vision is across a battlefield scattered with the evidences of creative defeat—"Banked voices slain!" But it is a holy struggle, and the voices are a choir's.

The "Atlantis" section of *The Bridge* celebrated high buildings and towers, which became a symbol of aspiration and achieved vision. Returning to this imagery in pagodas and campaniles, eastern temples and bell towers for churches, Crane continues to insist on the religious and aspiring nature of poetry by the introduction here of religious architecture in a surrealistic scene that faintly recalls the "Falling towers" passage in "What the Thunder Said." As the reveille (continuing the battlefield imagery of the preceding lines) is a summons to rise, the word emphasizes here, in a line of frenzied excitement bordering on delirium, the desperate quality of the poet's aspiration. It was a desperation Crane had learned in his struggle with *The Bridge*, seeing the vision elude him and its promises turn to ashes.

But if his vision was fragmentary, it was all he had of life; it was both his love and his hell:

> And so it was I entered the broken world
> To trace the visionary company of love, its voice
> An instant in the wind (I know not whither hurled)
> But not for long to hold each desperate choice.
>
> My word I poured I poured. But was it cognate, scored
> Of that tribunal monarch of the air
> Whose thigh embronzes earth, strikes crystal Word
> In wounds pledged once to hope—cleft to despair?

There is a reference here to the lovers Paolo and Francesca, hurled aimlessly in infernal winds, clasped in each others arms. The cruelty of the line

> But not for long to hold each desperate choice

exists in Crane's growing belief that he had betrayed his vision and his powers. What seemed to him his creative inconstancy is expressed here in imagery that wells up from the growing frustration, in his last years, of his increasingly aimless sexual encounters. He envied the lovers the eternity of their embrace, even in hell.

The sixth verse gives us what are possibly the most moving lines of the poem. Crane handles the dual Christian and pagan implications of his verse with much skill. "My word I poured." "Word" here has a theological significance that is almost immediately developed. The "tribunal monarch," as I have already said, is Apollo. Were his poems, Crane asks, embodiments of that vitality or life force of the sun, suggested here in the reference to Apollo's embronzing thigh? Then, capitalizing Word, he shifts it to its Christian meaning, associating, in a fine act of compression, the word of the poet with the creative fiat of God. As the wounds of Christ brought hope, must the ordeal of the poet be hopeless? Is it (returning to Apollo in the musical term) "cleft to despair"?

The last four verses are technically the most original, as they are also the most difficult and the most personal. They provide us with Crane's final comment and judgment on his own practice as a poet, and on the possibilities of vision:

> The steep encroachments of my blood left me
> No answer (could blood hold such a lofty tower
> As flings the question true?)—or is it she
> Whose sweet mortality stirs latent power?—
>
> And through whose pulse I hear, counting the strokes
> My veins recall and add, revived and sure
> The angelus of wars my chest evokes:
> What I hold healed, original now, and pure . . .
>
> And builds, within, a tower that is not stone
> (Not stone can jacket heaven)—but slip
> Of pebbles—visible wings of silence sown
> In azure circles, widening as they dip
>
> The matrix of the heart, lift down the eye
> That shrines the quiet lake and swells a tower . . .
> The commodious, tall decorum of that sky
> Unseals her earth, and lifts love in its shower.

To recapitulate briefly: the poet, dedicated to an absolute, a Platonic vision, must necessarily fail to achieve it in his art. Crane had learned that the tower of absolute vision was much too lofty for him to climb in his poetry, and he realized this with peculiar clairvoyance at the close of his life when he seemed to be running down in a frenzy of neurotic debauchery. The steep encroachments of his blood seemed to be not only qualifying but destroying his poetic vision. Crane turns, there-fore, from Apollo, whose fierce exactions he cannot satisfy, to the instruc-tion of a lowlier, more human, guide, "she /Whose sweet mortality stirs latent power." This woman is not merely an abstract personification like the Pocahontas of *The Bridge*, she is a gracious evocation from the very center of Crane's own being, and she beckons him back to an acceptance of those creative limitations no poet can escape, but which *The Bridge* had desperately tried to deny. Crane is intimately aware of her in ways that suggest she is not, indeed, physically separable from Crane himself, but is an emblematic concentration of the feminine qualities of submission and humility in his own nature. Crane counts the beats of her pulse, but it is important to observe that the throbbing is in his own veins. She faintly recalls, in her identification with Crane, the nostalgic, nameless yearning he had expressed in "Southern Cross" and embodied in his picture of

> . . . homeless Eve,
> Unwedded, stumbling gardenless, to grieve
> Windswept guitars on lonely decks forever.

This rather exceptional Eve, unwedded and an outcast (Crane's own condition), he describes as "docile, alas, from many arms/ . . . wraith of my unloved seed!" She is less the object of his desire than his feminine counterpart and (in the guitar image) the burden of his songs. In what Brom Weber has called Crane's "womanless life," this focusing of the female elements in his nature—acceptance, passivity, acquiescence, humility—in terms of a symbolic woman is an astonishingly original way of encompassing the full circle of human experience which is necessary to achieve the final vision towards which the poem is directed, and which is explicitly described in the tenth verse. Crane's technical achievement here is more startling and original than Eliot's invention of using the male-female consciousness of Tiresias in *The Waste Land* to attain a somewhat similar goal.

The woman of "The Broken Tower" is differentiated at once from the swaying shadows of the second verse. Her "sweet mortality" relates to the bee and honey imagery of perfect song, but simultaneously qualifies the reference by the idea of limit implicit in "mortality." The presence of the qualities she represents provides a regenerating influence on Crane's vision: "What I hold healed, original now, and pure." The agony he has endured so long subsides before the Angelus, which teaches submission to the creative Word: "Be it done unto me." This is the lesson that he can only learn from woman, and the sweet lady of his poem suddenly looks towards him in the guise of the Virgin.

From this new feeling of wholeness and integrity the poet builds a new vision in which there is an interaction between heaven and earth—a vision in which both the Apollo of absolute song and the lady of "sweet mortality" play their parts. The Angelus, prayer of prophecy and submission, rings the key of the last two stanzas, and they are verses composed of humilities and quiet acceptances. A slip is a pier to which ships come for docking and unloading. The word suggests here Crane's willingness to accept what his vision brings to his poetry without the frenetic attempt to force his experience, as he had done for so long. It is worth noting that the circling wings of the ninth verse recall the circling gull of the "Proem," which was a metaphorically successful prophecy of vision in *The*

Bridge before that vision collapsed. In a sense Crane has returned in almost the last lines he ever wrote to a new beginning and a better vision than the old.

There are two aspects to poetry, then: its godlike aspiration, symbolized by the sun imagery, and its human limitations, embodied in the evoked lady of the seventh and eighth verses. Neither aspect can exist successfully without the other. The last verse deals in opposites which, in the imagery, live harmoniously together. Thus, "lift down" represents a poised balance between the two directions and tendencies. The "eye" is both the eye of the poet and the eye of heaven, the sun. Now that Crane understands that absolute vision can be approached only through the limiting and perhaps distorting perspectives of mortal vision, he draws closer to the possibility of genuine vision than he had ever been before, and one word does service both for the poet's eye and for the sun. This eye, or symbol of vision, shrines a lake—feminine symbol of acquiescence and passivity; but it also swells a tower—a masculine, aggressive symbol. Both symbols are sexual and implicitly contain the images of the god and the earth-bound lady, between whom union is now seen as possible. The blending of these constitutes the resolution, and the heaven of the poet's imagination. The last two lines show the interaction once again of the two tendencies, but it is the god imagery, the sky and the sun, which remains the stronger, though only complete in its acceptance of earth and limitation.

There is something oddly unsatisfactory about the state of Crane criticism today. Crane is readily accorded the rank of "major" American poet, but, the accolade having been given, usually in the most general terms, the talk then continues to anatomize the structural defects of *The Bridge*, the threadbareness of Crane's intellectual tradition, the inadequacy of his myth, or the occult obscurity of his imagery. One wonders how anyone dare call such a fellow, whom everyone is engaged in showing up, a "major" poet. The practical result has been that Crane is less read today than any other American poet of comparable importance. It is essential to understand the large defects of his poetry, and the critics who have outlined them have only performed their function in doing so. But on the positive side there is still a good deal to be said, and this is largely concerned with the complex beauty of Crane's best imagery, and the effectively original organization of his best poems. Yet on these points there has been comparative silence.

Crane himself is largely responsible for this state of affairs. His early admiration for P. D. Ouspensky and the higher consciousness, and his scattered remarks about a new dynamics of metaphor, and a use of symbols outside the rational order, have not encouraged a close scrutiny of what he was doing on the level of practice. Crane's poetry shows an unusually strong rational bias, which his blueprints for the structure of *The Bridge* should indicate, even if other evidence were lacking. Through most of his career it is probable that he misunderstood the nature of his own genius, for his theoretical statements on logic and metaphor sometimes seem to apply more aptly to *Ash Wednesday* or to Wallace Stevens' work than to his own, which is essentially different from either. The importance and beauty of "The Broken Tower" partly arise from the new depth of Crane's intuition into the creative process of his own mind, and from his willingness to accept it at last without forcing it into something larger than itself. It shows us Crane working his way into a new wisdom.

The organization of the poem clearly employs no new order of logic, no suprarational use of symbols. It is an extremely difficult piece to cope with at first, but it gradually becomes clear that its difficulty is similar to what an early reader of Hopkins would have experienced. It is chiefly a matter of extraordinary verbal and syntactical compression, and the occasional elimination of nonessential words. In Hopkins' case such metaphorical compression has been called Shakespearean, and the term seems to me no less applicable to certain verses of this poem. Nor do I find a strained relationship between Crane's symbols and the reality they signify. The bells and the tower correspond at least as naturally and as tautly to the poet's voice and vision as Hopkins' windhover corresponds to Christ. Allen Tate has written: ". . . with poetry which is near us in time, or contemporaneous, much of the difficulty that appears to be in the language as such, is actually in the unfamiliar focus of feeling, belief, and experience which directs the language from the concealed depths that we must laboriously try to enter." The difficulty of much of Crane's language is easily resolved by an application of those disciplines with which critics have been so ready and so adept in the case of Crane's contemporaries. Crane's poetry will not again have many readers until we cease to take Crane at his word and forget all that he said about the new dynamics of poetry and its new logic, its new use of symbols, and P. D. Ouspensky. These are will-o'-the-wisps, and only distract us from the more deeply traditional ways in which the originality of Crane's poetry, at its very best, enlarged and enriched the resources of language.

HARVEY GROSS

Hart Crane and Wallace Stevens

I make no strong case for pairing these two poets other than that they both possess the "American sensibility." As poets they are as different in technique and temperament as Tennyson and Browning. Their dissimilarity, in fact, may serve critical generalization; in the dialectic of extreme opposition, Red and White, Left and Right, often exhibit comparable qualities. Hart Crane represents the American writer brutally scarred by his experience, and critics call him alienated; Wallace Stevens kept a fastidious distance between himself and "real life." He has also been called alienated. We may often wish Crane could submerge his turbulence and allow the poetry to sing through, unencumbered by the mud and silt dredged up from the sunless bottoms of rivers and seas. We may often wish that Stevens' poetry were less fictive, less of the sun and the moon, of "the formulations of midnight"; that it admit a subject larger than poetry itself. But the wishes of critics, set against the achievement of Crane and Stevens, are paltry things; the poets gave themselves magnificently, and it is ungrateful to ask for something else. If the wishes of critics were horses, all poets would be riding Shakespeare's Pegasus.

On one matter Crane and Stevens do approach each other; neither had a gift for the "plain style"; each sought after the incantatory power of words, the authority of rich and rhythmic language. In attempting to characterize the style of both poets, the word "rhetorical" comes immediately to mind. Although rhetoric has fallen into disrepute—many poets misunderstood Pound to have said poetry should be as flatly written as prose—twentieth-century poetry has often made use of resounding rhetoric; Yeats, Thomas, Eliot, when occasion and need make it appropriate, do not avoid Shakespearean or even Miltonic vividness. Too much has been made of "verse as speech" and the "conversational idiom"; it is not the low-keyed poems in gray language which raise the hairs on the back of the neck and set the stimulus singing along the ganglia.

The implications for prosody are clear. Rhetoric can only be sustained by consummate rhythmic control; the great masters of rhetoric in English, Shakespeare and Milton, have also been the greatest masters of metric. Rhetoric is language with more senuous surface than conceptual substance; it becomes the job of prosody, then, to keep rhetoric from flowing into pure sound or dissolving into pure image. Rhythm, the container in which time is contained, tells us how an idea feels; rhythm will rescue for cognition what may never receive articulate verbal expression, what rhetoric may overstate or conceal.

Crane's rhetoric is often self-defeating. It stems from injured sensibility, from a stupendous reaction to experience, or from simple ignorance. When Crane is in control of his rhythm, however, we can overlook rhetorical excess and exalt with him in the joyous use of language. Stevens' rhetoric is not often amazed reaction to experience and never ignorance; rather, it is diffidence: an effort to bring, without philosophical pompousness, the indefinable to definition. Stevens' purest rhetoric, his infamous use of nonsense syllables, has irritated many; but it is precisely here that we frequently discover Stevens bringing the subtlest thought and feeling into view:

> We say: At night an Arabian in my room,
> With his damned hoobla-hoobla-hoobla-how,
> Inscribes a primitive astronomy
>
> Across the unscrawled fores the future casts
> And throws his stars around the floor. By day
> The wood-dove used to chant his hoobla-hoo
>
> And still the grossest iridescence of ocean
> Howls hoo and rises and howls hoo and falls.
> Life's nonsense pierces us with strange relation.
> (Notes toward a Supreme Fiction)

Stevens' rhetoric, the hoobla-hoobla of "life's nonsense," forms part of his meaning, piercing us "with strange relation." Stevens' rhetoric does not always come off; the relations may remain persistently, stubbornly strange as they do in the opening lines of "Credences of Summer":

> Now in midsummer come and all fools slaughtered
> And spring's infuriations over and a long way
> To the first autumnal inhalations, young broods
> Are in the grass . . .

But so gripping are the rhythms here, so compelling the movement, that we almost forget our syntactical bafflement (is *come* noun or verb?), and our wonder about what particular fools were slaughtered and why. The rhythm affects our inner perception with a feeling of ripeness and fullness of time and that sense of continual change which penetrates all life, all reality.

I

> . . . after the erection of the Chinese Wall of Milton,
> blank verse suffered not only arrest but
> retrogression.
>
> (T. S. Eliot, "Marlowe")

The distinction of Eliot's prosody erected its own "Chinese Wall." A poet, coming under its shadow, could write his heart out, strain to clamber over the wall—as did Hart Crane. The tone and texture of Crane's verse are notably uneven; we are frequently jarred by the crudity of his rhythms, his inability to discover the appropriate metrical form for his feelings. Much that is rhythmically bad in Crane's poetry has its origin in Eliot's unassimilated influence: Crane never learned to master the delicate balance between "fixity and flux" which sets Eliot apart from the large numbers of his imitators. Crane did discover a metrical idiom congenial to his talent, but he first broke his head against The Chinese Wall.

Here is Crane's version of Eliotic ennui and urban despair:

> Behind
> My father's cannery works I used to see
> Rail-squatters ranged in nomad raillery,
> The ancient men—wifeless or runaway
> Hobo-trekkers that forever search
> An empire wilderness of freight and rails.
> Each seemed a child, like me, on a loose perch,
> Holding to childhood like some termless play.
> John, Jake or Charley, hopping the low freight
> —Memphis to Tallahassee—riding the rods,
> Blind fists of nothing, humpty-dumpty clods.
> ("The River" from *The Bridge*)

And here is the passage Crane was, consciously or otherwise, using as his model:

> A rat crept softly through the vegetation
> Dragging its slimy belly on the bank
> While I was fishing in the dull canal
> On a winter evening round behind the gashouse
> Musing upon the king my brother's wreck
> And on the king my father's death before him.
> (The Waste Land)

Crane maintains a steady iambic beat; the lines are clinched with resonant rhymes. Crane's language intends to express something of *Waste Land*-ish hopelessness and horror, of the desolate landscapes behind the gashouse and the cannery works, but the couplets almost bounce with good-humored vitality. We wonder if Crane's intention might not be parody here: as if he were deliberately trying to show there is life and energy behind the gashouse yet!

The Bridge gives other evidence of Crane's struggle against the Eliotic mode. Occasionally Crane gets close to the spirit of Eliot's technical discoveries, but his discomfort with freer rhythms leads him into awkward rhyming and odd locutions:

> So memory that strikes a rhyme out of a box
> Or splits a random smell of flowers through glass—
> Is it the whip stripped from the lilac tree
> One day in spring my father took to me,
> Or is it the Sabbatical, unconscious smile
> My mother almost brought me once from church
> And once only, as I recall—?
> ("Van Winkle" from The Bridge)

The third line is beautifully sprung by the trochaic third foot; the next line, with its doggerel meter and rhyme, wrecks the passage. Again I offer a corresponding passage from *The Waste Land*, not for odious comparison, but to show how intensely personal Eliot's rhythms are:

> *Dayadhvam:* I have heard the key
> Turn in the door once and turn once only
> We think of the key, each in his prison
> Thinking of the key, each confirms a prison . . .
> (The Waste Land)

Crane knew what he was up against, playing Eliot's gambits. In letters to Allen Tate and Gorham Munson, he assesses his situation, vis-à-vis Eliot:

I have been facing [Eliot] for *four* years,—and while I haven't discovered a weak spot yet in his armour, I flatter myself a little lately that I have discovered a safe tangent to strike which, if I can possibly explain the position,—goes *through* him toward a *different goal*. You see it is such a fearful temptation to imitate him that at times I have been almost distracted. . . . In his own realm Eliot presents us with an absolute *impasse*, yet oddly enough he can be utilized to lead us to, intelligently point to, other positions and 'pastures new.' Having absorbed him enough we can trust ourselves as never before, in the air or on the sea.

However, I take Eliot as a point of departure toward an almost complete reverse of direction. His pessimism is amply justified in his own case. But I would apply as much of his erudition and technique as I can absorb and assemble toward a more positive, or (if [I] must put it so in a skeptical age) ecstatic goal. I should not think of this if a kind of rhythm and ecstasy were not (at odd moments, and rare!) a very real thing to me.

Crane quarrels with Eliot's temperament; he could not *feel* what Eliot felt but suggests that Eliot's techniques might be used to express his own more exuberant, more violent nature. Unfortunately Eliot's metrical techniques, his subtle and limpid rhythms, were hardly suited to Crane's emotional make-up and even less suited to Crane's subjects. And Crane did not have Eliot's ear for conversation, the gift for rendering contemporary speech. The overheard conversations and interpolated monologues in *The Bridge* are fashionable pastiche effects and now sound dated. The distance between Crane and verse-as-speech was considerable; note the unevenness of tone and uncertain rhythm in this passage:

> "I ran a donkey engine down there on the Canal
> in Panama—got tired of that—
> then Yucatan selling kitchenware—beads—
> have you seen Popocatepetl—birdless mouth
> with ashes sifting down—?
>   and then the coast again . . ."
>   ("Cutty Sark" from *The Bridge*)

Crane does not maintain convincing speech cadence; the last line shifts suddenly into formal hexameter, breaking cleanly at the sixth syllable:

> with aśh | es síft | ing dówn—? ‖
>   and theń | the coást | a gáin . . .

The final lines of "Cape Hatteras" explode down the page in fine Imagist disorder; it looks like authentic visual prosody:

> Yes, Walt,
> Afoot again, and onward without halt,—

> Not soon, nor suddenly,—No, never to let go
> My hand
>   in yours,
>   Walt Whitman—
>   so—

The fermatas for the eye function aurally, but the lines scan as regular iambics. We have the curious case of a perfectly conventional syllable-stress meter masquerading as the wildest free verse. Crane's prosodic posing conceals a pedestrian rhythm and an embarrassingly maudlin sentiment.

The example of Crane underlines a continuing assertion of this book: that prosody has neither decorative nor semantic functions apart from the work it does as a conveyer of feeling. As long as Crane used, or tried to use, Eliot's rhythms, he was expressing feelings inimical to his own temperament. He could not adapt Eliot's loosened metric to what he had to say. His view of the world did not include Eliot's particular horror and despair. Crane's gift, like Whitman's, was ceremonious and rhetorical; his true poetic *métier* was the apostrophe, the classic form of lyric celebration. His best works are set pieces: the "Proem: To Brooklyn Bridge," the "Voyages," and the magnificent conclusion to "The River."

In these poems we observe a sureness of prosodic technique; the rhythms neither falter nor prove embarrassing to the concepts. The meter Crane settles on is a traditional pentameter which lends itself to the cadences of invocation. The form may seem limiting; it restricts Crane to only a few octaves of feeling. But Crane's development as a poet, up to the time he leaped from the S. S. "Orizaba," was perfectly congruent with the meter in which he accomplished his best work. Actually, he had absorbed from Eliot and others more technique than his sensibility and experience could possibly transmute into first-rate poetry. Or, to put it differently, he possessed metrical knowledge which his emerging powers as a poet could not put to use.

Crane's true metrical idiom was the unashamedly rhetorical line of the Elizabethans. If Eliot at a crucial point in his career found the relaxed blank verse of Jacobean dramatists suited to his moods, so Crane discovered in Marlowe and Jonson rhythms consonant with his exuberance and awe. Here Crane celebrates the Brooklyn Bridge:

> O harp and altar, of the fury fused,
> (How could mere toil align thy choiring strings!)
> Terrific threshold of the prophet's pledge,
> Prayer of pariah, and the lover's cry,—

Again the traffic lights that skim thy swift
Unfractioned idiom, immaculate sigh of stars,
Beading thy path—condense eternity:
And we have seen night lifted in thine arms.

Under thy shadow by the piers I waited;
Only in darkness is thy shadow clear.
The City's fiery parcels all undone,
Already snow submerges an iron year . . .

O Sleepless as the river under thee,
Vaulting the sea, the prairies' dreaming sod,
Unto us lowliest sometime sweep, descend
And of the curveship lend a myth to God.
                    ("Proem: To Brooklyn Bridge")

Earlier we suggested that the success of a prosody might be measured by what a poet can get away with. Crane's rhythm minimizes his uncertain, almost haphazard syntactical progression. Perhaps, by definition, the apostrophe requires no explicit grammar; the understood subject of every sentence is The Bridge, and every verb links the poet to his love. But without the binding meter, the omission of verbs and uncertain use of reference would be destructively apparent.

Crane's "mighty line" also overrides his flawed diction and conceals his queer metaphorical mixtures; carried along by the excited movement, we are not disposed to wonder what *unfractioned idiom* means, what precisely is intended by the image. *Vaulting the sea*, or whether a neologism such as *curveship* is defensible. Similarly, possessed, even drugged by Crane's rhythms, we are apt to overlook obvious errors in the choice of words; *wrapt* in the fifth line below (from *Voyages II*) has grotesque connotations:

And yet this great wink of eternity,
Of rimless floods, unfettered leewardings,
Samite sheeted and processioned where
Her undinal vast belly moonward bends,
Laughing the wrapt inflections of our love . . .

Crane meant *rapt*—his misspelling may be a case of homonymic confusion. Again, the sounding rhythms conceal an ill-contrived syntax: every line is a shifted construction; images drift and float off, cut from their grammatical moorings. Crane's derangement of language is the result of his Dionysiac methods of composition, the raging of his personal demon, and his commitment to Symbolist practice. But the flaring heat of Crane's rhythm, the absolute energy of his genius, fuses the second stanza of *Voyages II*:

> Take this Sea, whose diapason knells
> On scrolls of silver snowy sentences,
> The sceptered terror of whose sessions rends
> As her demeanors motions well or ill,
> All but the pieties of lovers' hands . . .

In three lines we find compacted grammatical ambiguity (is *knells* verb or noun?), a wild synaesthesia (*diapason* is *seen* on scrolls of snowy sentences), and Shakespearean cliché (*sceptred terror*).

These two stanzas appear to live on their prosody alone; the emotional force and solemn dignity of their rhythms seem, on first impact, independent of what the language is saying. But the metrical craft surprises with its sudden relevance; eternity's wink is felt as the spasmodic tremor of an inverted third foot:

And yét | this gréat | wínk of | e tér | ni tý . . .

We note other prosodical details. With few exceptions the lines are heavily end stopped. Crane unconsciously feels for rhymes: *bends* in the first stanza is echoed by *rends* and *hands* in the second stanza; *knells* is echoed by *ill*. The last two stanzas modulate into new clarity; aided now by syntactical closeness, a grammatically precise handling of imperatives, the metrical pressure forces the poet into prophetic lucidity as he foretells his own death by water:

> Mark how her turning shoulders wind the hours,
> And hasten while her penniless rich palms
> Pass superscription of bent foam and wave,—
> Hasten, while they are true,—sleep, death, desire,
> Close round one instant in one floating flower.
>
> Bind us in time, O Seasons clear, and awe.
> O minstrel galleons of Carib fire,
> Bequeath us to no earthly shore until
> Is answered in the vortex of our grave
> The seal's wide spindrift gaze toward paradise.

Perhaps Crane's greatest sustained passage is the concluding section of "The River." Syntax and meter are exactly suited here to Crane's feelings of relentless movement and religious awe:

> Down, down—born pioneers in time's despite,
> Grimed tributaries to an ancient flow—
> They win no frontier by their wayward plight,
> But drift in stillness, as from Jordan's brow.

You will not hear it as the sea; even stone
Is not more hushed by gravity . . . But slow,
As loth to take more tribute—sliding prone
Like one whose eyes were buried long ago

The River, spreading, flows—and spends your dream.
What are you, lost within this tideless spell?
You are your father's father, and the stream—
A liquid theme that floating niggers swell.

Damp tonnage and alluvial march of days—
Nights turbid, vascular with silted shale
And roots surrendered down of moraine clays:
The Mississippi drinks the farthest dale.

O quarrying passion, undertowed sunlight!
The basalt surface drags a jungle grace
Ochreous and lynx-barred in lengthening might;
Patience! and you shall reach the biding place!

Over De Soto's bones the freighted floors
Throb past the City storied of three thrones.
Down two more turns the Mississippi pours
(Anon tall ironsides up from salt lagoons)

And flows within itself, heaps itself free.
All fades but one thin skyline 'round . . . Ahead
No embrace opens but the stinging sea;
The River lifts itself from its long bed,

Poised wholly on its dream, a mustard glow
Tortured with history, its one will—flow!
—The Passion spreads in wide tongues, choked and slow,
Meeting the Gulf, hosannas silently below.

If, as Eliot points out, Marlowe "commenced the dissociative process which drew [blank verse] farther and farther away from the rhythms of rhymed verse," it was Crane who worked blank verse back into the rhythms of rhymed verse, and then attempted to revive rhymed verse as a major form. In these "heroic quatrains" from "The River" Crane discovers the prosodic form most congenial to his genius. His failures in freer rhythms and unrhymed verse point to the unformed, highly uneven quality of his genius—he had nowhere attained full powers before his death—and to a striking conflict of *Zeitgeist* and sensibility. Crane wanted to follow the "conversational mode" and prose syntax which Pound and Eliot espoused as *the* twentieth-century prosody (though their individual practice diverged widely from their professed ideals); he found himself, like those post-Miltonic writers of blank verse, Thomson and Warton, behind the unscalable Chinese Wall.

ALAN TRACHTENBERG

The Shadow of a Myth

In the winter of 1923, Hart Crane, a twenty-four-year-old poet living in Cleveland, announced plans to write a long poem called *The Bridge*. It was to be an epic, a "mystical synthesis of America." Crane had just completed *For the Marriage of Faustus and Helen*, a poem which sought to infuse modern Faustian culture (the term was Spengler's, designating science and restless searching) with love of beauty and religious devotion. Now, confirmed in his commitment to visionary poetry and feeling "directly connected with Whitman," Crane prepared for an even greater effort: to compose the myth of America. The poem would answer "the complete renunciation symbolized in *The Waste Land*," published the year before. Eliot had used London Bridge as a passageway for the dead, on which "each man fixed his eyes before his feet." Crane replied by projecting his myth of affirmation upon Brooklyn Bridge.

In the spring of 1923, Hart Crane left his father's home in Cleveland, and from then until his suicide in 1932, lived frequently in Brooklyn Heights, close to "the most beautiful Bridge of the world." He crossed the bridge often, alone and with friends, sometimes with lovers: "the cables enclosing us and pulling us upward in such a dance as I have never walked and never can walk with another." Part III of *Faustus and Helen* had been set in the shadow of the bridge, "where," Crane wrote, "the edge of the bridge leaps over the edge of the street." In the poem the bridge is the "Capped arbiter of beauty in this street," "the ominous lifted arm / That lowers down the arc of Helen's brow." Its "curve" of "memory" transcends "all stubble streets."

From *Brooklyn Bridge: Fact and Symbol.* Copyright © 1965 by Alan Trachtenberg. Oxford University Press.

Crane tried to keep Brooklyn Bridge always before him, in eye as well as in mind. In April 1924 he wrote: "I am now living in the shadow of the bridge." He had moved to 110 Columbia Heights, into the very house, and later, the very room occupied fifty years earlier by Roebling. Like the crippled engineer, the poet was to devote his most creative years to the vision across the harbor. In his imagination the shadow of the bridge deepened into the shadow of a myth.

I

The Bridge, Crane wrote, "carries further the tendencies manifest in 'F and H.' " These tendencies included a neo-Platonic conception of a "reality" beyond the evidence of the senses. The blind chaos of sensation in the modern city apparently denies this transcendent reality, but a glimpse of it is available, through ecstasy, to the properly devout poet. Helen represents the eternal, the unchanging; Faustus, the poet's aspiration; and the "religious gunman" of Part III, spirit of the Dionysian surrender (sexual as well as aesthetic) necessary for a vision of the eternal. The threefold image constitutes what Kenneth Burke has called an "aesthetic myth"—a modern substitute for "religious myth." The poet's impulse toward beauty is a mark of divinity. A part of the myth, and another "tendency" of the poem, is what Crane called its "fusion of our time with the past." The past is represented by the names Faustus and Helen; the present by the data of the poem: the "memoranda," the "baseball scores," and "stock quotations" of Part I; the jazz dance of Part II; the warplanes of Part III. The present fails to live up to the past. But the poet, a "bent axle of devotion," keeps his "lone eye" riveted upon Helen; he offers her "one inconspicuous, glowing orb of praise." At the end, in communion with the "religious gunman," he accepts and affirms past and present, the "years" whose "hands" are bloody; he has attained "the height/ The imagination spans beyond despair."

The idea of a bridge is explicit in the closing image; earlier, as I have indicated, it had appeared in fact, leaping over the street. In the projected poem, it will leap far beyond the street, but its function will be similar: an emblem of the eternal, providing a passage between the Ideal and the transitory sensations of history, a way to unify them.

In the earliest lines written for the new poem, the bridge was the location of an experience like that which ends Faustus and Helen: the imagination spanning beyond despair.

And midway on that structure I would stand
One moment, not as diver, but with arms
That open to project a disk's resilience
Winding the sun and planets in its face.

Expansive center, pure moment and electron
That guards like eyes that must look always down
In reconcilement of our chains and ecstasy
Crashing manifoldly on us as we hear
The looms, the wheels, the whistles in concord
Tethered and welded as the hills of dawn . . .

Somewhat like Wordsworth on Westminster Bridge, here the poet experiences harmony, his troubled self annihilated in a moment of worship. Subsequently Crane developed a narrative to precede this experience. In the narrative, or myth, the poet, like Faustus, was to be the hero, and his task a quest—not for Helen but her modern equivalent: Brooklyn Bridge.

Although the bridge lay at the end of quest, it was not, like the grail in *The Waste Land*, simply a magical object occupying a given location. It does not wait to be found, but to be created. That is, it represents not an external "thing," but an internal process, an act of consciousness. The bridge is not "found" in "Atlantis," the final section of the poem, but "made" throughout the poem. In "Atlantis" what has been "made" is at last recognized and named: "O Thou steeled Cognizance." Its properties are not magical but conceptual: it is a "Paradigm" of love and beauty, the eternal ideas which lie behind and inform human experience.

If we follow the poet's Platonic idea, to "think" the bridge is to perceive the unity and wholeness of history. In the poem, history is not chronological nor economic nor political. Crane wrote: "History and fact, location, etc., all have to be transfigured into abstract form that would almost function independently of its subject matter." Crane intended to re-create American history according to a pattern he derived from its facts. His version of American history has nothing in common with the ceremonial parade of Founding Fathers and bearded generals of popular culture. The poet's idea, and especially his distinction between history and "abstract form," is closer to what the anthropologist Mircea Eliade describes as the predominant ontology of archaic man—the myth of "eternal return." According to Eliade, the mind of archaic man sought to resist history—the line of "irreversible events"—by re-creating, in his rituals, the pre-temporal events of his mythology, such as the creation of the world. Unable to abide a feeling of uniqueness, early men identified, in their rituals, the present with the mythic past, thus abolishing the present as an autonomous moment of time. All events and actions "acquire a value," writes Eliade, "and in so doing become real, because they participate, after one fashion or another, in a reality that transcends them." The only "real" events are those recorded in mythology, which in turn become models for imitation, "paradigmatic gestures." All precious stones are precious because of thunder from heaven; all sacred buildings are sacred because they are built over the divine Center of the world; all sexual acts repeat the primordial act of creation. A non-precious stone, non-sacred building, a non-sanctified act of sex—these are not real. History, as distinct from myth, consists of such random acts and events, underived from an archetype; therefore history is not real and must be periodically "annulled." By imitating the "paradigmatic gesture" in ritual, archaic men transported themselves out of the realm of the random, of "irreversible events," and "re-actualized" the mythic epoch in which the original archetypal act occurred. Hence for the primitive as for the mystic, time has no lasting influence: "events repeat themselves because they imitate an archetype." Like the mystic, the primitive lives in a "continual present."

The Bridge is a sophisticated and well-wrought version of the archaic myth of return. The subject matter of the poem is drawn from legends about American history: Columbus, Pocahontas, Cortez, De Soto, Rip Van Winkle, the gold-rush, the whalers; and from contemporary reality: railroads, subways, warplanes, office buildings, cinemas, burlesque queens. Woven among these strands are allusions to world literature: the Bible, Plato, Marlowe, Shakespeare, Blake; and most important, to American artists: Whitman, Melville, Poe, Dickinson, Isadora Duncan. The action of the poem comprises through its fifteen sections, one waking day, from dawn in "Harbor Dawn," to midnight in "Atlantis." Through the device of dream, that single day includes vast stretches of time and space: a subway ride in the morning extends to a railroad journey to the Mississippi, then back in time, beyond De Soto, to the primeval world of the Indians, then forward to the West of the pioneers. In a sense, the entire day is a dream; the poet journeys through his own consciousness toward an awakening. He seeks to learn the meaning of American history which, in so far as that history is inseparable from his own memories, is the meaning of himself: Cathay, which designates the end of the journey, or the discovery of a new world, Crane wrote, is "an attitude of spirit," a self-discovery.

Thus in no sense of the word is The Bridge a historical poem. Its mode is myth. Its aim is to overcome history, to abolish time and the autonomy of events, and to show that all meaningful events partake of an archetype: the quest for a new world. In this regard the importance of Walt Whitman requires special notice. For among the many influences that worked upon Crane, few were as persuasive as Whitman's.

In "Passage to India," we have seen, Whitman identified the quest for wholeness—the "rondure"—as the chief theme and motive of American life. In Whitman's version of history, man was expelled from Eden into time: "Wandering, yearning, curious, with restless explorations,/ With questions, baffled, formless, feverish." Divided into separate and warring nations, at odds with nature, historical man was a sufferer. Now, however, in modern America, the end of suffering was in sight. The connecting works of engineers—the Suez Canal, the Atlantic Cable, the Union Pacific Railroad—had introduced a new stage; the separate geographical parts of the world were now linked into one system. The physical labors of engineers, moreover, were spiritual food for the poet; the "true son of God" recognized that by uniting East and West such works completed Columbus's voyage. Now it was clear: The "hidden" purpose of history was the brotherhood of races that would follow the bridges and canals of modern technology.

Crane was not interested principally in Whitman's social vision, but in his conception of poetry as the final step in the restoration of man's wholeness. Not the engineer nor the statesman nor the captain of industry, but the poet was the true civilizer. Translating engineering accomplishments into ideas, the poet completed the work of history, and prepared for the ultimate journey to "more than India," the journey to the Soul: "thou actual Me." Thus the poet recognized that all of history culminated in self-discovery; and he would lead the race out of its bondage in time and space to that moment of consciousness in which all would seem one. That moment of "return" would redeem history by abolishing it. In short, Crane inherited from Whitman the belief in the poet's function to judge history from the point of view of myth.

Whitman himself appears in "Cape Hatteras," which represents a critical phase of the action of The Bridge. In the preceeding sections, the poet had set out to find Pocahontas, the spirit of the land. With Rip Van Winkle his Muse of Memory, and the Twentieth Century Limited his vehicle, he moved westward out of the city to the Mississippi, the river of time. Borne backward on the stream, he found the goddess, joined her dance of union with nature, and thus entered the archetype. Now he must return to the present, to bridge the personal vision of the goddess and the actuality of modern America. An old sailor (possibly Melville) in a South Street bar and an apparition of old clipper ships from Brooklyn Bridge in

"Cutty Sark," are reminders of the quest. But the old has lost its direction; the age requires a renewal.

"Cape Hatteras" is the center of the span that leaps from Columbus to Brooklyn Bridge. The sea voyages are now done, the rondure accomplished. Now, a complacent age of stocks, traffic, and radios has lost sight of its goal; instead of a bridge, the age has created "a labyrinth submersed/ Where each sees only his dim past reversed." War, not peace and brotherhood, has succeeded the engineers, and flights into space are undertaken, not by poets but by war planes. "Cape Hatteras" poses the key questions of the poem: "What are the grounds for hope that modern history will not destroy itself?" "Where lies redemption?" "Is there an alternative to the chaos of the City?"

The answers are in Whitman's "sea eyes," "bright with myth." He alone has kept sight of the abstract form, the vision of ultimate integration. His perspective is geological; he stands apart, with "something green,/ Beyond all sesames of science." Whitman envisioned the highest human possibilities within the facts of chaos. It was he who "stood up and flung the span on even wing/ Of that great Bridge, our Myth, whereof I sing." He is a presence: "Familiar, thou, as mendicants in public places." He has kept faith, even among the most disastrous circumstances of betrayal. With his help, the flight into space might yet become "that span of consciousness thou'st named/ The Open Road."

"Cape Hatteras" introduces the violence and the promise, the despair and the hope, of modern life. It argues for the effectiveness of ideals, for the power of Utopia over history. The poet places his hand in Whitman's, and proceeds upon his quest. Returning from the sea in "Southern Cross," he searches for love in "National Winter Garden" and "Virginia," for community and friendship in "Quaker Hill," and for art in "The Tunnel." He finds nothing but betrayal: the strip tease dancer burlesques Pocahontas, the office girl is a pallid Mary, the New Avalon Hotel and golf course mock the New England tradition, and the tunnel crucifies Poe. But throughout, the poet's hand is in Whitman's, and at last, having survived the terrors of "The Tunnel," he arrives at the bridge.

II

Brooklyn Bridge lay at the end of the poet's journey, the pledge of a "cognizance" that would explain and redeem history. To reach the bridge, to attain its understanding, the poet suffered the travail of hell. But he emerges unscathed, and ascends the span. In "Atlantis" he reaches

Cathay, the symbol of sublime consciousness. The entire action implies a steady optimism that no matter how bad history may be, the bridge will reward the struggle richly. Such is its promise in the opening section of the poem, "Proem: To Brooklyn Bridge."

> How many dawns, chill from his rippling rest
> The seagull's wings shall dip and pivot him,
> Shedding white rings of tumult, building high
> Over the chained bay waters Liberty—
>
> Then, with inviolate curve, forsake our eyes
> As apparitional as sails that cross
> Some page of figures to be filed away;
> —Till elevators drop us from our day . . .
>
> I think of cinemas, panoramic sleights
> With multitudes bent toward some flashing scene
> Never disclosed, but hastened to again,
> Foretold to other eyes on the same screen;
>
> And Thee, across the harbor, silver-paced
> As though the sun took step of thee, yet left
> Some motion ever unspent in thy stride,—
> Implicitly thy freedom staying thee!
>
> Out of some subway scuttle, cell or loft
> A bedlamite speeds to thy parapets,
> Titling there momently, shrill shirt ballooning,
> A jest falls from the speechless caravan.
>
> Down Wall, from girder into street noon leaks,
> A rip-tooth of the sky's acetylene;
> All afternoon the cloud-flown derricks turn . . .
> Thy cables breathe the North Atlantic still.
>
> And obscure as that heaven of the Jews,
> Thy guerdon . . . Accolade thou dost bestow
> Of anonymity time cannot raise:
> Vibrant reprieve and pardon thou dost show.
>
> O harp and altar, of the fury fused,
> (How could mere toil align thy choiring strings!)
> Terrific threshold of the prophet's pledge,
> Prayer of pariah, and the lover's cry,—
>
> Again the traffic lights skim thy swift
> Unfractioned idiom, immaculate sigh of stars,
> Beading thy path—condense eternity:
> And we have seen night lifted in thine arms.

Under thy shadow by the piers I waited;
Only in darkness is thy shadow clear.
The City's fiery parcels all undone,
Already snow submerges an iron year . . .

O Sleepless as the river under thee,
Vaulting the sea, the prairies' dreaming sod,
Unto us lowliest sometime sweep, descend
And of the curveship lend a myth to God.

The setting of "Proem" in the harbor and lower Manhattan area is distinct, though the point of view shifts a good deal within this area, from a long view of the Bay and the Statue of Liberty, to an office in a skyscraper, down an elevator into the street, into a dark movie house, and then to the sun-bathed bridge. The view of the bridge also changes, from "across the harbor," in which the sun appears to be walking up the diagonal stays, to the promenade and towers as the bedlamite "speeds to thy parapets." Later the point of view is under the bridge, in its shadow. The shifting perspectives secure the object in space; there is no question that it is a bridge across a river between two concretely realized cities.

At the same time, the bridge stands apart from its setting, a world of its own. A series of transformations in the opening stanzas bring us to it. We begin with a seagull at dawn—a specific occurrence, yet eternal ("How many dawns"). The bird's wings leave our eyes as an "inviolate curve" (meaning unprofaned as well as unbroken) to become "apparitional as sails" (apparitional implies "epiphanal" as well as spectral and subjective). Then, in a further transmutation, they become a "page of figures." As the wings leave our eyes, so does the page: "filed away." Then, elevators "drop us" from the bird to the street. In the shift from bird to page to elevator, we have witnessed the transformation of a curve into a perpendicular, of an organism into a mechanism—wings into a list of numbers. "Filed away," the vision of the curve, identified with "sails" and voyages, has been forgotten ("How many" times?), like a page of reckonings. The quest for a vision of bird and sails resumes in the cinema, but, as in Plato's cave, the "flashing scene" is "never disclosed." Then, the eye finds a permanent vision of the curve in the "silver-paced" bridge.

The bridge has emerged from a counterpoint of motions (bird vs. elevator; sails vs. "multitudes bent") as an image of self-containment. Surrounded by a frantic energy ("some flashing scene . . . hastened to again"; "A bedlamite speeds . . .") the bridge is aloof; its motions express the sun. Verbs like drop, tilt, leak, submerge describe the city; the bridge is rendered by verbs like turn, breathe, lift, sweep. Established in its own visual plane, with a motion of its own, the bridge is prepared, by stanza seven, to receive the epithets of divinity addressed to it. Like Mary, it embraces, reprieves, and pardons. Its cables and towers are "harp and altar." The lights of traffic along its roadway, its "unfractioned idiom," seem to "condense eternity." Finally, as night has extinguished the cities and thereby clarified the shadow of the bridge, its true meaning becomes clear: its "curveship" represents an epiphany, a myth to manifest the divine. Such at least is what the poet implores the bridge to be.

In "Proem," Brooklyn Bridge achieves its status in direct opposition to the way of life embodied in the cities. Bridge and city are opposing and apparently irreconcilable forms of energy. This opposition, which is equivalent to that between myth and history, continues through the remainder of the poem; it creates the local tensions of each section, and the major tension of the entire work.

This tension is best illustrated in "The Tunnel," the penultimate section of the poem. After a fruitless search for reality in a Times Square theater, the protagonist boards a subway as "the quickest promise home." The short ride to Brooklyn Bridge is a nightmare of banal conversations and advertisements: "To brush some new presentiment of pain." The images are bizarre: "and love/ A burnt match skating in a urinal." Poe appears, his head "swinging from the swollen strap," his eyes "Below the toothpaste and the dandruff ads." The crucified poet, dragged to his death through the streets of Baltimore, "That last night on the ballot rounds," represents how society uses its visionary devotees of beauty.

If the "Proem" promised deliverance, "The Tunnel" seems to deliver damnation; its chief character is a Daemon, whose "hideous laughter" is "the muffled slaughter of a day in birth." The Daemon's joke is that he has inverted the highest hopes and brightest prophecies: "O cruelly to inoculate the brinking dawn/ With antennae toward worlds that glow and sink." The presiding spirit in the tunnel, he represents the transvaluation of ideals in modern America.

At the end of "The Tunnel," the protagonist leaves the subway and prepares, at the water's edge, to ascend the bridge. His faith, like Job's, is unimpaired. Job endured the assault of Satan, uttered no complaints, and in the end profited by an enlightened understanding, albeit an irrational one, of the power of his God. It is revealing—although it has been largely unnoticed—that Crane's epigraph to The Bridge is taken from Satan's reply to God in Job, 1.7: "From going to and fro in the earth, and from walking up and down in it." The words might be read to indicate the theme of voyage, but their source suggests a richer interpretation: the omnipresence of evil, of the Daemon of "The Tunnel." Job's only defense

is unremitting faith in his own righteousness and God's justice. And the
same holds for the poet: faith in Whitman, his own powers, and in his
bridge.

III

To keep the faith but not close his eyes to reality was Hart Crane's chief
struggle in composing *The Bridge*. Reality in the 1920's—the age of jazz,
inflated money, and Prohibition—did not seem to support any faith let
alone one like Crane's. It was a period of frantic construction, of competition for the title of "Tallest Building in the World," won in 1930 by the
Empire State Building. That tower had climbed the sky at the rate of a
story a day to the height of a hundred and two floors. Elsewhere, Florida
experienced a hysterical real-estate boom. In 1927 the first cross-country
highway announced the age of the automobile. The same year, Lindbergh
crossed the Atlantic. And in the same decade, the movie palace spread
into neighborhoods.

    In certain moods, Crane was possessed by the fever of the period:
"Time and space is the myth of the modern world," he wrote about
Lindbergh, "and it is interesting to see how any victory in the field is
heralded by the mass of humanity. In a way my Bridge is a manifestation
of the same general subject. Maybe I'm just a little jealous of Lindy!" But
the over-all effect of the direction of American life did not accord with his
myth. From 1926 to 1929, years during which his own physical and
emotional life deteriorated noticeably, Crane searched for a way to acknowledge the unhappy reality of America without surrendering his faith.
The changes he made in the final poem of the sequence—the poem he
had begun in 1923 and altered time and again—disclose the accommoda-
tion he reached.

    At first, as I have indicated, the finale projected an intense
experience of harmony. As his conception of the bridge took shape, he
changed the ending accordingly, weaving into it the major images developed earlier, which are mainly nautical and musical. He reorganized the
section into a walk across the bridge, and incorporated many structural
details of the cables and towers. "I have attempted to induce the same
feelings of elation, etc.—like being carried forward and upward simultaneously—both in imagery, rhythm and repetition, that one experiences
in walking across my beloved Brooklyn Bridge."

        Through the bound cable strands, the arching path
        Upward, veering with light, the flight of strings,—

Taut miles of shuttling moonlight syncopate
The whispered rush, telepathy wires.
Up the index of night, granite and steel—
Transparent meshes—fleckless the gleaming staves—
Sibylline voices flicker, waveringly stream
As though a god were issue of the strings. . . .

Sheerly the eyes, like seagulls stung with rime—
Slit and propelled by glistening fins of light—
Pick biting way up towering looms that press
Sidelong with flight of blade on tendon blade
—Tomorrows into yesteryear—and link
What cipher-script of time no traveller reads

Rhythm and imagery convey a real bridge as well as an "arc synoptic": the walk across the span recapitulates the experience of the concluding day.

In stanza six, at the center of the roadway, the poet attains his vision. It's midnight; night is lifted "to cycloramic crest/ Of deepest day." Now, as "Tall Vision-of-the-Voyage," the bridge becomes a "Choir, translating time/ Into what multitudinous Verb": it is "Psalm of Cathay!/ O Love, thy white pervasive Paradigm. . . !" This moment is the climax of the poem. In the six stanzas which follow, Crane interprets the "multitudinous Verb" as the explicit action of reaching Cathay. He achieves this through predominant images of voyage; the bridge becomes a ship which, in stanza seven, "left the haven hanging in the night." The past tense modulates the tone of the entire section, for we are now "Pacific here at time's end, bearing corn." We have left the physical bridge, and are transported to another realm, a realm which fuses land ("corn") and water ("Pacific")—or Pocahontas and Columbus. The implied image is clearly that of an island, much like the "insular Tahiti" of the soul which Ishmael discovers to his salvation in Melville's *Moby-Dick*. The *Pequod* too had rushed ahead "from all havens astern." In stanza eleven, the poet like the lone survivor of Ahab's madness, finds himself "floating" on the waters, his visionary Belle Isle (Atlantis) sustaining him. In the last stanza, still addressing the bridge, he floats onward toward Cathay. The passage has been made "from time's realm" to "time's end" to "thine Everpresence, beyond time." Like Melville, Crane began his spiritual voyage in the North Atlantic, plunged into older waters, and nearing Cathay, recovered the even older shores of Atlantis. East and West have merged in a single chrysalis.

The language of the closing six stanzas of the section has the resonance of a hymn; it includes some of Crane's most quoted epithets: "Unspeakable Thou Bridge to Thee, O Love." But the oracular tone is bought at an expense. The opening six stanzas were dominated by the physical presence of the bridge and the kinetic sense of moving across it; the last six, having left the "sheened harbor lanterns" behind, remove to a watery element. And as the bridge becomes a symbolic ship, we sense an underlying relaxation. It is true that the language remains rich, even rugged ("Of thy white seizure springs the prophecy"). But the hyperbolic imagery itself seems an effort to substitute verbal energy for genuine tension. The original tension, between the poet-hero and history, seems to be replaced by an unformulated struggle *within* the poet, a struggle to maintain a pitch of language unsupported by a concrete action. For the climactic action of the entire poem had already occurred, when at the center of the span, the poet names the bridge as "Paradigm." The rest is an effort, bound to prove inadequate in the nature of the case, to say what it is a paradigm of. Thus the poet, full of ponderous (and, we sense, conflicting) emotions, sails away from the harbor, detaching the myth from its concreteness. And the bridge achieves its final transmutation, into a floating and lonely abstraction.

IV

The dissolution of the bridge as fact—and the subsequent drop in the poem's intensity—was perhaps an inevitable outcome of the poet's conflict between his faith and reality. In the summer of 1926, suffering an attack of skepticism about his "myth of America," Crane stated the problem in his own terms. "Intellectually judged," he wrote to Waldo Frank, "the whole theme and project seems more and more absurd." He felt his materials were not authentic, that "these forms, materials, dynamics are simply non-existent in the world." As for Brooklyn Bridge: "The bridge today has no significance beyond an economical approach to shorter hours, quicker lunches, behaviorism and toothpicks." A month later he had recovered his faith. "I feel an absolute music in the air again," he wrote to Frank, "and some tremendous rondure floating somewhere." He had composed the "Proem," in which the bridge stands firmly opposed to the cities. He had beaten back the nightmarish view of the bridge, and could now proceed with his aim of translating a mechanical structure into a threshold of life.

But Crane could not dismiss the nightmare. He had to account for it, and he did so in a subtle fashion. Later in 1926 he arrived at the title for his last section: "Atlantis." Until then, it had been "Bridge Finale." The destination of the protagonist's journey, like Columbus's, had been called Cathay, the traditional symbol of the East. Atlantis was the sunken island of the West—older even than the Orient. What does Crane intend by his new title? Does he mean to identify East and West? Or to introduce the idea of the decline of greatness at the very moment his hero's journey is accomplished? What precisely does Atlantis add to our "cognizance" of the bridge?

The fable of Atlantis had been as important as Cathay to the discovery of the New World. Originally, it was a somewhat mystical legend told by Plato in *Timaeus* and *Critias*, concerning a land in the western ocean (the Atlantic), founded by Poseidon, god of the sea. Once all-powerful, the nation had grown lustful, and was punished for its pride with earthquakes and floods; in a single day it sunk forever. But the legend remained, and during the fifteenth century, was popular among sailors. The island was believed to be the place where seven Portuguese bishops, fleeing the Moors, had founded seven golden cities. Sailors hoped to rediscover this land, where Christians still lived in piety and wealth. To discover Atlantis, or to reach Cathay—these were the leading motifs among the navigators who sailed westward in the fifteenth century. No one, not even Columbus, dreamed that an entirely new world lay between the sunken world and the legendary riches of the Orient.

Crane thus had historical grounds for identifying Atlantis and Cathay. As it turned out, the discovery of America proved both legends to be illusions: neither had the geographical position attributed to it by Renaissance navigators. Both, however, remained active myths—Cathay inspiring the revived theme of the Northwest Passage in the nineteenth century, and Atlantis even yet arousing speculation. Crane had indicated early in the composition of his poem that Cathay would stand for "consciousness, knowledge, spiritual unity"—material conquest transmuted into "an attitude of spirit." What does Atlantis stand for?

The answer is complex. When we learn from Plato that the Atlanteans possessed a land with a great central plain, "said to have been the fairest of all plains, and very fertile," the resemblance to America is striking. Further, we learn that they were a race of highly inventive builders, who intersected the island with a vast system of inland canals. They had invented basic tools, farming, and the alphabet. Their proudest creations, however, were bridges—a series of bridges, in fact, which led over the canals toward the exact center of the island. There, a monumental bridge opened upon the gate to a temple, the shrine of Poseidon.

This was Atlantis in its glory. But, Plato revealed, the glory did not last. The "divine portion" faded away, and human nature "got the upper hand." The people grew prideful, avaricious, imperialistic. And most of all, they grew blind to their own failings—blind to the loss of their true powers.

Crane wove references to the sunken island throughout the fabric of the poem. They appear in "Cutty Sark" as the old sailor's memory of "the skeletons of cities." They recur forcefully in "The Tunnel" in two echoes of Poe's "The City in the Sea": "And Death, aloft,—gigantically down," and "worlds that glow and sink." And they emerge explicitly in stanza eleven of the finale:

> Now while thy petals spend the suns about us, hold—
> (O Thou whose radiance doth inherit me)
> Atlantis,—hold thy floating singer late!

In the preceding line, the bridge was addressed as a sea creature— "Anemone." Here, the poet invokes the floating form, now called Atlantis, to sustain his faith. In the following stanza, the last of the poem, the poet passes "to thine Everpresence, beyond time," as the "orphic strings . . . leap and converge." Then:

> —One Song, one Bridge of Fire! Is it Cathay,
> Now pity steeps the grass and rainbows ring
> The serpent with the eagle in the leaves . . . ?
> Whispers antiphonal in the azure swing.

The question *may* indicate doubt that the bridge does in fact represent the "mystic consummation" of Cathay; more likely, it indicates wonder. The antiphonal whispers through the cables of the disembodied bridge could hardly be negative. Atlantis, the bridge-anemone, had answered the prayer and held the "floating singer late."

How did the sunken island earn such a high function? Where did it get the "radiance" to bestow upon the poet? The answer lies once more in Plato's account. The people of Atlantis had indeed become blind in their pride and materialism—but not all of them. "To those who had no eye to see the true happiness, they still appeared glorious and blessed at the very time when they were filled with unrighteous avarice and power." Some, however, retained "an eye to see," and these few recognized baseness as baseness. The still radiant ones kept their "precious gift" of the "divine portion."

It is now clear what Crane meant. His Cathay, his moment of supreme awareness, was a moment of Atlantean "radiance." With an "eye to see," he perceived the bridge as more than stone and steel, as a "mystic consummation." He perceived the gift embodied in the bridge. The inhabitants of the Daemon's dark tunnels could no longer see—no longer make out the shape of the future within the chaos of the present. These are the people for whom the bridge was nothing but "an economical approach." They represented the loss of radiance, the sinking of Atlantis.

Crane used the Atlantis legend, like the epigraph from Job, to maintain a double insight: the promise of redemption and the actuality of evil. As long as he held the double view, as long as he was able to affirm the myth while condemning the actuality of his culture, he would not sink. To this end he required a bridge to rise above the wreckage of history—to rise above itself—and be a pure curveship. The purity was essential; the bridge could harbor no ambiguities. Hence its symbolic radiance became the only enduring fact of Hart Crane's Brooklyn Bridge.

THOMAS A. VOGLER

A New View
of Hart Crane's Bridge

Most of the early critical comments
on *The Bridge* agreed on the final verdict of the poem as a magnificent
failure—magnificent in its lyrical evocation of mood, and a failure in its
attempt to provide an epic or mythic expression of the movement of
American history. During the last decade, more favorable estimates of the
poem have appeared. But these comments share with the earlier ones an
emphasis on Crane's own statements of purpose and achievement in
writing the poem. What is surprising is that so few attempts have been
made to approach the poem from a different point of view. Criticism
should aim at setting a poem in as many illuminating contexts as possible;
the context of the poet's conscious intentions is only one of the many
possible contexts and one of the more suspect contexts at that. Poets are
notoriously poor critics of their own work, and instances of poets writing
"better than they knew" are almost commonplace. The fact that Crane
did not produce a poem widely recognized as an epic, although avowedly
attempting one, or a poem discovering a secular "myth to God," although
that was his fervent hope, does not leave the reader with the choice of
seeing the poem as a failure or, as some devotees would have it, as a
mystical success which must be taken on faith.

If one approaches *The Bridge* without a precommitment to Crane's
own statement of its theme, it is possible to find in it a theme which
provides a high degree of organic unity. The poem is a search or quest for a

From *The Sewanee Review* 3, vol. 72 (Summer 1965). Copyright © 1965 by The University
of the South.

mythic vision, rather than the fixed, symbolic expression of a vision firmly held in the poet's mind. The vision sought is one that will be based on a knowledge of a glorious past, and will provide a bridge from that past to the hopeful future, in spite of the dearth of hopeful signs in the actual present. The poem is highly subjective in language and content, and understandably so, because the quest is a personal quest, the search of the poet for a vision that will satisfy his *own* needs. But Crane also saw the problem of the poet as reflecting the central problem of the society in which he lived, and the poet's solution to the problem—if he could achieve one—as having consequences far beyond the poet's own private life.

Against the background of the poet's daily cycle from Brooklyn to Manhattan and back, essentially a closed, hopeless, and discouraging routine, the poet carries on his quest, ranging into the past of his country and his own youth for signs of an immanent regeneration, signs of hope on which to base an optimistic vision of the future. The poem labors to move from a state of desire to one of conviction, to see in the curve of the Bridge the arc of a rainbow promise not dependent on any text or tradition, but on the poet's own power to see into the nature of things. If the mystic sees "On the earth the broken arcs; in the heaven, a perfect round," then Crane is far from mysticism in his desire to build his arcs of earthly materials and to see them meeting, not in heaven, but in the future.

The "Proem" begins with the dawn of the poet-office-worker's day, set against the background of the Bridge and its suggestion of controlled, unspent motion and freedom. In contrast with the vague impression of freedom glimpsed in the seagull's flight, an atmosphere of oppressive routine builds up in the next two stanzas, and the two moods are alternated in a violently contrapuntal arrangement. The seagull disappears with its "apparitional" curve, leaving the poet deceived, like the viewer of a cinema, by a "panoramic sleight." He turns to the more free, and hence more stable ("Implicitly thy freedom staying thee!"), Bridge. The contrast suggests that the freedom of the Bridge will not prove apparitional like the gull's flight, but it is only a suggestion; and the deception of the first image hovers behind the second as an unrealized possibility.

In the fifth stanza a suicide suggests both the oppression of "subway scuttle, cell or loft," and one way, at least, of finding in the Bridge a path to freedom. Another way out is indicated, however, by the identification of the Bridge with the accoutrements of a new religion, and with the "Terrific threshold of the prophet's pledge." The last stanza seeks to realize this other way of escape by addressing the Bridge directly, seeking its aid in finding a "myth to God." It becomes increasingly clear throughout the poem that the myth to God is an attitude of mind rather than an allegoric organization of symbols. The Bridge, as symbol, is not to help him discover the attitude, but to support and confirm an otherwise unpredictable mood by basing it on a stable vision. The main function of the "Proem," in terms of the whole, is to set the background of the poem: despair with the present, a longing for freedom, the possibility that the vision will prove as "apparitional" as a "panoramic sleight," and the desire to find a hopeful organization of experience, a myth that will enable the poet to avoid the "bedlamite's" end.

The "Ave Maria" is presumably a dream which the poet has at dawn, just before awakening. The fluidity of the links between sections does not require any more rigorous time-scheme than the reader's realization that all the sections take place in the poet's mind during the course of a single day, against the background of past thoughts and experiences. In the "Ave Maria" Columbus is seen just before arriving in Spain, after discovering America. The first thing that should be noticed is that the poet has identified himself with Columbus, described Columbus as engaged on a quest, and located him at a very precise moment in that quest. Columbus is returning successfully from a venture that depended, as much as anything else, on faith. He is bringing "word" of a "dim frontier"—a new world and a new era of history—to the old world, the past. Crane picks the return stage of the voyage for a definite reason, for he sees his own attempt to sustain a vision as a return to the world of the present after a timeless moment of vision. It is in this return to reality that the vision, and the poet's faith in it, will receive the true test, as the true test of Columbus is shown here to be in his return to Spain. The metaphor will be repeated throughout the poem, in the many examples of attempts to return from somewhere with something of value. Even though Aeneas was not returning in the literal sense that Columbus was, the voyage of the *Aeneid* and Aeneas' goal lie behind the structure of the poem as a basic analogy for Crane's conception of his own quest. Directed by a vision of his destiny, Aeneas was returning to the main-stream of history after the debacle of Troy. Crane hopes that he will return from his dream through the gates of horn to find the dream a waking reality in the day ahead, and that he will walk across the Bridge towards home with the dream a secure vision. But he is also disturbed by his knowledge of the other gate for dreams, and by his knowledge of the many adventurers who never returned from their searches for Eldorado or Cathay.

Columbus is not seen completing his voyage, but rather at the crucial moment when success is finally assured. In "faith, not fear,"

Columbus appeals to "Madre Maria," who "Merges the wind in measure to the waves." The waves then become a "Series on series, infinite," and eyes can "enclose/This turning rondure whole." In answer to the appeal, "Madre Maria" has given a vision which transforms the hostile sea into a benevolent sign of the continuity of past, present, and future. In the remainder of this section God is addressed directly by the poet-as-Columbus in a way which reflects a realization of still another force guiding the explorer. God is apart from man, omnipotent and cruel in his love for man, subscribing "holocaust of ships," yet "urging through night our passage to the Chan." God is here the fierce Elohim of the Hebrew Scriptures; He is a "Hand of Fire," and to Him Columbus gives thanks for the "teeming span" which was at the same time the source of all his hardships and his bridge to the "word," to the new land and the future. The poet's identification with Columbus becomes complete, for all the terms of his quest are symbolically interchangeable with those of Columbus' quest. The poet too will try to find his "Madre Maria" in a series of elusive, mythical female figures, and will have to come to terms with a "Hand of Fire" in the "interborough fissures" of his own mind in "The Tunnel" section. But, for the present, the poet is still in the midst of the teeming span, looking for stray branches among salty teeth; he hopes to have found in Columbus' voyage such a branch, a symbol of hope and token of success.

In "The Harbor Dawn" the poet begins his secular, historical quest for the equivalent of Columbus' "Madre Maria." In a "waking dream" in a "wavering slumber," he has a vision of a sexual union with Powhatan's daughter:

> your hands within my hands are deeds;
> my tongue upon your throat—singing
> arms close; eyes wide, undoubtful
> dark
> drink the dawn—
> a forest shudders in your hair!

The vision is still only a dream, although now a "waking dream," but it is hopefully a prefigurative dream for which the poet can find some embodiment in his coming day. The dream-dimension of this symbolic fertilization of the seed that Columbus brought to the new world has its negative aspect too, and Crane does not hesitate to suggest it. The union occurs "while sirens/Sing to us, stealthily weave us into day." In the vision to come, the poet must overcome the possibility that his union is apparitional. Although the poet here has a clear impression of his bride's function, and of the similarity between that function and the comfort "Madre Maria" gave Columbus, he still has no concrete image or vision of her. He must wake from the dream to find his bride in time ("time recalls you to your love") and to discover her identity:

> Who is the woman with us in the dawn? . . .
> whose is the flesh our feet have moved upon?

The transition from dream prefiguration of the vision to actual search for the vision is a slow one in the poem. Crane moves from the dream in "Ave Maria," to the waking dream in "The Harbor Dawn," to the Sleepy Hollow region of consciousness in "Van Winkle," before he finally touches firmly on the "20th Century" in "The River." In the last stanza of "The Harbor Dawn" he emphasizes once more that in this stage of his quest he is still "under the mistletoe of dreams," while a star "As though to join us at some distant hill—/Turns in the waking west and goes to sleep."

The first two lines of "Van Winkle" encompass the whole of the continent, from "Far Rockaway to Golden Gate," and the history of the continent is identified with the poet's personal history as the transition to the past is made in terms of the poet's childhood. It was in his childhood when he, like the land, first felt the influence of Pizarro and Cortez, Priscilla and Captain Smith. The land itself, symbolized by Pocahontas, is to be his equivalent of Columbus' "Maria." But the poet must discover first "those whose addresses are never near," who know her "without name," before he can find Maquokeeta in "The Dance," who will hopefully help him to "see her truly." Before he finds "those," in the figures of the hoboes of his childhood, he touches still another intermediate state of consciousness in the figure of Rip Van Winkle. The sub-section ends with an explicit identification of the poet with the awakened Rip as he starts his subway ride to work:

> Keep hold of that nickel for car-change, Rip,—
> Have you got your *"Times"*—?
> And hurry along, Van Winkle—it's getting late!

Unlike Columbus, Van Winkle is memorable precisely because he lacked an adequate link between the past and future. He woke to find himself out of time, in a world incommensurable with his past, and was a pathetic rather than a triumphant figure. The doubts implied here help explain the urgency ("It's getting late!") of the final stanza, and the importance of the "nickel for car-change" that the poet-as-Rip must keep as he begins his trip. It is the same coin that will play the "nickel-in-the-slot piano" in

"Cutty Sark," and it is the coin pressed into the subway slot in "The Tunnel." It is the nickel of his memories and experience, which is all he has to pay his way in his journey through time.

As the "grind-organ" of almost automatic "recall" turns over in the poet's mind, it revives what are to be the two most important memories in the whole poem:

> Is it the whip stripped from the lilac tree
> One day in spring my father took to me,
> Or is it the Sabbatical, unconscious smile
> My mother almost brought me once from church
> And once only, as I recall—?

There are two memories here, one of Crane's father in the act of punishing him, and one of his mother *almost* bringing him a genuine ("unconscious") smile "from church." These memories, unlike the others, are put as questions, and we cannot understand this sub-section, or the poem, without realizing what the "it" refers to in both cases. In the image of his father, he is asking if *this* is his equivalent to the Elohim of Columbus; he may even be asking the psychological question whether this is the source of his need to find now, in his adult life, some means of assimilating this early experience into a pattern of benignity. With the mother's smile, Crane is asking the same two-part question. Is this the best he can find for his own "Maria," or is this the real source of his need for such a figure? With the mother, there is much more of a feeling of hesitancy and doubt than with the father. At the beginning of his search for the real (not anonymous) Pocahontas, he is forced to recall a failure of love in his own life, and to express the failure in terms that anticipate a similar failure in the poem. The mother "almost" brought the smile. The union was "almost" achieved, as the smile "flickered through the snow screen, blindly," but it proved illusional.

The first twenty-three lines of "The River" are a burlesque on the confusion and tawdriness of the poet's twentieth-century environment. In this "Limited" century only an express train "makes time," in a deliberately degrading sexual pun, over the land which Crane hopes to see as Pocahontas, the giving female lover. The train whizzes by, leaving "three men, still hungry" for a different knowledge of time and the land. The tramps the poet remembers from his childhood are "Time's rendings, time's blendings" who have been left behind, like Van Winkle, by the passing of time, or have deliberately chosen their way of life as an escape from the pressures of contemporary life. The poet is able to identify himself as a child with them, but rejects their way out as being too passive, lacking faith in a higher vision. They are "Blind fists of nothing, humpty-dumpty clods."

In spite of their inadequate grasp of time, however, they do know a body under the wide rain, as the poet knew the body of the land in his youth: "O Nights that brought me to her body bare!" This is still a "knowing her without name," without the full recognition the poet seeks, but it is a start. Although the tramps do not fully grasp time, so as to accept it, they do have a "Strange bird-wit, like the elemental gist/Of unwalled winds," which enables them to count "The river's minute by the far brook's year." This puts them in an ambiguous, intermediate position in terms of the poet's quest. Their "Strange bird-wit," or mythic sense, enables them to know "her," although anonymously, and to know time, in a cyclical, seasonal sense. But they lack a more imaginative vision of time as the River, time moving forward bearing everything with it towards a final end:

> The River, spreading, flows—and spends your dream.
> What are you, lost within this tideless spell?

The remainder of the sub-section is an elaboration of the forces of time, identified with the River, which carries with it all the "Damp tonnage and alluvial march of days," as it flows over DeSoto's bones, past the whole history of the continent, to the sea.

In "The Dance" the poet proceeds to make us the relationship between time and the River which he has discovered. He must now reverse the River's flow, return up the River and back in time to the consciousness of the Indian with "Mythical brows," who "knew" his gods directly as part of the natural physical world. The attempt to return is necessary for it is "Then you shall see her truly—your blood remembering its first invasion of her secrecy." The reversal of time in "The Dance" is not a rejection of the sense of time expressed in "The River," but an attempt to return to the source of time, to achieve the primitive mythic state of consciousness, and then to rejoin time and return to the present, equipped to cross it in safety with both the mythic recognition of the female figure and the fully-developed sense of time as the River. This is the significance of the name "Maquokeeta," for the Indian is an embodiment of the mythic sense and the name means, literally, "Big River."

As he returns upstream, he "learns" the mythic mode of conscious-ness. He is able to see Pocahontas, dressed as a bride, and accompanied by the sign of blue that Columbus associated with his "Madre Maria." As the explorer's vision calmed and linked the waves in the "Ave Maria," so the poet's vision of Pocahontas turns the waves of the River into "laughing chains the water wove and threw!" He finds the star that left him "As though to join us at some distant hill" in "Harbor Dawn," and, as the star bleeds immortally into the dawn, he touches his feet to the ground in union with the land. At the end of his journey, he is confronted with the ritualistic execution by fire of Maquokeeta, the tribal king. The experience that Maquokeeta is undergoing, which Crane attempts to enter into with him, is a simultaneous wedding dance of union with Pocahontas and a ceremonial dance of death for the execution. The air is blue, as it should be for the union, and Maquokeeta is identified with the sphinx-like immortality of the snake, becoming like one of the snakes in "Van Winkle," that "flittered from under the ash heap day/After day" and "flashed back at your thrust, as clean as fire." In the death of Maquokeeta, Crane sees for the first time that his own experience is to be a dying into life before he can achieve a poetic image of the rebirth of America. In some intuitive sense the disappearance of the Indians and their tribal morn has been essential, and even beneficial. The freedom of the Indian's spirit, his most desirable attribute, can survive the passing of time and be his gift to a later generation:

> Though other calendars now stack the sky,
> Thy freedom is her largesse, Prince, and hid
> On paths thou knewest best to claim her by.

As the final stanza shows, the poet has been able to collapse time and space, to cross the time barrier in order to gain spiritual nourishment from the past. His problem now is to return, to establish a continuity of the Indian's spirit through history, and to find the pattern of his own rebirth after his visionary death with Maquokeeta.

In the "Indiana" section, the spirit of the Indian is symbolically transferred to the pioneer boy Larry, for the Indian was doomed to extinction as he was pushed out by the white man. The doom can be read in the Indian mother's eyes, which "were not black/But sharp with pain," as she passes the pioneer mother who is returning east. Crane, as the pioneer mother, holds up the infant in passing to receive the spirit from the Indian. The spirit passes to the boy, and not the mother, for she already represents the decline of the pioneers, which the boy must overcome. She "found God lavish there in Colorado/But passing sly," and can report only a "dream called Eldorado," which yielded nothing but "barren tears."

Crane's identification with the mother at this point, rather than with the boy, is significant, for it identifies him with the pioneers' decline, left with only the hope that Larry will

Come back to Indiana—not too late!
(Or will you be a ranger to the end?)
Good-bye . . . Good-bye . . . oh, I shall always wait
    You, Larry, traveller—
                            stranger,
                                son,
                                    —my friend—

There is a note of desperation in the mother's voice as she bids
farewell to her stranger-son, hoping that he will preserve his freedom *and*
return with it; "You'll keep your pledge;/I know your word," she says. But
in the next section there is to be a loss of the "word" as Crane has
attempted to define it.

In "Cutty Sark" the poet, at the end of his day, meets a sailor lost
in time. Like the last of the Kentuckians, whom he represents, the sailor
is unable to remain on the body of the continent ("No—I can't live on
land—!") and has thus lost the union with Pocahontas which Crane had
tried to establish. His eyes have changed from the "engaging blue" of the
"Indiana" section, for they are now either green or made to appear green
by the bar lights shining on them. The loss of the "blue" and the loss of
the ability to stay on the land represent the final resignation of the
attempt to find an equivalent to Columbus' "Madre Maria." The best the
poet can do with the nickel he kept "for car-change" is to play "O
Stamboul Rose—dreams weave the rose!", which degenerates into:

ATLANTIS ROSE *drums wreathe the rose,*
the star floats burning in a gulf of tears
and sleep another thousand—
                            interminably
long since somebody's nickel—stopped—
playing—

The sense in which the River "spends your dream" seems clear now. Time
has conquered the vision; the nickel has run out; the star that was to join
him ("Harbor Dawn") now "floats burning in a gulf of tears," and he is
ready to give up time "and sleep another thousand" years.

Outside a wharf truck nearly ran him down
—he lunged up Bowery way while the dawn
was putting the Statue of Liberty out—that
torch of hers you know—
I started walking home across the Bridge . . .

The light of day has put out the poet's "waking dream" as effectively as the torch of the Statue, and the section ends the first movement

of the poem right where it started, in the sorry present. The poet's historical excursion has only succeeded in reaffirming the spiritual poverty of his existence, while setting it against earlier generations whose freedom makes his lack all the more oppressive.

The remainder of the section is a lament for the lost mythic vision, identified with the "clipper dreams indelible and ranging,/baronial white on lucky blue!" that "turned and left us on the lee." "Where can you be?" the poet asks of the ships that have failed, like his dream, to return in time with the symbolic suggestions of their parabolic course across the blue sea. The ships are gone, and with them their word, the power of their names: *"Taeping,"* the Pacific; *"Ariel,"* who at the Master's bidding calmed the storm; *"Rainbow,"* the ever-returning sign after the storm. Only the *"Nimbus"* and the *"Leander/*(last trip a tragedy)" seem now to have been named with a truly prophetic vision.

The poem is now ready for a basic change in direction, and what happens between the frustrated "walking home" in "Cutty Sark" and the final subway dive under the river in "The Tunnel" is a preparation for the recognition that the loss of vision is *itself* to be the mark of the "sounding heel" of the Elohim on him. The new possibility opened for the poet is that acceptance of the failure of his vision, as part of the "incognizable Word," can be the means of transcending that failure, as his acceptance and participation in the death of Maquokeeta was an attempt to transcend it by seeing it as the preparation for a rebirth. The next three sections, and the beginning of "The Tunnel," will repeat again and again in varying form the message of the vanished clipper ships, of the lost smile of the lost vision and the failed historical quest. But at the same time they attempt to lay the groundwork for an affirmative vision of the poet's present state that will hold, in spite of the failed quest.

Crane begins "Cape Hatteras" with a deliberately abortive exploration of new materials, metaphors of air flight, with which to identify his vision. He knows that the airplane flew only to crash, like the "monoplanes/We launched with paper wings and twisted rubber bands," recalled in "Van Winkle." The physical conquest of space is doomed in advance to fail as a metaphor for the poetic vision, as his earlier attempt to use Columbus failed in spite of his "faith" in it.

Before accepting the airplane's conquest of space as a basis for his faith in the future, the poet turns in an aside to Walt Whitman, "the "Meistersinger" who "set breath in steel," whose intense faith in the future and in science and the machine is directly relevant to the context. The poet wants to be another Whitman, but is unsure of himself and unsure of the basis of his faith in the "new universe." Ironically, Crane is turning to Whitman for support of a vision which he knows must collapse—at which point he will turn to Whitman again, and in a different sense, for the confidence he needs to overcome the collapse. Crane is distinguishing between Whitman's confidence in industry and the machine, and Whitman's transcendent acceptance of "Time absolutely," which he hopes will overcome the misuse of the machine that he is now forced to recognize.

Against the magnificent potential of the plane, whose pilot bears a "Sanskrit charge/To conjugate infinity's dim marge—/Anew. . . !" (like the "pledge" left with Larry by his mother in "Indiana"), the poet must contrast the present aftermath of the war, the "dim past reversed," which has for the time being shunted the conquest of space into a means of destruction. The poet then attempts to identify "man's perversity" as exhibited in the World War with that of the Civil War, an example Whitman had to face in his own experience. This is not an appeal to the "Strange bird-wit" of Whitman, to the Whitman who shared the spirit of the tramps in "The River," for that is the Whitman-esque vision that has failed him so far in the poem. He now needs the Whitman who will enable him to see "Easters of speeding light" in the plane's plunge to destruction, to achieve a vision of "the rainbow's arch—how shimmeringly stands/ Above the Cape's ghoul-mound."

> Yes, Walt,
> Afoot again, and onward without halt,—
> Not soon, nor suddenly,—No, never let go
>   My hand
>   in yours,
>   Walt Whitman—
>   so—

The final "so—" seems hesitant, or at least questioning, as if the strained overwriting of much of the apostrophe shows more desire to believe than actual belief in the vision offered. This weakness eats away at the final affirmative power of the poem and forces us to keep in mind the ambiguity inherent in contrasting a presently accepted vision with a formerly accepted, but now rejected, vision. The nature of the movement here is still the same shift with which the poem began, from the "apparitional flight" of the gulls to the "more stable" bridge, which nevertheless changes, too, as it is looked at differently. Crane could not have avoided taking note of Whitman's own warning, in "Whoever you are holding me now in hand," that "The way is suspicious, the result uncertain, perhaps destructive. . . ." Yet he was willing to take the chance, for he had to become that follower if he could. Whitman's equanimity in the face of death and catastrophe is what Crane needed at this stage of his quest, and would need even more in the final transition from "The Tunnel" to "Atlantis."

The "Three Songs" begins with a quotation from Marlowe's *Hero and Leander* which is meant to recall the lost clipper ship and the lost dream in "Cutty Sark." The "Songs" are a summation, or synecdoche, of the quest begun at the first of the poem for a "Madre Maria" in Crane's own experience and in the history of the country. They recall and re-emphasize the intense desire that motivated the quest and suggest, more clearly than the earlier poem had, the reasons for the failure of that quest.

Religious or secular, the sexual element is inevitable in visionary poetry of the kind Crane was consciously trying to write. The idea of a vision, as fulfilled, consummated union and harmony, inevitably calls forth the sexual symbol or metaphor. But the "Three Songs" quite deliberately begin with an expression of *past* desire. They are to be the opposite of the usual sexual fulfillment, an expression of frustrated desire, of protracted and painful longing, looking for and failing to find its object.

The "Southern Cross" begins with an expression of the poet's past desire. He "wanted" the "nameless Woman of the South, No wraith, but utterly." The Woman is nameless, for the dream-vision of "Harbor Dawn" had not identified her. And the poet wants her "utterly" in the sense that implies reciprocity, some answering sign such as that given Columbus in the "Ave Maria." But the consummation the poet desires is doomed, even before he considers the problem of naming the Woman, for she is apart:

> High, cool,
>   wide from the slowly smoldering fire
> Of lower heavens,—

If his Woman was the first mother, she has now become "homeless Eve,/Unwedded, stumbling gardenless to grieve." There is nothing left of the beauty of natural motherhood that the original Mother, Eve, might have had before she was forced from the garden. The thought of the lost beauty is enough "to grieve/Windswept guitars on lonely decks forever," and to reduce the poet's mind to churning spittle as he contemplates his crumbled vision:

> And this long wake of phosphor,
>   iridescent
> Furrow of all our travel—trailed derision!
> Eyes crumble at its kiss. Its long-drawn spell
> Incites a yell. Slid on that backward vision
> The mind is churned to spittle, whispering hell.

The "long wake of phosphor" is here a deliberate echo of the poet's confident belief, in "The Dance," that "I could see/Your hair's keen crescent running," and it points up the contrast between the poet's voyage to the dawn of history in that section and his voyage to the dawn here. The memory of his desire is almost more than he can bear, but he goes beyond that memory to recall the deceit the "nameless Woman" had practised on him in his dream:

> All night the water combed you with black
> Insolence. You crept out simmering, accomplished.
> Water rattled that stinging coil, your
> Rehearsed hair—docile, alas, from many arms.
> Yes, Eve—wraith of my unloved seed!

The poet's image of a mother was a deceit, "Rehearsed" and passed on to him "from many arms." He has confused memory and assimilated conventions with a direct visionary perception of reality. The ideal Mother, the "nameless Woman" who could have conceived and borne in the Garden, is a wraith; his seed were "unloved" because a fallen woman gave birth to him and to his vision. He can find no Mother, no "Madre Maria," to give him the smile of recognition that he desired, for she does not exist.

The "National Winter Garden" shows the failure of the poet's attempt to approach his "nameless Woman" as a bride rather than a mother. His inability to find any dimension but the sexual, where he had hoped to find a metaphor for a spiritual state of consciousness, leads him to a vicious sexual parody of his spiritual quest. He begins with the only "word" that he is to receive from the Magdalene, the "Outspoken buttocks" that invite him to join "the necessary cloudy clinch" of "The world's one flagrant, sweating cinch." The physical is the "one" union that the "world" has to offer. In the second stanza the "salads in the brain" emphasize the confusion that the presence of lust in the poet causes in his search for the bride. Even though his sensually practiced eye can pick a blonde "neatly through the smoke," he is always waiting for "someone else" to satisfy his other desire. The "final ring/When all the fireworks blare" destroys the consummation in the sacred marriage by reducing it to the perspective of sex in a cheap novel. And the poet is forced to the destruction, because always, before he can cross the threshold to his vision of spiritual union, he is forced to recognize "some cheapest echo" of the union in his physical lust. The "tom-tom scrimmage with a somewhere violin" burlesques his own mythic dance in "The Dance" by turning it, too, into the language of cliché and the rape of the "word."

The Magdalene is beyond expression of emotion, either through tears or through the "smile" that had been so important an anticipation in Crane's earlier search. The immortality symbol of the snake is seen as nothing but a string of beads, "turquoise fakes on tinselled hands"; and the poet waits "that writhing pool" in vain, for the sign that will calm and order the waters. The discrepancy between the desire and the physical fact is finally so extreme that the poet must "flee her spasm through a fleshless door." But if he has lost his vision, he has also gained something in perspective; he has recognized lust as a necessary part of his experience. Each "comes back to die alone" on the "empty trapeze" of the Magdalene's flesh, to generate another life rather than to be reborn. This "burlesque of our lust—and faith" must be accepted in whatever affirmation he is finally to reach.

The last Song, "Virginia," considers the possibility of finding a secular equivalent for the religious figure of the Virgin Mary, a mother and bride without participating in "The world's one flagrant, sweating cinch." But if the vision of a union with his "nameless Woman" as bride is destroyed because the poet's experience can produce only a "burlesque" of the union, then the identification of the Woman as a "Saturday Mary" is even more difficult. The poet is "still waiting" for the experience that will give him the vision. He can call to her, as he has been doing throughout the poem:

> O blue-eyed Mary with the claret scarf,
> Saturday Mary, mine!

But Mary remains in her "high wheat tower," inaccessible to the poet below in the sexual world, "Where green figs gleam/By oyster shells!" Pocahontas was a "Princess whose brown lap was virgin May" ("The Dance"), and the poet once thought that accessibility to her lap and preservation of her virginity were not incompatible. Now, standing "High in the noon" of broad day, he cannot find the elements of his dream-vision on "Prince Street" below the tower. Yet there are "Forget-me-nots at windowpanes" (referring to the window of his waking dream in "Harbor Dawn"), and he does not finally reject the desire so much as he emphasizes the impossibility of attaining it on the basis of previous experience. "What are you going to do?" he asks. "Let down your golden hair!" he pleads. But there is no response, and she is left behind as an image of his unsatisfied desire:

> Out of the way-up nickel-dime tower shine,
> Cathedral Mary,
>   shine!—

In "Quaker Hill" the poet turns from the visionary Woman whom he had not experienced to two female writers with whom he has achieved a kind of union in the shared experience he finds expressed in their works. Isadora Duncan and Emily Dickinson suggest to him the acceptance of a world in which "no ideals have ever been fully successful," as comparable to the acceptance of the fall season as a thing of beauty in which "The gentian weaves her fringes." The section continues the palinode on his earlier conception of the mythic mode of perception, but there are also indications of the kind of vision towards which he is turning. He begins with the apparently serious assertion that only cows have a true "perspective" of existence, for they

> . . . see no other thing
> Than grass and snow, and their own inner being
> Through the rich halo that they do not trouble
> Even to cast upon the seasons fleeting
> Though they should thin and die on last year's stubble.

They do not need to enhance the passing of time or the seasons through a bovine mythopoeia. It is enough for them to see only grass and snow and "their own inner being," to accept what they see, and to accept the consequences of their immediate experience, without seeking other terms as a reference for their acceptance. The cows are "awkward, ponderous and uncoy," but they do not need to boast of their "store of faith," nor to find and affirm a mythic vision in order to accept their existence.

The poet does not know "Who holds the lease on time and on disgrace?/What eats the pattern with ubiquity?", but he does know that he must accept the loss of his "kinsmen and the patriarch race" as an irrevocable fact, as the cows accept the grass and snow and their own death. He now feels able to "Shoulder the curse of sundered parentage," to accept the inevitable separation between him and his visionary parent-images of the Father and the Mother, and the historical sundering of Pocahontas and Maquokeeta. Since the separation was already inherent in the concept of the punishing Father, apart and unapproachable, this element alone of Columbus' voyage is still available to the poet as the "word" he seeks. He slowly comes to the realization that, like the cows, like Isadora Duncan and Emily Dickinson, he must accept the limitations of his present existence and find in them the means to his salvation:

> So, must we from the hawk's far stemming view,
> Must we descend as worm's eye to construe
> Our love of all we touch, and take it to the Gate
> As humbly as a guest who knows himself too late,

His news already told? Yes, while the heart is wrung,
Arise—yes, take this sheaf of dust upon your tongue!
In one last angelus lift throbbing throat—
Listen, transmuting silence with that silly note

Of pain that Emily, that Isadora knew!
While high from dim elm-chancels hung with dew,
That triple-noted clause of moonlight—
Yes, whip-poor-will, unhusks the heart of fright,
Breaks us and saves, yes, breaks the heart, yet yields
That patience that is armour and that shields
Love from despair—when love forsees the end—
Leaf after autumnal leaf
                                break off,
                                                descend—
                                                                descend—

The "Gate to which he must take his humble offering of experienced reality looks forward to the "Gates of Wrath" through which he must pass in "The Tunnel," as the "last angelus" looks backward to the Angelus sung around "the cordage tree" in the "Ave Maria," just before Columbus became aware of the "sounding heel" of the Elohim. Crane is now ready to enter the "Tunnel" and find evidence of the "sounding heel" in his own life. He now hopes to see his error of vision as an experience which both breaks and saves, as one that "breaks the heart, yet yields/That patience that is armour and that shields/Love from despair."

"The Tunnel" begins with still another résumé of the earlier, misguided portion of the poem, as the poet ironically describes the "nightly sessions" at "Columbus Circle," which he reaches by going "up Times Square." This is ground the poet has covered before; so he can now express the whole process through a few well-chosen puns. "You shall reach them all [the nightly dream sessions]," he says, only to "find the garden in the third act dead," as he had found it dead in the "Three Songs." There is a moment's hesitation before entering the subway, as he considers whether or not he should walk a bit first. But the decision is made for him as he finds himself "preparing penguin flexions of the arms" so as to "Be minimum" to meet the crowds of the dead he will find below. The larger transition here is towards an exploration of an inner state of consciousness; he is now ready, like the cows of "Quaker Hill," to ignore the "grass and snow" and to explore his "own inner being."

The state of the mind represented by the subway is seen as a consequence of urban life ("And so/of cities you bespeak/subways"). And the poet accentuates his descent into the region of his "inner being" by contrasting it with quoted snatches of dialogue which refer to his former quest:

> "Let's have a pencil Jimmy—living now
> at Floral Park
> Flatbush—on the Fourth of July—
> like a pigeon's muddy dream—potatoes
> to dig in the field—travlin the town—too—
> night after night—the Culver line—the
> girls all shaping up—it used to be—"

Each of these apparently random outbursts refers to the earlier poem. Jimmy was the father of Larry in "Indiana" and the pioneer he represented is living now in a fallen garden ("Floral Park") in the city ("Flatbush"). The "Fourth of July" is a flashback to the political beginnings of the nation ("I'm a/Democrat," insists the continuation of Larry in "Cutty Sark"), and the "pigeon's muddy dream" is a reminder of the dream-vision of the "Strange bird-wit" or mythic consciousness of the earlier poem. The salesman is mobile, like the tramps, and sees his vision "night after night" of "the girls all shaping up." The whole passage is a burlesque of vision as "it used to be" for the poet.

Now the poet must recant this earlier vision ("Our tongues recant like beaten weather vanes") in order to find the "answer" that "lives like verdigris, like hair/Beyond extinction, surcease of the bone," in still another repetition of the now familiar affirmation-by-contrast, begun in the poem's first two stanzas. The "repetition" in burlesque form of the earlier mistaken vision "freezes." Freezes what? The implied answer is the poet's blood, in which he had found his passionate hope for the fulfillment of the dream-vision. The desire *still* lingers; so the poet offers still another purgatorial repetition:

> "what do you want? getting weak on the links?
> fandaddle daddy don't ask for change—IS THIS
> FOURTEENTH? it's half past six she said—if
> you don't like my gate why did you
> swing on it, why *didja*
> swing on it
> anyhow—"

> And somehow anyhow swing—

The "nameless Woman" of his dream-vision throws his desire in his face, taunting him with his eagerness to swing on her gate rather than to press through the "Gates of Wrath." These are the sounds of "The phonographs of hades in the brain," that reduce "love" to "A burnt match skating in a urinal." To this musical accompaniment, the poet must now "TAKE THE EXPRESS" that "made time" over the land in "The River,' leaving him behind.

The vision the poet achieves at this point is one he has often had ("Why do I often meet your visage here?") but until now has been unable to accept. In these "interborough fissures of the mind" Poe replaces Whitman as an index of the poet's experience. He does not reject the "acceptance" of Whitman so carefully prepared for in "Cape Hatteras," but he finds in the agony of Poe's last night a closer analogue for his own emotional state:

> And when they dragged your retching flesh,
> Your trembling hands that night through Baltimore—
> That last night on the ballot rounds, did you
> Shaking, did you deny the ticket, Poe?

The poet is hovering on the verge of losing his faith completely and wonders if Poe gave up the ticket under comparably agonizing circumstances. Everywhere he turns, he finds images of death and despair:

> For Gravesend Manor change at Chambers Street.
> The platform hurries along to a dead stop.

For a moment he catches a glimpse of hope in the "intent escalator," which "lifts a serenade" upwards, and in the riders whose eyes shift from their shoes to the heavens bursting "suddenly in rain." But as the train begins "Taking the final level for the dive/Under the river," he is still aboard, still striving to find an acceptable meeting-point for his vision and his symbols. In the birdless region of the car "Newspapers wing, revolve and wing," in harsh contrast to the "seagull's wings . . . shedding white rings of tumult" in the "Proem," while blank windows synaesthetically gargle incomprehensible "signals through the roar." He finds only a "Wop washerwoman" with "bandaged hair" to match against the proud image of Columbus. But the question he asks her shows that he still has not completely frozen his desire for a consummation of the dream-vision:

> O Genoese, do you bring mother eyes and hands
> Back home to children and to golden hair?

The next two stanzas are a condensation of the whole argument that we have attempted to follow from "Cape Hatteras" on. In the first, the desire to find his vision, even in the degraded "Wop washerwoman," is finally recognized as something he cannot purge; even though he can mock and burlesque it as a form of deception:

> O cruelly to inoculate the brinking dawn
> With antennae toward worlds that glow and sink;—
> To spoon us out more liquid than the dim
> Locution of the eldest star, and pack ·
> The conscience navelled in the plunging wind,
> Umbilical to call—and straightway die!

His vision of "worlds that glow and sink" is balanced on "brinking dawn" that can never become full day. It is an unavoidable working of his "conscience" that produces visions. "Umbilical to call," which must nevertheless "straightway die." The poet's "shrill ganglia" are "Impassioned with some song we fail to keep." Failure to keep the song is death, and yet even in death he feels:

> . . . the slope,
> The sod and billow breaking,—lifting ground,
> —A sound of waters bending astride the sky
> Unceasing with some Word that will not die. . . !

The "Word that will not die," even though every particular embodiment of the vision the poet finds must die, is the vision of his continually reborn desire to find a vision. For an instant he is able to see himself as Sisyphus, and to accept that vision, because his hands can "drop memory" of his failure, leaving only the recognition of continually reborn desire. But there is a glimpse of a further step, in which the hands may be "drawn away, to die." This is the ultimate failure of the desire itself, the final "Kiss of our agony" that he would then have to bear. In a last prophetic vision he sees the "Hand of Fire" gathering him into that final agony. The "Kiss of our agony" is one that "takest all," from the songs "we fail to keep" even to this last vision of reborn desire. "It still interests me to affirm certain things," Crane had said in a less passionate context, and now he is contemplating even the loss of that "interest" as something which must be born in time, and accepted as part of the cruel "parable of man."

The final section of the poem, "The Atlantis," must seem at first incongruous with "The Tunnel" in its return to the Bridge as an acceptable symbol. Many readers have found the section confusing and overwritten in the light of the despair and resignation of "Quaker Hill" and "The Tunnel," reacting negatively and superficially to the animistic vision of the Bridge which it suggests. The conflict of tone, between the meaning we have been following through the poem's development and the triumphant enthusiasm of this section, which seems to suggest that the poet has reached his goal, does not "ruin" the section or the poem. It is, I think, a genuine poetic summation of the lived-through experience of seeking a vision, which is the functional theme of *The Bridge*. "The Atlantis" was the first part of the poem to be written, and its heady ecstasy was originally to be led up to, somehow established, and justified by the main body of the poem. Now, it takes its place as the beginning *and* end of the poem's struggle, an "Atlantis" of the mind, which the poet can neither find and occupy securely, nor stop searching for. It is the vision of the unbaptized poets in Dante's Limbo, whose affliction is to live without hope in a state of desire.

The first three stanzas re-establish the Bridge as a symbol of the harp suggested in the "Proem." The harp's music is beautiful but ethereal. The fourth stanza suggests that only the poet, who has suffered and met experience head-on, can hear the Bridge's song and read its meaning. His eyes can turn

> —Tomorrows into yesteryear—and link
> What cipher-script of time no traveller reads
> But who, through smoking pyres of love and death,
> Searches the timeless laugh of mythic spears.

The poetic ecstasy increases until the poet makes a claim for his vision palpably at odds with what he has actually experienced. The Bridge is assigned a symbolic meaning which it cannot bear within the context of the poem as written; it belongs, rather, to the poem the poet hoped to write, to the vision he hoped to achieve:

> Tall Vision-of-the-Voyage, tensely spare—
> Bridge, lifting night to cycloramic crest
> Of deepest day—O Choir, translating time
> Into what multitudinous Verb the suns
> And synergy of waters ever fuse, recast
> In myriad syllables,—Psalm of Cathay!
> O Love, thy white, pervasive Paradigm. . . !

With the seventh stanza the poet begins moving towards the actual limited vision which he has expressed in the poem that came to be written:

> We left the haven hanging in the night—
> Sheened harbor lanterns backward fled the keel.
> Pacific here at time's end, bearing corn,—
> Eyes stammer through the pangs of dust and steel.

But there is still the Bridge in the poet's mind, the "Thou" that "leadest from time's realm/As love strikes clear direction for the helm." The ninth

stanza contains a hint of the vision which the poet actually experienced in
"The Tunnel":

> With white escarpments swinging into light,
> Sustained in tears the cities are endowed
> And justified conclamant with ripe fields
> Revolving through their harvests in sweet torment.

Even while making his extravagant claims of having searched "the timeless laugh of mythic spears," the poet indicates the absence of a firmly
assured vision. "Thy pardon for this history," he asks, as if to excuse the
doubts his suffering has caused. "Hold thy floating singer late!" he pleads,
as if conscious that this vision he is trying to sustain is in danger of
disappearing once more into the teeming span. "Is it Cathay," he asks in
the final stanza, that the "orphic strings" sing?

> Now pity steeps the grass and rainbows ring
> The serpent with the eagle in the leaves. . . ?
> Whispers antiphonal in azure swing.

As Orpheus lost Eurydice when he turned to look at her, the poet,
we feel must lose this vision after the poetic ecstasy of expression
passes. The "arching strands of song," the "humming spars" and
"chimes," the vision "terrible of drums," which was "like an organ,"
does in fact give way, when faced with the question, to ambiguous and
undecipherable whispers. In one line the ethereal verbosity of the
ambiguous vision is almost completely redeemed. The poet has returned
to the "Sibylline voices" the "flicker, waveringly stream," in a confession
that he can never *know* whether or not "a god" is "issue of the
strings."

Crane liked to think of himself as the Virgil of the new world, but
his true desire was to be its Aeneas, to complete a voyage from the
shattered world of Troy to a new beginning in Rome, connecting the
two worlds by a destiny that made success inevitable, if only the voyager
held true to the vision of his goal. The criterion of "success" for a
poem of this kind should not be whether or not the poet actually achieves
the vision he seeks, nor whether or not the vision is acceptable to the
reader in the precise terms the poet offers. It should be the degree of
poetic honesty and skill the poet exhibits in pursuing his quest. The
quest itself may end in failure, as it did for the Romantics, with whom
Crane has his most obvious and important similarities. But, regardless of
outcome, the expression of a man as poet, trying by sheer will and faith
to find an acceptable purpose and meaning in his life, is still one of

the most inspiring themes a poet can attempt. It may prove after all to be the "heroic argument" or epic theme of our age, for it is the closest we have come to a theme that can excite anything like an epic response from our poets.

JOSEPH RIDDEL

Hart Crane's Poetics of Failure

Hart Crane's last poem, "The Broken Tower," is so confused with the sensational events of his last days that it is hard to consider the poem apart from the man. On the whole, it seems wise not to try to, for this is a poem which dramatizes, once and for all in our time, the pathetic gesture of a man dying into his work. In other words, it seems to do just what Crane's life was dedicated to—it turns the self into a poem, or almost so. For like so many of Crane's visionary poems, it renders not apocalypse but the failure of vision. To purify the self that has fallen into a "broken world," the poet wills a new "tower" in which his being is reconstituted: a purified inner space, a marriage of self and other, the fulfillment of his subjectivity in the object, an escape from time. Yet Crane ends not by creating that "tower"—or at least, not by achieving it as a visionary poet must, in the style of the poem—but by reconfirming his role as poet and hence affirming the future possibility of creating that new "tower." In short, like all of Crane's poems, it catches the poet in his act of being a poet, pursuing the dream that lies always before him. Its true subject is the viability of the poet's means, his language, by which alone he and the vision are to be fulfilled as one.

Aspiring through language ("My word I poured. But was it cognate . . . ?") to transcend the "broken world," to achieve the "pure" in the "crystal Word," Crane realizes once again the difference between his words, which are the world's, and the "crystal Word," which seems always

From English Literary History 4, vol. 33 (December 1966). Copyright © 1966 by Johns Hopkins University Press.

just beyond his grasp. Yet the triumph of failure attends the willed vision at poem's end, where Crane finds momentary consolation in the meaning of his search, his quest through words, which has become his life. He finds himself buoyed up once more by his faith in his method, by his capacity to be possessed by language and purified by it. But he discovers, too, why he must forfeit his hope of ever achieving that purity; why, as he had hinted to himself in earlier poems, the visionary poet was destined to fail and thus was condemned again and again to "pour" forth words that hold him to the world even as they hold within themselves logos. To put it another way, Crane's desire to transmute the temporal self into pure space—to purify himself virtually into the form of a poem—is rewarded by a vicious yet vital irony, in which the poet finds himself to share the ultimate failure of his method because he is condemned to repeat it incessantly in time.

This is, I think, the crucial paradox that explains Crane's limitations, and answers for his alleged visionary style. It is no less a quality which separates him from the optimum vitality of Whitman and from the apocalyptic style of Rimbaud, both his acknowledged masters. But recently, a group of critics, trying to revive so-called "Cosmic Poetry," have more or less apotheosized Crane for qualities he more desired than possessed. This critical reaction, though by no means dominant nor persuasive, has formulated a poetics, or a critical stance, which cannot be ignored because it is so symptomatic of a modern problem. The reaction is predominantly against Eliotism, and in general against a formalistic, intellectual poetry; these critics have come to accept Crane, in terms which he himself set forth, as the direct heir of Whitman and the immediate forerunner of the "New Paganism." His style, formed so deliberately in opposition to Eliot's and, ironically, so unquestionably influenced by it, becomes the norm of a poetry that is at once "religious, physical, passionate, [and] incantatory." More important, what Eliot and Pound had created as the "official" style of their age, the hard and dry and impersonal, is replaced by a new "official" style, no less contrived for its appearing spontaneous. It is a style measured not by wit nor sharp paradox, but by orderly constellations of incoherent images, by highly condensed and vaguely orphic metaphors, and by personal symbols which emerge into public meaning only by the very fact that they ascribe to some archetypal significance. It is a style that "starts with the sun" yet uses words of the world, though as if to admit Nietzsche's prophecy that language could be purified of the world's appearance only by turning it into music. If Crane's is taken to be its norm, however, then there is more of a priority on recurrent patterns, image clusters, and internal linkages of a mathematical and mechanical kind than anything the Eliotics conceived. For all the talk about organicism, the "New Paganism," at least in the mode Crane represents, produces something more like a machine or a formula. In any event, Crane's poetry is less Whitmanesque than Poesque, less organic than mathematical, in Valéry's sense of what Poe's poetics reveals. That Crane presumes to be an orphic poet, in the profoundest mythical sense, is one thing; the self-consciousness with which he goes about playing that role, and creating its style, is another.

There is, then, another and I think necessary way of looking at Crane's poetry than as "cosmic." For however much Crane talked of vision, of myth, and the like, however much he aspired to discover the pure language latent in the world, his poems are basically post-romantic and post-symbolist: they are poems in which the poet rehearses the act of creating the poem, poems in which life is explored and virtually lived by holding it within the intense focus of the moment of its creation—poems, that is, which create a world rather than discover one. If the poet lives his life, as Crane seems to have, for the single purpose of transforming himself back into the pure moment of his origin, then the poem may well become a doubly transformative act. The poet seeks self-transcendence by willing a return to his beginning. In fact, Crane's theme, like Poe's, would seem to be nothing less than the creation myth itself, to which his own poetic act is analogue. Whatever, the poem becomes a quest for permanence, which is achieved only in the achievement of the perfect poem, hence never. The poet may presume to set himself at the cosmic center, and like Orpheus to speak with the power of the cosmic urge out of the nothingness of the One. He is more likely to be involved in a very human enterprise, conducted at a higher intensity than is ordinary: the pursuit of himself, the definition of himself in his role as poet and, in Crane's particular case, as shareholder of the primordial mysteries. Like Orpheus, he is the victim of those he presumes to serve; or in other words, his role is that of victim to the very mysteries he harbors and sings.

Crane's poems do often achieve a constellated structure of recurrent images—the curve and circle imagery of The Bridge for example—but what kind of vision these manifest patterns represent is, to say the least, ambiguous. Surely it is more something desired than something possessed and known; surely Crane's "new" language, admitting its occasional brilliance, is anything but pure, his universe of images anything but apocalyptic. L. S. Dembo, in a most thorough reading of The Bridge, has shown how the pattern of imagery as well as the thematic progress of the poem leads his poet-quester not to vision but back to the world that defiles visions. The quester's vision sustains him not because it is grasped, but because it remains tantalizingly always before him, as possibility; it is his only when he has shared it with the world, that is, when he, like Columbus in "Ave Maria," has introduced it into history and thus exposed it to inevitable corruption and travesty. In *The Bridge's* several sections, the vision invariably precedes the poem or is to follow it. A great many of these individual pieces spring from the anxiety (like Columbus') over whether the glimpsed vision can be communicated at all. For the poet's role is not so much to have the vision—Crane would seem to say with Blake that the poet by definition has had it in that he is poet—as it is to convey it to a world that must corrupt it. Crane's poet-quester lives to be sacrificed in his role, for he is to be destroyed with his vision. The enemy is history. And yet, to go one step further, he restores the vision, purifying it of history, in his act of sacrificing himself to it, in the suffering that attends the rejection of the Word by the world.

Crane's poems confess the torture of the poet who, to articulate the Word, must contend with history and its words. He has to restore the Word, then, by becoming it in his own sacrificial act. Crane's search for a language has its analogue clearly in the metaphor of Christ: the Word given, betrayed, and subsequently left to the world in words. The poetic vision he expressly desires to evoke—it is, in effect, identical with his new language—inevitably turns back upon itself, for the desire is never to be fulfilled. Dembo points up the analogy between Crane's distraught poet and Nietzsche's tragic vision of the poet-hero who fulfills himself only in his defeat. Here is the crucial passage from *The Birth of Tragedy*: ". . . tragic myth, through the figure of the hero, delivers us from our avid thirst for earthly satisfaction and reminds us of another existence and a higher delight. For this delight the hero readies himself, not through his victories but through his undoing." Yet it is not simply, as Dembo says, that Crane's frustrated quester celebrates his undoing by an indifferent but redeemable philistine world, though he does this; nor that in adapting, for his later poetry, the mask of the Nietzschean hero and discarding that of the impotent clown, Crane desired to give stature and dignity to the poet as modern hero, though above all he longed for a dignity befitting the exalted role of poet. The paradox runs deeper, and is to be explained perhaps only by determining why in the mythical strategy of his poems the sacrifice of Dionysus had to be superimposed upon the sacrifice of Christ. And beyond that, why it is the sacrifice and not what should plausibly follow it, resurrection, that ultimately engages Crane; why, that is, Crane's poetry, which so passionately aspires to redeem history, by way of denying it, ultimately takes the only life it has from the pathos of the poet's failure to redeem it.

Crane aspires, in short, to write the poem that reaches beyond poetry, and yet it is in poetry, which clings tenaciously to history and its corruptions, that the poet claims his sacrificial identity. His defeat becomes necessary not so much as an affirmation of his dignity as poet, as the very act of his being. He is a seeker and sufferer rather than a finder. And while Crane may, even must, cling to his belief that the Absolute exists not only in the particulars of the world but beyond (just as he clings to a belief in his ability to articulate it and hence to join the two in One in the poem), he is like Poe in respect to his doubt over the price one must pay for the act, the sacrifice of self. And like for Poe, that act becomes his real theme, in which the marriage of subject and object implies the loss of subject. But the subject in Crane insists on surviving even in its own nothingness, surviving, that is, in the faith of its ultimate reconciliation and apotheosis: the clown in "Chaplinesque"; the lover in "Voyages"; the quester in "For the Marriage of Faustus and Helen"; the poet in "Praise for an Urn," whose poem aspires to its own apotheosis and fails of self-confidence; the bedlamite, the pariah, Columbus, Maquokeeta, the drunken sailor, his fellow American artists, and a host of other masks in *The Bridge*. But the end of these poems deliver, instead of vision, only the desperately renewed faith that it is still possibly available. They redeem the poet's vocation, and return him to his proper role, as voice of the Absolute he feels within himself and as seeker after the Absolute that exists in the world. In other words, his role is to re-unite the two in one, in poetry. The end for Crane's poems, it seems, was to justify the need for further poems, in which, ultimately, self and world might become one.

What Crane had finally to confront, perhaps unconsciously, was the fact that his failure lay in his method—the very method that had become his identity. The creative act itself is the true subject of these poems, the life of the poet-quester-visionary-lover-seeker whose role is as futile, yet as necessary, to himself as Sisyphus'. Like the Poe of the *Symbolistes*, who reappears in the "Tunnel" section of *The Bridge*, to have lost oneself to the world in quest of a way beyond it gives one a meaning and a purpose, in that it affirms alienation as prelude to transcendence. In the poet, as Crane idealizes him, resides the power to recognize the Word become flesh; his role is to transform that flesh back into the Word. But the transformative act, in that it will not yield to the easy explanations of dogma, is a suffering and a sacrifice of his own self. The flesh will not let go easily, and neither will the poem, for the poem, like life, is painfully real, and the vision, though glimpsed in that it is felt, remains problematic. The danger for a poet like Crane, however, is not that the vision may not be realized, but that his faith in it, and hence in himself, may wane. For then the very thing that sustains him, the need to pursue the vision, the need that calls forth the poem and verifies the poet's identity, betrays him to the enemy—history.

The poet's role in history (or better perhaps, his obligation to history) has a paradoxical effect on Crane's form. For the visionary poet, while he expressly denies history, must acknowledge it in the very act of trying to transform it. Crane's talent, almost every commentator on his poetry has remarked, was essentially lyrical. Yet it was virtually certain that, given his obsession with temporality, Crane would aspire to write an epic—or more accurately, to turn history into myth, to collapse the epic and the lyrical forms, by way of presenting not only the ideal that must in-form history but the very act of transformation by which the ideal is purified of history. *The Bridge*, clearly, is neither epic nor, as Crane suggested, a myth of America. It is aptly described, as Poe described the *Iliad*, as a series of lyrical poems, each one rehearsing a basic pattern of the poet's defeat by and sacrifice to an indifferent world which will not receive his word. But Crane's aspiration was, nevertheless, to transmute history into myth, by way of proving that the myth subsumed history. One method, pointed up by Eliot in his essay on *Ulysses* and by the practice of *The Waste Land*, was to telescope the individual quest with the archetypal: witness Crane's explanation of the Faust-Helen parallel in the essay "General Aims and Theories," and his various rationalizations, in letters to friends and sponsors, of the uses of mythical-historical archetypes in *The Bridge*. As he moved from the short, intense lyric toward the cluster of lyrics stretched upon a mythical-historical frame, he had to create a persona (of the poet-quester) who could be involved in both time and eternity, or who, in other words, was at once personal and archetypal. Circumscribed by history, this persona was nonetheless cognate with the poet-hero-victim of all time, archetypes of the poet in the guise of mythical or historical anti-heroes: with Faust, with Columbus, with Whitman and Poe and Emily Dickinson (fellow victims in the same sequence of history), with Rimbaud—in short, with the artist-*diabolus* whom history betrays because he denies history its privileges and priorities. The archetype of poet-quester becomes the archetype of visonary-victim, Dionysus-Christ. (Crane no less than Eliot could not really abide nor trust in the single, separate self of Whitman; Whitman soon became Poe, betrayed, perhaps self-betrayed, and denied by history. Unlike Eliot, he had only the archetypal self of artist-outsider to fall back on. Similarly, poetry for him was a method of telescoping personal history with the recurrent or mythical event in which history transcends itself. The distinction might be that Eliot preserves the illusion of historical time in his "tradition," while Crane is impatient with particular events that make up the logos except as they, like Columbus' voyage, can be reduced to the one truth they symbolize.) What the modern self shared with his prototype, however, was not vision so much as the commitment to pursue vision. The poem itself—*The Bridge* in particular—rather than elevating historical events into epical elaboration, thereby admitting the purposefulness of the many within the One, reduces history to a primary mythical pattern, thereby bespeaking the poet's distrust of history. This accounts, I think, for the confusions which attend Crane's very personal use of American history. He is not interested in history as such at all, except in that it offers evidence of the recurrent and universal pattern that obsessed him. American history was not so much a myth to him as an *ur*-myth, not history so much as a cosmic syndrome of the Absolute. In that sense alone did his particular involvement with it, and victimization by it, have meaning.

If Crane's use of history is arbitrary, therefore, this is just as it must be; for his role as he assumes it is to transform history into its absolute form before it transforms him into anonymity. This is what, in effect, Roebling had done in manifesting his vision of the bridge, which for Crane was a work of art, the marriage of form and power, even if it was destined to be received by a skeptical world only as a technological feat. The power of transformation rests, Crane would insist, with the poet, not as in Eliot with history. And therein is revealed Crane's true theme and problem. If the transformative act is history's, the poet is forced at one and the same time to acknowledge history and deny his creativity. But if the act is his, or through him, he may grasp his identity even in his undoing. For it is only through him that history can have meaning. The poet's identity rests in his method, a method which he must exercise in history but which he hopes will lead him beyond, to the meaning of history's dynamics; which is to say, he finds history in himself alone.

His method, as a mode of his being, exists as I previously indicated to reach beyond and thus to deny itself—a paradox Crane appears to have lived to the end. The paradox is perhaps more evident in Crane's early, short lyrics. Poems like "Praise for an Urn" and "Legend" explore the sacrificial nature of the creative act and the anxiety of almost certain failure. "Black Tambourine" identifies the poet with the "black man," exiled in "some mid-kingdom, dark," which is bounded on one side by the transcendent world available to his imagination, "his tambourine," and on the other by his primordial "carcass," the origin and end of his mortal self. But to the world (of self-consciousness) he is outcast and slave, neither accepted by it nor willing to accept it, isolated by time (like the Negro by history) in an absurd space. "Chaplinesque" regards the artist's pratfalls and evasions as a kind of sacrificial gesture, the compromise of one fact to preserve another—an inner integrity set against the world the poet disdains (because it is one he never made) yet aspires to purify. Even *The Bridge* celebrates at its very center the quester's ultimate triumph in his withdrawal from and return to the history that destroys him; in "The Dance," which makes the poem's completest retreat into the mythical past and back toward the primal moment, the sacrifice of Maquokeeta is at once an end and a beginning. It is a fulfillment of his role, the moment in which he is given to history which in turn will obscure and defile his meaning.

Beyond those early minor poems which state the condition, however, lay the necessity for vigorous reponse, evident certainly in *The Bridge* but likewise in several poems written at about the time Crane was formulating his large work. The response is manifest, as Dembo points out, in the shift of masks from impotent clown to engaged poet-quester, from the comic to the tragic vision. But in the end, one has to argue, the tragic vision returns to the comic or serio-comic, as is curiously evident in two poems I should like to explore in depth: "The Wine Menagerie" and "Lachrymae Christi." They are more truly poems in Crane's proper mode than is *The Bridge*, and they reveal clearly the problems he would face, and fail to overcome, in trying to write a poem that presumes to deal with history as apocalypse.

II

Harriet Monroe, closing off her correspondence with Crane about the obscurities of "At Melville's Tomb," testily observed that the poem "reeks with brains." Crane has seldom been accused since of an excess of brains, though it should be evident that the affected spontaneity of his poetry is outweighed by self-conscious contrivance and intellectual allusiveness. But Crane's allusions, whether indebted to Eliot or, more plausibly, derived from the quasi-intellectual mysticism of writers like Ouspensky, whom he was reading with careless fervor, intends something quite opposite Eliot's. If for Eliot the myth of history (i.e., tradition) may be an analogue (if not the Incarnation) of the divine order, for Crane it must be made, in and through the poet's words, to distill the pure Word. History, for Crane, is simply the energy of the Word issuing into particular forms. If for Eliot allusion is the method by which the individual talent delineates that enduring past to which the present self is heir and on which it modestly builds, for Crane it is the process by which the poet searches the fragments of history for its Absolute. If for Eliot allusion manifests an escape from personality, for Crane it is the apotheosis of personality, his version of cosmic personalism in which the Word is seen to realize Itself as person and poet. Eliot's history takes on perspective and the illusion of chronology and movement; it is authentically historical, even if in the end it proves to be immediate rather than continuous. Crane's history, on the other hand, is always subsumed by the *ur*-myth, the ideal of Unity. Eliot's history is at once corrupt and redeemable; Crane's is not so much corrupt as corrupting.

The effects on form and style are corollary. Crane's long poems do not develop, they recur. They pivot upon the eternal event, which the poet is constantly reliving. The persona of *The Bridge* is no protagonist, is involved in no *agon* except the recurrent event of his quest and failure. The compressed images, the ellipses, the forcefully collapsed syntax and metaphors—all reveal a poem which tries to deny the temporality of language, to distill the pure logos from the dross of the world's words. At the same time, this style calls attention to its own processes, and the stresses of its effort. If Eliot's language, especially in his later poetry, orders itself toward the formal rhythms of music, and points forward to the ultimate stillness upon which all is centered, Crane's aspires toward spontaneity and the illusion of creative release into the dynamics that pervade all meaningful forms—e.g., the Bridge as still motion. Paradoxically, it is acutely self-conscious; it "reeks with brains" at its most illogic extremes. But—and this is the crucial point—it achieves, or seeks to, an intensity of rhythm and movement that overrides intellect and purifies it. The poem aspires toward the tranquillity and silence of "belle isle" (monistic union), but the language ironically will not let go, and ultimately disdains the end in which it would consume itself. The new language, that is, reconciles subject and object, id and ego, in that it is the bridge by which alone the self passes from one world to the other, from alienation to home and back again.

In "The Wine Menagerie," for example, stylistic compression vies with some rather indirect allusiveness to evidence this process. The telescoped metaphors just fail to conceal the obvious scene, a bar, even as they fail to render adequately the dramatic evolution of vision. But that is just the point. The heady release, under the inspiriting effects of wine, leads to a new freedom and wholeness that is in itself a wrapt confinement. The images of the opening two stanzas turn upon this paradox, the transformation of time into space. For the redemption of sight frees an interior self which is at the same time pure and violent (the id that is both creative and destructive), and in turn transforms the impurities of real things into the purity of images. Yet the poet is "conscripted," even en-wombed, by the very bottles that contain the wine of his release:

> Invariably, when wine redeems the sight,
> Narrowing the mustard scansions of the eyes,
> A leopard ranging always in the brow
> Asserts a vision in the slumbering gaze.
>
> Then glozening decanters that reflect the street
> Wear me in crescents on their bellies. Slow
> Applause flows into liquid cynosures:
> —I am conscripted to their shadows' glow.

Indeed, this lacerating paradox controls the entire poem. The redemptive wine releases a Dionysian self that is "conscripted" by its own dual nature. Not only the "leopard" but the "glozening decanters," which contain the poet's image in their womb-like "bellies," point forward to the new "thresholds" he will affirm—"thresholds" in which "freedom" is circumscribed by "Wine talons." Stanzas three through six extend the paradox of the opening two: the refracted images of the dance are animal and violent, yet surely Dionysian, and they suggest, in a painful way, the sacrifice of self attendant upon the transformative act. The scene manifests all the violence of a rape, contained within a drabbly sham interior (space) and attended by the nightmare image of the serpent (time, but no less the destructive-creative primal force that is the union of subject and object), which circumscribes the speaker's vision. If on one level the scene does violence to the vision, it is no less the arena of the "I's" necessary act. In other words, the redemption implied in the poem's first line, this release from one kind of seeing (commonsensical) into another, is a freedom to undergo the agony of a generative act. The "urchin" who enters the scene in stanza five comes like a supplicant to the mysteries of the revel to which he is likewise victim. The dance contrasts rudely with his innocence, but is nonetheless the complement of it. For the "urchin," like the poet, is an outsider whose innocence must be sacrificed if he is to be an insider. What he knows, or is to know, is the revelation imaged in stanza six, in which "roses shine" between "black tusks," a metaphor of the Dionysian season, Spring, and the paradox of creation in destruction.

What, then, are the "New thresholds, new anatomies!" of the two succeeding stanzas?

> New thresholds, new anatomies! Wine talons
> Build freedom up about me and distill
> This competence—to travel in a tear
> Sparkling alone, within another's will.

Until my blood dreams a receptive smile
Wherein new purities are snared; where chimes
Before some flame of gaunt repose a shell
Tolled once, perhaps, by every tongue in hell.

The poem may be remotely connected with the love affair Crane described so ardently to Waldo Frank in a letter dated April 21, 1924. "Lachrymae Christi" certainly is: it was written a short two months before the letter and incorporates the ambiguous guilt and idealization of that "affair." But "The Wine Menagerie" was completed almost a year-and-a-half afterward. The ecstatic (but no less conscripting) transport within "another's will" is to be understood only in the context of the tear-smile imagery. In *The Birth of Tragedy* Nietzsche describes the dismemberment of Dionysus in terms of the agony of individuation, the division of the One into the many, like the "separation into air, water, earth, and fire." Individuation, he continues, "should be regarded as the source of all suffering, and rejected. The smile of this Dionysos has given birth to the Olympian gods, his tears have given birth to men." He remarks further that individuation was in the Elusinian mysteries the "root of all evil," while art signified reintegration. The movement in the above stanzas, through a "tear/Sparkling alone" toward the "new purities" of a "receptive smile," re-enacts the Dionysian cycle, which Nietzsche speaks of as a special kind of transformative act: "No longer the *artist*, he [in the ecstasy of his dance] has himself become a *work of art*," and in turn he becomes for his worshipers, like Orpheus, the object of violent desire. From the individuation and consequent suffering that gives birth to the poem, through the agony of the creative (re-creative) act which destroys the self, to the ecstasy of the "receptive smile," the imagery records an act of recomposing the self into a work of art: the reuniting of subject and object, self and other. But in this poem the "smile" only beckons, is not fully achieved, and the momentary "freedom" distilled in the sacrificial act exists but to be destroyed—again like Dionysian wholeness. The compressed and highly oblique metaphors of the last two stanzas can only suggest other forms of fragmentation, and particularly, in the images of beheading, the new cycle of Dionysian frenzy which must lead endlessly from wholeness to individuation and back again.

Yet the tragic rhythm, as the last couplet suggests, is more aptly comic. The freedom achieved in the moment of the poem—those "New thresholds, new anatomies"—is betrayed by the world's ruddy "tooth" and the "treasons of the snow," by time. And the poet becomes an "exile," an individual, once more in order to fulfill himself. Inevitably, the poem ends on the note of individuation and exile, not of ecstasy. While the symbolist poem should ideally conclude with vision or silence, with "new anatomies" evoked, the modernist poem must celebrate victory in defeat. The cycle of Crane's poem is not from the One to the many back to the One, but from fragmentation toward ecstasy and back again. The "new purities" of the Dionysian smile are not the poet's possession, but his compulsion. They are dreamed, not realized, except in the sense that one knows them only in the moment he knows he needs them. Unlike the symbolist poem, Crane's moves toward a threshold (the verge of unity) within the self rather than beyond the self; the ecstatic moment for him—at the center of the poem—is a moment of integration desperately grasped, in the act of making the poem, which precedes betrayal and exile. The "new purities" are "snared"; the "freedom" is built up around him by "Wine talons." His moment of integration is attained by transforming the kind of violence that marks stanzas three and four into pure form, "a shell." He aspires toward "new purities" of a "receptive smile," while the masculine actor of the earlier stanzas "takes her" with the "forceps" of his smile, an act in which "an instant of the world" is *unmade*. But the one act precedes the other; the time-space tomb must be unmade if the self is to be released into a womb of "new purities," from which, of course, must follow another birth or individuation. Confined by one world (time-space), the poet must dream new ones, to be "snared" only at the expense of self. But the "tooth implicit of the world" pursues and destroys the wholeness of vision and of the self, giving the self back itself and its agony. Like Dionysus, the poet must not possess but be possessed, and realize himself in losing himself. He can "travel" in a "tear," "within another's will," but only for the instant of his poetic act, his "dream." Yet even that for the poet means he must lose himself. The smile is earned at the price of tears, to which there is an inevitable return; at poem's end, the poet is once more an alien in reality, the exile.

The mark of a Crane poem is almost always this kind of turbulence and violence. It turns not on the language of paradox, but on the paradox of his act which anticipates the undoing of the actor. The Dionysian smile of rapture (which gives birth to the Olympian gods) is achieved in the agony of his fragmentation; the recognition of wholeness lies in our recognizing how far we have fallen from it, and yet how the poem returns us to it. Similarly, Crane's exile, a wondering Aeneas returned to the hellish world and its betrayals, pays the price of vision, which is not had except that it is lost. Was Marianne Moore so wrong, we might ask, to change the title of the poem to "Again" when she published it in the *Dial?*

Within this kind of context it is possible to understand the larger rhythms, and some of the obscurer particulars of "Lachrymae Christi." Crane's most incoherent poem, stylistically his most outrageous, "Lachrymae Christi" is to be understood primarily in the sense of its being only one more version of the one poem Crane could write. The imagery is at once more blatant and more inward than in the usual Crane effort; and unlike *The Bridge*, it is not long enough for motifs, images, and symbols to recur into coherence and clarity. Preceding "The Wine Menagerie," and less open than that poem, "Lachrymae Christi" is illuminated, at least in part, by the later piece. It moves from smile to smile through the agony of sacrifice and tears, and ends in the ecstatic moment of anticipated self-transcendence. The concluding image of Dionysus' "Unmangled target smile" is a vision of wholeness anticipated in the moment of fragmentation, and the image in the opening stanza of the "unyielding smile" is the blank expressionlessness of a sterile world into which the fragmented self is born, another kind of death. Between the two, between his birth into the modern landscape (a figure of absolute dualism) and his release into the ecstatic unity of death, lies the poet's creative ground. He must generate the one out of the other; he must, as Crane puts it in his most notorious essay, "acclimatize" the machine (of time). The middle of the poem is just that generative and purifying yet self-destructive act.

If the tears of Christ (and by metamorphosis, of Dionysus) are the wine which redeems agony, the "benzine/Rinsings" of the opening stanzas are anything but sacramental. They are venemous, sterilizing, death-rendering; they negate the ground of life, and compel the sacrifice of the creative act. It is difficult, given the syntactical dislocations, the paren-thesis, and the stanza break, to respond to the poem's opening sentence, which runs half-way through the second stanza. The analogy between the "Rinsings" and the "Immaculate venom" must certainly image, however, the impotent landscape in which the generative energy is contained—the body of the creative soul, the dualism of id-ego. And this energy is frankly, if obliquely, imaged as sexual. The illogic of the metaphor "venom binds" manifests the tension between vital and sterile, organic and inorganic. The imagery of evolving Spring, which follows, is the imagery of sexual violence, a destruction of the virgin innocence (a sterility in itself) that is paradoxically necessary to the fulfillment of that virginity. (Similarly, the crucifixion of Christ and the riving of Dionysus are essential to their fulfillment, the former an Apollonian illusion, the latter the stirrings of ecstatic transcendence; likewise, the analogy be-tween poet and his fulfillment in the poem.) Here, then, we can possibly understand the metaphor of the "Immaculate venom" which "binds/The fox's teeth"; for if the violence of sexual energy fragments in order to generate life, that which "binds" this energy is at once pure (immaculate and Apollonian) and sterilizing (venomous). Moreover, the complex associations of the immortal serpent, the sexual serpent, the serpent of intellect and time, and the serpentine dance of Dionysus begin to accumulate upon the double vision of the sacrificial and the generative act.

The agony of the creation results not only from the act of making the Word flesh (though that birth is agony enough), but anticipates the further consequences of regaining the Word from the flesh, the crucifixion. Thus the initial birth, the coming of the many out of the One, the individual self out of nature into isolation, is both fulfillment and betrayal. Here, in the paradox of the Nazarene's tears which distill "clemencies" even as they evidence the violation of innocence, we have Crane's variation on the fortunate fall. The poet, like the Nazarene, is given to the world, sacrificed to it; he does not assume his role, it is thrust upon him. He is the world's innocence and its redemption. But in his suffering and death, there is not "penitence/But song," the perpetual flow of redemptive waters by which alone the world survives the ravishments of its birth. Death (or the tunnelling worms of time, again associated with "venom" and "vermin") is fulfillment in that it frees the self from time into the work of art.

Hence, the poet (and the poem) survives his betrayal by resolving the paradox of it. The resolution is once again, as in "The Wine Menagerie," locked parenthetically in the poem's center:

> (Let sphinxes from the ripe
> Borage of death have cleared my tongue
> Once and again; vermin and rod
> No longer bind. Some sentient cloud
> Of tears flocks through the tendoned loam!
> Betrayed stones slowly speak.)

Paraphrase is difficult, but not altogether impossible. The condensation of images, indeed, is explicable both within the development of the poem and within the context of Crane's intellectual habit. Clearly enough, the passage turns upon the release of a submerged or pent-up energy, a primal force, into articulation, the freeing of the self into words, the surge of id into ego forms. For the first and only time in the poem, Crane uses the personal pronoun, underscoring the identification of poet with Nazarene. But more pronounced is the explicit association of the mystery with death, the analogy with the Christian paradox and the sexual pun of the death that is a birth. Oneness, then, is death, which binds and completes life; and death is power, potential life.

The clarification of particular images or symbols, however, is no easy task, in part because the strategy of the poem is to distill a new language, the language of primal force residual in the baser elements of the world's words. One can only pick at the parts, describe the arrangements and the possible relationships into which the parts coalesce. "Borage" must be read in the context of the title. A medicinal herb, it is likewise the source of a cordial wine, thus linking with the ambiguities of the title. The "sphinxes," on the other hand, combining in their dual nature both the spiritual and the animal, are the proper source of the mystery of the One that issues into the violent dualism of life. They are at once containers ("Let" in the sense of concealing) of the elemental and the elemental itself (that from which all is "Let," the pent-up source that must be released). They contain the mysterious and sacred energy (on the level of the poem's sexual metaphor, the id) which being released (individuated) is at once creative and destructive. But released it must be, and through the poet and at his expense—for that is his role. The full explanation owes something, no doubt, to a passage in *Tertium Organum*, where Ouspensky quotes from Madame Blavatsky to the effect that "Adam Kadmon is *humanity*, or humankind—Homo Sapiens—the SPHINX, i.e. 'the being with the body of an animal, and the face of a superman.' " But it may likewise call to mind Emerson's "Sphinx" (as well as his use of the figure in *Nature* and the essay "History") who manifests at once nature's mystery and the poetic mind which will free her by unlocking her enigma. Surely the metaphorical pressure here implies a oneness of the vital mysteries and the self which in giving them voice frees both, the life emerging from death at the expense of the primal Unity, but no less at the expense of the Christian myth of death.

Similarly the metaphor of the binding "vermin and rod," which picks up the earlier "venom" even as it suggests the caduceus and its multiple associations: both curative and releasing (Christ the Physician), but also emblematic of the sexual bifurcation and violent reunion that are the paradoxical source of creation. Crane's intellectual preferences may once more provide a clue, this time a passage out of a book he had earlier read with enthusiasm, Remy de Gourmont's *Physique de l'Amour*: "I don't know whether anyone has ever remarked that the caduceus of Mercury represents two serpents coupled. To describe the caduceus is to describe the love mechanism of ophidians. The bifurcated penis penetrates the vagina, the bodies interlaced fold on fold while the two heads rise over the stiffened coils and look fixedly at each other for a long time, eye gazing into eye." In the generative moment the paralysis is broken: the creative release issues into a flow (a "cloud/Of tears") at once spiritual and sentient, the metaphor of natural rebirth (of individuation, but literally of the nature's coming to life in the spring). The things of nature fragment Nature, yet fulfill Her wholeness only by destroying it; or in Nietzsche's terms, nature rises to celebrate her reconciliation with her lost child, man.

Indeed, the subsequent movement of the poem implies nothing else but the process of individuation. And the poem turns back in the end to fulfill the Nietzschean process almost to the letter. For individuation, which is a necessary manifestation of the Word, portends betrayal, but no less the reunion of man and nature. Rather than rounding off the poem in terms of the Christ analogy (as he did in an earlier version), Crane metamorphoses Christ into Dionysus, and for a very good reason. For the one signifies the necessity of history, and its Apollonian dream, the other the transformation which denies history. Analogously with Dionysus' tears, which in Nietzsche's version of the myth give birth to man, Christ's symbolize the fortunate fall, the simultaneous betrayal and rationalization of individuation. But Dionysus' smile is the fulfillment of himself, not of the Father, and a triumph of the One. The vision of Crane's poet is not to be redeemed by divine fiat; the betrayal of our birth must be its own redemption. Thus Dionysus' "Unmangled target smile," that rapture or ecstasy which as Nietzsche indicates emerges "at the shattering of the principium individuationis," becomes the emblem of wholeness, of art, toward which life aspires. In betrayal lies the necessity of vision. Yet the smile of Dionysus, one notes, is not an achieved and communicated vision in the poem; it is the ecstasy of anticipated fulfillment. For the moment of the poet's betrayal and dismemberment is, like Dionysus', as inevitable as his transcendence, and indeed is essential to it; the moment, in truth, is his fulfillment. It is not just that one must precede the other in sequence; the one is the other. The tears of Christ (history's betrayal) are redeemed by Dionysus' smile (which denies history). But the fulfillment of the "smile" is always a "target," the unmangled or unmediated vision always the promise of suffering and its balm. The poem, like The Bridge, would confront Spenglerean pessimism, an enduring problem for Crane, by transforming history's incessant motion into the myth of an on-going cycle, realized through the voice of the Dionysian self. Crane indicates, thereby, that the cycle (and history) is manifest only in the coming and going of the individual self—the poet as word and as flesh, the poet as sufferer returned again and again to the deathly landscape of history's changes and the perfidies attendant upon his role as keeper of the Word, the ground of being.

III

The consequences of Crane's vision are as obvious in his life as in his style. The method arrives at an impasse, condemning the poet to a repetition that can only be sustained by an heroic expenditure of energy upon intense and forced moments. There was not in Crane's poetics, so like his temperament, the economy that allowed a conservative expenditure of that energy—like Wallace Stevens' "violence from within" that would adjust itself to contain and counter rather than deny the "violence without." What finally happens to Crane, one wants to say, is that he became the ultimate victim of history, and the constant cycle of renewal-defeat upon which his poems turned led finally to an exhaustion rather than a revival of his energies. What is victimized is his faith in the inexhaustible energy of self; in effect, the failure of *The Bridge* to articulate in some vague way the principle of the conservation of energy in recurrence suggests pathetically his own exhaustion. But this is no less a failure of method—a method, again paradoxically, contrived like Poe's upon what I should like to call, tentatively, the "poetics of failure."

The "poetics of failure" may be manifest in two different but complementary effects. The poet may posit an idea of the visionary poem as self-transcending, and hence aspire toward a poetry which either denies itself or destroys itself. Or he may get hung up on the paradox of the poem which wills its own end, because he and the poetic method have become one. These are two kinds of symbolism in effect: Mallarmé's on the one hand, Poe's on the other. The Poe of *Symbolisme* wills the former, the poem as dream, but most often achieves the latter, the poem as a quest which leads the poetic self through the terrifying landscape of its mortality. The one wills the ecstasy of silence, the other experiences the darkness of blackness. And in a sense, the two represent the dilemma of American poetics. Even Emerson's unruffled cosmic optimism issued in a poetics of failure. Confronted by the contradiction that the poet should be "the man without impediment," but that history had never yet nor never could produce that man, he had to fall back upon the poem which anticipated what it could not yield: "Thus journeys the mighty Ideal before us; it never was known to fall into the rear. No man ever came to an experience which was satiating, but his good is tidings of a better. Onward and onward!" Poe reveals the consequences of reflecting too long on the ungraspable, though he too takes it as the true impetus for poetry: "There is still a something in the distance which he has been unable to attain. We have still a thirst unquenchable, to allay which he has not shown us the crystal springs. This thirst belongs to the immortality of man. It is the desire of the moth for the star. It is no mere appreciation of Beauty above." Still, Emerson's cosmic optimism, admitting that "poetry was all written before time was" and the fault of any one poem lies in man's translations, had to confront the limitations of language. He had to live in the faith that his poetics would someday have its poet. But in the meantime, if the pure poem was not yet to be written, the poet's responsibility was to prepare himself to write it. For his own part, Emerson wrote poems which almost literally were dedicated to defining what this poet must *be*, not to rendering what this poet does *see*. They are essentially verse essays in poetics, poems which explore the role of the poet but never dare to assume that role. And this is as true of poems like "Woodnotes" and "Monadnoc" as of those explicit poems about ideal poets like "Bacchus," "Saadi," and "Merlin." In a sense, Emerson was writing Poe's "Israfel," an optative poem, in the optimum mode. But in so doing he made poetry as large as life, in that he made it a mode of preparing for the end. Between what his poet could and should do lay an abyss Emerson never really crossed, nor even confronted.

The point is this: the only possible solution to the poetics of failure, which is essentially the minority report upon symbolism, is some kind of post-symbolist adjustment. One possibility is to substitute the process of the poem for any transcendental end it may aspire to reach. Resolution, in other words, is available in a poetics like Whitman's, in which the seeking self and the end sought become the same thing, contained as they are within an Hegelian faith in the rightness of whatever is, in the rightness of history as mythic process. In short, it is the resolution which disclaims the problem. Or resolution may lie in a post-transcendental, humanistic poetics like that of Wallace Stevens, which, denying resolution, throws the poetic self back upon the resources of an all-too-human imagination that can discover its identity only in the act of relating itself to otherness. There, at the center of himself, the poet must learn to live in the act of creating not the Word but himself. Either that, or retreat into a myth of history that does not so much absolve the self as subsume it to the larger purposes of history. This is Eliot's response, which begins by denying that poetry can redeem us, except by teaching us to sit still in the eternity of history.

For a poet like Crane, however, there is ultimately no resolution: neither the broken world into which he falls nor the pure world he envisions is convincingly real for him, and hence no reconciliation of the two suffices, even were it possible. The poetic self, trapped in one and longing for the other, finds itself and its method denied by both. For not only is the self betrayed, the poetic method is betrayed; or better, it betrays itself at every turn. The betrayal is manifest on several levels. The recurrent event demands an ever-renewed language; the language of the "broken world" must be constantly re-purified, until at last the poet betrays himself into ingenuity. It is not, and cannot be, as he says, that there is *a* language to be discovered. For once it is had and given to the world the world corrupts it, as well as the giver. The language must constantly be renewed, and this finally becomes the poet's onus. He might begin with the enthusiastic proclamation that he is possessed by language, and with a faith that this language is the revealed truth, that the Word is the force *in* the world. But the fact that came home to Crane very early was that each embrace of the unknown, even if it brought him momentary ecstasy, was consummated in loss. He was always returned to his one responsibility: to the words of the world which repeatedly obscure the true Word they severally contain.

The history of *The Bridge* is a history of renewed assaults upon his theme, until finally, as Crane was to admit in moments of despair, the writing of the thing became an exhaustive burden rather than, as it was to be, the ultimate of transport. Characteristically, he wrote the last section first, the section which carried him to the threshold of vision. Then he got down to his true theme, the quest and its ultimate frustration. He might have recognized something very like this within the individual sections. In the guise of searching history for its idea, he was celebrating his own method, by which alone, his poetics insisted, history could be cleansed. And since the method fulfilled itself only in defeat, it failed ultimately to sustain him, demanding re-engagement to the point of diminishing returns. In the end, his resources of energy were rapidly exhausted, even before his resources of language, if we are to judge from "The Broken Tower."

Unlike Eliot, Crane could not adopt his method to his life, to make the process of searching a discipline of waiting; nor could he, like Stevens, find his method an end in itself, the act of the mind in search of the supreme fiction which finally discovers that the supreme has being only in the mind seeking and hence creating it. Perhaps in "The Broken Tower" Crane caught a glimpse of that possibility. But when that poem fell, as he mistakenly thought, on deaf ears, Crane suffered the ultimate betrayal of his method. For if the need to communicate his vision to the world had always been his one compulsion—and in effect, the essence of his vision—the threat of utter solipsism was intolerable in that it would cut him off once and for all from the world he disdained. Yet here alone, in isolation from the world, could the Word be pure. In the end, ironically, he needed the very world he and his language denied, and in revenging himself upon it, he betrayed himself into the silence his method at once paradoxically sought and feared. What is left, the very tentative new language of his canon, displays enough of the corruption, and of the purity, to remind us of his heroic pathos.

R. W. B. LEWIS

"For the Marriage of Faustus and Helen"

Athree-part poem of roughly 140 lines, "For the Marriage of Faustus and Helen," occupies a key position in Crane's career suggestively similar to that of *Endymion* in the career of John Keats. Like *Endymion*, "Faustus and Helen" is the poet's first venture into the long (or perhaps one should say the longer, the more deliberately ambitious) poem, after a number of masterful but carefully restricted short lyrics. More importantly, the venture itself is, in both cases, the very motif of the poems resulting. Sir Sidney Colvin's summary of *Endymion*—a "parable of the poetic soul in man seeking communion with the spirit of essential Beauty in the world" —applies readily enough to "Faustus and Helen"; though Crane's poem is less a parable, with distinctive narrative ingredients, than a prayerful meditation. The search of Endymion ("the human soul, the poet, or the poetic imagination," in the words of W. J. Bate) for Cynthia, the moon-goddess and representative of ideal beauty in Keats's poem is to a telling extent re-enacted in the search of Crane's Faustus ("the symbol of himself, the poetic and imaginative man of all times," as Crane explained) for Helen (the symbol of an "abstract 'sense of beauty' ").

I do not present this fundamental similarity as evidence of poetic influence, though some influence may exist. But what is more striking is the archetypal nature, not only of Crane's poem, but of his poetic development—something that, for me at least, contains an insinuation

From *The Poetry of Hart Crane: A Critical Study.* Copyright © 1967 by Princeton University Press.

about *the* poetic career as such, and the phases it seems inevitably to pass through. There are, of course, major differences between Keats and Crane generally, and between *Endymion* and "Faustus and Helen" in particular: differences of idiom and of method, and larger ones of the dialetical movement characteristic of each poet. There are also further deep affinities—especially in the shared idea of the poetic construct, any poetic construct, as an instance (as Crane once put it) of "power in repose"—that I shall want to come back to. Meanwhile, let me simply stress the turning-point—the poetic breakthrough, if you will—comparably achieved by the two poems. For Crane, the turning-point was so radical and complex, and raises so many questions about his technique and his temperament, his habitual procedure and even his "philosophy," that I shall allow myself to linger over "Faustus and Helen" a good deal more than, in another perspective, it might seem to deserve.

Crane apparently hit upon the general notion of his poem in April 1922, when he was still living in Cleveland and working for the advertising firm of Corday and Gross: "inventing metaphors for water heaters and sundry household conveniences" as Horton puts it; a *métier* by no means unrelated to "Faustus and Helen." By the middle of May, he had painfully written a nearly final version of the first twelve lines of Section I; but then, in his usual manner, he abandoned that section and went on to Section II, which he finished with unexpected speed in early June. Returning to the first part, he made (he told Munson on June 18) "a good start on it," but he was beginning to have doubts "about the successful eventuation of the poem as a *whole.*" The doubts persisted. He was able to feel on August 17 that the first part was "about right now" (though the stanza beginning "The earth may glide diaphanous to death" was not added until September); and he could even show a few lines of Section III ("Corymbulous formations of mechanics" and so on). But six weeks later, he proposed issuing the two completed sections as independent and unconnected poems, the first to be called "For the Marriage of Faustus and Helen," and the second "The Sirens of the Springs of Guilty Song."

As the concluding section came slowly into being, however, the work began to reveal to its author an at least sufficient harmony. "I've just about finished the last part," he remarked on January 20, 1923; and by February 7, he was confidently describing the poem's overall structure to Waldo Frank and pointing out "a few planks of the scaffolding." In short, "Faustus and Helen," like many of Crane's shorter writings, grew out of a curiously haphazard and seemingly piecemeal method of composition. But though there are rough patches along the way, the poem moves—it begins, progresses, and ends—with a kind of splendid clarity. It is the product without question of a shaping power that is at last fully in command, a power that bends the individual sections into a most compelling design.

Crane himself, on the rational level, was not very clear about the nature of that design; and the compositional fits and starts probably reflect a certain gap between a firm imaginative grasp and a degree of rational confusion. I have already remarked that, when Crane erred in his appraisal of his own poems, it was more often than not because he underestimated his achievement. His comments on "Faustus and Helen" and his outlines of it suggest that he never quite realized what he had done. He was enormously excited by the feeling that he was doing, that finally he had done something, very big; and the excitement became almost uncontrollable when Allen Tate and Waldo Frank contended (according to Crane's report) that he had proved himself the greatest American poet then alive with "Faustus and Helen," and when Gorham Munson added "the astounding assertion that the poem was the greatest poem written in America since Walt Whitman" (which, by the way, it very well may have been). But while at work on it, he explained glutinously to Munson that his poetic purpose was "to evolve a conscious pseudo-symphonic construction toward an abstract beauty that has not been done before in English." He alluded elsewhere, and more cogently, to the "graduation from the quotidian into the abstract" in Section I, and he implied in his retrospective summary for Frank that Section III ended in a restatement of that same "graduation."

All this is misleading. "Faustus and Helen" is more truly and profoundly Platonic than Crane understood (though I do not mean to suggest any direct Platonic influence, nor, as I shall say, that of any other formal metaphysic). It does indeed move to the rhythm of an ascending dialectic, moves from a poetic definition of the visible and temporal world—as experienced, say, in the Cleveland of 1922—to a vision of a world of timeless beauty. But then, just as in Plato's *Republic* myth the philosopher's mission brings him back down into the dim cave of the actual, so in "Faustus and Helen" the poet and poem turn of necessity downward to confront and to celebrate the here-and-now. "For the Marriage of Faustus and Helen" is not only a prothalamium for the wedding between the poet and ideal beauty; it is also a song for the reconciliation and marriage between two dimensions of existence. Its continuing subject, indeed, is nothing other than the visionary redemption of this actual world; and in this respect it is a vast expansion on the brief thematic hint at the close of "Chaplinesque," when the empty ash can was transformed for an instant into a grail of laughter.

Section I transcends the realm of time, of "bloodshot eyes" and "troubled hands" to conclude in a hymn of "praise" for Helen (*ideal beauty*) and her realm of "hourless days." But Section III, hence the poem as a whole, ends with a magnificent imperative in which everything that had earlier been transcended is re-entered, accepted, eulogized:

> Distinctly praise the years, whose volatile
> Blamed bleeding hands extend and thresh the height. . . .

Those first four words deserve to be put into italics. More than anything else Crane ever wrote, they announce his fundamental attitude toward the world man lives in, and his own mature conception of the profession of poetry.

II

"Praise" is perhaps the key word in the poem, and "Faustus and Helen" is in one perspective an autobiographical work. It declares the mood of praise that Crane was everywhere voicing in his letters during the months of composition, and that he was erecting into a first principle, even the prime subject, of poetry. It was at this time—over the months in 1922—that Crane turned decisively away from the kind of poetry that he recognized as dominant among his contemporaries: the poetry, as he called it, of "humor and the Dance of Death" (by "humor," meaning Laforguian irony and Eliotic wit). He told Allen Tate to follow the "upward" direction evident in one of Tate's recent poems; and he went on: "Launch into praise" (an obvious early version of the "Faustus" phrase just quoted). "*You* are the one who can give praise an edge and beauty, Allen. You have done so well in a couple of damnations, that I feel confident in you." "I cry for a positive attitude," he exclaimed to Charmion Wiegand in January 1923. "When you see the first two parts of my 'Faustus & Helen' . . . you will see better what I mean."

In March, with "Faustus and Helen" completed and *The Bridge* stirring almost violently in his imagination, Crane wrote Munson that he had "lost the last shreds of philosophical pessimism during the last few months," and that he felt himself "quite fit to become a suitable Pindar for the dawn of the machine age." Remarks like those no doubt sounded willfully immature to most of Crane's literary colleagues, as they explored and proclaimed the cultural death that had visited or was about to visit the waste land of the age. Forty years later, when one has perhaps been sufficiently exposed to every mode and degree of "philosophical pessimism," such remarks may strike us instead (they strike me) as invigorating and restorative, and as being grounded in a decidedly arguable estimate of the fundamentally hopeful and praiseworthy condition of things.

They were, of course, grounded as well in more personal elements. Crane's mood of praise, here as always, emanated from the simple sense of his own creative capability; he regularly transferred to the external world his alternating confidence and despair about his own abilities. But in the present case, there was a prior cause for his feeling of immense creative potential. It now appears probable that the immediate source of Crane's shift of spirit was something like a mystical seizure—of the sort that, according to his biographers, Whitman also underwent one morning in the early 1850's, that led rapidly to the 1855 *Leaves of Grass* and that Whitman recollected tranquilly in the fifth section of "Song of Myself":

> I mind how once we lay such a transparent summer
> morning. . . .
> Swiftly arose and spread around me the peace and knowledge
> that pass all the arguments of the
> earth,
> And I know that the hand of God is the promise of my own,
> And I know that the spirit of God is the brother of my own,
> And that all men ever born are also my brothers, and
> the women my sisters and lovers,
> And that the kelson of the creation is love.

Crane may have had that passage and the experience behind it in mind when he told Munson, in the letter about "philosophical pessimism," that "I begin to feel myself directly connected with Whitman . . . in currents that are positively awesome in their extent and possibilities." Crane's own experience, as he described it, was more purely visionary and egocentric than Whitman's; it was more a matter of the radiated consciousness, and it was less charged than Whitman's with the sense of the human family, of the universal binding power ("kelson"—a line of jointed timbers) of love, and the intimate presence of the Godhead. It soon gave rise, however, to the Whitmanian conviction that, as Crane put it, "in the absolute sense the artist *identifies* with life," and the corollary belief that "we must somehow touch the clearest veins of eternity flowing through the crowds around us"; to some extent in "Faustus and Helen" and to every extent in *The Bridge*, it led to a passionate search for the Godhead.

The event took place in January or February 1922; and this is Crane's account of it, to Munson, in June of that year:

Did I tell you of that thrilling experience this last winter in the dentist's chair when under the influence of aether and *amnesia* my mind spiraled to a kind of seventh heaven of consciousness and egoistic dance among the seven spheres—and something like an objective voice kept saying to me—'You have the higher consciousness—you have the higher consciousness. This is something very few have. This is what is called genius'? A happiness, ecstatic such as I have known only twice in 'inspirations' came over me. I felt the two worlds. And at once. As the bore went into my tooth I was able to follow its every revolution as detached as a spectator at a funeral. O Gorham, I have known moments in eternity. I tell you this as one who is a brother. . . . Today I have made a good start on the first part of 'Faustus and Helen.'

"I felt the two worlds. And at once." This experience stimulated by anaesthetic, Crane later sought to repeat through the stimulus of alcohol—and not, as it seems, altogether ill-advisedly. Philip Horton, in his fine discussion of this aspect of Crane, quotes William James on the power of alcohol to arouse man's "mystical faculties": "Sobriety diminishes, discriminates, and says no; drunkenness expands, unites and says yeas. It is in fact the great exciter of the Yes function in man."

It is also, of course, an exciter of the negative function and can arouse man's pugnacious and destructive faculties as well as his mystical ones. On the whole, though, it did intensify Crane's yea-saying impulse, for a number of years anyhow; even if Crane might have pondered Emerson's admonition on the subject. In "The Poet," Emerson, after citing the ancient belief that the poet writes "not with the intellect alone but with the intellect inebriated by nectar" and after observing that "this is the reason why bards love wine, mead, narcotics, coffee, tea, opium, the fumes of sandalwood and tobacco," goes on to argue that "never can advantage be taken of nature by a trick," and reminds us of Milton's saying that "the lyric poet may drink wine and live generously; but the epic poet, he who shall sing of the gods and their descent into men, must drink water out of a wooden bowl."

But the new or visionary quality in "Faustus and Helen" and the poems that followed it was not only the result of a mystical experience and the product of an "intellect inebriated by nectar." It also reflected Crane's growing escape from his artistic bondage to T. S. Eliot and Laforgue. Crane's relation to Eliot was both contradictory and continuing. He once said that he had read "Prufrock" twenty-five times, "and things like 'Preludes' more often"; after an initial disappointment with *The Waste Land*, he went on, as he acknowledged, "to read and re-read" it incessantly; *The Bridge*, conceived in part as an answer to *The Waste Land*, echoes it at several turns. But at a relatively early stage, Crane sensed a fundamental difference between Eliot and himself, an urgency to escape from Eliot's "overwhelming question" and the Prufrockian and waste-land moods that characterized Eliot's poetry in those years. It was something more than the ambitious restiveness of a somewhat younger generation, though it partook of that. Crane put it as honestly as he knew how in a letter to Munson, in January 1923, when "Faustus and Helen" was nearly done. The passages have been quoted frequently, but they should be placed in context here:

> You already know, I think, that my work for the past two years (those meagre drops!) has been more influenced by Eliot than any other modern. . . . There is no one writing in English who can command so much respect, to my mind, as Eliot. However, I take Eliot as a point of departure toward an almost complete reversal of direction. His pessimism is amply justified, in his own case. But I would apply as much of his erudition and technique as I can absorb and assemble toward a more positive, or (if [I] must put it so in a skeptical age) ecstatic goal. I should not think of this if a kind of rhythm and ecstasy were not (at odd moments and rare!) a very real thing to me. I feel that Eliot ignored certain spiritual events and possibilities as real and powerful now as, say, in the time of Blake. Certainly the man has dug the ground and buried hope as deep and direfully as it can ever be done. He has outclassed Baudelaire with a devastating humor that the earlier poet lacked.
>
> After this perfection of death—nothing is possible in motion but a resurrection of some kind. Or else, as everyone persists in announcing in the deep and dirgeful *Dial*, the fruits of civilization are entirely harvested. Everyone, of course, wants to die as soon and painlessly as possible. Now is the time for humor, and the Dance of Death. All I know through very much suffering and dullness (somehow I seem to twinge more all the time) is that it interests me to still affirm certain things. That will be the persisting theme of the last part of "F & H" as it has been all along.

The moments of joy were, as we see, odd and rare, punctuation marks in periods of "very much suffering." But Crane's chief assertion—that "nothing is possible in motion but a resurrection of some kind"—should no more be attributed to sheer personal temperament than the death-consciousness that it repudiates and that Crane was perfectly willing to assume to be "a very real thing" for Eliot. At this moment, in fact, Crane was not making a statement primarily of personal inclination, but a prediction of sorts about an inevitable curve in cultural attitude and literary expression—toward a freshened awareness of "certain spiritual events and possibilities." In his own generation, it was Crane himself who followed such a curve.

He did so in part, as the passage hints, by shifting his poetic allegiance from Eliot to William Blake: though not at all the Blake whose essential failure—because he lacked "a framework of accepted and traditional ideas"—Eliot had regretfully made public in a brief essay of 1920. It was much rather the poet Crane encountered, in September 1922, in S. Foster Damon's impressive critical study *William Blake: his Philosophy and Symbols*. Crane had apparently begun to read Blake as early as 1917—"You know how much Blake has always interested me," he said to Munson, in commenting on Damon's book. But in the latter, by which Crane confessed he was "especially thrilled," Crane could find the poetry he had been looking for: a supreme example of the visionary imagination, and poetry which looked at once into and through the immediate and visible world; highly personal poetry in a highly personal idiom which at the same time projected a majestically hopeful myth of world history.

III

Affirmation was indeed "the persisting theme" of "Faustus and Helen." Yet paradoxically the affirmative impulse was almost undermined in advance by devices at the start of the poem that reflected Eliot's continuing influence. The point is worth laboring a little. Crane had not fully perceived the way in which Eliot's "erudition and technique" were inseparable from that very sense of cultural and spiritual decay that Crane was bent on denying, that they had been developed to convey that sense and could not readily be applied "toward an opposite goal." In another letter of this period, Crane accused Eliot of believing that "happiness and beauty dwell only in memory." This was of course a serious reduction of Eliot's attitude (though we remember that he was talking about the Eliot prior to "Marina" and "Ash Wednesday"); even so, Crane could not have altogether grasped the fact that Eliot's erudite quoting from the great literature of the past was a technique for suggesting, by ironic juxtaposition, some portion of that belief. If he had, he would not have begun his anti-Eliotic hymn of praise to the present world with so Eliotic a gesture—a title that recalls Marlowe's *Doctor Faustus* and a long quotation from Ben Jonson's *The Alchemist*, items which seem at first glance to pose a familiar ironic comparison between past splendor and present degradation.

As to the figures named in the title, once he had selected them, as Brom Weber remarks, "Crane redeemed himself by immediately disregarding them." There are few if any vibrations of Marlowe in the poem; and Faustus and Helen are, in Crane's explanation to Frank, "the symbol of myself, the poetic and imaginative man of all times," and the symbol of an "abstract 'sense of beauty.' " A careful reading of Scene XIII in *Doctor Faustus*, where Helen is magically conjured up, would only muddle the reader of Crane's poem; far from wanting to offer Helen "one inconspicuous orb of praise," as Crane's Faustus does, Marlowe's wants the lady to be his paramour and finds heaven in her thoroughly physical embraces. The epigraph (from *The Alchemist*, IV, 5) is more bothersome yet.

> And so we may arrive by Talmud skill
> And profane Greek to raise the building up
> Of Helen's house against the Ismaelite

and so on for five more lines packed with names of Old Testament figures and Biblical exegetes. A number of ingenious explanations suggest themselves, both of the relevance of the Jonson passage and the effect it produces when conjoined with the titular reference to Marlowe. But the fact is that the Jonson passage is pure Jabberwocky. In the play, it is spoken by Dol Common, a lively whore with a talent for chicanery, who is pretending to a religious fit as part of a scheme to gull Sir Epicure Mammon, a gentleman of awe-inspiring erotic fancy. The confusion is compounded: for the Jonsonian scene is a flamboyant parody of the meeting between Faustus and Helen in Marlowe's play. Crane thus confronts us with a bewildering complex of ironies as headnotes to a poem the whole drive of which is to get beyond irony.

The poem itself is more self-sufficient and less devious than those headnotes might lead one to expect. Its initial difficulty is due in part to a language that is often doing several things at once, and sometimes pointing in more than one direction at a time. Then, too, there is the poem's structural method, what Joseph Frank might call its "spatial form"—whereby the full import of a word or phrase is bestowed retroactively by the later appearance of a nourishingly correlative or a suggestively opposite word or phrase. "The baked and labeled dough" in the poem's second line, for example, must wait thirty lines for "the white wafer cheek of love" to give it final meaning (an image of spiritual flabbiness)—even though mental doughiness is conveyed at once, and even though the immediate context invests "dough" with its slang meaning of money (hence an image of the money-grubbing temper).

All this has to do with what Crane, several years later, would call "the logic of metaphor" and would describe as "the so-called illogical impingements of the connotations of words on the consciousness," and the "combinations and interplay" of such connotations "in metaphor." In Section I of "Faustus and Helen," metaphor is the transporting agent on the journey enacted from this everyday world to a world of absolute beauty. If we let our logical faculty relax for a while, and if we permit the connotations of the words in the opening stanzas to impinge freely on our consciousness and to combine and interact—what we will then experience is the poetic creation of a world: this world.

It is a world which is crowded and confused (multitudes, stacked, numbers, crowd) but where relationship is lacking (divided, partitioned; by later implication, fragmentary). Its voice is vulgar and contradictory ("Smutty wings flash out equivocations"); its spirit is dully unchanging, backward-looking, cliché-ridden (accepted, memoranda, stock quotations). It is, in fact, a world that has become one huge stock market; or better, a world that Crane's poetry skillfully transforms into a huge stock market, as the business-office references to stacked partitions, memoranda, and stenographic smiles lead into the Wall Street idiom, to stock quotations (a phrase which does double duty), numbers, margins, curbs, and corners. This is Crane's original way of releasing a large historical insight. Contemporary America has become a stock-market culture, and in "Faustus and Helen I" we see the process in action.

The movement from that world to the realm of Helen is not abrupt; it is rather, in Crane's phrase, a steady "graduation from the quotidian." Even in the thick of the quotidian, the mind, normally assailed by equivocations of smutty wings, sometimes feels itself "brushed by sparrow wings"; the imagination stirs to those "spiritual events and possibilities" that Crane spoke of to Munson. Such higher possibilities are "rebuffed" from the main walks of life; they inhabit the margins of life, its curbs and corners (those otherwise Wall Street words likewise doing double duty). And in the evening, they retreat—and we follow them in imagination—into a place ("somewhere") that, though not yet Helen's world, is a partial version of it, a promise and an indication. It is "virginal perhaps" rather than smutty; if not integral, it is "less fragmentary" than the partitioned and divided setting of the usual day; as against the "baked" feeling of the asphalt world, this evening world is "cool." And from its vantage point, the journeying spirit can catch a glimpse of the home of ideal beauty:

> There is the world dimensional for
> those untwisted by the love of things
> irreconcilable.

I hear a slight stress on the word "there." "*There* is the world I seek, that other dimension of experience that is accessible to anyone not wedded to the equivocal, not committed to unresolvable conflict as the truth of life and thought; to anyone who does not find irony to be the one true mode of expression."

IV

The lines about "the world dimensional" are sometimes cited as evidence of the sizable influence upon "Faustus and Helen" (and perhaps on the lyrics that followed) of *Tertium Organum*, a turgid work of mystical philosophy by the Russian speculator, P. D. Ouspensky. The claim seems to me improbable, on both particular and general grounds. *Tertium Organum*, which became available in America in 1920, was undoubtedly fashionable in some American literary circles in the early 1920's and intermittently thereafter. But for one thing, most of the sentence just quoted was as we remember composed early in 1921 as part of a grab-bag poem, "The Bridge of Estador"; and this was apparently some time before Crane had heard of Ouspensky's book, even if we accept Weber's conclusion that Crane had the book in his hands "before the end of 1921 at the very latest, if not earlier." The best evidence is that *Tertium Organum* was on Crane's shelf in late 1921 and that Crane glanced at it, as one does, but that he did not really look into it for more than a year. It was not until mid-February of 1923—when "Faustus and Helen" was finished—that Crane wrote Tate: "I have also enjoyed reading Ouspensky's *Tertium Organum* lately." I see no reason not to take Crane's subsequent statement literally: namely that Ouspensky's "corroboration of several experiences in consciousness that I have had gave it particular interest." "Corroboration" sounds like the right word: and of personal experiences, one assumes, like that undergone in the dentist's chair when Crane "felt the two worlds. And at once."

    In Philip Horton's deft summary, Ouspensky's "conception of the spiritual decay of humanity under two centuries of scientific materialism and the imminent emergence of a new order of consciousness," along with his "view of art as the beginning of wisdom and the artist as visionary"— all this could appeal mightily to Crane and to the New York friends upon whom he later urged a reading of Ouspensky. But Crane's own enthusiasm was short lived. When those same friends went on to adopt the bizarre discipline of the Ouspenskyite Gurdjieff, who brought his mystical and conversionary dances to America in 1924, Crane signed off at once. He found the "Hindu antics" ridiculous, and he withdrew from the whole business so completely that his friends became, as he would recall, "hermetically sealed to my eyesight," while he himself was left by them "to roll in the gutter of my ancient predispositions." Crane's most important dispositions were always toward poetry, and not to mystical flailings nor to any mode of philosophizing, however he might be momentarily diverted by the splurging arguments of an Ouspensky.

The important fact is that there was virtually nothing in *Tertium Organum* that Crane could not find—had not already found—in the poetry of William Blake, or in Blake's younger Romantic contemporaries, or in Whitman or (expressed yet more suitably for his purpose, as I shall argue) in Emerson. Blake can stand, here, for that entire tradition, and one reason for quoting Horton's summary of Ouspensky is that it applies so well to Blake—in Crane's phrase, Ouspensky "corroborates" Blake. The purpose that came into view with "Faustus and Helen" was defined by Crane, in April 1923, by means of a quotation from Blake's *Jerusalem* (from "To the Christians"). Crane had been talking about how one might arrive at a knowledge of "the essence of things," when such essences are not to be found in the physical mass and bulk of things, but "are suspended on the invisible dimension." We get at them, Crane proposed, in the manner recommended by Blake:

> I give you the end of a golden string
>   Only wind it into a ball,—
> It will lead you in at Heaven's gate,
>   Built in Jerusalem's wall.

This is the way of poetry, and it indictes the way of the criticism of poetry: which must re-wind the "golden string" of metaphoric language, and so follow the imagination into its own heavenly kingdom. But it is not the way of philosophy, and here is the nub of the more general issue.

Crane, as he insisted time and again, was simply not responsive to systematic philosophic thought, not versed in it or attracted by it; and he did not regard the articulation of philosophic thought as any part of the poet's function. To those who either demanded that he acquire a metaphysic or who imputed one to his writings, Crane tended to reply, as he did with much cheerful pugnacity to Yvor Winters, after Winters' review of *White Buildings:*

> If you knew how little of a metaphysician I am in the scholastic sense of the term, you would scarcely attribute such conscious method to my poems (with regard to that element) as you do. I am an utter ignoramus in that whole subject, have never read Kant, Descartes, or other doctors. It's all an accident as far as my style goes.

That was in May 1927. A year before, Crane, in a letter to Munson, had made an ambitious effort to state his theory of the relation between poetry and knowledge. "In so far as the metaphysics of any absolute knowledge extends," he wrote, "poetry . . . is simply the concrete *evidence* of the *experience* of a recognition (*knowledge,* if you like)." Poetry, he went on, "can give you a *ratio* of fact and experience, and in this sense it is both perception and the thing perceived." That is to say: it can be both the fact, whatever the fact might be—let us say, the existence of God—and the concretely expressed experience of that fact. Crane felt that one should not ask more of poetry than a ratio of that kind. One should not ask the poet to confront directly the problem of God's existence. Poetry does not "logically enunciate such a problem or its solution"; it gives instead "the real connective experience, the very 'sign manifest' on which rests the assumption of a godhead."

Granted such views and intentions, Crane did not pore often or late over volumes of philosophy. He did read the *Dialogues* of Plato, probably more thoughtfully and carefully than any other philosophic writing. What he honored in Plato was "the architecture of his logic," the "harmonious relationship" of his statements "to each other." "This grace," he said, "partakes of poetry." But for Plato, Crane pointed out, grace was subordinate to rational inquiry, and even, for example, Socrates' demonstration of the dialectical ascent to beauty was a rational excursion and not transferable to poetry; he felt that Plato was quite right, in his own view, to banish the poets from the republic. For the rest, Crane shows only peripheral and temporary contacts with unsystematic or "poetic" fragments of philosophizing: a brief, minor interest in Ouspensky; something of Nietzsche but not much (bits of *The Birth of Tragedy* drift in the neighborhood of "Faustus and Helen III" and "Lachrymae Christi"); conceivably some pages of William James. Some sort of philosophical and theological scheme may and very likely should be used (with tact) to illuminate Crane's poetry, as long as it is remembered that Crane's poetry was not composed to illuminate *it.* For real sustenance, Crane went not to philosophy or theology but to poetry; not to the work of the intellect but to the work of the imagination—earlier evidence of *"the experience* of a recognition."

What was being recognized, in Crane's case, was not only a time-less reality, but the connection between such a reality and the temporal world. From "Faustus and Helen" on, Crane's poems were what he called them: "connective experiences," the experience being visionary and the connections being established by the resources of poetry. If this were what people meant by "metaphysical poetry," Crane was willing to accept the label. In the letter to Winters, Crane said:

> Since I have been "located" in this category by a number of people, I may as well go on alluding to certain (what are also called) metaphysical passages in Donne, Blake, Vaughan, etc., as being of particular appeal to me on a basis of common characteristics with what I like to do in my own poems, however little scientific knowledge of the subject I may have.

With poets like "Donne, Blake, Vaughan, etc."—to whom one can add Keats, Shelley, Melville, Whitman, and one or two others—Crane in part intuited an existing tradition, and in part created a tradition with which he could affiliate. In drawing upon that tradition, Crane inevitably drew upon some of the philosophical ingredients—primarily a loose and shifting Platonistic strain—reflected in it: but it was always the poetry that affected him.

This is something one may admire, regret, or simply observe. In our time, when intellectual systems are in such great and serious demand, the absence of a solid conceptual framework behind Crane's poetry has been unduly regretted, while the presence of a potent and resourceful poetic tradition has been insufficiently observed. I suspect that the majority of poets have proceeded pretty much the way Crane did, and have found their bearings in earlier poetry rather than in formal philosophy or theology. There is much to be said for Northrop Frye's flat contention that no poet ever, really, "takes over" a ready-made system of ideas; though it goes without saying that some poets are born into a luckier culture than others. But we may have been misled by the immeasurably influential example of T. S. Eliot, who visited upon other poets and upon a whole generation of readers a profound and thoroughly valid belief in his personal requirement of an orderly intellectual scheme wherewith to assess in poetry the "futility and anarchy" of the age. For Crane, in any event, there was coherence enough for *his* needs in the tradition of visionary poetry.

V

The reference to "the world dimensional" in "Faustus and Helen I" is followed by an image of the poet, coming home of an evening in a streetcar, suddenly envisioning Helen "across the aisle." "The street car device," Crane told Frank, "is the most concrete symbol I could find for the transition of the imagination from quotidian details to the universal

consideration of beauty—the body still 'centered in traffic,' the imagination eluding its daily nets and self consciousness." But the symbol is
unsatisfactory. The phrase "lost yet poised in traffic" is enough to define
an incipient vision, with "traffic" reinforcing the implications of "stacked"
and "multitudes"; the streetcar, as an *actual* means of transportation, is a
rhetorical confusion. The transition desired is better effected by the
contrasts that begin to burgeon and intertwine: contrasts involving Hel-
en's physical aspects taken as symbols; her smile, her eyes, her hands, her
body. Helen's "half-riant" expression (an unlucky Whitmanism) replaces
the artificial "stenographic smiles" of stanza one. Her "eyes across the
aisle" flicker with "prefigurations," as against the "million brittle, bloodshot eyes" of the finite world; and, also as against that mob of eyes, the
poet will bend upon Helen "a lone eye. . . . One inconspicuous glowing
orb of praise"—a lone eye, perhaps, because the other eye remains fixed
upon the lower realm. The hands of Helen contrast with the "troubled
hands" that press toward her; and her body is seen in a moment of ecstatic
sexual sublimation above "the body of the world" as it weeps in the dust.

In short, as the vision of Helen comes into view, the actual world
reveals by contrast its qualities of ugliness and desperation. For now it is
morally and spiritually measured ("counted") by the emerging figure of
Helen. Now her hands can

> . . . count the nights
> Stippled with pink and green advertisements.

So measured, the world of offices and finance, later of "steel and soil,"
appears shrouded in a darkness lit only by advertising signs. It appears
troubled; it is morally compromised and psychically wounded ("this bartered blood"). It is fallen and anguished:

> . . . the body of the world
> Weeps in inventive dust for the hiatus
> That winks above it, bluet in your breasts.

The world's body weeps because, in the hiatus between Helen's breasts
that winks far above the world, it recognizes the hiatus between the
actual and the ideal—and longs to close the hiatus through love. It
recognizes, too, the remote but complete experience of love Helen herself
is undergoing, as her own body seems exalted in a sort of celestial orgasm:

> Reflective conversion of all things
> At your deep blush, when ecstasies thread
> The limbs and belly, when rainbows spread
> Impinging on the throat and sides . . .

In the compact summary of "Faustus and Helen" which Crane sent Munson in January 1923, he indicated that this is the phase of "Love" in the first section, following those of "Meditation" and "Evocation" and leading to the final phase of "Beauty." Helen has undoubtedly become a figure of intense love-in-action, and of a love that transforms reality; yet such concrete eroticism may seem to accord ill with the ideal and hence presumably bodiless or at least virginally pure figure the poem is moving toward. But Crane has not lost his poetic way. For one thing, the goddess who moves in and out of "Faustus and Helen" is a recognizably traditional being; she resembles, for example, the goddess in Keats's *Endymion*, as Harold Bloom has described her: a "contrary Goddess . . . both virginal and wanton"; a figure, in short, who corresponds to the inseparable and contradictory desires of man. In "Faustus and Helen I," there is even a hint of carnal frivolity about her. The verb "winks"—following "half-riant" and in contrast with "weeps"—startlingly suggests the erotic mockery which, in "Voyages II," the god-like and moonward-bending sea (that "great wink of eternity") would direct upon the limitations of human love. For another thing, it is a significant part of Crane's intention to body forth the ideal in terms of the actual: in order to accomplish a "reflective conversion" of the actual; in order to establish by means of poetry the organic continuity and connection between the two dimensions. The contrasts we have been noting are in fact the elements that must eventually be connected or married; this is the very point and aim of "Faustus and Helen." In Section II of the poem, it is the wanton goddess who is celebrated; here, in the final stanzas of Section I, we move on and upward beyond "Love" to "Beauty" to observe and praise the pure and distant figure ("you who turned away once, Helen"). But finally, Crane wants to suggest that the two divinities are parts of a single being; he wants to present the evidence of experiencing "the two worlds. And at once."

The troubled and bleeding body of the actual world appears to be dying ("The earth may glide diaphanous to death"). The poet—climbing through metaphor, and by means of the poetic "inventions" discovered in the "dust" of the actual and indeed (for Crane) only to be discovered within that fallen sphere—transcends the dust and the blood to enter the domain of Helen. Here, unlike the crowded quotidian world with its multitudes and numbers and bloodshot eyes, is a "world which comes to each of us alone"; here in this white world, having passed from the dark, congested human city through a series of "white cities" (moments in the graduation toward ideal beauty), the poet finds a place beyond time ("hourless days") and change ("continuous"). But just as Helen herself had been described in resonantly physical detail (breasts, limbs, belly, throat, sides), so her remote realm and the poet's reverential experience of it are described in language borrowed from the lower world of "steel and soil" so ardously transcended—in terms of planes, axles, and companion ways. Helen's city is, as it were, the factories of heaven: or it is made to seem so by the art of Crane's poetry. The effect of that art is, in the poetic sense, to redeem the fallen world; not, finally, to transcend and abandon it, but—before "Faustus and Helen" is through—to find the means of praising it; in one of the oldest and greatest of theological formulae, not to destroy it but to perfect it.

VI

The process continues spiritedly in Section II. Here the fallen world is explored—not as a domain of tears and death, but of dance and laughter; if not a world redeemed, at least a world redeemable. The very act of falling appears as a necessary adventure; and the presiding goddess is "The siren of the springs of guilty song." By paying homage to that charming wanton, the poem learns to smile at the human and fleshly frailties which she represents and the sense of guilt is exorcized, the "groans of death" silenced, by song itself. The world is, so to speak, being made ready by poetry for the poetic grace it will receive in the final section.

This middle portion of the poem is more closely related to the whole of "Faustus and Helen" than Crane understood, and it develops in a way rather different than he implied. In "General Aims and Theories" of 1925, Crane made much of his intention in "Faustus and Helen" to "embody . . . a contemporary approximation to an ancient human culture or mythology," and to build "a bridge between so-called classic experience" and the "confused cosmos of today, which has no formulated mythology yet for classic poetic reference or for religious exploitation." As examples of these approximations and bridgings and as part of an effort to recapture in modern terms what he called the Greek idea of beauty, Crane said that he "found 'Helen' sitting in a street-car; the Dionysian revels of her court and her seduction were transferred" (in Section II) "to a Metropolitan roof garden with a jazz orchestra" and so on. This sounds as though Crane were fuzzily attempting to borrow Eliot's technique of bringing "classic experience" and mythology to bear upon the confused modern cosmos; but Crane's comments on this occasion shed more darkness than light. Homer's Helen, for example, did not indulge in Dionysian revels, either in Sparta or in Troy; perhaps Crane was thinking vaguely of Shakespeare's Helen in *Troilus and Cressida,* a young woman decidedly fond of revelling. Homer and Greek culture generally contribute no more to Section II than Marlowe does to the poem as a whole. Section II announces itself not by Eliotic usages of ancient myth but through the immediate energy and collision of its imagery.

The scene is indeed a metropolitan roof garden, where brass instruments glitter and resound hypnotically ("Brazen hypnotics glitter") and humans dance with gay abandon ("Glee shifts from foot to foot").

> This crashing opéra bouffe,
> Blest excursion! this ricochet
> From roof to roof.

This was the feel and tempo of Crane's own life at one time: "the old bivouacs of New York days," as he recalled them to Munson in January 1923, "when I ricochet-ed 'from roof to roof' without intermission." More largely, it was the way human life itself felt to Crane at this time: a dance, and not a Dance of Death, but a dance of joyful life. He wrote Tate while at work on Section II, "Perhaps it is useless, perhaps it is silly,—but one *does* have joys." As earlier he had testified to the difficulty of expressing any strong personal emotion at all at a time when critical fashion favored the resolutely impersonal, so now he acknowledged the problem of expressing the experience of joy. "The vocabulary of damnations and prostrations has been developed at the expense of these other modes . . . it is hard to dance in proper measure." Crane's dance motif would reach its turbulent climax in the summer of 1926, when, feeling that he was dancing on dynamite," he composed the portion of The Bridge called "The Dance."

Here, in "Faustus and Helen," as he said to Tate, he was aiming mainly at "an idiom for the proper transportation of Jazz into words! Something clean, sparkling, elusive!" The idiom in Section II sparkles and eludes, though it is not what is normally meant by "clean" as applied to poetic language (stripped, uncluttered, pure); and it is jazzy only as language can be jazzy but not as jazz is jazzy. Crane's efforts to contrive verbal analogues of jazz were usually, as here, unsatisfactory. But this is not to say that the swift and bouncing rhythms of Section II, leading as they do into the more assertive movement of the final stanzas, are not in their own way arresting. They serve very well as the musical vehicle of Crane's statement about fallen man.

In an unattractive but poetically justified image at the end of the first stanza, we hear that "nigger cupids scour the stars." The Negro jazz musicians thus function as exciters of love: but of the erotic love proper to *this* world and not of the "white wafer cheek of love" touched in Section I;

Cupid, as Crane might surprise us by knowing, was the Roman version of Greek Eros. And as the dance, the stormy music ("snarling hails of melody"), the exuberant horseplay ("Rhythmic ellipses lead into canters") continue through the long night ("Until somewhere a rooster banters") —the poem begins to establish its attitude toward that kind of love and this kind of world. In a frame of mind at once innocent and daring, Crane issues his invitation to join him in yielding to temptation:

> Greet naively—yet intrepidly
> New soothings, new amazements
> That cornets introduce at every turn—
> And you may fall downstairs with me
> With perfect grace and equanimity.

It is an invitation to sin with grace; to fall morally and to fall hard and far (from the roof to the bottom of the stairs) without quite losing one's moral balance, or one's sense of humor. There follows the parallel invitation to take the moral plunge into the dangerous waters of experience, while the more cautious sit at home on dry land, safely law-abiding:

> Or, plaintively scud past shores
> Where, by strange harmonic laws
> All relatives, serene and cool,
> Sit rocked in patent armchairs.

The relatives (I assume a pun here: both uncles and aunts, those symbols of the super-ego, *and* something opposite to the absolute nature of Crane's thrust into life) are serene and cool; but it is a false kind of coolness, not a coolness beyond heat as in Section I but an absence of heat. The laws they live by look strange from the point of view of the dancing or the plunging life; shortly, in Section III, that rocking-chair existence will appear as an unending "meagre penance." Crane thus announces his attitude toward the life of conventional and self-protective piety. In so doing, he presents his exhilarated version of "the fortunate fall"—that notion so central to the American literary tradition: namely, that what orthodox morality regards as sinful conduct and a re-enactment of the Fall of Man is in fact the necessary and hence the fortunate experience that begets genuine human maturity. And like Henry James Senior, who gave one of the most vigorous accounts of the fortunate fall and who also (like Crane) found eloquent support for his convictions in William Blake, Crane very rapidly dissociates himself from those who, obsessed with man's fallen condition, saw in it only a condition of death:

> While titters hailed the groans of death
> Beneath gyrating awnings I have seen
> The incunabula of the divine grotesque.
> This music has a reassuring way.

This music, the kind Crane is composing and celebrating, is reassuring—by contrast precisely within the other sounds Crane had been hearing, the mournful music of the "poetry of damnation" as he had called it, or the ironic music of "humor and the Dance of Death," a definition exactly parallel to the first of the lines just quoted. This life-affirming music is as remote from the death-dance as the smiles of the youthful goddess—in the final stanza—are from the ironic "titters" that Crane unfairly attributed to some of his contemporaries. While the latter, Crane contends, were greeting the death of culture with elegant wit, he himself in the excitement of his dance ("Beneath gyrating awnings") caught the first traces and manifestations ("incunabula") of an unorthodox goddess ("the divine grotesque").

It is this goddess ("still so young"), this delightful temptation to moral danger (this "siren of the springs of guilty song") that is smiled upon and taken to heart in the closing lines of Section II. In accepting her, "we" are accepting our own fallen condition:

> Let us take her on the incandescent wax
> Striated with nuances, nervosities
> That we are heir to: she is still so young,
> We cannot frown upon her as she smiles.

"Striated" means striped or streaked. There is something here of the moral sympathy Crane would direct toward the denizens of "The Wine Menagerie": "poor streaked bodies wreathing up and out"; streaked or striated with Crane's way of suggesting moral taintedness, like Eliot's "maculate," spotted. But it is a taintedness that Crane accepts. The siren's guilty song will be played upon the streaked or grooved and ardent human phonograph ("the incandescent wax"—an image related to the later one in "The Tunnel"—"The phonographs of hades in the brain"). It is a song for human life to dance to; it will lighten and alleviate the shadings and anxieties, the frailties we inherit as human beings. As the goddess of our frailties is thus evoked, as in metaphor she wings her way across "the guarded skies," Crane completes the first account of his maturing attitude toward the fallen world.

VII

In Section II, the element of guilt in the guilty song is exorcized (as I have said) by the sheer intensity of song itself; as though Crane were elaborating in advance the brief credo—his essential credo about the celebrational nature of life and poetry—he would put forward two years later in "Lachrymae Christi":

> Not penitence
> But song. . . .

In the concluding stanzas of "Faustus and Helen," the song swells into a music as powerful as any in modern poetry. But during much of Section III, the movement is alternately heavy, portentous, and jumpy. The imagination has to work through an acknowledgment of tragedy, a memory of war, an awareness of massive destruction, before it can arrive at the hymn of praise—and praise very "distinctly" of this ravaged world—that it longs to utter. Crane was right to reduce the pace of the final section, as he had originally planned it. "I shall not attempt to make it the paragon of SPEED that I thought of," he informed Munson in August 1922; "I think it needs more sheer weight than such a motive would provide"; and Section III, for all its climactic ecstasy is notably weightier than the preceding sections. Crane said later about the second section that it was "a sensual culmination," and so it was. But in retrospect, that dancing excitement was obviously not a culmination on anything *but* the sensual level. Here, as in *The Bridge*, Crane's imagination refused to jump prematurely to the phase of final rejoicing. Other and much more sombre realities had to be faced before the world of time could be truly and persuasively celebrated; and other connections had to be made.

Death, and death on an enormous scale, was a fact of recent history in 1922; tragedy of an immense scope was a very real event; no poet attempting to write responsibly could evade those matters or content himself with making fun of the death-consciousness they had caused. Crane's personal knowledge of the First World War had been restricted to a short hitch in a Cleveland munition plant; and he was too young, his life had been too provincial, and his education too limited for him to participate in the vast vision of cultural disaster shared by Eliot and others. He could only work with what he knew and what he had. "Faustus and Helen III" is a valiant effort to examine the grounds of Eliot's "philosophic pessimism," and to give expression to the widely different judgment of history and human possibility that Crane nonetheless held.

As Crane attempts to squeeze such broadly ranging considerations into a relatively small poetic space and into his own congenitally tucked-in idiom, the poetry grows exceedingly complex; though the central development is magnificently clear—the irresistible drive of "the imagination . . . beyond despair." "It is so packed with tangential slants, interwoven symbolisms," Crane told Munson, "that I'm not sure whether or not it will [be] understood." He presented the following little chart of the section: "Tragedy, War (the eternal soldier), Résumé, Ecstasy, Final Declaration," and we can usefully take those words as the titles respectively of the first; the second and third; the fourth; the fifth and sixth; and the seventh stanzas. But even with so much guidance, Section III remains challengingly obscure. It merits and it rewards a fairly detailed inspection.

The subject of the opening stanza is—characteristically—not tragedy but the transcendence of tragedy. Death is the central figure: death seated close beside the poet in the darkness, and addressed in three successive images. Death is the "capped arbiter of beauty in this street" —the force (capped like a gunman or a soldier) that determines the fate of beauty *in this street,* in this temporal and mortal world; but that has, by implication, no authority over ideal beauty. Death is next the representative ("delicate ambassador") of the manifold dead, those cut down by war: who nonetheless return to make their presence felt once more—

> . . . intricate slain numbers that arise
> In whispers. . . .

There is a probable reminiscence here of the seventh of John Donne's "Holy Sonnets":

> . . . arise, arise
> From death, you numberless infinities
> Of soules. . . .

And the probability is strengthened when the grand conclusion of Donne's tenth "Holy Sonnet"—"And death shall be no more; death thou shalt die"—becomes plainly audible behind the third of the apostrophes to death in Crane's poem:

> . . . religious gunman!
> Who faithfully, yourself, will fall too soon.

Donne was talking quite literally about the eternal life, about the defeat of death and the literal resurrection of the dead that was the promise of Christian doctrine. Crane—and the contrast is a significant contrast of epochs—is expressing his private conviction about psychological and spiritual resilience, and in a way that he would shortly paraphrase for Munson:

"After this perfection of death—nothing is possible in motion but a resurrection of some kind." The phrase "in motion" even helps explain the reference in the stanza under discussion to the "motor dawn" that the street is "narrow[ing] darkly into." At this moment of perfect darkness and the sense of death, a resurrection of some kind must of necessity be in motion, a motion symbolized and driven by the dawn. There was (Crane felt) simply nowhere else for the human spirit and for poetry to go.

Death that eternal and hence "religious" killer will "fall," the poem continues,

> And in other ways than as the wind settles
> On the sixteen thrifty bridges of the city:
> Let us unbind our throats of fear and pity.

The death of death (that is, of the death-consciousness) will be no quiet and gradual affair, like the wind settling on a city's bridges; it will be an occasion for triumphant song. Crane told Waldo Frank that "the Fall of Troy, etc." was "also in" this section, and it may be that Troy was one intended referent of the city which has fallen and on whose ruins the dust (wind) slowly settles; not that Troy, so far as I know, was ever said to have sixteen bridges; it sounds more like New York. But the key word here, I fancy, is "thrifty": a word that eventually combines with "meagre" to suggest the worst kind of death that Crane could imagine, that self-withholding lifeless life that is really a death-in-life, and that, in Section III, is radically distinguished from the self-*giving* manner of the "lavish heart" and of the "substance . . . spent beyond repair." The latter is the life of praise, of the song that "our throats" can utter once they are loosed from the tragic emotions that currently clutch at them. The emotions mentioned are, of course, Aristotle's classic pair—pity and fear; emotions which, according to the *Poetics* are first aroused and then healthfully purged out of us by the experience of tragedy. Crane says somewhat the same thing: "Let us unbind our throats of fear and pity"; but his whole attention is on what happens after that, on the death-denying song that follows.

But there is more to be confessed before that song. The next portion is devoted to "War (the eternal soldier)," and it presents a ruthlessly concentrated and imagistically agitated account of a machine-gun attack by a World War I fighter aircraft, from the perspective of the pilot. Phrases stammer like bullets: "corymbulous formations of mechanics," "spouting malice/Plangent over meadows"; and they send us hurriedly to the dictionary, a volume even more indispensable for "Faustus and Helen III" than is usual with Crane. "Corymbulous," for example, is a rare botanical term meaning "clustering": hence, clustering formations of aircraft. "Corymbulous" also associates with a surprising number of coun-trified allusions in the later stanzas of Section III: hill, meadows, boughs, blue plateaus, stubble, wine, delve, and thresh; not to mention "mounted cities" and "saddled sky." The number is surprising until we realize that Crane is building a small pattern of pastoral imagery that serves at once to reduce the tragic to the pathetic, and to suggest something alive, glowing, continuing, in contrast with the dark, mechanized world of city streets; a process that would recur more expansively and with a somewhat different emphasis in *The Bridge,* when Crane's pastoral imagination engaged what he there called the "iron age."

The effect is obliquely Virgilian: for in the *Aeneid,* Virgil, good gentleman-farmer that he was, also sought the effect of "violence clothed in pathos" (Crane's phrase for the passage under discussion) by introduc-ing into the bloodiest or most grandiose moments an image drawn from the humble and the rustic life—as when Vulcan, great Lord of Fire, rises and goes to his furnaces in the similitude (Book VIII) of a housewife who must "eke out her slender livelihood" and so rises early to "poke the drowsy embers upon the earth." It is the pastoral context in "Faustus and Helen III" that explains the conversation or shrinkage of the deathdealing fighter-pilot into a frontier cowboy (or perhaps a militant cowboy, an old-time cavalry officer) saddling the sky and mounting it like a horse. The same context justifies, I think, the description at once poetically harsh and humanly touching, of the "torn and empty houses" as resem-bling "old women with teeth unjubilant"—houses with gaping holes in their walls, staring upward like old peasant women in whose gaping mouths there appears no smile of flashing teeth. "Unjubilant" stands in opposition to the jubilation shortly to come in Section III; just as the phrase "spouting malice," which brilliantly transforms the wicked rattle of the machine-gun into a vicious outpouring of human hatred, provides a polar opposite to the outburst of laughter and praise of man at the poem's end.

The evocation of the then recent First World War is thus typically constructed by dislocating and realigning the elements under intense rhythmic pressure. But—and this is the important point—Crane, by means of his particular realignment, has virtually won in advance the poetic and emotional victory he is aiming at. The floral and pastoral imagery removes or at least softens a good deal of the historical horror (i.e., the immediate source of the prevalent death-consciousness); and what remains of that horror is undercut, poetically and emotionally, by the language Crane selected. The definition of the war experience is,

accordingly, a careful prologue to Crane's statement of his own attitude to
history in the fourth stanza, "Résumé":

> We did not ask for that, but have survived,
> And will persist to speak again before
> All stubble streets that have not curved
> To memory. . . .

There has been a period of ferocious ill-will in human affairs, and
of a force of destruction that nothing, not even a "hypogeum" (underground or underwater vault: hence "of wave or rock") could hold out
against. We were part of it; we flew the airplanes and "our flesh remembers." But we did not desire war nor ourselves declare it: this is Crane's
insistent twenty-four-year-old contention. It was not an expression of *our*
feelings and ambitions (that is, of Crane's generation and of those like-
minded with him). And so, having survived, we will persist, not in
brooding over the post war waste land, but in uttering from liberated
throats a different song. "Stubble," another country word that means the
stumps remaining in the ground after reaping, is a good adjectival noun
for bombed streets; and the qualifying phrase, "that have not curved to
memory," after its primary meaning of "have not disappeared altogether,"
seems to have as its secondary meaning an insinuation about Eliot's *Waste
Land* verdict on the decline of the West. Crane and his hopeful fellows,
the poem at this stage implies, will speak to those who (in the
"Chaplinesque" phrase) "can still love the world," who can listen because
they can believe in the future; those whom the very real shock of a world
war has not caused to retreat into nostalgia and the belief (as Crane said
with blunt inaccuracy about Eliot) that "happiness and beauty dwell only
in memory."

But Crane's title for this part of "Faustus and Helen III"—"Résumé"—
indicates his intention here not only of striking an attitude toward the
present and future but of recapitulating earlier moments in the poem. The
"stubble streets that have not curved / To memory" remind us perhaps of
the asphalt and the memoranda of Section I; is is time, anyhow, to
remember and re-encounter Helen, as Crane thereupon does. He will, he
goes on, speak to those who have not enlisted on the side of memory—

> . . . or known the ominous lifted arm
> That lowers down the arc of Helen's brow
> To saturate with blessing and dismay.

The syntax of those lines is puzzling. But we may venture the paraphrase
that Crane will address himself to those who, on the one hand, have not

succumbed to nostalgia and yet, on the other hand, have never experienced nostalgia's antidote, the vision of beauty. The vision has become potent and ambiguous. In connection with "ominous," "lowers," and "dismay," Helen's arm seems lifted to strike and she herself to glower (formerly she blushed and winked); one denies her only at one's risk, while even to acknowledge her is (as in Section I) to be at first smitten with dismay at the revealed ugliness of the actual. But her hand is also lifted in benediction; and in the next two stanzas, the world is increasingly blessed.

This is the poem's moment of "Ecstasy," in Crane's chart, though the résumé also continues to the recollection of imagery and attitudes from Section II. There have been many abstruse speculations about the items that introduce this moment—

> A goose, tobacco and cologne—
> Three winged and gold-shod prophecies of heaven
> The lavish heart shall always have to leaven
> And spread with bells and voices, and atone
> The abating shadows of our conscript dust.

"Three winged," be it noted; not (as the typescript shows) "three-winged," a printer's mistake that has started endless analytic hares. The items have been take as medieval emblems, though of what only Crane is thought to know; or as debased instances of religious symbolism; or as somehow corresponding to the "druggist, barber and tobacconist" of Section I, though, as a rapid count will show, this leaves either the druggist or the barber in charge of the goose. But there is a hard specificity about the references, and I suspect that the best guess is to see the goose, tobacco, and cologne as Crane's way of getting down to fundamentals. They are the "few herbs and apples" (the derivation, I am reasonably sure, is conscious and direct) that Emerson described himself as hastily snatching in his poem "Days"—a poem that Crane had already echoed in his own "Pastorale." But where Emerson mocked himself for asking so little of life, Crane is arguing that, enroute to ecstasy, we must take the most commonplace elements that the world has to offer as prophecies of heaven. He is implying, in a way that Emerson would have thoroughly approved, that we must (as Emerson put it in *Nature*) learn to "perceive the miraculous in the common." We must see these commonplace elements as reflectors of perfect beauty ("gold-shod" looks forward to the emblematic "gold hair" of Helen in the next stanza). If the heart is lavish enough—sufficiently "unthrifty"—it will leaven (that is, it will have a transforming influence upon) those earthly items; it will make audible in them bells ringing and voices raised in song. It will

> . . . atone
> The abating shadows of our conscript dust.

These lines are a marked if tightened transfiguration of phrases from
Section I:

> this bartered blood . . .
> the body of the world
> Weeps in inventive dust. . . .
> The earth may glide diaphanous to death.

Now the dust of the fallen world is undergoing atonement, and our fading
spirits ("abating shadows") are, along with the diaphanous earth, being
rescued and redeemed.

They are being rescued and redeemed, of course, by the poetic
imagination, once it has consummated its marriage with an envisioned
ideal of beauty. The world we know, to say it most flatly, is being saved by
poetry: by and in this very poem as it has evolved and as it now moves
toward its climax. As the phase of "Ecstasy" continues, gathering momen-
tum, it is the imagination that is seen as the source of laughter and the
warrant for praise. The mention of Anchises and Erasmus, in the penultimate stanza, may halt us temporarily, if we remember too closely what we
know about Anchises and Erasmus; but I think we can hear in those
names high-sounding references to every great achievement of which
mortal man has been capable *except* the achievement of the imagination
and its ally, the lavish heart. (The worksheet bears out this reading; and
indeed Crane's earlier version strikes me as superior to his final one.) As
against the grand achievements of Anchises and Erasmus, who had restored what had been destroyed (had re-gathered the "blown blood and
wine," presumably of shattered Troy and the shattered Catholic and
Eucharistic culture), the poetic imagination is summoned by Crane to a
comparable but perhaps mightier task—a new kind of re-unification, that
of the fragmented elements ("scattered wine") of the contemporary epoch:

> Delve upward for the new and scattered wine,
> O brother-thief of time, that we recall.
> Laugh out the meagre penance of their days
> Who dare not share with us the breath released,
> The substance drilled and spent beyond repair
> For golden, or the shadow of gold hair.

Death and the human imagination are fraternal thieves of time,
each stealing it away with even more finality than "procrastination" in
Young's famous *Night Thoughts* aphorism. In death, time comes to a stop;

by the imagination, the entire temporal sphere is transcended. There follows the culminating rejection of the unimaginative life: the life already defined, in Section II, as one of thrift, safety, moralism. That deadly existence, that life of dreary penance, that spirit that does not dare to risk breathlessness ("Know, Olympians, we are breathless" Crane had exclaimed in the preceding section), that fears nothing so much as prodigality of any kind: all this is laughed at; and the poet becomes the prodigal son, willing to seem to waste his spiritual and physical substance in riotous living if he can catch a glimpse even of the shadow of golden hair, of Helen's beauty.

And so the poem arrives at its "Final Declaration":

> Distinctly praise the years, whose volatile
> Blamed bleeding hands extend and thresh the height
> The imagination spans beyond despair,
> Outpacing bargain, vocable and prayer.

Music like that almost overpowers analysis; it is one of the finest passages in twentieth-century poetry. But its greatness comes in part from its success in bringing to a supreme climax and conclusion images and elements and attitudes that had made up so much of the stuff of the poem to this moment. What is singled out for praise is just that transitoriness, that culpability and woundedness that Section I had established as characteristic of the temporal world. That blamed and bleeding world, that world bloodied by war and condemned by man, is worthy of praise; for the poetic imagination (as it "Delve[s] upward for the new and scattered wine") sees it extending to the height of the ideal world, continuous with the ideal, beautified and perfected by the ideal. And, so delving upward, the imagination arches beyond despair, and arches too beyond "bargain," beyond the stock-market world where bargains are struck and blood is bartered; even beyond human utterance and beyond prayer. But in the splendor of its vision, it is after all the years that it returns to praise—the irradiated years.

SHERMAN PAUL

The Long Way Home

At almost every stage, *The Bridge* was a controversial poem. Criticism—opposition—seems to have mounted in ratio to the degree of its completion, and on publication it was for the most part greeted with openly hostile reviews, the most damaging, Crane felt, by his friends Yvor Winters and Allen Tate. Tate had already expressed his basic strictures in the Foreword to *White Buildings*, which he wrote during the year in which he had lived and quarreled with Crane; and Winters, who had reviewed *White Buildings*, had accepted Tate's "evaluation and definition of Hart Crane's genius" and made it his point of departure. Their criticism—and that of Munson in *Destinations* (his essay on Crane is subtitled "Young Titan in the Sacred Wood")—is similar, having for its grounds an appreciation of Eliot's account of the modern sensibility and the ethical-religious demands made on poetry by the New Humanists, who, in the years Crane devoted to *The Bridge*, had again become prominent and powerful. With the later criticism of Crane by R. P. Blackmur, these vigorously held and expressed views—position papers in the contemporary debate on the modern spirit—created the perspective in which *The Bridge* and the imagination that fashioned it have almost always been treated. With this encumbrance of criticism it has been difficult to see the poem freshly, or, as Bachelard would say, in an open, "admirative" way, but this is what we must now try to do.

How splendidly the dedicatory poem opens and fills its imaginative space with the reverberations of its images—images whose invitation to poetic reverie can hardly be surpassed.

From *Hart's Bridge*. Copyright © 1972 by The Board of Trustees, University of Illinois. University of Illinois Press.

> How many dawns, chill from his rippling rest
> The seagull's wing shall dip and pivot him,
> Shedding white rings of tumult, building high
> Over the chained bay waters Liberty—

The poem begins with the renewal of creation and with its own birth. And in its beginning is its end. The point of departure is the place of return. *The Bridge,* constituted by all that occurs between "Proem" and "Atlantis," describes a circle, the most pervasive figure of the poet's world.

The opening lines evoke a familiar prospect—New York harbor as it may be seen at dawn when looking seaward from Brooklyn Bridge—and express the sense of liberation, the dilation of spirit, afforded by it. In pitch and rising rhythm suspending on "Liberty," they strike up for a new world, for the freedom and creation—the freedom of creation—depicted in the movement (flight, soaring, and dance) of the seagull, Crane's tutelary bird. ("Constantly your seagull ['the white bird'] has floated in my mind," he told Gaston Lachaise, "and it will mean much to me to have it.") This is not the scavenging gull of *Paterson IV,* but the gull of "The Wanderer," a poem opening also in New York harbor and treating a poet's dedication to America and to the renewal of creation, a poem whose importance to Crane may have been hinted at in the epigraph from Job with which he introduced *The Bridge.* Its kin are many, among them the bird with whose free spirit Wordsworth identifies in *The Prelude* and the hawk in Thoreau's *Walden:* symbols of "all that's consummate and free," of the self, fulfilled in and liberated by the powers of imagination and spirit.

The scene, like that of "Crossing Brooklyn Ferry," is eternally recurring and warrants faith in the future. ("How many" suggests this, and "shall" invokes the future, bends the poem toward it.) The coming of dawn—the radiant hope of beginnings insisted on by the writers of *The Seven Arts* group—is the expectation of the poem. But the dawn does not come of itself so much as through the agency of the seagull, as the effulgence of its motion. The bird is harbinger, creator. It rises from the waters "Shedding white rings of tumult"—shedding light, white circles of perfect harmony—and the dance of its being, its "building high," enacted in the poem's movement, is an upward vortex, while the "tumult" is its cry of birth and creative play as well as a reminder of the downward vortex, the chill and darkness, the "rest," from which it has ascended. This light-giving flight brings to view—may be said to create—the Statue of Liberty and is, in itself, an act of liberty, the free action of the spirit over the "chained bay waters. . . ." Accordingly, as the imagery of the last stanza indicates, it is a paradigm of the bridge.

Seagull and statue intertwined: the importance of this bright wonderful image is stressed by the brevity of its appearance. "Liberty" also
"forsake[s] our eyes" with the departure of the gull; it, too, becomes
"apparitional." And what was actual thereby becomes visionary, a presence to be pursued, like the woman of "The Harbor Dawn." We are
permitted only a glimpse of the goddess, the first in the poet's pantheon to
be presented, although historically she may be the last, assuming all that
Crane invests in the more prominent Mary and Pocahontas. "Liberty"
stands in the harbor welcoming the voyager, a supreme image of homecoming for Crane, who spoke his double need—for response and imaginative freedom, security and risk—in "To Liberty":

> Out of the seagull cries and wind
> On this strange shore I build
> The virgin. . . .

And just as the image of the ascending gull recalls the moth of his earliest
poem, so these lines of explicit comment on the initial stanza of "Proem"
recall "C 33" and the fledgling poet's justification and devotion: "O Ma-
terna! To enrich thy gold head / And wavering shoulders with a new light
shed." At the beginning of The Bridge, the poet, looking to sea, counts
on poetry, an energy of the self, to liberate him and to bring him home.

Turning on "Liberty," the poem itself describes a curve like the
"inviolate curve" of the gull and quickly enacts a momentous transition
from space to confinement, imaginative liberty to routine, reality present
(beheld) to reality lost (remembered, imagined in interior space, longed
for)—from dawn, that is, to "day," the working day, which fails the
expectations of the dawn by being dark. With remarkable compression,
the second stanza places us in the business world of "Faustus and Helen"
and "Recitative." And the gull, who in its flight "forsake[s] our eyes" (and
all the affirmative possibilities of the self), is now assimilated to "sails," an
image as white and fleeting ("apparitional") that evokes the spacious past
of discovery and sea adventure (the world of "Ave Maria" and "Cutty
Sark") and, in the context of an office worker's reverie, represents the
deepest longing of the soul. What the "inviolate curve" of the gull intends
and the sail summons us to is deferred ("filed away" covers it too) until we
are freed, as in "Faustus and Helen," from the routine that characterizes
modern civilization (suggested also by paper work, finance, skyscrapers,
and machinery). Then we may seek the "world dimensional," that
"somewhere / Virginal perhaps, less fragmentary, cool."

Only with this pursuit in mind does the poet distinguish himself
from the "multitudes" for whom he speaks, and then in order to propose

an object worthy of their desire. Though the first three stanzas represent a diminuition in intensity of seeing—from beholding to dreaming to fantasizing passively—there is no diminishment of its necessity. The poet subscribes to the belief, from Proverbs, that where there is no vision the people perish. When he thinks of "cinemas" it is not only because he associates "panoramic sleights" with the gull's vanishing flight, but because, even though they ultimately cheat the multitudes, they show their inextinguishable desire for the true magic of revelation. Though in their removes from the source (object) of vision—the light of some "flashing scene / Never disclosed"—the multitudes are in Plato's cave, they are also in church—the church that the movies, especially remarked in the twenties, had become. Their attitude ("bent toward," where "bent" is read as "kneel" and "toward" is read as a transcendental preposition) is religious, albeit secular and parodic, and prepares us for the revelation of the bridge, a true object of devotion, which the poet, moving from darkness to light and from disappointment to fulfillment, discloses in all of its radiant splendor:

> And Thee, across the harbor, silver-paced
> As though the sun took step of thee, yet left
> Some motion ever unspent in thy stride,—
> Implicitly thy freedom staying thee!

The image is vital, not mechanical: the bridge, an organic structure, has what Louis Sullivan called "mobile equilibrium"; and as a roadway for the sun it is an arc of the cosmic circle. And it recalls the dawn-bringing gull of stanza one. "Thee" rhymes with "liberty." The poet, in showing us the path of the soul to reality, restores the epiphanic glory of the beginning. Again the poem is at peak, and now the bridge becomes its focus, to be variously characterized in the next five stanzas and invoked in the concluding two.

Before turning to these stanzas something more should perhaps be said about the third stanza. It works to distinguish the poet from the "multitudes" but, as "Van Winkle" shows, its imagery carries his private burden. The most notable thing about it is the violated curve of desire, the terrible want always frustrated (refused: "Never disclosed"), a pattern of expectation and disappointment first traced in the poet's case in his boyhood. In "Van Winkle," where memory flashes it out of his own dark depths, he remembers

> . . . the Sabbatical, unconscious smile
> My mother almost brought me once from church
> And once only. . . .

It flickered through the snow screen, blindly
It forsook her at the doorway, it was gone
Before I had left the window. It
Did not return with the kiss in the hall.

In this episode, the poem—and the poet's quest—has its origin. "Forsake": "forsook." And in considering the bridge to which he directs our attention, it may help us understand the deification and celebration of this answerer.

Stanzas five to nine are a litany—a catalog somewhat in Whitman's fashion—of the attributes and occasions of the bridge. In the first, the bridge provides a platform for spiritual release, in this instance the death leap of the "bedlamite" who has fled the subway (the "Tunnel," or inferno of industrial civilization and of isolation), ascended the parapets of the bridge, and there, "shrill shirt ballooning," like a gull, taken flight. The concluding line—"A jest falls from the speechless caravan"—is Whitman-like in its matter-of-fact tone and cadence, and perhaps in its ambiguity. For "jest" may refer to the bedlamite as well as to the kind of remark called forth in moments of extremity. That it "falls," in contrast to the "ballooning" shirt—both arrested in the instant of the poet's own "flashing scene"—conveys a positive value even though the negative is present. "To die," as Whitman said, "is different from what any one supposed, and luckier."

The next stanza maintains the values established in stanzas one and four. Significantly, the bridge is set against the artifacts with which the poet defines modern civilization: Wall Street, a dark confining metallic space associated with the mechanical by the image of the acetylene torch—that is, by the busy construction of skyscrapers, these conveyed in the images of "rip-tooth" and of towering (yet "cloud-flown": gull-abandoned) derricks. The bridge, again, is not presented in its mechanical but in its vital aspect. Though it is a part of the scene (seen), the very center of it, it belongs to another world: to the eternal, spiritual, pristine, spacious, natural world of the "North Atlantic," the cool new world of the harbor dawn, as the further contrast of "noon" and "afternoon" suggests. And even now, in the frenzy of modern life, the bridge responds to the spirit ("breathe") and is "still," at peace.

Crane wrote Waldo Frank that, in "Atlantis," which he was again working on in January 1926, the bridge was becoming "a ship, a world, a woman, a tremendous harp. . . ." It is world and ship here, and both are related to each other. "Cables breathe" is descriptively accurate in respect to the actual bridge, just as "flashing scene," in an earlier stanza, is in respect to the movies of that time. Crane is invariably true to the actual, and his bridge, just as "flashing scene," in an earlier stanza, is in respect to the movies of that time. Crane is invariably true to the actual, and his metaphors, accordingly, are never far-fetched. In the context of ocean setting ("North Atlantic"), "cables" acquire nautical significance, and animated by "breathe" (breath), they evoke the image of sails. And so the bridge is a ship—sailing ship, and gull—and the world it belongs to is both natural (spiritual) and past. The bridge is a curve of time, simultaneously past-present-future. It exists in the present as a vital presence of the past, and the future it portends will possess values—new only because rediscovered—that are associated with the past.

The progression of this litany is most clearly one of increasing religious identification; of mounting fervor, too, culminating in stanza eight and subsiding in the wonderful peace of stanza nine. In stanza seven, the weakest, the bridge is asserted to be a redemptive agency—again because vital ("Vibrant"). The referents are vague ("that heaven of the Jews," "guerdon," "accolade"), but evoke religious and archaic associations, chiefly those of chivalric times, and do the work of transition. What the poet asserts, however, is what he hopes to receive ("reprieve and pardon"). Syntactical parallelism and rhyme indicate what is important to him: "Accolade thou dost bestow"; "Vibrant reprieve and pardon thou dost show." The bridge neither withholds nor hides, and its accolade is conferred by embrace.

Such is the logic by which the bridge becomes the answerer of stanza eight and the holy mother of stanza nine. In stanza eight the wonder of

> O harp and altar, of the fury fused,
> (How could mere toil align thy choiring strings!)

is heightened by the immediate recollection of Blake's great poem to creation, "The Tyger," no image of which is employed by Crane, the association being achieved instead at a deeper level by "fury fused" and the interrogatory character of the parenthetical exclamation. Blake's poem speaks in these lines for Crane's awareness of the terrible but joyous energies and awful grandeur of art, of the difficulty of synthesizing (to use his theoretical word for "fuse") the contraries of experience. It speaks for Roebling's achievement and that of his own "song." By joining the mechanical (the forge of creation) and the natural (the tyger), Blake's poem also confirms the mysterious double nature of the bridge, Crane's tyger, burning brightly in the darkness of the next stanza, but in a way moderated perhaps by the moderating stanza of Blake's poem:

And when the stars threw down their spears,
And water'd heaven with their tears,
Did he smile his work to see?
Did he who made the Lamb make thee?

The evocation of divinity is powerful in Crane's lines—"Terrific," used in the sense of awe-inspiring, is fitting. For the bridge, framed by divinity, is also the instrument with which we entreat divinity: an instrument of religious celebration ("harp and altar") and the "threshold" from which the prophet, pariah, and lover launch their petitions—the "pledge," "prayer," and "cry" whose answers, imputed here, are assured in the next stanza, which concludes the sentence begun by the poet's outcry.

Now with the coming of night the masculine divinity of creation becomes the feminine divinity of love, or rather we see this aspect of divinity's nature, a nature similarly presented in "Ave Maria." Night overtakes the poem without our knowing it, but, as in "Faustus and Helen," it is a time consecrated by woman. Not Helen, however, but Mary is associated with the "traffic lights," which move across the bridge, delineating it—"immaculate sigh of stars, / Beading thy path"—even as the continuous movement "condense[s] eternity," reveals the radiant bridge fully, in its supreme office: "And we have seen night lifted in thine arms." This image of the mother, recalling the pietà, is among the greatest in Crane's work. It is the culminating image of his litany and is presented as the revelation hitherto undisclosed ("we have seen"). In the curve of lights from pier to pier, the bridge, which is more commonly recognized as spanning the abyss, is represented as sustaining the darkness of the world. Its most powerful meaning for Crane—he ascribes eternity to it—is in its upholding arms.

And so he invokes in it his dark time. The concluding stanzas may be considered separately, even though they fulfill the development of the litany, because in them the poet speaks *in propria persona,* thereby focusing the poem, hitherto focused on the bridge, on himself—on his own position in respect to the bridge and his need for its spiritual agency. At the end of the poem we find him awaiting the dawn of its beginning. (He is not waiting passively, but, as "I waited" suggests, humbly.) We have moved through an entire day—the temporal span of The Bridge (as also of "Song of Myself")—and now move out of the darkness into the rest of The Bridge. We stand beneath the bridge, in its shadow, not, as at the end, in "Atlantis," on it; for "the darkness," as Crane maintained, is part of the poet's business: the condition and point of departure for a journey, a trial, a passage into light. The time is probably late December, past Christmas (the "fiery parcels" of the brightly lit Manhattan skyline are "all undone"), and past midnight. Yet the winter solstice, the darkest time, portends the light, just as Christmas portends redemption and the gentle, purifying snow (submerging "an iron year") the blessing of love.

Of these hopeful changes—of the vital process that brings them to pass—the bridge is guarantor, an eternal wakefulness ("O Sleepless") overseeing the restless movement of history ("the river"). Always in motion, it has life, a cosmic energy like that of the sun, which earlier "took step of thee" and whose diurnal course over the continent is now represented by its "inviolate curve": "Vaulting the sea, the prairies' dreaming sod." Again the bridge figures as part of the circle of life; and it is an awakener, not merely vaulting the prairie but bringing forth—the hope of *The Seven Arts* critics—its hidden life. Its magnitude and height above us comport with divinity, but so does the dovelike nature of its spirit ("sometime sweep, descend" recalling the seagull), which the poet, finally, petitions: "Unto us lowliest sometime sweep, descend / And of the curveship lend a myth to God."

With this personal request, psychological-spiritual meanings are added to the geographical points (east and west) of the poem. The poet asks for intervention of spirit, for his own quickening by the divinity he recognizes and celebrates in the world. For the act of descent empowers the poem, "a myth to God" ("descend" rhymes with and controls the meaning of "lend"); it complements the upward flight of the seagull, a "curveship" too. And these visible motions of spirit, like the poem the poet wishes to create, are the "concrete *evidence* of the *experience* of a recognition"; they are instances of "the real connective experience, the very 'sign manifest' on which rests the assumption of a godhead." We should not invest "myth" too heavily, certainly not with the religious and philosophical expectations of Crane's friends. The poem is concerned with myth but is itself not necessarily mythic. Nor is it religious, though Crane said that "the very idea of a bridge . . . is a form peculiarly dependent on . . . spiritual convictions." It does not aspire to anything so grand (and doctrinal), but merely to poetry, an "affirmation of experience," and an affirmative experience of the kind Williams rendered in "The Wanderer":

> And with that a great sea-gull
> Went to the left, vanishing with a wild cry—
> But in my mind all the persons of godhead
> Followed after.

"Proem: To Brooklyn Bridge" is an invocatory prayer—an equivalent perhaps of the traditional invocation to the muse—that also does the work of Whitman's "Inscriptions." It introduces us to the poet's themes and to the "thematic anticipations" noted in part by Frederick Hoffman. More formally integrated with the poem than "Inscriptions," it does more. In many significant ways it is a single version of the entire poem: an instance of its situation, duration, landscapes, mediating consciousness, poetic (symbolic) action, and "logic of metaphor." In naming the bridge, it centers and localizes the poem, establishes a point in history and geography, in time and space; and in invoking the bridge, it begins the symbolization upon which the success of the poem depends. No more ludicrous than the Eiffel Tower, the bridge is a symbol, of the order of Whitman's "grass," that acquires meaning by participating in concrete situations. In speaking of the frequently expressed wish of overcoming the "meaningless life of our industrial society . . . [by] introducing value through creating new symbols," Dorothy Lee addresses the problem Crane recognized in writing "Proem": "symbols in themselves have no value, and they cannot convey value to a situation. Only after they have participated in a situation can they have value, and then only in so far as the situation itself holds value." Since individual experience initiates this acquisition of meaning, the poet, for whom the bridge already possesses meaning at the beginning of the poem, speaks for himself and enables us, by means of the poem (to invoke, in this instance, is to evoke), to enter his experience and come into his meanings. And since a symbol "grows in meaning, and even changes in meaning," he will present the bridge in various situations, as he does so exemplarily in "Proem" by using the cubist technique of shifting perspectives, a technique that brings much together in the name of the bridge and represents one of the ways in which the entire poem, the poet's journey of consciousness, becomes a totality of meaning, the "Word" of a simultaneously apprehended "logic of metaphor" as well as the warrant of his identification with life.

"*O clemens, o pia, o dulces Maria.*" With these words of Columbus' prayer, William Carlos Williams concluded "The Discovery of the Indies," a chapter of *In the American Grain* that Crane probably read when it first appeared in *Broom*, in March 1923. His "Ave Maria," a dramatic monologue of the returning Columbus, also concludes with a prayer, one that celebrates God's work in the discovery even as it speaks the mariner's thankfulness for homecoming to Spain after the terrible trials of passage. Placed in respect to homecoming rather than, with Williams, to discovery, the prayer (and the prayerful nature established by the title of the poem) provides a transition from "Proem." For like the poet of "Proem," Columbus, isolated and alone, is represented as enduring a dark time and petitioning divine help; he has found the New World ("It is morning there") but now, like the dawning world of "Proem," it has been lost in the darkness of the present and, even for him, has become "apparitional," a wonderful event of the past. The homeward voyage to report the discovery ("I bring you back Cathay") is depicted as a test of faith, an act decreed by God, who "dost search / Cruelly with love." In every respect, all the more so in its time of difficulty, "Ave Maria" shows the Christian orientation provided by what critics of modern secularism and disintegration, like Waldo Frank, called the medieval synthesis. It offers a contrast to the present in The Bridge ("A period that is loose at all ends, without apparent direction of any sort") at the same time that Columbus, the only person in the poem other than the mother of "Indiana" who is permitted the autonomy of monologue, becomes an example of the kind of discovery and heroic perseverance which by imaginative identification the poet assimilates to himself.

The presence of Columbus is perhaps inevitable in a poem so much concerned with the redemption—or rediscovery—of America. (This, in fact, is the theme for which Columbus is spokesman in the concluding dialogue with Cervantes in Waldo Frank's Virgin Spain, whose title refers to Mary, to Spain, the immaculate "mother of beginnings.") When Crane first outlined The Bridge for Otto Kahn, he began it with Columbus and moved forward chronologically—and dialectically—through Pocahontas and Whitman, its three major figures. He did not seem to consider the disjunctions of time that he later employed nor the movement of consciousness that contained them. Yet this is what makes "Ave Maria" both a historical starting point and a present occasion in the mind of the poet. Though the monologue, in language suitable to the speaker (sometimes, as with Williams, in words from Columbus' journal), presents a world of its own distant from the poet, it is still immediately there, known in its language by the "contact," as Williams would say, it affords. The separateness of that world—the differing conceptions of deity, cosmos, geography—marks its distance, conveys the poet's sense of time, though in his dream it is timeless. And in its placement between "Proem" and "The Harbor Dawn," the episode belongs to the poet; it is not merely the formal beginning of a poem on America but the first episode in the poet's act of remembering (remembering, awakening, and discovering, for much of his discovering is remembering); it is his historical "ground," something still vital in which he participates, something very much related to the present time and to his concerns. For it is a historical representation of loss—what better example of discovery, loss, even "betrayal"?—a loss also told in "Proem" and "The Harbor Dawn" and subsequent parts of the poem.

When we say that "Ave Maria" is a historical starting point we mean not only that here, with Columbus' discovery, American history begins but that here is the beginning of "history" in America. This is the sense in which Claude Lévi-Strauss uses "history" when he remarks, in *Tristes Tropiques,* that until the discovery "the New World was spared the agitations of 'history'. . . . For "history" is an intrusive force, one that Crane, with the particular sensitivity to its consequences shown by other writers of his time, identifies when he says, in the context of the lost (or hidden: overlaid) timeless world of the Indian, "always the iron dealt cleavage!" Columbus, according to Lévi-Strauss, "risked the only total adventure yet offered mankind," but in doing so he introduced "history," opened America to the "shallowness which characterizes the history of the New World in modern times." He betrayed it to the ravaging greed (symbolized by the westward movement, the gold rush, the railroad, and the skyscraper) against which, in "Ave Maria," he warns Ferdinand ("Yet no delirium of jewels!"; "Rush [not] down the plenitude"). Columbus, then, begins a history of spoliation and loss at the same time that he reminds us, if only in the phrase "Indian emperies," of a primitive world antedating "history," a world whose "lesson," Lévi-Strauss tells us, "may even come to us with a millenary freshness. . . ."

Its lesson—of "contact" (Williams), harmony (Frank), sacrality (Rosenfeld)—came to Crane with millenary freshness; and by manipulating time, the very element that destroys the work—myths, religions—of man, he tried to bring it to us. To treat time disjunctively is to negate its linearity, its irresistible historical dimension, the "viewpoint" that Crane told Otto Kahn one could get in "any history primer." He preferred "a more organic panorama, showing the continuous and living evidence of the past in the inmost vital substance of the present." For the "purely chronological," he said, was "ineffective from the poetic standpoint"— that is, would not enable him to do what he wished to do in the poem: recover time and, with it, the sacred ground, or possibility, of a new beginning.

At the end of *Virgin Spain,* the "history" begun by Columbus ends with the disappearance of the White Towers of America; as the sun sets in the west, the sky in the east is *"suddenly aflame with sunrise."* Crane may have acknowledged this apocalypse by calling the concluding poem of *The Bridge* "Atlantis." Yet his expectation of the dawn, though as great as Frank's, was never expressed in such Wagnerian fashion. It depended, instead, on radical change in perspective, on awareness of the circular rhythms of man and nature, on the realization that, as Lévi-Strauss learned, "The golden age which blind superstition situated behind or ahead of us is *in us."* The possibility of a new beginning for which Crane speaks is underwritten by the mind and nature, by the similarity of *experience* so often emphasized by the logic of metaphor of his poem—for example, in the hierophany of the seagull's flight experienced by the poet in "Proem" and that of the " 'The Great White Birds' " experienced by the Indians in "Ave Maria."

In speaking of his own "pioneering" in *The Bridge,* Crane explained to Otto Kahn that, in what followed "Ave Maria," he was working backward from the present (or down) to "the nature-world of the Indian." When he said that he was treating the "Myth of America," he meant both the recurrent pattern—the impulsion—of our "history" and the mythic, or aboriginal, world beneath it. This is the double aspect, represented in *The Bridge* by the interplay of linear and circular imagery, to which he refers in telling Waldo Frank that "to handle the beautiful skeins of this myth of America—to realize suddenly, as I seem to, how much of the past is living under only slightly altered forms, even in machinery . . . is extremely exciting." Much of the excitement of writing (and reading) *The Bridge* comes from discovering this new world. For Crane's passage, like Whitman's in "Passage to India," is "back . . . to primal thought"; his is the voyage of the "mind's return, / To reason's early paradise. . . ." And perhaps his passage follows that of Columbus because, in Whitman's poem, Columbus ("History's type of courage, action, faith") is said to have opened the way to the greater work of the poet—to those reconciliations and reunions whose all-inclusive example is that of "Nature and Man . . . disjoin'd and diffused no more." That Crane turned to Mexico after completing *The Bridge* is understandable; there he actually reached, as he once said of "The Dance," "the pure mythical soil . . . at last!"

Crane's conception of Columbus owes something to Williams (the "wonder-breathing" discoverer, not despoiler, of Beautiful Thing) and something to Waldo Frank (the "mystic mariner" overwhelmed by "faith, not fear"). But it owes most to Whitman, to "Passage to India" and perhaps to "Prayer of Columbus." Of more significance than the verbal evidence—"rondure," "teeming," "athwart," for example—is the fact that Columbus' prayer in "Ave Maria" is in spirit so much like Whitman's apostrophe to God in section eight of "Passage to India," a poem in which the poet celebrates both the sacrality of the universe and the soul's desire to go beyond, to voyage forth and come to rest in God. To reach, to return to, "affection's source" is Whitman's goal; he can only be satisfied by "love complete," as he says in the stanza from which Crane took the epigraph to "Cape Hatteras":

> Reckoning ahead O soul, when thou, the time achiev'd,
> The seas all cross'd, weather'd the capes, the voyage done,
> Surrounding, copest, frontest God, yieldest the aim attain'd,

> As fill'd with friendship, love complete, the Elder Brother found
> The Younger melts in fondness in his arms.

A similar desire for the assuagement of the "trembling heart" concludes "Ave Maria" and is expressed in lines that visually reach forward into the poem and are recalled once more (in "O Hand of Fire") at the close of "The Tunnel." For the poet they mark the beginning and the end of the rediscovery of America—and the soul's voyage—whose ecstatic goal is reached in "Atlantis."

And then Whitman confirms for the poet, in "Cape Hatteras," the faith (the trust) of which so much of the poet's journey is a test; confirms the faith in a meaningful, living universe of which Columbus provides the first touchstones. As a historical figure, Columbus may be said to represent the religious consciousness of medieval Christianity; for him the "medieval synthesis" is still a fact of experience, not a phrase to designate the falling-away of subsequent history. Of him, as a historical figure, it is perhaps sufficiently accurate to say that "being dedicated to divine will, [he] holds a vision of God that is integrated within the life he enacts, giving him the sense of a living universe and the sense of his own mission within the divine whole." But in the poem, in the poetry, it is otherwise: it is his renewed sense of a living universe, his sense of the cosmos itself as hierophany—this is his vision of God—that sustains his faith and steadies his dedication. Twice—on the return voyage and the voyage out—he is tested at sea, by chaos; and the monologue that tells of the stormy return and homecoming concludes with the prayer, a celebration of the mystery and power of God and of the glory of his universe. Here Columbus tells of the passage out—"through night our passage"—whose wonderful culmination certified the hierophanies he had witnessed (the corposant, "Teneriffe's garnet," the "teeming span" itself) and, considering "all that amplitude that time explores," was *his* discovery of cosmos. The discovery is revelation ("where our Indian emperies lie revealed") and accordingly, he says, "faith, not fear / Nigh surged me witless. . . ." Like the Indians who are moved by his ships to sacral awareness, he is moved by the dawn that discloses the New World, moved by his presence at creation: "I, wonder-breathing, kept the watch,—saw / The *first* palm chevron the *first* lighted hill." And a similar sense of cosmos—of order, of motion, and energy and the splendor of creation—is expressed in the brilliant lines that remind us of the poet's apostrophe to the bridge in "Proem" and of the epigraph from Plato that introduces "Atlantis" and the greater apostrophe of that poem:

> This turning rondure whole, this crescent ring
> Sun-cusped and zoned with modulated fire
> Like pearls . . .

This disposition that thy night relates
From Moon to Saturn in one sapphire wheel:
The orbic wake of thy once whirling feet,
Elohim, still I hear thy sounding heel!

Perhaps this explains the dramatic issue of the monologue: the return voyage to "bring you back Cathay"; not riches, as Crane explained to Otto Kahn, but the "word" (of a morning world) that had been revealed to Columbus ("For I have seen now what no perjured breath / Of clown nor sage can riddle or gainsay"), "Cathay," which Crane said was a "symbol of consciousness, knowledge, spiritual unity." The voyage to the New World is the ultimate trial of faith—wherever one discovers cosmos there is a new world—and Columbus is a hero of faith. Allusions to Captain Ahab's blasphemous voyage (corposants, compass, "gleaming fields") underscore his achievement; and he is especially important to a poet for whom such a victory is one of trust and involves Mary (mother), God (father), friends ("Be with me, Luis de San Angel") and perhaps lover ("Dark waters onward shake the dark prow free," which recalls "Voyages VI").

More resonant than any lines in the poem are those that evoke the ultimate world that answers the voyager:

. . .the far
Hushed gleaming fields and pendant seething wheat
Of knowledge. . . .

They recall the lines of Watt's hymn that Bildad sang as the *Pequod* plunged into the open seas ("Sweet fields beyond the swelling flood,/ Stand dressed in living green"), lines that Ishmael said never sounded more sweetly to him, "full of hope and fruition." And they recall the lines of Ceres' blessing in *The Tempest* cited by Crane in a letter to the Browns from California: "Spring come to you at the farthest / In the very end of harvest." How wonderfully they summon for us the earthly paradise that Columbus believed he had found, the "verdant land" from which Ishmael said we should never push off, the "fresh, green breast of the new world" that Nick Carraway, in *The Great Gatsby*, said "had once pandered in whispers to the last and greatest of all human dreams": all the images we cherish of Mother Earth, the sacred body risen from the sea, the "plenitude" to be worshiped, not violated or profaned. For the gleaming fields are cosmos (and beauty and knowledge), the bright living world created anew from the waters of chaos, darkness, and death. We may even, in considering the "pendant . . . wheat / Of knowledge," recall the evocation of the golden-haired Venus at the close of "Voyages." These images move us, and they move the poet, who, in the dream of "Ave Maria," is about to enter the "waking dream" of "The Harbor Dawn," where he himself discovers the New World by imaginatively possessing Powhatan's daughter.

Philip Horton justified Crane's use of the epigraph from Seneca because Columbus himself had cited it to show that he had fulfilled "an ancient destiny." But it confirms the poet's destiny as well. For "all of the terms of his quest," as Thomas Vogler says, "are symbolically interchangeable with those of Columbus' quest." Columbus' monologue is the poet's dream, which explains the most notable things about it: that the passage home provides the dramatic setting of the discovery; that the chaos that tests the "word" is under the dominion of a cruel Hebraic God, the father whose hand is fire and whose love requires the intercession of the mother ("O Madre María"); and that the mother to whom the poet appeals in "Ave Maria" is the tutelary divinity of his vision and its object, the paradise he wishes to discover and the homeland to which he wishes to return. Discovery is recovery because, as the poem tells us, the poet has been there before.

JOHN T. IRWIN

Figurations of the Writer's Death: Freud and Hart Crane

Let me begin by juxtaposing two passages—one from Freud, one from Hart Crane—as pretexts for discussing the way in which a writer deals with the inscribed image of his own death—both the certain death of his physical body and the possible death of the body of his work. The Freudian passage is a footnote to his essay "The Uncanny" (1919). After discussing instances of the uncanny "from the realm of fiction" and "imaginative writing," Freud turns, near the end of the essay, to another class of the phenomenon, the uncanny in real life, and offers a marginal example from his own experience:

> Since the uncanny effect of a 'double' also belongs to this same group it is interesting to observe what the effect is of meeting one's own image unbidden and unexpected. Ernst Mach has related two such observations in his *Analyse der Empfindungen* (1900). On the first occasion he was not a little startled when he realized that the face before him was his own. The second time he formed a very unfavourable opinion about the supposed stranger who entered the omnibus, and thought 'What a shabby-looking school-master that man is who is getting in!'—I can report a similar adventure. I was sitting alone in my *wagon-lit* compartment when a more than usually violent jolt of the train swung back the door of the adjoining washing-cabinet, and an elderly gentleman in a dressing-gown and a travelling cap came in. I assumed that in leaving the washing-cabinet, which lay between the two compartments, he had taken the wrong direction and come into my compartment by mistake. Jumping up

From *Psychiatry and the Humanities*, vol. 4 (1980), edited by Joseph Smith. Copyright © 1980 by The Forum on Psychiatry and the Humanities of the Washington School of Psychiatry. Yale University Press.

with the intention of putting him right, I at once realized to my dismay that the intruder was nothing but my own reflection in the looking-glass on the open door. I can still recollect that I thoroughly disliked his appearance. Instead, therefore, of being *frightened* by our 'doubles', both Mach and I simply failed to recognize them as such. Is it not possible, though, that our dislike of them was a vestigial trace of the archaic reaction which feels the 'double' to be something uncanny?

The Crane passage is taken from the opening section of his long poem *The Bridge*. Having described the bridge at dawn in the first four stanzas of "To Brooklyn Bridge," Crane suddenly shifts the mood in the fifth stanza with the description of a suicide:

> Out of some subway scuttle, cell or loft
> A bedlamite speeds to thy parapets,
> Tilting there momently, shrill shirt ballooning,
> A jest falls from the speechless caravan.

It is obvious enough how the bedlamite's leap from the Brooklyn Bridge into the East River can be read, retrospectively, as a foreshadowing of Crane's own suicidal leap from the deck of the S.S. *Orizaba* into the Caribbean Sea some two years after *The Bridge*'s publication. The prefiguration becomes even more striking when we recall that in the poem's final section, "Atlantis," the image of the bridge metamorphoses into that of a ship, its cables transformed into "cordage," its girders into "spars," with the seafarer Jason aloft in its rigging. Moreover, if one considers the poet Weldon Kees's presumed suicide from the Golden Gate Bridge in 1955 and John Berryman's 1972 leap from the bridge over the Mississippi River in Minneapolis in light of the reference to the Golden Gate at the beginning of the "Van Winkle" section and the image of the poet's body floating down the Mississippi in "The River," then *The Bridge* seems prefigurative not only of Crane's fate but of the fate of a certain type of lyric poet in twentieth-century America.

Obvious as the foreshadowing of Crane's suicide is in the passage from *The Bridge*, it is much less obvious that the passage from Freud presents an image of the writer's death—indeed, that it presents, in its tale of Freud's not recognizing his mirror-image, any image of death at all. Yet I would argue that the passage can be so interpreted on at least three counts. First of all, Freud characterizes both Mach's experience and his own as an encounter with a double. Earlier in the essay, discussing Otto Rank's study of doubling, Freud had remarked how the figure of the double, which had originally been "an insurance against the destruction of the ego, an 'energetic denial of the power of death' " (1919), reversed its significance when primitive man passed the stage of primary narcissism. The double changed from "an assurance of immortality" into "the uncanny harbinger of death." In encountering one's double, then, one meets the prefiguration or foreshadowing of one's own fate, one's own fatality. Secondly, both Mach and Freud report that, on first seeing their doubles, they failed to recognize them as images of themselves. Since it is literally impossible to imagine one's own death, to imagine the end of imagining or think the absence of thought, one always conceives of one's own death as if it were the death of another—one's consciousness still being in existence as onlooker. If we grant, then, that any image of one's own death always implies this continued presence of oneself as observer of the image, then to see one's image in a mirror and not to recognize it is perhaps as close as we can come to depicting the loss of self-consciousness, the absence of the self as observer. Thirdly, what Mach and Freud each saw was a mirror-image—that is, a spatial double—but what Freud also encountered at some point, as the note makes clear, was a temporal doubling, in that his own experience was a repetition of Mach's earlier experience. In reading Mach's account of not recognizing his mirror-image, Freud encountered Mach as a double. Since Freud doesn't comment on *this* double, are we to assume that he didn't recognize the doubling between himself and Mach, just as he and Mach hadn't recognized their mirror-images? It would be a curious lapse, but no more curious than the footnote itself; for to put it bluntly, there is something fishy about the note, something oddly strained about Freud's introducing Mach's experience into the essay, as if Freud needed corroboration of his own somewhat far-fetched story. Mach's account of not recognizing his image occurs in the first chapter of *The Analysis of Sensations*, in a footnote to his remark that "Personally, people know themselves very poorly":

> Once, when a young man, I noticed in the street the profile of a face that was very displeasing and repulsive to me. I was not a little taken aback when a moment afterwards I found that it was my own face which, in passing by a shop where mirrors were sold, I had perceived reflected from two mirrors that were inclined at the proper angle to each other.
>
> Not long ago, after a trying railway journey by night, when I was very tired, I got into an omnibus, just as another man appeared at the other end. "What a shabby pedagogue that is, that has just entered," thought I. It was myself: opposite me hung a large mirror. The physiognomy of my class, accordingly, was better known to me than my own.

The Analysis of Sensations was first published in 1886 (though it contained material that had appeared in print as early as the 1860s), and by 1906 the book was in its fifth edition. Freud cites the second edition

(1900). Mach died in 1916, and Freud completed his essay "The Uncanny" in the middle of 1919, publishing it in autumn of the same year. Though there seems to have been no direct personal contact between Mach and Freud, Thomas Szasz has argued, in his introduction to *The Analysis of Sensations*, that Freud was "much influenced by the general *epistemological* outlook inherent in Mach's psychological writings. This, particularly as it involved his views concerning the relationship between physics (medicine) and psychology, Freud borrowed from Mach. Indeed, perhaps Mach's prestige and authority may have even handicapped Freud, and the other founders of the science of psychoanalysis, from fully realizing the physicalistic basis upon which they have placed psychoanalysis. Szasz also contends that in *The Analysis of Sensations* Mach had anticipated some of the fundamental concepts of psychoanalysis. In a letter dated June 12, 1900, to his friend Wilhelm Fliess, Freud refers to Mach's book:

> Do you suppose that some day a marble tablet will be placed on the house, inscribed with these words:
> 'In this house on July 24th, 1895, The Secret of Dreams was revealed to Dr. Sigmund Freud.'
> At this moment, I see little prospect of it. But when I read the latest psychological books (Mach's *Analyse der Empfindungen*, second edition, Kroell's *Aufbau der Seele*, etc.) all of which have the same kind of aims as my work, and see what they have to say about dreams, I am as delighted as the dwarf in the fairy tale because 'the princess doesn't know.'
>
> (Freud, 1887–1902)

Commenting on this passage, Szasz notes that

> Mach, at this time, was a full Professor in the University of Vienna, and he had already achieved world-renown as a physicist and philosopher. Yet, Freud referred to him as if he were a psychologist and an expert on dreams. Surely, it is true that *The Analysis of Sensations* does not contain anything of value concerning dream-psychology. Nor was it addressed to this topic. Freud, as we know, had much coveted the social recognition which a regular professorship at the outstanding University of Vienna implied. . . . he selected—presumably not without reason—Mach's somewhat unrelated work with which to compare what he felt was his *magnum opus. The Interpretation of Dreams*, it must be remembered, was also his first psychological book written alone. He thus compared his work—in his own mind and to his friend—with that of the well-recognized University professor, Mach, in order to prove its originality and worth.

As further evidence of Freud's general sensitivity to the question of influence versus originality in his work, consider the following passage from *An Autobiographical Study* (1925):

Even when I have moved away from observation, I have carefully avoided any contact with philosophy proper. This avoidance has been greatly facilitated by constitutional incapacity. I was always open to the ideas of G. T. Fechner and have followed that thinker upon many important points. The large extent to which psycho-analysis coincides with the philosophy of Schopenhauer—not only did he assert the dominance of the emotions and the supreme importance of sexuality but he was even aware of the mechanism of repression—is not to be traced to my acquaintance with his teaching. I read Schopenhauer very late in my life. Nietzsche, another philosopher whose guesses and intuitions often agree in the most astonishing way with the laborious findings of psychoanalysis, was for a long time avoided by me on that very account; I was less concerned with the question of priority than with keeping my mind unembarrassed.

Yet, twenty-five years earlier, in his letter to Fliess, Freud was clearly concerned with the question of priority, concerned with the fact that on July 24, 1895, he knew "the Secret of Dreams" while, to judge from the 1900 edition of *The Analysis of Sensations,* the famous Ernst Mach still didn't know the secret. And as the reference to the "marble tablet" shows, he was concerned about whether his own originality would ever achieve public recognition. It is significant that in the passage from *An Autobiographical Study* in which Freud denies the influence of Schopenhauer and Nietzsche on his work, he freely acknowledges the influence of Fechner, just as Mach freely acknowledged Fechner's influence in *The Analysis of Sensations.* Mach notes in the preface to the first edition that "My natural bent for the study of these questions received its strongest stimulus twenty-five years ago from Fechner's *Elemente der Psychophysik* (Leipzig, 1860)." And in the book's final chapter he says that "Fechner's psychophysics, which have had so important an influence, did not fail to stimulate me exceedingly at the time," though one of the aims of *The Analysis of Sensations,* as Mach makes clear, is to separate his own work from Fechner's, to distinguish his notion of "*the complete parallelism of the psychical and the physical*" from "Fechner's conception of the physical and psychical as two different aspects of one and the same reality."

Now putting the question of influence aside for a moment, we can say that, just as there is a philosophical line of thought that runs from Schopenhauer to Nietzsche to Freud, a recognizable similarity in their psychological insights that Freud openly acknowledged, so too there is a scientific line of thought that runs from Fechner to Mach to Freud, a recognizable similarity in their questioning of the relationship between the physical and the psychical that Freud openly acknowledged in the case of Fechner and privately acknowledged in the case of Mach (the letter to

Fliess). For our purposes, then, it is important to distinguish between the question of influence and the question of priority. Though Freud denies the influence of Schopenhauer and Nietzsche, the very necessity, the very appropriateness, of such a denial is an admission that many of Schopenhauer's and Nietzsche's insights into human motivations and the mechanisms of the psyche are similar to his own and precede his own writings, often by many years. As a rhetorical defense against this feeling of his work's having been anticipated, of its not being original, Freud distinguishes between the "philosophical" nature of Schopenhauer's and Nietzsche's work, which he deprecatingly characterizes with such words as *guesses* and *intuitions*, and the scientific nature of his own work, "the laborious findings of psychoanalysis."

What is uncanny, or perhaps not so uncanny, is that Mach used the same strategy in *The Analysis of Sensations* many years earlier. At the very start of the book, Mach points out that "the physiology of the senses" has gradually abandoned "the method of investigating sensations in themselves followed by men like Goethe, Schopenhauer and . . . Johannes Muller" and has "assumed an almost exclusively physical character."

Though Mach acknowledges the helpfulness of insights drawn from philosophy and deplores any absolute separation between philosophy and natural science, it is clear that he classifies himself as a man of science and that, however useful his scientific findings may be to philosophy, "there is no such thing as 'the philosophy of Mach'." Just as Freud claimed to have formed conclusions resembling Schopenhauer's long before he had ever read Schopenhauer's work, so Mach says that it was "by studying the physiology of the senses, and by reading Herbart" that he "arrived at views akin to those of Hume," though at the time he "was still unacquainted with Hume himself." Moreover, aware that his scientific critique of the substantial existence of the ego and Nietzsche's philosophical critique of the ego might be interpreted as having the same ethical effect, Mach takes pains to point out that the "ethical ideal" which he believes will follow from a renunciation of the ego and individual immortality is "far removed" from "the ideal of an overweening Nietzschean 'superman,' who cannot, and I hope will not, be tolerated by his fellow-men."

Consequently, though Freud could logically distinguish his scientific work from the philosophical writings of Schopenhauer and Nietzsche, it would have been impossible for him to represent his research as being more scientific than Mach's, particularly when Mach had made use of the same invidious distinction between science and philosophy years before. What we are left with is a situation in which Freud, no matter what the influence of Mach's research on his own, would have been aware of the similarities in certain areas between his writings and Mach's prior writings and thus could have easily felt, granting his sensitivity to the question of priority as evidenced by his reaction to Schopenhauer and Nietzsche, that Mach's work called into question the originality of his own work in certain areas and thus threatened its survival. In short, it is a situation in which the temporal doubling between Freud and Mach would have presented Freud with an image of the possible death of parts of his own work by reason of their seeming to be merely psychoanalytic rephrasings of Mach's previous insights, a situation in which Freud not only would not have had at his disposal the rhetorical defense-mechanism that he used against Schopenhauer and Nietzsche but would have found in that very mechanism another example of Mach's priority.

With these considerations in mind, let us examine more closely the circumstances surrounding the composition of "The Uncanny." The essay, which was first published in the autumn of 1919, "is mentioned by Freud in a letter to Ferenczi of May 12 of the same year, in which he says he has dug an old paper out of a drawer and is rewriting it. Nothing is known as to when it was originally written or how much it was changed, though the footnote quoted from *Totem and Taboo* . . . shows that the subject was present in his mind as early as 1913. The passages dealing with the 'compulsion to repeat' . . . must in any case have formed part of the revision" (1919, editors' note). In discussing the uncanny effect of coincidences or "similar recurrences" as related to infantile psychology, Freud refers the reader to "another work, already completed, in which this has been gone into in detail, but in a different connection. For it is possible to recognize the dominance in the unconscious mind of a 'compulsion to repeat' proceeding from the instinctual impulses and probably inherent in the very nature of the instincts—a compulsion powerful enough to override the pleasure principle, lending to certain aspects of the mind their daemonic character, and still very clearly expressed in the impulses of small children; a compulsion, too, which is responsible for a part of the course taken by the analyses of neurotic patients. All these considerations prepare us for the discovery that whatever reminds us of this inner 'compulsion to repeat' is perceived as uncanny." The work to which Freud refers in this passage is *Beyond the Pleasure Principle*, which he had begun writing in March 1919. In the same letter to Ferenczi in which Freud mentions the essay on the uncanny, he reports that a draft of the longer work has been completed. However, Freud held back publication of *Beyond the Pleasure Principle* and continued to work on the manuscript through the early part of 1920, finally publishing it later that year.

In *Beyond the Pleasure Principle* Freud introduces what is perhaps his most controversial notion, the concept of a death instinct inherent in all living matter. As Freud indicates in the passage from "The Uncanny" quoted above, he was led to this concept by the observation that in the play of small children and in the actions of some neurotics there seems to be a compulsion to repeat that does not depend on the pleasurableness of the repeated action. More often than not, the repeated material is traumatic, and the repetition is an effort to master the trauma by transforming the original affront from something passively suffered by the individual into something which he actively initiates in the form of a repetition, and thus controls. The aim of this mastery is to reduce the level of excitation in the traumatized organism to what it was before the affront. Having identified this compulsion as "instinctual," Freud asks, "But how is the predicate of being 'instinctual' related to the compulsion to repeat? At this point we cannot escape a suspicion that we may have come upon the track of a universal attribute of instincts and perhaps of organic life in general which has not hitherto been clearly recognized or at least not explicitly stressed. *It seems, then, that an instinct is an urge inherent in organic life to restore an earlier state of things* which the living entity has been obliged to abandon under the pressure of external disturbing forces" (1920). The instincts are "an expression of the *conservative* nature of living substance," and the ultimate goal of the instincts, the ultimate "earlier state of things" which the compulsion to repeat seeks to restore, is the inorganic state from which life sprang, the state of zero excitation. Freud concludes that "If we are to take it as a truth that knows no exception that everything living dies for *internal* reasons—becomes inorganic once again—then we shall be compelled to say that '*the aim of all life is death*'." The death instinct is, then, not simply one type of instinct among others; it is the archetypal operating principle of all the instincts, of instinctual behavior. Even in the case of something as apparently opposed to death as the pleasure principle, Freud asserts, "The pleasure principle seems actually to serve the death instincts."

Clearly, in *Beyond the Pleasure Principle* Freud is only too aware of the controversial nature of this theory, that is, aware of the largely *theoretical* character of the notion of the death instinct. Thus, for example, the death instinct depends upon the assumption that death is the inevitable fate of living matter, that without exception "everything dies for *internal* reasons." If that is not true, then the death instinct is not the principle of all instinctual behavior. It may simply be one of two major types of instinct, its opposite being the sex instinct, the drive to reproduce life. Or if death is an accidental rather than a necessary feature of life, there may be no death instinct at all.

In section 6 of *Beyond the Pleasure Principle*, Freud surveys recent work in biology to see if any data exists that "would flatly contradict the recognition of death instincts;" and after reviewing the work of Weismann, Goette, Hartmann, Woodruff, Maupas, Calkins, and others, and noting "how little agreement there is among biologists on the subject of natural death," he judges that there is no data which would rule out the possibility of a death instinct. What is significant in this procedure is not only Freud's turning to biology "to test the validity of the belief," but the ambivalent way in which he handles this scientific evidence. Freud was aware that the "theoretical grounds" on which his notion of a death instinct was based could just as easily be characterized as "speculative" or "philosophical." By seeking evidence from a natural science like biology, Freud makes his own position seem less philosophical. But there is also a danger in this procedure; for though Freud was ostensibly searching for data that might contradict his theory, he was also looking for any evidence that might support it. Yet biological data that was similar enough to his own theory to be supportive, might also turn out to be preemptive of his discovery, revealing that his notion of a death instinct had been anticipated by the natural sciences. Freud's strategy is to represent the biological data which he cites as being like, but not too like, his own theory. Thus, in dealing with Weismann's work, he notes "the striking similarity between Weismann's distinction of soma and germ-plasm" and his own "separation of the death instincts from the life instincts," but he points out that "the appearance of a significant correspondence is dissipated as soon as we discover Weismann's views on the problem of death." However, in one of his citations of scientific opinion, Freud reveals a significant link between the reading he had been doing for this section of *Beyond the Pleasure Principle* and the essay he was writing on the uncanny. He says,

> According to E. Hering's theory, two kinds of processes are constantly at work in living substance, operating in contrary directions, one constructive or assimilatory and the other destructive or dissimilatory. May we venture to recognize in these two directions taken by the vital processes the activity of our two instinctual impulses, the life instincts and the death instincts? There is something else, at any rate, that we cannot remain blind to. We have unwittingly steered our course into the harbour of Schopenhauer's philosophy. For him death is the 'true result and to that extent the purpose of life,' while the sexual instinct is the embodiment of the will to live.

The passage attracts our interest for a variety of reasons. First, it is a clear example of Freud's effort to chart an "original" course between the

Scylla and Charybdis of natural science and philosophy, represented here by the work of Hering and Schopenhauer respectively. Second, it is an equally clear example of his sensitivity to the question of priority and repetition in his writing, his sensitivity to the fact that he has "unwittingly" (does that mean "unconsciously"?) repeated an insight from Schopenhauer's philosophy, a repetition that "we cannot remain blind to" (who had tried to remain blind to it?). Finally, and most important, the reference to Hering recalls the context within which Freud, in the essay on the uncanny, discusses the compulsion to repeat and mentions the existence of a longer work on the subject—*Beyond the Pleasure Principle.* At that point in the essay, Freud has been giving examples of the uncanny effect of coincidences, of "similar recurrences," and the example which immediately precedes his suggestion of the link between the uncanny and the compulsion to repeat is this: "suppose one is engaged in reading the works of the famous physiologist, Hering, and within the space of a few days receives two letters from two different countries, each from a person called Hering, though one has never before had any dealings with anyone of that name" (1919). Obviously, the person who was "engaged in reading the works of the famous physiologist, Hering" at that moment was Freud himself. To judge from the reference in *Beyond the Pleasure Principle,* Hering's works were among the texts in natural science which Freud was surveying for data that might contradict or support the notion of a death instinct. And what seems likely is that the reason the physiologist Hering was on Freud's mind at the time he was writing "The Uncanny" is the same reason that Ernst Mach was on his mind: that besides surveying works in biology and physiology, Freud read certain psychophysical works as well, and that among these he reread Mach's *The Analysis of Sensations,* which, according to the letter to Fliess, he had first read almost twenty years earlier. Thus, just as Hering emerged from Freud's survey of scientific data on natural death to become an instance of uncanny recurrence, so Mach emerged from the same survey to become an example of uncanny doubling.

The likelihood that Freud was reading psychophysical texts at the time is confirmed by the fact that the opening section of *Beyond the Pleasure Principle* includes, as part of a discussion of originality in research, a lengthy quote from Fechner. Freud says,

> It is of no concern to us in this connection to enquire how far, with this hypothesis of the pleasure principle, we have approached or adopted any particular, historically established, philosophical system. We have arrived at these speculative assumptions in an attempt to describe and to account for the facts of daily observation in our field of study. Priority and

originality are not among the aims that psycho-analytic work sets itself; and the impressions that underlie the hypothesis of the pleasure principle are so obvious that they can scarcely be overlooked. On the other hand we would readily express our gratitude to any philosophical or psychological theory which was able to inform us of the meaning of the feelings of pleasure and unpleasure which act so imperatively upon us. But on this point we are, alas, offered nothing to our purpose. . . .

We cannot, however, remain indifferent to the discovery that an investigator of such penetration as G. T. Fechner held a view on the subject of pleasure and unpleasure which coincides in all essentials with the one that has been forced upon us by psycho-analytic work. [1920]

Freud then goes on to quote a passage from Fechner's *Einige Ideen zur Schöpfungs- und Entwicklungsgeschichte der Organismen* (1873). What interests us here is that Freud characterizes the similarity between Fechner's "view on the subject of pleasure and unpleasure," and his own concept of the pleasure principle, as a "discovery," as something that he had recently become aware of, thus suggesting that he had only recently read or reread Fechner's book. (Perhaps Freud's willingness to acknowledge the similarity between the pleasure principle and Fechner's view of pleasure and unpleasure is due to the fact that Freud himself was about to advance beyond the pleasure principle in the development of his thought.)

Further evidence suggesting the likelihood that Mach's *The Analysis of Sensations* was one of the works which Freud searched for data that might bear on the death instinct is to be found in the book itself. Mach says in the preface to the first edition that he is "under especial obligations to those investigators, such as E. Hering, V. Hensen, W. Preyer and others, who have directed attention either to the matter of my writings or to my methodological expositions," and he adds that though his "natural bent for the study of these questions received its strongest stimulus twenty-five years ago from Fechner's *Elemente der Psychophysik*," his "greatest assistance" was derived from Hering's work. Throughout the book, Mach frequently refers to the scientific contributions of Hering and Weismann, and at one point, in discussing Hering's notion of an unconscious memory inherent in cells and simple organisms that accounts for the hereditary transmission of information by cells and thus the repetition of functions by the organisms which they compose, Mach is led to discuss Weismann's notion of "death as a phenomenon of heredity." (If death is a phenomenon of heredity, that is, a "memory outside the organ of consciousness," does that mean that death is an instinct?)

Clearly, the connections between Mach's work and the work of most of the scientists whom Freud mentions in section 6 of *Beyond the*

Pleasure Principle are so close that it would have been virtually unthinkable for a researcher as meticulous as Freud not to have included *The Analysis of Sensations* in his survey of scientific literature on natural death. What this all means, then, is that at the time when Freud quoted, as a footnote to "The Uncanny," the passage from *The Analysis of Sensations* in which Mach tells the story of not recognizing his double, Freud had in all likelihood been rereading Mach's book in the context of the death instinct and the compulsion to repeat.

Now just as meeting one's double is, as Freud notes, an image of death, so too a "coincidence" or "similar recurrence" like that which Freud points out between Mach's uncanny experience and his own is also an image of death, because it recalls the "inner compulsion to repeat" —that is, the death instinct. Yet the only comment Freud makes on these similar experiences is: "Instead, therefore, of being *frightened* by our 'doubles', both Mach and I simply failed to recognize them as such. Is it not possible, though, that our dislike of them was a vestigial trace of the archaic reaction which feels the 'double' to be something uncanny?" (1919). Rather, is it not possible that Freud's footnote on Mach represents an irruption of the uncanny within the essay on the uncanny? Is it not possible that the footnote is "a vestigial trace" of an act of repression? Freud points out in the essay that "the uncanny (*unheimlich*) is something which is secretly familiar (*heimlich-heimisch*), which has undergone repression and then returned from it. And concerning the uncanny in real life, he says, "an uncanny experience occurs either when infantile complexes which have been repressed are once more revived by some impression, or when primitive beliefs which have been surmounted seem once more to be confirmed." Is the footnote, then, which remarks an interesting but seemingly insignificant similarity in the experiences of Mach and Freud, the trace left by Freud's repression of a more important, and a more disquieting, sense of the similarity between himself and Mach, a similarity Freud would have confronted in rereading *The Analysis of Sensations?*

If Freud's footnote is such a trace, then it should send us back to *The Analysis of Sensations* to examine the context in which Mach tells the story of meeting his double. It occurs in the opening chapter during Mach's discussion of the ego as a temporary unity, as being "only of relative permanency."

> The apparent permanency of the ego consists chiefly in the single fact of its continuity, in the slowness of its changes. The many thoughts and plans of yesterday that are continued to-day, and of which our environment in waking hours incessantly reminds us (whence in dreams the ego can be very indistinct, doubled, or entirely wanting), and the little

habits that are unconsciously and involuntarily kept up for long periods of time, constitute the groundwork of the ego. There can hardly be greater differences in the egos of different people, than occur in the course of years in one person. When I recall to-day my early youth, I should take the boy that I then was, with the exception of a few individual features, for a different person, were it not for the existence of the chain of memories. Many an article that I myself penned twenty years ago impresses me now as something quite foreign to myself. The very gradual character of the changes of the body also contributes to the stability of the ego, but in a much less degree than people imagine. Such things are much less analyzed and noticed than the intellectual and the moral ego. Personally, people know themselves very poorly. When I wrote these lines in 1886, Ribot's admirable little book, *The Diseases of Personality* (second edition, Paris, 1888, Chicago 1895), was unknown to me. Ribot ascribes the principal role in preserving the continuity of the ego to the general sensibility. Generally, I am in perfect accord with his views.

The ego is as little absolutely permanent as are bodies. That which we so much dread in death, the annihilation of our permanency, actually occurs in life in abundant measure. That which is most valued by us, remains preserved in countless copies, or, in cases of exceptional excellence, is even preserved of itself. In the best human being, however, there are individual traits, the loss of which neither he himself nor others need regret. Indeed, at times, death, viewed as a liberation from individuality, may even become a pleasant thought. Such reflections of course do not make physiological death any the easier to bear.

One can imagine Freud rereading this passage—almost twenty years after his remark in the letter to Fliess that *The Analysis of Sensations* was one of "the latest psychological books" having "the same kind of aims as my work"—and experiencing an uncanny sensation similar to that of seeing what one had thought was another person turn out to be one's own image. Mach was a physicist interested in psychology who worked on psychophysical parallelism, Freud a neurologist interested in psychology who worked in psychoanalysis. Each felt that important insights into his own work had been anticipated by philosophers, and each took pains to distinguish his own scientific findings from philosophical intuitions. But in the passage quoted above, the similarity between Mach and Freud must have seemed to Freud, at the precise moment when he was working on "The Uncanny" and *Beyond the Pleasure Principle*, almost overwhelming. As an example of how completely one's ego changes over a period of years, Mach reports the experience of looking at articles he had written twenty years earlier and finding them "quite foreign" (alien? dead?) to himself; and then, three sentences later, as a footnote to the statement that "Personally, people know themselves very poorly," he tells the story of not recognizing his mirror-image on two separate occasions. The association is clear: one's writings are an inscribed image of the self similar to one's mirror-image, and just as Mach has had the experience of looking at essays he had written twenty years earlier and not recognizing himself, so he has also had the experience of seeing his mirror-image and not recognizing himself.

The essay in which Freud refers to Mach's story was an old paper Freud had dug out of a drawer and was rewriting. Further, the Mach text that contains the story was one that Freud had read twenty years earlier. Thus, in rewriting an old paper on the uncanny during the middle of 1919, Freud was confronting an earlier written image of himself at the same time that he was reexperiencing the twenty-year-old written image of Mach in *The Analysis of Sensations.* Add to this the fact that, immediately after the sentence containing the footnote about not recognizing his double, Mach calls attention to his *own* revision of his original text, remarking that "When I wrote these lines in 1886, Ribot's admirable little book, *The Diseases of Personality* . . . was unknown to me." What Freud read in 1900 and quoted in 1919 was the second edition of *The Analysis of Sensations*—that is, Mach's own encounter with an earlier written image of himself. And the result of Mach's retrospective encounter was that an earlier book (Ribot's), which Mach had been unaware of at the time of the first writing, had to be acknowledged, in the second edition, as putting part of Mach's text in question on the grounds of both priority and broader knowledge—a moment that would have rendered transparent Freud's own concerns about originality and priority in rereading Mach. And Freud would not even have had the excuse Mach had in regard to Ribot, for Freud was aware of *The Analysis of Sensations* from the very beginning of his psychoanalytic writing. When Mach then goes on to remark that what "we so much dread in death, the annihilation of our permanency, actually occurs in life in abundant measure," he points out what seems to be a deathlike, unconscious operating principle in the self. And when he proceeds to distinguish between those valuable traits in the self which are "preserved in countless copies" and those traits whose loss is not to be regretted, and then relates this natural process by which traits die out of the self during life to the notion that "at times, death, viewed as a liberation from individuality, may even become a pleasant thought," he seems not only to make a distinction similar to that between the life instincts whose aim is survival and the death instincts whose ultimate aim is annihilation, but also to associate the instinct to survive with the act of writing, with that which "remains preserved in countless copies."

Suffice it to say that if Freud, at the time when he quoted Mach's story of doubling in "The Uncanny," was rereading *The Analysis of Sensations* in light of the death instinct and the compulsion to repeat for the survey of scientific data in *Beyond the Pleasure Principle*, then the context in which Mach tells of not recognizing his mirror-image would have fulfilled in Freud's case all the criteria of an uncanny experience in real life—an experience that would have been much more uncanny than the one involving the coincidental repetition of Hering's name which Freud reports in the essay. More uncanny because more threatening, for the experience could well have aroused Freud's fear that the similarity between Mach's insights and his own (which would have been threatening enough in itself to Freud's sense of his own originality) was *not* coincidental, the fear that Freud had absorbed more of Mach's ideas in his original reading of *The Analysis of Sensations* than he had realized, and that he had been unconsciously influenced by Mach's work in his own subsequent writings, until, in rereading Mach, he confronted that anxiety-ridden similarity and repressed it, the footnote on Mach being the trace of the repression.

Now, based on the hypersensitivity which Freud exhibits, in his published writings and his correspondence, to the question of priority and originality, it is no great insight to suggest that Freud suffered from an originality neurosis, nor much more of an insight to point out the connection between such a neurosis and the castration complex. For the threat in an originality neurosis is that the writings of an older man (Mach was Freud's senior by eighteen years), through their similarity and priority, preempt the possibility of originality for the younger man's writings and thus threaten the survival of the younger man's work—that is, they prefigure the death of the younger man's written corpus, prefigure it in this instance in a doubly uncanny manner through Mach's anticipation of the death instinct. The similarity between Mach's insights and Freud's would, then, fall into that category of experiences which are uncanny because they revive repressed infantile complexes, in this case the threat posed by the father to the son's potency and viability, the son's feeling of being a passive repetition of the original. In such a case, Mach could easily symbolize for Freud all those writers whose prior work Freud felt to be a threat to his own originality.

One such writer, Nietzsche, is a particularly menacing presence in both "The Uncanny" and *Beyond the Pleasure Principle*, and there is evidence to suggest that Freud's intellectual relationship to Nietzsche was tinged with oedipal anxieties. (In the triangle of Nietzsche, Lou Andreas-Salomé, and Freud, the role of intellectual mentor to the beautiful, intelligent Lou had been played first by the older man, Nietzsche, and then by Freud, and to judge from their correspondence one of the things that Lou and Freud discussed was the resemblances between Nietzsche's thought and Freud's.) In the essay on the uncanny, Freud refers to the uncanny effect of "the constant recurrence of the same thing . . . through several consecutive generations," and again, to the uncanny theme of "the unintended recurrence of the same thing." And in *Beyond the Pleasure Principle,* discussing the "daemonic" character which the compulsion to repeat gives to the actions of some neurotics, he remarks,

> This 'perpetual recurrence of the same thing' causes us no astonishment when it relates to *active* behaviour on the part of the person concerned and when we can discern in him an essential character-trait which always remains the same and which is compelled to find expression in a repetition of the same experiences. We are much more impressed by cases where the subject appears to have a *passive* experience, over which he has no influence, but in which he meets with a repetition of the same fatality.

Clearly, the allusion in each of the instances quoted is to Nietzsche's concept of "the eternal recurrence of the same" from *Thus Spoke Zarathustra,* part 3 (1884). The impulse which Freud evokes by the names "the compulsion to repeat" and "the death instinct" is, broadly speaking, an aspect of the same dynamic principle that Nietzsche named "the eternal recurrence of the same," just as Freud's "life instincts" or "sex instincts" are an aspect of the principle that Nietzsche named "the will to power." It is Zarathustra's role to proclaim two related concepts—the eternal recurrence of the same and the overman—concepts that are related because the overman is that theoretical being who is capable of willing the eternal recurrence of the same, capable of changing the endless recurrences of time and the death which time inevitably brings from something passively suffered to something actively willed, of raising that repetition (which seeks to return to an original state of sameness) from an unconscious compulsion to a conscious desire. Yet something very much like that is what Freud proclaims in *Beyond the Pleasure Principle,* for in identifying the death instinct (that compulsion to repeat whose ultimate goal is a return to the quiescence of the inorganic state), Freud tries to raise it from the instinctual level to the level of thought. In enunciating the principle that *"the aim of all life is death,"* that man's destiny is not personal immortality in an otherworld, Freud, like Nietzsche, aims to do away with the complex network of metaphysical illusions that are based on the belief in personal survival, aims to reconcile man to the reality of the human condition, an aim which Freud pursues in such later works as *The Future of an Illusion* (1927).

Yet in *The Analysis of Sensations*, published two years after *Zarathustra* (part 3), Mach, in denying the permanency of the ego and "individual immortality," aims at a similar clearing away of illusions, as indicated by the title of the first chapter, "Introductory Remarks: Antimetaphysical." His assertion that "The ego is just as little absolutely permanent as are bodies" might well have seemed to Freud an echo of the moment when Zarathustra's animals, discussing the eternal recurrence and the overman, tell Zarathustra, "The soul is as mortal as the body." It is precisely because Mach is aware of the apparent similarity, in terms of the effect on human conduct, of Nietzsche's antimetaphysical critique and his own that he goes out of his way to distinguish "the ethical ideal" which will be founded on the impermanency of the ego and the renunciation of individual immortality from "the ideal of an overweening Nietzschean 'superman'," he who wills the eternal recurrence of the same. Freud would have confronted, then, in *The Analysis of Sensations*, not only Nietzsche's seeming priority in this area of thought, but also what appeared to be Mach's prior attempt to circumvent that priority.

If the footnote on Mach in "The Uncanny" is the "vestigial trace" of an act of repression, if it marks the burial place, the encrypting of the image of the possible death of Freud's written corpus, then there are various ways in which the footnote's cryptic message can be translated. Through its symbolic language the footnote may say: just as Mach didn't recognize his double, so I don't recognize my double (Mach); turnabout is fair play; if Mach is not wrong in doing this, then I am not wrong in doing the same thing to Mach. (The footnote would then imply that though Mach is prior to Freud, he is no more original than Freud, for Mach has his own threatening predecessors whom *he* has tried to repress.) Or the footnote may say: just as Mach was not afraid of his own double, but simply disliked his appearance, so I am not afraid of my double (Mach), I simply don't like his looks. (However, Freud himself hints that this dislike of the double's appearance masks an original fear.) Or the footnote may say: if we let the similarity between Mach's experience of not recognizing his double and my own experience stand for all the recognized and unrecognized similarities between my work and the work of previous writers, then I hereby declare that those similarities are not significant enough to be included in the body of the text, they are of marginal importance. (The threat to the written corpus would thus be expelled from the body of the text and "buried in a footnote.") Yet Mach's own account of not recognizing his double was also given in a footnote to *The Analysis of Sensations*. Is Freud, then, repeating Mach once more in the very attempt to repress the fear of repeating Mach? The structure of Freud's footnote—the spatial doubling involved in each man's encounter with his mirror-image, which is in turn temporally doubled by the way Freud's experience repeats Mach's, which is itself a doubling of Freud's encounter with Mach's written image in *The Analysis of Sensations*—is like a house of mirrors; its doubling of doubles seems to insure that whichever way we translate the note's cryptic message, whichever way Freud tries to repress his fear of repeating Mach, Freud ends up repeating a strategy that Mach himself had previously used. The act of repression reinscribes the feared repetition that it is meant to repress, thus assuring the cycle of re-return and re-repression.

Keeping this structure in mind, let us turn back to the passage from Hart Crane's *The Bridge*. If in Freud's text we found that a quotation about the uncanny effect of doubling seemed to be a trace, a veiled image, of the writer's repressed fear of the death of his work, might we then expect to find that Crane's description of the bedlamite's leap from the Brooklyn Bridge, a form of death that seems to be an uncanny prefiguration of Crane's own suicide by drowning, contains a veiled quotation? Presenting itself as a kind of summation and commentary upon the American symbolist tradition, *The Bridge* abounds with quotations from, and allusions to, the works of Whitman, Poe, Melville, and Emily Dickinson. Moreover, Whitman and Poe appear as characters in "Cape Hatteras" and "The Tunnel" respectively. Yet it is not to any of these major writers that the faint echo in Crane's description of the suicide directs our attention, but rather to a minor nineteenth-century American poet. When Crane characterizes the bedlamite's death with the words, "A jest falls from the speechless caravan," we seem to recall somewhere in American poetry another silent "caravan" associated with death. I refer, of course, to the closing lines of William Cullen Bryant's "Thanatopsis," the most famous passage from Bryant's most famous poem and a standard text for memorization in American schools for decades. At the end of the poem—which seeks to assuage the fear of death through the love of nature, showing that the natural world which nurtures us continues this care by providing us our final resting place—the poet says:

> So live, that when thy summons comes to join
> The innumerable caravan, which moves
> To that mysterious realm, where each shall take
> His chamber in the silent halls of death,
> Thou go not, like the quarry-slave at night,
> Scourged to his dungeon, but, sustained and soothed

By an unfaltering trust, approach thy grave,
Like one who wraps the drapery of his couch
About him, and lies down to pleasant dreams.

Whether Crane's "speechless caravan" is a conscious or unconscious echo of Bryant's "innumerable caravan," at least one critic, R. W. B.
Lewis, has suggested that *The Bridge* does indeed owe a conscious debt
of influence to another Bryant poem, "The Fountain." And I would
contend that that debt, which is by no means an inconsiderable one, was
of a particularly threatening character to Crane. In "The Fountain,"
Bryant depicts the historical alteration of the American landscape through
the changes which the woodland fountain has witnessed in its natural
setting over the years. At least two sections of *The Bridge*—"The River"
and "The Dance"—appear to owe part of their general conception and
certain descriptive details, as well as their tone of visionary union with the
Indian world, to Bryant's account of the Indians being supplanted by the
white settlers. The reworking of descriptive details is perhaps the easiest of
these to illustrate. Thus, Bryant's depiction of the felling of the woods by
the white man's axe—"Then all around was heard the crash of trees /
Trembling awhile and rushing to the ground"—is echoed in Crane's
description of the thunderstorm in the forest—"The oak grove circles in a
crash of leaves." While Bryant's "ranks of spiky maize / Rose like a host
embattled" is echoed by Crane's address to the rain-god Maquokeeta, "Lo,
through what infinite seasons dost thou gaze— / Across what bivouacs of
thine angered slain, / And see'st thy bride immortal in the maize?"

Yet these debts are minor compared to the debt that Crane appears
to owe to the conclusion of Bryant's poem, where, in imagining the future
of the land, Bryant associates four image patterns whose symbolic interaction becomes a major structural element in *The Bridge*. "The Fountain"
ends:

> Here the sage,
> Gazing into thy self-replenished depth,
> Has seen eternal order circumscribe
> And bound the motions of eternal change,
> And from the gushing of thy simple fount
> Has reasoned to the mighty universe.
>
> Is there no other change for thee, that lurks
> Among the future ages? Will not man
> Seek out strange arts to wither and deform
> The pleasant landscape which thou makest green?
> Or shall the veins that feed thy constant stream

> Be choked in middle earth, and flow no more
> For ever, that the water-plants along
> Thy channel perish, and the bird in vain
> Alight to drink? Haply shall these green hills
> Sink, with the lapse of years, into the gulf
> Of ocean waters, and thy source be lost
> Amidst the bitter brine? Or shall they rise,
> Upheaved in broken cliffs and airy peaks,
> Haunts of the eagle and the snake, and thou
> Gush midway from the bare and barren steep?

The four image patterns linked here are: first, the circularization of power ("the motions of eternal change" are "circumscribed and bound" by the concentric circles of the pool which, by turning the power back upon itself, makes it self-replenishing); second, the fountain; third, the sinking/rising of the land; and fourth, the eagle and the snake.

The image of the circle dominates *The Bridge*, its great emblem being the arc of the bridge above the river and the arc of the tunnel below, the two together forming the circle of eternity through which the river of time flows. For Crane the circularization of power is, broadly speaking, a Platonic motif—the notion that energy turned back upon itself controls or orders itself without the loss of energy, like a fountain whose jet fills a circular pool that catches the water and replenishes the source of the fountain. Or like the suspension bridge whose counterbalanced forces Crane evokes as a "motion ever unspent in thy stride,/ Implicitly thy freedom staying thee!" But Crane also draws on Henry Adams' image of circular power, the dynamo, in passages that evoke the deadening mechanization of the circle. In "Cape Hatteras" he addresses the dynamo as "O murmurless and shrined / In oilrinsed circles of blind ecstasy!" and transferring this mechanistic image of the circle to the universe, Crane writes:

> But that star-glistered salver of infinity,
> The circle, blind crucible of endless space,
> Is sluiced by motion,—subjugated never.
> Adam and Adam's answer in the forest
> Left Hesperus mirrored in the lucid pool.
> Now the eagle dominates our days, is jurist
> Of the ambiguous cloud. We know the strident rule
> Of wings imperious. . . .

Crane later describes the propellers of the imperious eagle-airplanes as "marauding circles." In the passage quoted above, the circular power that Crane opposes to the blind, mechanical circles lies in the concentric rings of the lucid, mirroring pool of the intellect. Adam's answer to the "blind crucible of endless space" is language—the naming of the evening star, Hesperus, that leaves it mirrored in the pool of the mind. The circular power of language is further embodied in the self-referentiality of the poem; for though the bridge referred to in the poem is ostensibly the Brooklyn Bridge, it is also the poem called *The Bridge*. The poem's subject is the act of symbolization considered as a bridge between mind and world and between mind and mind. The bridging or bridgeship that the poem thematizes is wholly linguistic. Thus it is that the litany of names applied to the bridge in the opening and closing sections of the poem, many of which make no sense if the referent is the real Brooklyn Bridge, are perfectly comprehensible if the referent is the symbolic bridge, the bridge of symbolization.

Crane's use of the second and third image patterns—the fountain and the sinking/rising of the land—can best be illustrated by starting with a passage from "The River" in which Crane depicts the submersion of the Indian world by the white settlers:

> The old gods of the rain lie wrapped in pools
> Where eyeless fish curvet a sunken fountain
> And re-descend with corn from querulous crows.
> Such pilferings make up their timeless eatage,
> Propitiate them for their timber torn
> By iron, iron—always the iron dealt cleavage!
> They doze now, below axe and powder horn.

Crane's symbol for the ideal land that the original settlers of America dreamed of, the ideal land that has been submerged by greed and material-ism but that might some day reemerge, is the island continent of Atlantis, the beautiful, favored land that sank beneath the sea. As Plato tells the story in the *Critias*, the island of Atlantis belonged to the sea-god Poseidon. Enamored of a maiden named Clito who lived on a hill at the center of the island, Poseidon "fortified the hill where she had her abode by a fence of alternate rings of sea and land, smaller and greater, one within another. He fashioned two such round wheels . . . of earth and three of sea from the very center of the island, at uniform distances. . . . The island left at their center he adorned with his own hand . . . causing two fountains to flow from underground springs, one warm, one cold, and the soil to send up abundance of food plants of all kinds." At first, Poseidon's descendants by Clito were virtuous; they "found the weight of their gold and other possessions a light load. Wealth made them not drunken with wanton-ness." But in later generations the people of Atlantis took "the infection of wicked covetousness and pride of power," and for this they were punished by the gods—their island vanished beneath the waves.

In the "Cutty Sark" section, Crane associates Atlantis, a sunken land of Platonic concentric circles at whose center were fountains, with the sperm whale, whose islandlike body rises and sinks beneath the sea and bears a fountain in its back. In *Moby-Dick*, the chapter describing the whale's spout is called "The Fountain," and clearly Melville is the proper allusive background here, for this section of *The Bridge* begins with an epigraph from one of his poems and the sailor in "Cutty Sark" is described in terms reminiscent of Ishmael:

> Murmurs of Leviathan he spoke
> and rum was Plato in our heads . . .
>
> "—that spiracle!" he shot a finger out the door . . .
> "O life's a geyser. . . ."

Like Atlantis, the whale with the fountain in its back symbolizes for Crane that bountifulness of nature which has been submerged and almost destroyed by human greed and by a blind will-to-power whose goal is the absolute domination of physical nature. As a counterpoint to the narrative line of "Cutty Sark," the song of "Atlantis Rose" weaves into the text its image of *"teased remnants of the skeletons of cities— / and galleries, galleries of watergutted lava."*

The fourth image pattern, the eagle and the snake, is an almost universal symbol of the bounding extremes (the highest and the lowest), while the conjunction of the eagle and the snake, as in the feathered serpent, is a symbol of the coincidence of opposites. The image, which can be found in contexts as various as the Mexican flag and *Thus Spoke Zarathustra*, is used by Crane as a symbol of the spatial and temporal integration of the idealized nature-world of the Indians. In "The River" the poet senses the presence of the virgin body of the continent, the maiden Pocahontas, beneath the commercial disfiguration of the land and says,

> . . . I knew her body there,
> Time like a serpent down her shoulder, dark,
> And space, an eaglet's wing, laid on her hair.

This image leads immediately into the passage describing the Indian rain-gods who "lie wrapped in pools" containing a "sunken fountain," and it prepares us for the moment in "The Dance" when the rain-god Maquokeeta, with "eagle feathers" down his back, arrives as the thunderbird during the rain dance—that is, the snake dance—to fertilize the virgin land, feathered serpent and fountain both being symbols of fertilization and harmonious union. "The Dance" ends with the image of "The serpent with the eagle in the boughs." The modern, mechanical parodies of the eagle of space and the serpent of time are the death-dealing airplanes of "Cape Hatteras" and the nightmarish serpent-train of "The Tunnel"; yet in the final section, "Atlantis," Crane reaffirms his belief that the inseminating power of the poetic word, the phallic bridging power of language, can raise the ideal land with its bountiful fountains and harmonious concentric rings, the land where "rainbows ring / The serpent with the eagle in the leaves."

I have discussed Crane's use of these related image patterns at some length not only to show how substantial a debt Crane owes to Bryant's poem, but also to show how far he has surpassed Bryant in his complex interweaving of these images. Indeed, Crane has so completely transformed the minor art of his source into the major art of his own poem that it is difficult to see how he could feel threatened enough by his debt to Bryant to repress it, particularly when he acknowledges in *The Bridge* his debts to much more talented and, one would presume, more threatening writers, such as Whitman and Poe. Yet I would suggest that it is precisely in Crane's strategy of thematizing his literary debts to writers like Whitman and Poe that the repression of Bryant is rooted; for one of the things that Crane aims at in portraying himself as Whitman's younger brother in "Cape Hatteras" and in confronting the image of his own physical death through the image of Poe's death in "The Tunnel" is what we might call "achievement by association." Crane treats these and other major nineteenth-century American writers as if he were their rightful heir and prospective equal. The possibility that there exists any lesser poetic context in which his work could be interpreted is never entertained for a moment in the poem. It would not matter, then, how much Crane had transcended Bryant's use of these same images; the strategy of *The Bridge* would simply not admit the appropriateness of any comparison between Crane and Bryant.

Yet I would argue that the echo of Bryant's "Thanatopsis" in "To Brooklyn Bridge," considered as a vestigial trace of Crane's repressed debt to Bryant, depends upon an even more complicated mechanism of repression. In comparing the contexts of Crane's "speechless caravan" and Bryant's "innumerable caravan," one is struck by a curious reversal. Crane's caravan moving across the Brooklyn Bridge clearly represents the living, while Bryant's caravan journeying to "the silent halls of death" just as clearly represents the dead, yet Crane attributes to the living caravan a quality generally associated with the dead—speechlessness—while he describes the bedlamite's suicidal death as a linguistic act, a jest (in the sense both of a joke and a heroic deed). Now if we label the various elements in these two poetic contexts, we come up with a list like this: (1) a crowd of people moving across a bridge; (2) the vast numbers of the dead; (3) the living described as if they were dead, that is, the speechlessness of the living dead; and (4) suicidal death as a linguistic act of ambiguous significance. Keeping these elements in mind, let us look at the passage in "The Tunnel" where Crane, during the nightmarish subway ride under the river, explicitly confronts his own physical death in the image of Poe's death:

> And why do I often meet your visage here,
> Your eyes like agate lanterns—on and on
> Below the toothpaste and the dandruff ads?
> —And did their riding eyes right through your side,
> And did their eyes like unwashed platters ride?
> And Death, aloft,—gigantically down
> Probing through you—toward me, O evermore!
> And when they dragged your retching flesh,
> Your trembling hands that night through Baltimore—
> That last night on the ballot rounds, did you
> Shaking, did you deny the ticket, Poe?
>
> For Gravesend Manor change at Chambers Street.
> The platform hurries along to a dead stop.
>
> The intent escalator lifts a serenade
> Stilly
> Of shoes, umbrellas, each eye attending its shoe, then
> Bolting outright somewhere above where streets
> Burst suddenly in rain . . .

What catches our attention in this passage is the phrase "each eye attending its shoe," an echo of one of the most famous passages in Eliot's *The Waste Land*. Evoking the living dead of the modern metropolis, Eliot writes,

> Unreal City,
> Under the brown fog of a winter dawn,
> A crowd flowed over London Bridge, so many,
> I had not thought death had undone so many.
> Sighs, short and infrequent, were exhaled,
> And each man fixed his eyes before his feet.

The line "I had not thought death had undone so many" is, as Eliot points out in a footnote, an allusion to the moment in canto 3 of *The Inferno* when Dante sees the living dead, those "who lived without blame, and without praise" and thus, refused by both heaven and hell, "have no hope of death" yet lead a "blind life so mean, that they are envious of every other lot" (Dante Alighieri). And the next line—"Sighs, short and infrequent, were exhaled"—is an allusion, as Eliot again points out in a note, to the moment in canto 4 of *The Inferno* when Dante, having entered the first circle of hell, first sees the dead and notices that they speak no words, but only sigh. We recall that in between these two moments Dante is refused passage across the dismal river into hell by the steersman, Charon, because Dante is not dead, and that at the end of canto 3 Dante loses consciousness and reawakens at the beginning of canto 4 on the other side of the river, the loss of consciousness apparently being a symbolic death which allows his entrance into the realm of the dead.

Now one can see how Crane's allusion to the passage from *The Waste Land* is meant to associate the lifeless swarms in the subway with the living dead of Eliot's "unreal city" and those of Dante's inferno, as well as to associate Crane's subway journey under the East River with Dante's passage across the dismal river into hell, both poets symbolically enacting their own deaths. But what is particularly significant for our purposes is that the passage from *The Waste Land*, with its allusions to Dante, contains all the elements that we had enumerated in the comparison of Crane's "speechless caravan" and Bryant's "innumerable caravan": the crowd flowing over the bridge; the vast numbers of the dead; the speechlessness of the living dead; and an individual death that is both self-willed and linguistic, that is, symbolic. Whereas the death in "To Brooklyn Bridge" was a suicide described as a linguistic act, a "jest," Crane's confronting of his own fate through the image of Poe's death, and Dante's fictive loss of consciousness in order to enter the world of the dead are both symbolic deaths, each poet's self-willed imaging of his own fate. Yet I have suggested that the description of the suicide in "To Brooklyn Bridge" is also an image of the poet's death—a more or less literal image of Crane's suicide by drowning and a veiled image of his feared death as a poet due to the unoriginality of his work—an unoriginality symbolized by quotation, by the repetition of prior work. What this suggests in turn is an analogy between the "self-willed" character of death in an actual suicide on the one hand and in a writer's symbolic representation of his own death on the other. But what we make of this analogy depends in this case on what we make of the similarity between the image pattern evoked by the echo of Bryant's "Thanatopsis" in the description of the suicide and that evoked by the echo of Eliot's *The Waste Land* in

Crane's imagining of his own fate. Could it be that the really menacing presence for Crane in *The Bridge* is not Bryant but Eliot?

We do know from Crane's correspondence that from its inception *The Bridge* was meant to be a reply to the pessimism of *The Waste Land,* an "affirmation of experience, and to that extent . . . 'positive' rather than 'negative' in the sense that *The Waste Land* is negative," as Crane said in a letter to Selden Rodman in May 1930 (*Letters*). Crane's myth of the inseminating power of the poetic imagination, its power to resurrect Atlantis and its fertile fountain, is meant to counterbalance Eliot's myth of the impotent Fisher King and the drying up of the land. In the year he began work on *The Bridge,* Crane wrote to Gorham Munson:

> You already know, I think, that my work for the past two years (those meagre drops!) has been more influenced by Eliot than any other modern. . . .
>
> There is no one writing in English who can command so much respect, to my mind, as Eliot. However, I take Eliot as a point of departure toward an almost complete reverse of direction. His pessimism is amply justified, in his own case. But I would apply as much of his erudition and technique as I can absorb and assemble toward a more positive, or (if [I] must put it so in a sceptical age) ecstatic goal. . . . Certainly the man has dug the ground and buried hope as deep and direfully as it can ever be done. . . .
>
> After this perfection of death—nothing is possible in motion but a resurrection of some kind. Or else, as everyone persists in announcing in the deep and dirgeful *Dial,* the fruits of civilization are entirely harvested. Everyone, of course, wants to die as soon and as painlessly as possible! Now is the time for humor, and the Dance of Death. All I know through very much suffering and dullness . . . is that it interests me to still affirm certain things.

In another letter to Gorham Munson some three years later (March 5, 1926), Crane announced the completion of the "Atlantis" section:

> the finale of *The Bridge* is written, the other five or six parts are in feverish embryo. They will require at least a year or more for completion; however bad this work may be, it ought to be hugely and unforgivably, distinguishedly bad. In a way it's a test of materials as much as a test of one's imagination. *Is* the last statement sentimentally made by Eliot,
>
> > "This is the way the world ends,
> > This is the way the world ends,—
> > Not with a bang but a whimper."
>
> is this acceptable or not as the poetic determinism of our age?! I, of course, can say no, to myself, and believe it. But in the face of a stern

conviction of death on the part of the only group of people whose verbal sophistication is likely to take an interest in a style such as mine—what can I expect? However, I know my way by now, regardless. I shall at least continue to grip with the problem without relaxing into the easy acceptance (in the name of "elegance, nostalgia, wit, splenetic splendor") of death which I see most of my friends doing.

Yet in a letter to Waldo Frank only three months later (June 20, 1926), the doubt that Crane expressed to Munson had turned into a general disillusionment with the project of *The Bridge:*

Emotionally I should like to write *The Bridge;* intellectually judged the whole theme and project seems more and more absurd. A fear of personal impotence in this matter wouldn't affect me half so much as the convictions that arise from other sources . . . I had what I thought were authentic materials that would have been a pleasurable-agony of wrestling, eventuating or not in perfection—at least being worthy of the most supreme efforts I could muster.

These "materials" were valid to me to the extent that I presumed them to be (articulate or not) at least organic and active factors in the experience and perceptions of our common race, time and belief. The very idea of a bridge, of course, is a form peculiarly dependent on such spiritual convictions. It is an act of faith besides being a communication. . . . however great their subjective significance to me is concerned— these forms, materials, dynamics are simply non-existent in the world. I may amuse and delight and flatter myself as much as I please—but I am only evading a recognition and playing Don Quixote in an immorally conscious way.

. . . The bridge as a symbol today has no significance beyond an economical approach to shorter hours, quicker lunches, behaviorism and toothpicks. And inasmuch as the bridge is a symbol of all such poetry as I am interested in writing it is my present fancy that a year from now I'll be more contented working in an office than before. Rimbaud was the last great poet that our civilization will see—he let off all the great cannon crackers in Valhalla's parapets, the sun has set theatrically several times since while Laforgue, Eliot and others of that kidney have whimpered fastidiously.

During the next four years of work on *The Bridge*, Crane's attitude toward the poem swung back and forth between intellectual disillusionment and emotional affirmation, a doubleness toward the work that is, I would suggest, reflected in his description of the suicide's leap from the bridge as a "jest." At times Crane thought that in projecting a modern epic of the American imagination he had involved himself in a quixotic delusion, a delusion that could only end in poetic self-destruction, a suicidal leap from *The Bridge*—either in the sense that he would be unable to finish his much-publicized epic or that the completed poem would turn out to be a ridiculous failure. In either case Crane thought that he would be a laughingstock, "a jest," and that his poetic career would be destroyed. Yet at other times Crane felt that the writing of *The Bridge* was a leap of faith, a leap which might or might not turn out to be suicidal, but which had to be made. He felt that he must run the risk of his death as a poet, the risk of becoming a jest, if he was to achieve the *beau geste* he projected; indeed, as the work progressed, he felt that the very taking of that risk was a *beau geste* in itself, that even if *The Bridge* turned out to be a failure, it would "be hugely and unforgivably, distinguishedly bad," that if the poem did not exhibit the power of imaginative achievement, at least it would indicate the scope of imaginative desire.

What is clear from Crane's correspondence is that the doubleness of his attitude toward the poem is directly related to the doubleness of his attitude toward Eliot. On the one hand, he admired Eliot's poetic artistry, but on the other he deplored his pessimism, that "perfection of death" which he found in *The Waste Land*. In writing *The Bridge*, Crane planned to use the poetic artistry of *The Waste Land* against the content of *The Waste Land*, planned to use Eliot's "erudition and technique" to achieve "an almost complete reverse of direction." Yet as Crane worked on *The Bridge* he seems to have realized that Eliot's artistic technique and the content of Eliot's poetry were not really two different things, that if one adopted the technique, then one got the pessimistic content along with it. Eliot's immediate poetic tradition was that of the French symbolists and the English decadents, a tradition that responded to the loss of belief in God and the ideal otherworld by making art the highest value in life. As Nietzsche says in *The Birth of Tragedy*, "it is only as an *aesthetic phenomenon* that existence and the world are eternally *justified.*" Or as Walter Pater says in the conclusion to *The Renaissance*, "we are all under sentence of death but with a sort of indefinite reprieve . . . we have an interval, and then our place knows us no more. Some spend this interval in listlessness, some in high passions, the wisest, at least among 'the children of this world,' in art and song. . . . Of such wisdom the poetic passion, the desire of beauty, the love of art for its own sake, has most."

Yet the problem with the religion of art is that what starts out to be life-enhancing ends up being life-negating. In his critique of the Christian afterlife, Nietzsche points out that the effect of the absolute valuation of the otherworld is the disvaluation of this world; in comparison to the ideal afterlife, the real life of the present is made to seem worthless. But what occurs in the religion of art is much the same: the aesthetic ideal tends to become located not in a fictive otherworld but in the historical past, a past whose accumulated riches must inevitably make the present seem worthless in comparison. The technique of fragmented cultural allusion employed by Eliot in *The Waste Land* and by Pound in *Hugh Selwyn Mauberley* and *The Cantos* involves the amassing of the past's riches against the present, the marshalling of the vast numbers of the great dead to do battle with the living dead. In a letter to Herbert Weinstock in April 1930, Crane said that it took him "nearly five years, with innumerable readings" to convince himself of "the essential unity" of *The Waste Land*: "And *The Bridge* is at least as complicated in its structure and inferences as *The Waste Land*—perhaps more so" (*Letters*). Yet it was Crane's use of the technique of fragmented cultural allusion in *The Bridge* that probably led him, after his enthusiastic start in composing "Atlantis," to write to Waldo Frank that "The form of the poem arises out of a past that so overwhelms the present with its worth and vision that I'm at a loss to explain my delusion that there exist any real links between that past and a future destiny worthy of it. The 'destiny' is long since completed, perhaps the little last section of my poem is a hangover echo of it—but it hangs suspended somewhere in ether like an Absalom by his hair" (*Letters*).

Setting out to make a positive statement about the unifying / vivifying power of the creative imagination in response to Eliot's pessimism, Crane located himself in that art-for-art's-sake tradition which posits the imagination as an absolute value, a tradition that makes art not just the highest value in life but a value higher than life, an aesthetic ideal to which the dedicated artist ends up sacrificing himself. In the hagiography of the religion of art as formulated by the French symbolists, Edgar Allan Poe is an early martyr, and it is Poe's martyrdom, the sacrifice of his life in pursuing his aesthetic ideal in a materialistic society, that Crane makes the image of his own fate in "The Tunnel."

Now it is one thing to die like Poe if one's works can live like Poe's, but it is quite another thing to die like Poe when one has begun to feel that the "past so overwhelms the present with its worth and vision" that no major artistic achievement is possible, that no present or future writing will ever be able to survive like Poe's. If one thinks that a " 'destiny' is long since completed," that "Rimbaud was the last great poet that our civilization will see," then the self-sacrifice of the artist's life to the aesthetic ideal, an ideal that can no longer be approached in any realistic sense, begins to seem like deluded self-destruction. Confronting this dilemma in the "Quaker Hill" section of *The Bridge*, Crane begins with an epigraph attributed to Isadora Duncan: "I see only the ideal. But no ideals have ever been fully successful on this earth"; and ends

> So, must we from the hawk's far stemming view,
> Must we descend as worm's eye to construe
> Our love of all we touch, and take it to the Gate
> As humbly as a guest who knows himself too late,
> His news already told? Yes, while the heart is wrung,
> Arise—yes, take this sheaf of dust upon your tongue!
> In one last angelus lift throbbing throat—
> Listen, transmuting silence with that silly note
>
> Of pain that Emily, that Isadora knew!
> While high from dim elm-chancels hung with dew,
> That triple-noted clause of moonlight—
> Yes, whip-poor-will, unhusks the heart of fright
> Breaks us and saves, yes, breaks the heart, yet yields
> That patience that is armour and that shields
> Love from despair—when love forsees the end—
> Leaf after autumnal leaf
> break off,
> descend—
> descend—

In trying to write a modern epic of the creative imagination, Crane had begun to feel like "a guest who knows himself too late,/His news already told." Though he could reconcile himself to the fact of physical death, the possible death of his work—that his poetry might be a "sheaf of dust"—was another matter. What defense, what armor or shield, was possible against the image of the death of his written corpus, an image that threatened to become a self-fulfilling prefiguration by destroying the affirming energy of his imagination through despair? Whatever that defense might be, it was clear that it would have to be a defense against Eliot, for Crane realized that in adopting Eliot's "erudition and technique" in order to make a positive statement whose antithetical starting point was the pessimism of *The Waste Land,* he had outwitted himself. Setting out to confute Eliot's pessimistic rule, Crane found himself in danger of becoming an example of that rule. Crane simply had to free himself and his poem from Eliot, but the problem was, that in terms of both technique and antithetical content, *The Waste Land* was so much a part of *The Bridge* that to repress Eliot directly, to psychically kill him, would destroy *The Bridge* and finish Crane as a poet. Furthermore, Eliot was one of the leaders of that "group of people whose verbal sophistication" Crane looked to for an appreciation of his complex style, that group whose influence he counted on to introduce his poem favorably to a wider audience. Crane sent "The Tunnel," with its image of Poe's death and its echo of The Waste Land, to Eliot at The Criterion, and Eliot published it. And in a letter (September 12, 1927) to his benefactor Otto Kahn, Crane bragged about this acceptance: "I have been especially gratified by the reception accorded me by The Criterion, whose director Mr. T. S. Eliot, is representative of the most exacting literary standards of our times" (Letters).

Faced, then, with both the need to free himself from Eliot's influence and the virtual impossibility of any direct repression or overt repudiation of Eliot, Crane, by one of those elliptical associations that characterize his poetic style, linked Eliot, whose Waste Land represented the "perfection of death," with Bryant, the poet of "Thanatopsis" and the "Hymn to Death," thereby superimposing upon one poet of death the repression of another poet of death. In this case, the echo of Bryant's "Thanatopsis" in the description of the suicide would be less a vestigial trace of the repression of Bryant than a trace of the mechanism by which Bryant and Eliot were associated so that the repression of Bryant could serve as the symbolic repression of Eliot. Considered from one point of view, the repression of Bryant would be overdetermined by the association with Eliot; while from another point of view, Bryant would serve as a screen-figure for Eliot, thus allowing the attempt to satisfy the wished-for repression of the modern poet of death but not allowing that direct negation or psychic killing of the antithetical double which would turn out to be the self-destruction of The Bridge. However, it would not, I think, be accurate to say that Bryant is simply a substitute for Eliot if by "substitute" one meant a figure whose sole purpose was to represent another figure. Bryant is present in The Bridge for other reasons than to serve as Eliot's scapegoat, and given the psychological mechanism of The Bridge, Bryant's repression would occur, Eliot or no. I would argue, then, that because of the associative link between Bryant and Eliot as poets of death, the image of Eliot is simply allowed to ride double on the preexisting repression of Bryant, so that the symbolic repression of Eliot occurs as if by coincidence, thus keeping uncompromised Crane's ambivalent attitude toward Eliot.

Granting all this, we are left, then, with the problem of how to translate the cryptic message of the suicide's leap from the bridge. If the echo of Bryant's "innumerable caravan" of the dead by Crane's "speechless caravan" is meant to characterize the people on the bridge as the living dead and thus equate them with the lifeless masses crossing London Bridge in The Waste Land, then the bedlamite's leap would be a rejection of the Eliotic bridge of sighs and its condemned masses. But what is the significance of that rejection? Does it represent an act of despair, a decision that it is better to be one of the dead than one of the living dead? Or does it represent an act of affirmation, an attempt to maintain the possibility of an aesthetic ideal to which the artist can sacrifice his life, an attempt to make one's own death the ultimate aesthetic (symbolic) act simply by demonstrating that death is not a meaningless event that we passively (impotently) suffer but an action to which meaning can be given by willing the form that one's death takes. In this case, the jest/*geste* would signify, through the self-destruction of the artist's power in his failed quest for an aesthetic absolute, the scope of the artist's desire; it would affirm the artist's belief that death is not a means to escape the condition of the living dead, but a means to join the great dead who, because they sacrificed their lives to their art, have survived in their works.

The same ambiguous significance that attaches to the suicide in the poem—an act of despair or an act of affirmation—informs Crane's own death as well, and it is in this context that a final comparison of Crane's and Freud's figurations of death may be made. Faced with death's loss of meaning because of the loss of belief in God and an afterlife, Freud and Crane attempt to preserve the meaningfulness of death without falling back into metaphysical illusions—attempt on the one hand to confront death realistically as the annihilation of the personal self, and on the other to keep death's obliteration of the individual bearer of meaning from putting death itself beyond the control of meaning.

Through his notion of an unconscious death instinct (which the notion itself raises to the level of consciousness in a dictum like "*the aim of all life is death*"), Freud tries to remove death from an area beyond human control (that is, the unconscious) by giving it a teleological significance within the myth of a natural return to origins (the living organism's instinctive compulsion to return to the inorganic state from which it originally derived), tries to change man's helpless passivity before the meaningless through/into the active control of naming. Yet the danger of this approach is that Freud's notion of death as the aim of life can easily be interpreted as a justification for suicide. Freud seems to address this possibility when he notes that the self-preservative instincts "are component instincts whose function it is to assure that the organism shall follow its own path to death, and to ward off any possible ways of returning to inorganic existence other than those which are immanent in the organism. . . . What we are left with is the fact that the organism wishes to die only in its own fashion. Thus these guardians of life, too, were originally myrmidons of death. Hence arises the paradoxical situation that the living organism struggles most energetically against events (dangers, in fact) which might help it to attain its life's aim rapidly—by a kind of short-circuit. Such behaviour is, however, precisely what characterizes purely instinctual as contrasted with intelligent efforts" (1920). Freud himself describes this as an "extreme view of the self-preservative instincts," one that needs to be balanced by other insights; but it is a view that reveals Freud's intention to preserve death's meaning by making death part of a natural design "immanent in the organism." In section 6 of *Beyond the Pleasure Principle* he is even more explicit. Discussing our "belief in the internal necessity of dying," Freud says, "Perhaps we have adopted the belief because there is some comfort in it. If we are to die ourselves, and first to lose in death those who are dearest to us, it is easier to submit to a remorseless law of nature, to the sublime Aranke [Necessity], than to a chance which might perhaps have been escaped."

In place of the Judeo-Christian notion of death's meaning, Freud proposes a scientific version of the Greek concept of willing (submitting to, concurring in) the sublime Necessity. Freud's project of raising to the level of will that "remorseless law of nature" whose biological expression is the death instinct clearly shows itself in his characterization of instinctual behavior as if it were volitional ("the organism *wishes* to die only in its own fashion"), as if the design inherent in this "law of nature" resulted from something like the Schopenhauerian "world will." Yet if the avoidance of those very dangers which would shorten the organism's natural path to death is precisely what distinguishes instinctual *as opposed* to intelligent behavior, then Freud's project of raising the death instinct to the level of intelligent action would seem to do away with this instinctual avoidance of an immediate achievement of the goal, would seem to make that shortening of the path to death "natural" for—immanent within—a self-conscious organism, one that knew its ultimate goal and could achieve it immediately by suicide. Freud realized that the correlative of the Greek notion of willing the beautiful Necessity was the equally Greek notion that what is best for man is never to be born and what is next best is to die soon. And the problem of suicide, implicit in raising the death instinct to the level of consciousness, remains unresolved in *Beyond the Pleasure Principle.*

One senses in Freud's project the influence of Nietzsche's *The Birth of Tragedy* and its ideal of Dionysian wisdom, of tragic joy in the annihilation of the personal self. Freud would have man will the sublime Necessity on the grounds of the reality principle; while Nietzsche would have man will the beautiful Ananke on aesthetic (nonmoral) grounds; yet for Nietzsche these aesthetic grounds *are* the reality principle, because in this world coming-to-be and passing-away result solely from the innocent play of opposites: "play as artists and children engage in it, exhibits coming-to-be and passing away, structuring and destroying, without any moral additive, in forever equal innocence. And as children and artists play, so plays the ever-living fire. It constructs and destroys, all in innocence" (*Philosophy in Tragic Age*).

Crane's attempt to preserve the meaningfulness of death by maintaining the possibility of the artist's self-sacrifce to an aesthetic ideal relies heavily on Nietzsche's thought (Nietzsche was one of Crane's favorite writers, and the adjective *Nietzschean* was one of Crane's highest terms of praise) and in particular on the notion found in *The Birth of Tragedy* that in song and dance the artist himself becomes his own work of art. Indeed, there is a sense in which Crane's most moving poem is the aesthetic figure of his own life; and that poem's most moving moment is its almost sacramental closure. Unlike the sacrifice of one's life to a religious ideal whose compensation is the survival of the self in a glorified afterlife, the sacrifice of the artist's life to an aesthetic ideal can have, as an annihilation of the self, only a prefigurative compensation, that is, a compensatory prefiguration. For both Freud and Crane, the ability to come to terms with the fact of their physical deaths involves the confrontation with the written figuration of that death; but the figuration of one's own death depends on an illusion (as a figure it implies the continued presence, as an observer of the figure, of the very self whose annihilation it depicts), an illusion that encrypts the sense of the self's survival in the image of its nonsurvival. But this compensatory prefiguration must itself, then, be protected from the image of its own possible death due to unoriginality. Thus, for the analyst as for the artist, the willing of the sublime Necessity, the acceptance of death as the annihilation of the personal self, depends precisely on the repression of the possible annihilation of the figure of that death, the written self.

DONALD PEASE

Blake, Crane, Whitman, and Modernism:
A Poetics of Pure Possibility

What of the poetics and metaphysics of the future tense, that strange resource whereby the human mind pre-empts a tomorrow which the living speaker will not experience and whose very existence is a piece of syntactic inference? Is poetry, in some fundamental sense, always part remembrance and part prophecy — the very reality of past and future being wholly a convention of language?

—GEORGE STEINER, *Extraterritorial*

W
illiam Blake has always been a problem for literary historians. Although his dates fall roughly within the romantic period, no philosophy of romanticism can adequately accommodate his visionary excesses. Utterly opposed both to the abstractive advances of empirical science and to the organicist resistance to those advances, inimical to Wordsworth as well as to Locke, Blake was the exponent of a vision that did not find a place in his age. Consequently, Blake's radically marginal status manages even today to disrupt the imperial ambitions of literary historians intent on placing him within a sequential framework. Immanent to a particular period, yet no less transcendent, Blake's poetry points beyond the givens of the familiar landscape in which

From *PMLA*, vol. 96 (January 1981). Copyright © 1981 by Modern Language Association.

it is located historically, points not to past elements in a literary tradition but to possibilities that do not yet exist. Blake always stands before rather than behind the historians—awaiting his place.

Blake's pull toward the future, however, has made him the ancestor of a peculiar literary tradition. His independence of his past has turned him into a forerunner of modernism, a tradition definable by its denial of historical continuity. Of course Blake's inclusion within the discourse of modernism only reiterates his nonsynchronous status. For a tradition eager to confirm the power of discontinuity, however, Blake's non-synchronism, as the sign of his epistemological break with the past, becomes a desirable trait. But Blake is no more settled in the modernist period than he was in the romantic. Indeed his presence in the later period exposes the contradiction at the very core of modernism: through its adoption of Blake, modernism both confirms its historical discontinuity and acknowledges a need to legitimize this discontinuity by locating its ancestral roots. Perhaps we should take a closer look at this paradox, since in the course of this essay we will revaluate Blake's placement within a "modernist" tradition.

Heuristically defined, modernism refers both to an act—without a past—and to a literature about that act. Because language is intrinsically mediational, modernist literature cannot *be* that act but can only be *about* that act. Thus modernism invariably traces a frustrating double movement; it can never coincide with the present moment, which is its subject. Paul de Man has described the situation with all the sympathy his irony allows:

> The continuous goal of modernity, the desire to break out of literature toward the reality of the moment, prevails in its turn, folding back upon itself, engenders the repetition and continuation of literature. Thus modernity, which is fundamentally a falling away from literature and a repetition of history, also acts as the principle that gives literature duration and historical existence.

However resourceful in illuminating the double sense of the word, this description still does not explain modernists like T. S. Eliot, who lament rather than affirm modernity's discontinuity with the past. But while such apparently eccentric responses may well give us reason to pause, a moment's reflection should suffice to prove that even they do not disrupt the modernist project so much as they activate its latent powers. For is not the feeling of discontinuity only the shadowy counter responses that is fated to accompany freedom from inherited patterns? Certainly the rhetoric of modernism makes this compensatory relation clear, for the joyful release from the "dead hand of convention" can find its balancing trope—after, that is, the inevitable recoil from the anarchic surrender to experience—only in an agonizing "disinheritance, a loss of tradition, belief, and meaning." Although these two responses—triumphant joy and bereft anxiety—most assuredly conflict, they do so more in a field of controlled tension than as mutual cancellations; we could even say that each ironically includes, gives duration to, the other.

Would we violate this balance of power if we argued that the sense of displacement from a past represses the anxiety over the even deeper loss of the present moment in the inevitable formalness of literature? While no one would deny literature its formal quality, the modernist must deny the conservative, authoritarian, "traditional" element intrinsic to all literary forms, even if the denial assumes the form of a sensed discontinuity with the past. But does the resultant sense of disinheritance conceal a wish to be free of form? Certainly the impasse engendered by the inherently generic, hence inevitably historical, quality of poetic forms has led many modernist poets to turn iconoclasm into art, to intermingle the conservative act of making forms with the rebellious act of decreating them or, somewhat less violently, of affirming the self-reflexive quality of the work. The poetry then withdraws all referential indexes and becomes a pure act of mind. But do not even these transformalist strategies, these self-reflexive, self-consuming, or self-enacting projects, all indicate a desire to reunite with the present moment? And, conversely, do not all these *causa sui* enterprises inevitably conceal, perhaps as their originating repression, the consciousness of their historicity, the awareness that they cannot be represented and present at the same time? Maybe the self-defeating quality of these projects becomes too clear when we reflect that even iconoclasm has a tradition; nevertheless, we need only consider the applicability of the terms "self-consuming," "self-reflexive," and "self-enacting" to poems throughout literary history to verify a lingering suspicion: all modernist strategies either have a past or make one possible as soon as they appear. Regardless of how hard modernists try, they cannot evade a *tradition* of the new.

We need not pursue this point too far, however, because it has already been preempted by Harold Bloom. With the strength engendered by the modernists' need to repress their precursors' influences, Bloom exploits the complex relations between past and present American and British poets to isolate their shared sense of a "strong" belatedness. Bloom's theory "solves" the dilemma of the joyfully spontaneous yet pathetically transitory modern poet by exposing the quest for originality as a repression of the poet's "election" by a precursor. Here I should like, however, to "swerve" quite consciously away from Bloom's powerful reversals and offer a perspective on his oedipal model, for our preceding discussion facilitates a surprising insight: *it is not the modernist poet in relation with the precursor but the poet in relation with the present moment that elicits the oedipal model.*

When we apply the logic of the Oedipus complex to what we have called the paradox of modernism we find that modernist poets, in their wish to coincide with the present moment, evoke a free origin; but their language inevitably blocks an unmediated relation with this origin and, consequently, instills a sense of belatedness. When Bloom confronts this modernist complex, with all the intimations of mortality endemic to it, he transforms it into an ephebe-precursor relationship, thereby equating the mediating or blocking aspect of language with a precursor. But such an equation overlooks the problem of a representational model of poetic language. By relocating the belated poet's wish in the precursor's poem, Bloom presupposes that the ephebe's desire must first have been actualized and not merely re-presented in that poem. Now if, as has been suggested, the later poet's desire to be original is really the desire to coincide with the radical originality of the present moment—the one act no literature, not even a precursor's, can ever bring to realization—Bloom has not resolved but only repeated, at one remove, the paradox of modernity. We might even say that Bloom himself has successfully repressed the modernist complex by oedipalizing it, for through the fiction of the precursor Bloom can fulfill the wish to achieve the full presence of the present as an unquestioned fact that is attainable, alas, only in the past.

Yet this paradigmatic modern wish, as a representative version of what Martin Heidegger calls the "will's revenge against time passing," needs to be questioned. Perhaps, following Heidegger's suggestion, we can relocate the problem of modernism, not in the poet's inevitably belated relation to the moment, but in the representational model of language itself and "the willing intrinsic to [the representational model], intent on . . . grasping and clutching the moment," although in vain. These preliminaries prepare the way for the argument that poetry need not be thought of as representing the present moment at all. Instead of conceiving of a poem as an actualized utterance or act, might we not describe a poem as what Barbara Herrnstein Smith has provocatively called a "possible utterance, what a poet might say"? Instead of mediating a present into a durative past, can a poem affirm time passing as a coming again—and a coming, not of what has been, but of what is ever more about to be? Could this self-surpassing project be not an attempt to represent and thus inevitably historicize a moment but rather the "predelineation of a possibility," not a reproduction of some cause but an activity generating ongoing possibilities, not a memory of a former satisfaction (not even of a precursor's satisfaction) or the anticipation of a future one but a free projection that can only take place as, and through, repetition? If we can conceive of a poetry of pure possibility can we revaluate a later poet's relation to a predecessor, not as a scene in which the earlier poet overwhelms the later poet with the power of his past accomplishments, but as one in which the earlier poet ceases to remain past and suddenly beckons the later poet from the position of the future to partake in the power of what can still be said in the earlier poetry? Since all these questions focus so insistently on the power inherent in possibility, they obviously require a reconsideration of the poet's prophetic capability, the power to make what remains unsaid speak. And this project necessarily returns us to William Blake, whose poetry, as we saw at the outset, still possesses a prophetic power no literary period, not even the modern, has purged or discharged into coherent meaning.

By now, though, we have discovered the power of what remains unsaid in Blake by contrasting it with the power modernism derives from its need to repress its presentiment that all present poetic saying has already been said. Indeed modernism's representative wish to partake of the originality of the moment has always already been countermanded by the very language that expresses this wish. We cannot, however, merely abandon the discourse of modernism as an expendable means to an end, for then Blake's poetry would not speak to the modern age at all; or, if it did speak, we would not have the ears to hear. To release Blake's power within the discourse of modernism, we must rediscover Blake through a modern poet who did not simply use Blake to legitimize his own sense of discontinuity. While many modern poets have avowed a relationship to Blake, Hart Crane is unique in his attitude; for he returns to Blake not to endorse his own modernity but to release himself from its hold, particularly from T. S. Eliot's dominant version of the modern sensibility. Thus I choose Crane as a paradigmatic modernist, because he is modern in an almost double sense: he perceives modernism as a loss of poetic possibility, and he feels alienated by modernism. According to the aforementioned preemptive logic of modernism, Crane's dispossession makes him more modern, not less, than his contemporaries: in his inability to be represented by the discourse of modernism, Crane partakes of the paradox of modernity itself. Crane feels his freedom compromised by the very discourse intended to express it, and he attempts to write his way out of the modernist dilemma through a re-vision of the poetry of his British ancestor William Blake and his American predecessor Walt Whitman.

Yet, as soon as we discover a possible solution to the dilemma of modernism, we are likely to feel the force modernism finds in what has already been said. Consequently, we cannot merely evade modernism by ignoring the question it poses about our procedure; we must also admit that our decision to recover Blake through Crane automatically embroils us in the modernist problematics of poetic influence. These problematics are best delineated by the following questions: How can Blake influence Crane without reducing Crane's poetry to the status of a repressed imitation? Can Blake's prophecies, written for and against his time, resolve Crane's modern dilemma without privileging Blake's poetry as a final solution? In short, how can a poet's vision escape compromise when the poet returns to the poems of another? Having acknowledged this perplexity, however, we cannot limit our discussion to these questions, for they suppress an even more fundamental problem. We shall use these questions that remain unasked although they insistently demand responses.

I

When we raise the problem of poetic influence, we raise the question Blake made the subject of an entire poem, that prophetic poem starkly entitled *Milton*. Before we begin a discussion of the influence Blake might have on moderns, then, we must consider his attitude toward the influence Milton's poetry had on him. Two different schools of literary historians have attempted to elucidate Blake's relation to his precursor John Milton. From the side of what we might call a literary history based on suspicion, Harold Bloom reads Blake's poetry in terms of Blake's fierce need to repress the influence of Milton; but this interpretation merely equates Blake's poetry with the exertions of Milton's Satan rather than analyzes Blake's recovery of a power in Milton's poetry beyond either the reach or grasp of Satan. On the side of a literary history of belief, Joseph Wittreich valiantly resolves to restore Blake to a tradition of epic prophecy that includes Milton; but this effort, despite the rhetorical power of the formulations of the genre Wittreich calls epic prophecy, leads to a reading of Blake's re-vision of Milton as a mere expansion of the same generic principles rather than as a revaluation of Milton's poetic project.

Since Bloom begins with the irrecoverable pastness of the precursor, his reading engenders the metaphor of Milton as a ghost haunting Blake with images of absence. But Blake did not regard Milton's vision as past; rather he saw through it to the prophetic vision it made possible. Indeed, Blake's sense of the difference between a ghostly and a prophetic voice led him to distinguish specters from what he called emanations.

Blake's vision of the prophetic Milton speaks not as a ghost (or what Blake called a "spectre") but as an emanation. An emanation, unlike a ghost, does not merely belong to a past world; instead it participates simultaneously in two temporal schemes. It always has already been envisoned; yet it must forever be reenvisioned. In contrast to a ghost, an emanation cannot haunt a person with a sense of the irretrievability of the past, for an emanation is what can be made of a poet's vision, not what the poet has made of that vision. It is a possibility for continued *re*-vision rather than the shell of an already completed artistic form. Not really even a form so much as the formative power, an emanation spontaneously surpasses every attempt to limit it to a single form. When Blake "converses" with Milton, he does business not with Milton's ghost, as Bloom suggests, but with Milton's emanation—the "visionary form dramatic" that Blake envisions as responsible for making his own prophecy possible.

Although Wittreich does not mistake emanations for specters, he still does not sufficiently discriminate text from context. Eager to delineate a continuous tradition of epic prophecy, he endorses the epic as the appropriate generic context for prophecy and then attempts to resolve Bloom's fierce oedipal rivalry by isolating it in the epic portion of the genre rather than in the prophetic.

> The epic poet enters into a contentious relationship with his predecessors and into a harmonious one with his culture, . . . on the other hand, the prophet asserts discontinuity between himself and his culture . . . and continuity between himself and his precursors.

Instead of dissolving Bloom's oedipal model, however, Wittreich only inverts and internalizes it, and at a lamentable expense. In conceiving a division between Milton's labors as an epic poet and his labors as a prophetic poet, a division bound to make the epic poet feel like the ghost of the prophet, Wittreich unintentionally creates a rift in the genre of epic prophecy, whose unity and continuity he is eager to delineate. Although we cannot here follow out the problems of a literary history based on such a model, we can expand on the model's basic insight—that the epic poet worked at cross-purposes to the prophet in Milton—because it is precisely Blake's complaint. Instead of resolving the contradiction into the controlled tension engendered by mixing disparate forms, however, Blake intensifies this opposition until he completely separates Milton's wish to be an epic poet from Milton's calling as a prophet; identifies the wish with the cycle of inferiority, jealousy, revenge, and self-righteousness that constitutes the representative epic action; and then annihilates this vicious cycle, together with the epic form, by recovering prophetic power.

Such a description unfortunately elucidates the overall action in Blake's *Milton* at the expense of his prophetic vision, since once the poem can be reduced to this isolable action, his prophecy does not fundamentally differ from Milton's epic plot, which also depends on the interaction of tyranny and rebellion. Moreover, by pitting Blake's prophecy against Milton's form, this interpretation has only revalidated the oedipal model invoked by Bloom and Wittreich. Should we wish to recover the force of Blake's prophecy, we must say more than that Blake prophesied against Milton's epic form or even against Milton's need for such a form; for a prophecy that merely reacts to a need, according to the complex intertwinings of desire, will not annihilate that need but only perpetuate it, though it is displaced, this time into the prophet's reverse need to react. While Blake made the inevitability of this doubly binding situation the subject of a major visionary element in *Milton,* he did not thereby subject himself to what he called the Orc cycle. Instead he dissolved the agencies of the need and thus supplanted its supremacy, along with the interplay of longing, possession, jealousy, and revenge that perpetuates the need.

But since how and why he dissolves these agencies are more germane to the true action of *Milton* than what he dissolves, perhaps we can renew our understanding of Blake's *Milton* if we reconsider his major complaint against Milton. We may recall that in his epigraph Blake echoes the last lines of Milton's invocation to the muse in *Paradise Lost.* Like Milton, Blake aspires "to justify the ways of God to men." But Blake's agreement with the latter part of this invocation only discriminates his disagreement with the earlier part, wherein Milton asks for his ". . . advent'rous song, / . . . to soar / Above th' Aonian Mount while it pursues / Things unattempted yet in prose or rhyme"; for in his preface to *Milton,* Blake diagnoses Milton's need to "soar above" previous epics as a sign that Milton was "curb'd by the general malady & infection from the silly Greek and Latin Slaves of the Sword." "We do not want either Greek or Roman Models," Blake continues, "if we are but just & true to our own Imaginations, those Worlds of Eternity in which we shall live for ever in Jesus our Lord." To Blake, Milton's use of the classical world as an ideology to be superseded by Christianity only diminished Milton's ability to use the Bible properly, that is, imaginatively; for Milton treated the "sublime of the Bible" in the same way that he treated the Greek world—not as true inspiration but merely as a style to be imitated, even if that imitation assumed the form of a supersession. But we cannot get a full sense of Blake's re-vision of Milton's poetry until we recall the second half of Milton's invocation:

> . . . what in me is dark
> Illumine, what is low raise and support,
> That to the highth of this great Argument
> I may assert Eternal Providence
> And justify the ways of God to men.

In Blake's reading, the two different charges to the muse constitute an opposition whereby Milton is "tempted" by his very wish to represent "things unattempted yet in prose or rhyme," and this temptation must itself be "illumined" before Milton can indeed justify God's ways to men.

Even this stark restructuring, however, cannot bring the issue raised by Milton's poetry clearly to light. For that we need the opening scene in *Milton*, where Milton listens to the Bard's song, since in this song Satan, rather than Milton, wishes to perform "as yet unattempted" deeds. Here, though, the particular deed assumes the form not of writing an epic poem but of taking over a harrow from an immortal named Palamabron and following behind Rintrah's plow. After Satan leads Palamabron's harrow and Palamabron supervises Satan's mills, terrible confusion results, and Los, the father of all three embattled parties, must call an assembly of eternals to adjudicate the case. As is usual in Blake's work, the narrative formulates almost nothing explicitly and leaves everything to the imagination; and since in the context of the entire scene it is Milton whose imagination would make sense of the action, we should interpret the scene in terms of Milton's imaginative project. Because theodicy is the central element in that project, perhaps we should interrupt the scene at the moment when justification becomes the central action. We discover not Milton but Satan justifying his ways against the charges of Palamabron:

> For Satan, flaming with Rintrah's fury hidden beneath his own mildness
> Accus'd Palamabron before the Assembly of ingratitude, of malice.
> He created Seven deadly Sins, drawing out his infernal Scroll
> Of Moral Laws and cruel punishments upon the clouds of Jehovah
> . . . Saying I am God alone:
> There is no other! let all obey my principles of moral individuality.
> (*Milton* I, Pl. 9, ll.)

The passage leads the intent listener, Milton, to a revaluation of his theodicy, not merely because Satan defends himself in echoes from Milton's epic poems but because these lines expose Milton's God as Satan in disguise. Thus the Bard's song suggests that Milton's true theodicy entailed justifying not God's ways to men but his own satanic wish to be God, a wish displaced—as in the first lines of his invocation to the muse—into the ambition to be greater than Greek or Roman models. So long as Milton tries to surpass Homer and Vergil, the wish to be "original," however it is disguised, continues to resound, though this time in the image of a displaced and vengeful Satan. In *Milton,* then, imitation (or memory) and revenge collaborate as the dual aspects of a single anxious complex, in which the experience of feeling belated, accompanied by a denial of the feeling, is discharged into a punishment of another's derivative posture. In short, the passage indicates that Milton, in wishing to outsoar the Greeks and Romans, only self-righteously continued their theme of arms and the man, though at the more pious level of a Christian crusader sanctioned by Divine Providence. By continuing this theme, Milton has imitated his classical predecessors after all. Perhaps to avoid this recognition Blake's Milton uses Satan (who cannot be believed) as the common translation (and, therefore, the common repression) for both the feeling of being derivative and the resultant need for revenge.

Though Milton's adaptation of epic and theological conventions in his poetry forever precludes his acknowledging these feelings, the Bard's song will not let him recognize anything else. Thus, in terms generated by Milton's invocation, one might say that the Bard's song functions as the inspiration that would "illumine" what is dark and "raise up" what is low—that inspiration which Milton had asked for but not received. In other words, Blake's Bard's song articulates the inspiration that Milton's finished poem did not. As a re-vision of *Paradise Lost* it gives voice to the poem that Milton could have written.

Blake's ability to revise *Paradise Lost* constitutes an insight central to his entire prophetic project and utterly transforms the conventional attitude toward a work of art. Since this attitude—which Blake would expect Milton, who wished to write the ultimate theodicy, to support— privileges the completed form of an artistic work, it is part of the vicious cycle of jealousy and revenge already described. In Blake's reading, Milton's need for a completed form only conceals his deeper wish to possess what all previous epics lacked, the final word on the matter of theodicy. Because in *Paradise Lost* Milton registers his triumph as revenge when he outsoars all previous epic efforts to possess, in effect, *his* truth in *their* form, his truth turns out to be the fear that his truth is derivative, not *his* but *theirs.* His suppression of this recognition takes the form of a defense against the fear that a paradisal state of utterly defended self-possession can be lost. To release Milton's poetry from the defensive reaction at work in (and *as*) its form, Blake must change Milton's relation with his created work. Blake's Milton, in fronting not what he had already written (the specter or ghost of creation) but what remains potential in it (his emanation), renews his relation with what can never be possessed or lost, the still active imagination.

After the Bard's song has unsettled his earlier formulations, Milton, no longer satisfied with his vision of paradise, exclaims:

> What do I here before the Judgment? without Emanation?
> With the daughters of memory & not with the daughters of inspiration?
> I in my selfhood am that Satan; I am that evil one.
>
> (I, Pl. 14, ll.)

Now this passage is meaningful enough as the one recognition Milton never had, but we begin to approach a much vaster dimension of its significance when we juxtapose its initial question, "What do I here before the Judgment? without my Emanation?" which anticipates a last judgment, with these lines from Blake's A Vision of the Last Judgment: "Error is Created, Truth is Eternal. Error or Creation will be Burned Up & then & not till then Truth or Eternity will appear. It is burnt up the Moment Men cease to behold it." Taken together these lines begin to illuminate the prophetic action in Milton; in the poem, Milton will bring both the created universe and his created epic poetry to a final judgment by ceasing to behold their outward forms. Before he can cease beholding these forms, which, as we have seen, constitute their imitative, derivative—in a word, satanic—element, he must behold some other dimension in them; and Milton begins to understand this other dimension when he descends to the valley of Beth Peor and, on seeing the immortal Urizen (who, on one level, is representative of the God of Paradise Lost), begins wrestling with him, "Creating new flesh on the Demon cold and building him/As with new clay, a Human form in the Valley of Beth Peor" (I, Pl. 19, ll). Here Milton utterly releases the priority he gave God in Paradise Lost. There God created man in His image; here Milton creates God in his. And the symmetry of these contrary activities releases a profound insight: God becomes a man so man can become as God. Because God and man exist as interchanging and interchangeable identities, neither can assume sole responsibility for the other. And if neither has priority over the other, but each coexists in and through becoming the other, neither God nor man need remain beholden to the psychology of jealousy that underpins the satanic universe. Through this insight Milton truly justifies, in the sense that he makes equal, the ways of God and man. This justification, moreover, signifies a final judgment, for when man becomes as God, he no longer beholds the outward creation; rather, he can participate in, and enjoy, the organized innocence of creating.

Earlier, to maintain the fiction of progression that any developing discussion of a work necessitates, we observed that Milton begins to comprehend this theodicy when he descends to the Valley of Beth Peor and proceeds to deepen his understanding until he reaches his final epiphany in Blake's Felpham Garden; but actually this recognition is immanent to, but not yet concretized in, the Bard's song, for at the most profound level Palamabron's harrowing means God's becoming a man (or the act of creation), while Rintrah's plowing signifies the correspondent clause that man can become as God (or the apocalypse). In Blake's view neither the harrowing nor the plowing can be done separately; instead the full sweep of the joint activities turns creation into revelation, while apocalypse, in its turn, can only reveal itself *through* creation. Creation appears separated from revelation only after Satan, eager to possess the outward show as his own, imitates Palamabron. When Milton understands what he hears in the Bard's song, he becomes—in accordance with the wonderful logic implicit in Blake's dictum that a man becomes (that is, "assumes the form of") what he beholds—all the dramatic agents in a series of recognition scenes, which are in their turn dramatizations of Milton's *act of understanding.* Perhaps it would be more accurate to say that since Milton in his epic poetry had already achieved a certain form of understanding, the renewal of his imagination takes the form of radical re-cognitions of those earlier scenes; and these re-cognitions, as in Beth Peor, materialize the elements missing in Milton's earlier understanding, the *plow* following the harrow, the *revelation* intertwined with the creation. According to the satanic logic of the Orc (or oedipal) cycle, however, even these re-cognition scenes can become forms that Milton might be tempted to possess as signs of his spiritual achievement. Consequently, he cannot stay beholden to any of them. Instead Blake's Milton must be ready to say, "I in my Selfhood am that Satan," not only to the main scenes in the already written poetry but to their ongoing revisions, including the ultimate recognition that John Milton is God become as man.

Ceasing to behold what he has created means beginning to behold what remains to be created. In the renewed rhythm of Blake's imagination, a scene dramatizing an epiphany is followed by a dramatic realization of the blind spots inherent in that epiphany, a realization in turn elevated to the level of epiphany. This sequence is the "progression" of Blake's re-vision of Milton. If, however, the "progression" depends on Milton's rejection of his every previous effort, does not this "progression" only revalidate the vicious cycle of revenge and imitation, though this time internalized and directed against Milton himself? And does not the cycle of rejection, with its perpetual recognition "I in my Selfhood am that Satan," lead to an infinite regress, an infinity of rejected forms? Perhaps in response to his own awareness of the force of these questions, Milton finds himself in a penultimate scene in which there is no longer a Satan to recognize. Yet again, since, according to Blake's economy of vision, seeking to behold one aspect of creation implies beholding another, Milton's act of turning away from his already created forms implies bringing to consciousness what he has not yet formed; he begins to behold, not what his forms have become, but the power that enables his forms to become other than what they are. In short, he begins to behold the estranged emanation that he at first calls Ololon. As if to emphasize the *undeveloped* as well as the willful aspect of Milton's labors, Ololon has the appearance of a twelve-year-old virgin. But Milton, unlike the Adam who deferred to the weakness of Eve's sex, does not modify the power of his vision to accommodate Ololon's adolescence; rather he thunders:

> . . . Obey thou the words of the Inspired Man,
> All that can be annihilated must be annihilated . . .
> To cast off the rotten rags of Memory by Inspiration,
> . . . imitation of Nature's Images drawn from Remembrance.
> These are the Sexual Garments, the Abomination of Desolation,
> Hiding the Human Lineaments as with an Ark & Curtains
> Which Jesus rent & shall now wholly purge away with Fire
> Till Generation is swallow'd up in Regeneration.
>
> (II, Pl. 40, ll; Pl. 41, ll.)

In this scene, Milton returns to the action in the Bard's song with a recognition of its implications. Of course, by playing Rintrah to Ololon's Palamabron, he reenacts their relationship. More important, by becoming rather than imitating Rintrah, he "annihilate[s]" the satanic masquerade. By asking, moreover, not to "soar above" all previous epics but to "cast off the rotten rags of Memory by Inspiration," he rescinds the first portion of his invocation to the muse. In other words, he separates all that is inspired from all that is derivative in his epic form. In this recognition of the undeveloped state of his epic labors (Ololon), Milton in effect converts what has become of them into their power to become again. But with this renewed cognition, Milton's emanation ceases to exist in the undeveloped form. In fact, it ceases to exist in any representable form at all. With Ololon converted into the formative power, spontaneously free of any formal constraint, the expression "I in my Selfhood am that Satan" no longer has any referent. So with nothing left to see, Milton is transformed into what he sees with, the active imagination: "One man, Jesus the Saviour, wonderful! round his limbs / The Clouds of Ololon folded as a Garment dipped in blood" (II, Pl. 42, ll). If Milton no longer has anything left to re-cognize but now identifies with the activity of the imagination and if this activity, which for Blake is synonymous with the Christ event, entails the intervolved process of creation and apocalypse, then Milton, in beholding the process of becoming, has become it.

This transformation does not resolve so much as it dissolves Milton's wish to soar above the work of his precursors. Once Milton partakes of the sheer process of becoming, nothing remains either to imitate or to lose. In the Blakean imagination, created forms are not representations of previously existing categories but particularizations of the process of becoming, which, in its capacity to rend apart every form intended to represent it, returns all creation to the status of mere possibility. For Blake, neither human subjects nor created forms can exist apart from this process, although they constitute its means of imaging itself. And if Milton has become identified with the imaging power, then his second wish, to illumine what is dark and raise up what is low, has not been fulfilled so much as elevated by the sheer power of illumination.

By way of summarizing, then, we might say that whereas Milton's epic was organized around the need to defeat a misguided figure, Blake's prophecy is organized around the disappearance of this need. Since, however, the need disappears, along with the created world, in that "moment" in Blake's A Vision of the Last Judgment when man ceases to behold creation, perhaps we should reconsider the Blakean moment at least long enough to contrast it with the passing moment in modernism that led us into this detour. On reflection, the Blakean moment differs fundamentally from the moment the modernist would find spontaneously historicized in language in that, like the opening scene in Milton, it never becomes past. Indeed, it was Blake's refusal to temporalize this moment that resulted in his resolutely nonnarrative form.

Since Blake views the preterit mode of narrative sequence as implicitly endorsing the sense of time passing and the resultant feelings of loss, jealousy, and revenge, he ignores sequential patterns and entirely disregards diachronic designs. He condenses his prophecy into a single recurrent scene instead of into line or sequence. In other words, he tells the same story in different ways; but he tells these different stories, as it were, at the same time. Thus, Blake does not spatialize time, stripping off its temporal dimension, but creates—to reverse one of Blake's favorite expressions—a particular minute. In attempting to comprehend this moment, though, we cannot limit it to any particular time or ascribe it to any particular action; for this moment recurs without ever settling down long enough to take place except as a recurrence. Like the flow of the ocean's surface, the moment changes, but without anything specific in it changing from one form to another. It is just always in the act of changing.

Since all scenes in *Milton* partake of the same time as the Bard's song, they all reenact that scene, though with different emphases and characters. They are the same seen differently. But if only the perception changes while the central action remains constant, perception must be the true action of *Milton*; or, as Blake would say, "The Eye altering alters all." Once perception is acknowledged as the true action, however, the scenes cannot be said to constitute actual events; rather they constitute ever-changing states of awareness or represent states of awareness as if they were actual events.

Because each scene portends a re-cognition, the action does not proceed with the past leading to the future. Instead the events of the song, narrated in the past tense, always seem to become more and more present—and in a double sense. First, in re-cognizing more in the song, the narrator and Milton make it appear more present; second, in "presentifying" (to use Husserl's term) only this song, the poem does not give a sense of time passing. The "now" of the poem remains oriented to a past event becoming increasingly present; and since Milton "adds" to the past by recognizing new dimensions implicit to the Bard's song, the past action *becomes an act in the present.* But this past event becoming present becomes not so much a fully realized event as an eventfulness always in the act of becoming.

Even when Milton's transformation into the figure of Christ occurs, none of the other scenes lapses out of the picture; therefore, to avoid the implication that *Milton* leads up to a culminative event, we might say that each additional scene replaces yet enhances the one before and *after.* What "finally" results then is not a present tense but a tensed present, an intensified moment full at both ends; and when we reconsider each scene from this double perspective, we cannot say whether each refers to a past event or to one about to occur. Each act potentially "means" every other in a poem in which nothing changes but everything interchanges, in which things possess not actuality but only ever-renewed possibility, in which nothing ever occurs but everything recurs.

In *Milton,* then, Blake discovers that the present moment is not a free origin with a recoverable presence after all but is already a repetition. Since it lacks any recoverable self-presence but only repeats the past and "recollects" the future, the present moment cannot, as modernism would have it, end up historicized by the mediation of language, for it is already doubly mediated. It repeats past and future, and this repetition constitutes the true being of the moment as pure *becoming.*

From this perspective, it cannot be only the repeated present moment in *this* poem that is thus transformed. Even Blake's own writings partake of this moment, for Blake brings them to judgment as well as re-cognizes them *through* the work of Milton. When Blake returns to Milton, then, he does not look back on the already actualized vision of a powerful precursor; he looks through the ever-repeated moment that made Milton's prophecy possible. What results is neither a "correction" nor an expansion but a *making prophecy possible.* Blake does not set out to be greater in the role of Milton; to do so would only unconsciously repeat the Orc cycle of tyranny and rebellion. Instead Blake's return enables him in his literature to experience, for example, the Second Coming with the knowledge that he did not possess this experience any more than did Milton but rather that it occurs again through the human imagination. To put this particular moment in its most dramatic context, we might say that in Blake the Second Coming precedes the Creation, so that all creation re-forms itself out of this first repetition.

In other words, Blake responds to the dilemma of modernism by revaluating the modernist moment. Like the postmodernist theoretician Jacques Derrida, Blake conceives of language as a differential relation between a potential and an already articulated significance. But whereas Derrida dissipates this potential into differentiation, Blake recovers the potential by conceiving of a "Word" that always already surpasses every form intended to signify it. In Blake's system, thus, it is repetition, not difference, that is original, and this original repetition functions through the power of the imagination.

Should we wish a minute particular to exemplify this abstract function, we need only concretize that moment when Milton ceases to behold already created matter and partakes of its process of figuration. I have described this process of figuration as the separative relation between man and nature; but now we must observe that it is a relation distinctively different from any other, for in it the means of relating entities (whether through separation or union) precedes all entities. In Blake, then, it is not mental ideas or archetypal mythic figures that are original; it is the self-divided relation of Palamabron and Rintrah, which, by imaging itself *through* all created forms, treats already actualized creation in the same way Blake treats Milton's epic, as memories awaiting reimagining. Thus the imagination overcomes every attempt to limit it to a single representation: as a relation *between two* terms, the imagination must always appear on the other side of any attempt to grasp it singly. To humanize this power, we can describe it as a self-overcoming will, which Blake calls Los, the figure who must surpass even that which he has not yet done.

Limiting the imagination to a single representation is a dissimulation of Satan, who memorizes, or fixes, the movement of imagination and pretends that he is *either* the creator *or* the outward form of creation. This pretense obviously only conceals the imagination's double motive, to have both the creator and the created partake of the figurative process; each is a repetition of the other, separated as well as united through the bond of the imagination. All fictions that deny this relation, including the modernist fictions of "representation" and "presence," result in what Blake considers a natural religion more indicative of the work of memory than of what he calls imagination. When he equates the Creation with the Fall and subjective man with Satan, Blake implicitly likens both representative creation and self-present subjectivity to mere distortions of the "Imaginative Word," which is not self-present but in between man and world, not an original presence or even a representation of presence but a pure meditation.

In keeping with the spirit of this vision, Blake recognizes Milton, not as a figure in the past, but rather as the ever-renewed power to re-cognize the word, the "ever-apparent Spirit of Prophecy." Consequently, Blake goes beyond interpreting Milton's written words to beholding the word Milton made possible, one that can never finally be written and yet that underwrites all other words, returning man and all utterances to the prophetic moment when vision gives way to re-vision in that state of pure possibility Blake calls *Milton.*

II

Unlike the modernist, then, Blake does not conceive of the relationship between the present moment and language in terms of loss. As we have seen, for Blake time never eventuated in a present moment. Because he never conceived of time achieving presence in a moment, presence could not be lost in a moment, as it is for the modernist. Because Blake did not believe poetry could be either used up or turned into an orthodoxy, he did not feel overshadowed by what an earlier poet had written. Quite the contrary, in imaginging what remained unactualized in a precursor's poetry, Blake felt a momentous influx of renewed power.

It was just this power, Blake's ability to remain emphatically apart from the defining orthodoxies of tradition, however, that won him the hostility of such moderns as T. S. Eliot, who could embrace their modernity only as an acknowledgment of their felt discontinuity from a past. Since Eliot could feel his present discontinuity only in contrast to the continuity he posited for a tradition, he could not tolerate the marginal status of Blake, whose "genius required . . . what is sadly lacked, [which] was a framework of accepted traditional ideas."

While Eliot considered Blake a bothersome, contrary element, worthy only of expulsion from an otherwise coherent, albeit irretrievably lost, tradition, Eliot's contemporary Hart Crane regarded Blake as a much needed alternative to the modernism that Eliot's sensibility had come to represent. Eliot, of course, denied any sign of this sensibility in his poetry, but the very insistence of the denial—registered, we might add, with uncharacteristic force—only confirmed the suspicion that a *dissociated* sensibility was at work as much in his personality as in his poetry.

We all know the "dissociation of sensibility" as Eliot's central doctrine and his major complaint against his age; but Charles Altieri, in an article intent on formulating a common mythos out of the conflicting schools of modernism, offers some insights fundamental to understanding how this sensibility functions as a poetic technique. After discussing Roman Jakobson's poetic theory at length, Altieri corroborates it only long enough to discern its inapplicability to Eliot by arguing that, whereas in Jakobson's theory a poem provides the occasion for a metaphor to add a dimension of depth to the sequential or metonymic displacements characteristic of ordinary discourse, Eliot's poetry reverses this procedure. In other words, Eliot strips metaphors of their depth dimension, thereby collapsing them onto a metonymical plane composed of displaced rather than interconnected elements. Perhaps the matter is more subtle than even Altieri indicates, however; for when we consider the famous opening lines from "The Love Song of J. Alfred Prufrock" (1915)—"Let us go then, you and I, / When the evening is spread out against the sky / Like a patient etherized upon a table"—we find that the passage shifts abruptly from a metonymic sequence based on the contiguity of "you and I" in the first line and of the evening foregrounded against the sky in the second to a metaphoric figure based on a similitude in the third. But Eliot does more than simply collapse this simile into metonymic fragments. By choosing a "clinical" scene as his means of joining together the evening and the sky, he effectively shakes the sky loose from the sublime associations traditionally connected with it, thereby letting it stand as a metaphor, but one sufficiently crippled in stature to seem in need of further support.

Eliot asserts his poetic intention, however, not only by dissociating his metaphors but by dislocating allusions, mythic schemata, and quotations from their informing contexts and then inserting them in poems utterly incompatible with their original import: he wanted to write a poetry so utterly alienated from the one tradition capable of assimilating it into meaning that it would affirm his need to recover a lost tradition—but to do so, alas, *outside* the poetry.

Thus Eliot's project made Crane's task clear: to overturn the dominance of Eliot's sensibility by restoring the metaphoric dimension to poetry as well as to the modern world. And since Blake, in his capacity of uncovering the unrecognized in seemingly every cognition, did not invent new metaphors so much as write with the metaphorizing power itself, his poetry seemed to Crane an appropriate alternative. Crane did not, of course, merely replicate Blake's vision; their poetry is as different as the ages they address. On deciding that the passive perception of nature was England's central error, Blake traced the source of the error back to the nature worship implicit in Milton's conception of paradise. And since Blake truly believed that poets embody the deepest sensibilities of their nations, he ventured to change England's perception by changing Milton's imagination; thus, we have seen, Blake's Milton exchanged the feeling of being beholden to nature for the capacity to create nature. With the advantages of a technology that subdued nature, Hart Crane's America, instead of feeling inferior to created nature, felt as if it had, through the very success of its progressive achievements, lost touch with its original urge to recover a relation with a new world. If Crane's need, as embodied in his poetry, was merely different from Blake's, it was precisely the reverse of Eliot's; for Crane, unlike Eliot, wished not to recover a relation with an old tradition but to renew America's relation with what remained radically new within it.

Although Crane shared Eliot's emphasis on desire rather than Blake's on the imagination, he used Blake's method of organizing images to achieve a perspective capable of reversing the dissociative effects of Eliot's desire. In The Waste Land Eliot detaches lyrics from their historical contexts and thereby reduces their initial intensity until they are finally indistinguishable from epigrammatic fragments, able to register only the point that they have become pointless. By contrast, Crane in *The Bridge* detaches from their historical contexts a series of American scenes—a dreamer who wakens to find his lover missing, a frontier mother hoping for the return of her son, a poet longing for a creative word—whose lyric potential he mobilizes by organizing them, as Blake did *Milton,* around an original scene of intense longing, that of Columbus hoping to return safely to Europe with his vision of the new world. By turning each scene into a reactivation of the longing experienced in every other scene, Crane turns Eliot's metonyms, with all their implicit dissociation, back into metaphors.

Had Crane, in his poetry, simply annexed Eliot's fragments into a significant context by adding a metaphoric overlay, though, he would have only added to the modernist culture's surplus of forever outmoded "significant formulations," which alienated Eliot to begin with. Crane wanted not to absorb Eliot's disconnected fragments back into the modern world but to change that world.

So when Crane chose the bridge as his dominant metaphor, he did not mean to limit its tenor to any single referent already existing in the world; instead, he meant to express his longing for a connective relation with a new world. Like the office worker in the proem, Crane sees the bridge as an expression of the longing to be free of every established pattern and routine relation. The bridge is an appropriate expression of freedom and longing because the office worker sees it not merely as an extension of the human wish for interconnection but also as a leap arrested in mid-stride, independent of both destination and point of departure. A site of passage, then, rather than a world in itself, the bridge, with its "ever unspent" power to pass over into something else, cannot betray the office worker's freedom by limiting it to a determinate goal. Through the workings of what Crane calls the "logic of metaphor," the bridge, as the image of freedom longed for as well as an expression of longing itself, reveals longing to be the very life of freedom. And since the life of this life, the "ever unspent" capacity of both freedom and longing to express themselves by passing over into something else, is best conveyed through the metamorphoses characteristic of the metaphoric process, perhaps we should say that *The Bridge* did not fulfill Crane's desire for the metaphoric dimension absent in Eliot's poetry but made this longing, which could never be satisfied by any single object, indistinguishable from the power of making metaphoric relationships.

For when we make this assumption we can begin to understand the logic behind the bridge's metamorphoses into, by turns, a curveship, waking dream, train, covered wagon, sailing ship, airplane, subway, and tunnel. As an expression of Columbus' wish to bring the Old World into connection with the New, the bridge assumes the form most expressive of this wish as reiterated throughout American history. But since the wish expresses itself through both these images and their agents, Crane intensifies its charge through their reiteration, until, in the "Atlantis" section of the poem, the images and their agents drop away and *longing itself assumes the appearance of a world.* And this world is not the New World Columbus discovered but a world "one shore beyond" anyone's capacity to attain it, the new world that remained a wish long after America became a historical fact.

III

Although Blake's visionary form provided Crane with a dramatic means of deliverance from Eliot's Waste Land, Blake's voice was less suitable for Crane's purposes. And if Crane became an apostate from Eliot's tradition by reforging Blake's images in the fire of his own desire, he became a certifiable heretic when he let those images resound in a voice akin to Walt Whitman's, for Eliot was even less sympathetic to Whitman's "claptrap" than he was to Blake's. Curiously enough, though, Eliot still felt threatened enough by Whitman's verse line to try to get rid of the voice. Analyzing "Burnt Norton," Roy Harvey Pearce, with characteristic force, exposes Eliot's need to distort Whitman's voice in that poem: "the Whitmanian mode is made to negate itself and generate its opposite—a wholly personal style takes on a grand impersonality."

But in shaking Whitman's line loose from his voice, Eliot did provide a monumental insight into Whitman, which we may best comprehend if we set it within the context of later breakthroughs in Whitman criticism. James E. Miller, Jr., broke with the academy's tacit policy of excluding Whitman from serious consideration when he articulated a deep structure in *Leaves of Grass* based on the transformations of Whitman's cosmic personality. After Charles Feidelson had demonstrated how this personality transposes all supposed entities into the single activity of self-making, Quentin Anderson and James M. Cox shrewdly observed that since this activity includes the reader, the agent within the poem is identical with the subject of the changes the reader undergoes while reading the poem. While all these critics privilege the personality of Whitman to one extent or another, Eliot, in separating it from Whitman's voice, explicitly exposes it as a persona for a voice; but it remained for Hart Crane to remark on this voice's special capacity "to bind us throbbing" with one sound, a capacity that sets Whitman's voice apart as that of the genius loci of America.

Although listening to the genius loci is prerequisite for any national bard, Whitman had neither Blake's Milton as an incarnation of the
genius loci nor, of course, Hart Crane's Whitman; instead of turning to a
precursor, Whitman invented a voice for America. After asserting that in
America each individual must feel a fusing relation with the world en
masse, Whitman could not cultivate the romantic poet's isolated point of
view or resurrect images from the poetic tradition; he had to create a new
yet vernacular poetry of separate equals, a poetry of the "fusing relation"
between individuals. Although I shall refine this point later, I might say
here that when Whitman discovered his form he did not write in the
vernacular so much as he became the vernacular Americans could communicate with. Having charged that "there be no school founded" on
him, Whitman never represented a philosophical position but instead
embodied the exchange of opinion leading up to one. He could not
establish a fixed identity for himself in his poetry, for if he had he would
have accepted the finality of separateness. In place of a fixed identity, he
created what might be called an "inter-subject," a subjectivity reducible to
neither self nor other and not even equivalent to intersubjectivity, but
rather a consciousness of the never-ending collocution between self and
other. Now, since dialogue presupposes such collocutions, perhaps we can
use it as a metaphor to indicate what we mean by an intersubject. In a
dialogue each person speaks from his or her own position, but that
position is always modified by the anticipated qualifications of a respon-
dent. Neither dialogue partner can hold onto a fixed position: both must
surrender their opinions and change their positions for the sake of finding
out the truth about the subject. If we can imagine this ever-changing
subject of the dialogue as a subjectivity, we can come close to understanding Whitman's persona in *Leaves of Grass*, for therein he is not a separate
person but a personification of the "common place" between persons and
things.

We might get a better sense of this subjectivity if we reiterate our
opening point that, though Whitman is the persona for a voice, this voice
precedes the separation into different identities. When Whitman sings,
"And what I assume, you shall assume" ("Song of Myself"), the "you" is
not a reader with an identity separable from the activity of reading the
poem: the "you" is virtually anticipated by the speaker before he can speak
a word. Or, as Whitman puts it, "Those are not the words, the substantial
words, . . . they are in you" ("A Song of the Rolling Earth"). In Whitman's poetry, "you" supplements "I" as the "latency" remaining unspoken
in every utterance; thus neither "I" nor "you" alone can constitute the
speaking voice. Only the profound relation *between* them can. When in

good voice, Whitman's speaker alternately anticipates his listener's responses and changes places with the listener, thereby producing a voice that by turns questions, exhorts, commands, swears, soothes, cons, screams, cozens, doubts, echoes, recriminates, and even downright gabs. In "Song of Myself," Whitman explains the resultant fusion of voices: "It is you talking just as much as myself, I act as the tongue of you, / Tied in your mouth, in mine it begins to be loosen'd." By alternately impersonating both sides of an implicit dialogue, then, Whitman's voice undergoes constant modulations, startling enough in their effects to be his voice's equivalent of the transformative power of traditional metaphor.

The power of this modulation, however, can be attributed to neither the speaker nor the "answerer" but only to the voice resulting from their fusion. From their voices, in other words, there "proceeds another eternally curious of the harmony of things." (Preface to the 1855 edition of *Leaves of Grass;* Whitman invokes such a voice at the end of the Preface.) Although Whitman describes the sound of this fusing voice, in its various intensities, as a "hum," "lull," "drift," and even "a barbaric yawp," he actually prefers this sound, which we could call the unspoken resonance of his words, to the individual words themselves: "The words of my book nothing, the drift of it everything" ("Shut Not Your Doors"). The words are only the "shreds," or the "debris," the outward form of the invisible and "unlaunch'd" poem that can never be written or *confirmed* into print because, like Blake's word of the imagination, it underwrites everything. Neither can it be accommodated into significance by an act of reflection. Instead, the word as voice displaces the privileged position of the exact, coherent meanings and replaces them with the copious flow of undifferentiated voices. For with Whitman, a poem ceases to be an image of something seen or a precise rendition of an emotion and becomes a confluence of "dumb voices." Like those echoes that sink into consciousness in the silences between speech, the resultant "lulls" are less sounds in themselves than re-soundings of already spoken words. So just as Blake privileged the re-vision of the word over any literal expression, Whitman gives priority to this re-sounding voice. In Whitman, however, these echoes seem to appear before the individual utterances and to re-sound through them.

To actualize such an *inter*locutive voice Whitman obviously had to develop innovations in form, and he abandoned the passive and active diatheses of the voice for a voice capable of saying, "I sing myself and celebrate myself." In this construction the "I" is an identity neither totally separated from its activity of singing, as it would be in the active voice, nor acted on, as it would be in a passive construction. Instead the "I" is, as Emile Benveniste writes of the subject in the "middle" voice, "inside the process of which he is agent . . . he achieves something which is achieved in him." But if Whitman's persona is located within this activity of singing and is, moreover, effected in each new song, Whitman can no longer be identified with a psychological identity that existed before these songs. Instead the intensity of the songs transformed Whitman's empirical ego into what he calls "that shadow," the "likeness" of his true self capable of appearing only within the interlocutive process effected in "caroling these songs" ("That Shadow, My Likeness"). Thus when Whitman wrote "I sing myself" he literally meant that his singing brought a self into being.

In other words, Whitman turned into the consciousness of singing—but a consciousness of a peculiar kind. Since, as we have seen, Whitman's voice marks the confluence of self and other, it partakes of all the sensual delight inherent in such fusion. So when Whitman incarnates the voice of *inter*locution, he does not remain a merely disembodied voice but becomes a "body electric," covered with "instant conductors all over"—not merely a speaking voice but a fully sensualized, listening, smelling, seeing, tasting, touching one, longing for renewed union with others. Perhaps, since only the sexual urge approaches the intensity of the consequent desire for union, Whitman uses sexuality as the appropriate metaphor for that desire. In both sexual and interlocutive intercourse, the self experiences itself as the interiority of the other; both the sexual and interlocutive selves incarnate the give-and-take of an interrelationship profound enough to make the one who gives indistinguishable from the one who takes. This is to say that the sexualized self, like Whitman's intersubject, incarnates the relation between persons rather than any individual identity; consequently, when Whitman speaks from out of that "body electric," he treats all his relationships in the world (and not merely his male relationships) as ones in which he touchingly ventures "the verge of myself, then the outlet again" ("Crossing Brooklyn Ferry").

The sexual metaphor, however, is only one way that Whitman emphasizes the interiority of the subject within the intersubjective process. Through an even more telling strategy, the "I"—when he appears after multiple predications—seems surrounded, even *spoken*, by natural processes before Whitman can speak about them: "Throwing myself on the sand, confronting the waves, I . . . taking all hints to use them" ("Out of the Cradle Endlessly Rocking"). But while the subject is definitely immersed in this atmosphere of confluent activities, he does not appear dominated by them; instead he merges with them as if he were no less fluid. This observation should not lead us to conclude what Whitman only liquefies himself, though, for in *Leaves of Grass* he manages to melt, perhaps evaporate, the most resistant objects into a merging flow. And this observation provides the key for understanding Whitman's catalog constructions; for in these, too, objective scenes surround Whitman, but without any one scene assuming visual priority, and without the group being distributed into a sequence of scenes to be considered one by one. These resonant scenes, by flowing into, even echoing, one another, displace the priority of the glance and render themselves finally *indistinguishable from spoken words*. Through this remarkable technique, Whitman effects a profound confusion of the senses, for in the catalogs he manages to so intertwine the acts of speaking and seeing that he seems to *speak seeing*.

So not just these catalogs but speaker, reader, and individual poems—in fact, all subjects and all objects—flow into the same "hum" of a "valvèd voice." All things are "eidolons" or "similitudes" of that fusing relation. Like Blake's "Imagination," Whitman's interlocutive voice serves as the original relation for all creation. While Blake's poems were images of the imaginative process, though, Whitman's are echoes of the "valvèd voice." In Whitman all things bespeak this "throbbing voice" and long to harmonize with its unspoken melody. But this voice can never be articulated, and it remains a pre-conception, presented in faint calls and intimations. Throughout the poem, Whitman's "I" as "you" partakes of the rapid transformation of this unspoken voice until the speaker departs into the unspeakably thin air, "effuses" into the "eddies and drift" of the unspoken voice of America's genius loci. For finally it is, not Whitman, but the universal fusing voice of America that flows out into the melodies of separate individuals; it is this pure performative that speaks through all the individual speech acts. As the unspoken resonance of these acts, the genius loci's words cannot be identified with individual utterances: instead the genius loci bespeaks the speaking of these utterances. As the reiteration of the power to speak antecedent to every individual expression, each utterance then looms up as a foreboding of what remains to be spoken. By emphasizing this unspoken resonance, Whitman's poems, like Blake's visionary forms, say more than any single speech act can sustain. In giving vista to these "passwords primeval," Whitman's utterances must always anticipate the answerer coimplicated in this separative relation. Thus Whitman's poems always address other poets, "answerers," who secretly speak their poems in response to Whitman's and thereby make good on his ever-elusive promise of a separate but equal relation:

Poets to come! orators, singers, musicians to come!
Not to-day is to justify me and answer what I am for
But you, a new brood, native, athletic, continental, greater than
      before known,
Arouse! for you must justify me.

                         ("Poets to Come")

IV

Although Crane's primary reason for returning to Whitman in the "Cape Hatteras" section of *The Bridge* was to assert his role as heir to the voice of America's genius loci, other reasons also come immediately to mind: he had to regain Whitman's true voice after Eliot's distortions; he wished to make explicit the implicit connection between Whitman's "Crossing Brooklyn Ferry" and his own poem; and he wanted an American song capable of matching the intensity of Columbus' profound cry of longing for a vision of the "Kingdoms trembling in the Naked Heart." But most important, he needed Whitman's sense of being in profound relation with all creation in order to get through his own imminent ordeal with the dissociated sensibility of the modern world.

Of course Crane's very need to return to Whitman occasions once again the question haunting this discussion: Does the presence of this powerful precursor threaten to make Crane seem ghostly by comparison? In their varied efforts to respond to this question, Crane's critics have proffered antithetical interpretations. While such critics as Joseph Arpad and M. Bernetta Quinn find in "Hatteras" Crane's realization of a Neoplatonic logos, Thomas Vogler and L. S. Dembo suggest that Crane's need to return to Whitman indicates his inability to get beyond the wish for such a word. Crane, of course, elicits both these responses in the antithetical structure of a poem whose terrific emotional oscillations range from ecstasy to despair and back again. But I think it is part of Crane's intention to evoke this either/or response as well as transform it.

As we recall, Columbus experienced just such an ambivalence when he was about to return to the Old World: he did not know whether he possessed a true vision of a new world or merely the wish for a vision. Similarly, Crane on Hatteras does not know whether his vision of America results from an actual vision of contemporary America or from a need to escape a world "where each sees only his dim past reversed." But just as Columbus' despair over solving the dilemma led to a reversal in his attitude toward the New World, so Crane's also undergoes a remarkable reversal. Remembering Whitman, he recalls the poet who in "Years of the Modern" and "Crossing Brooklyn Ferry" had in effect already experienced the present age in the past: "I am with you, you men and women of . . . ever so many generations hence. . . . Just as you feel . . . so I felt" ("Crossing Brooklyn Bridge"). Thus recalling Whitman's vision, Crane experiences his own present made past, thereby implicitly turning the New World into an old world awaiting renewal. If Crane's moment of decision in "Hatteras" seems to replicate Columbus' in "Ave Maria," we begin to recognize a difference when we reflect that this time Crane must look forward to returning to contemporary America with the word of *his* discovery.

A double repetition transpires. Crane repeats not only Columbus' quest to renew a world but also Whitman's intention to sing a new world into being. This relation with Whitman, however, suggests further complications. By feeling "ascensions of Walt" in himself, Crane can enter present-day America knowing it is a distortion of the age that Whitman had envisioned in years past. As a result of embodying Whitman's perspective, Crane achieves the uncanny effect of moving into his own present age with Whitman's *prior* vision of it.

Walt becomes, in other words, Crane's means of making the *new* world once again possible, but Crane does not return to Whitman's poetry as the final word. Nor does he recall Whitman's presence in the past. Since, as we have seen, Whitman's interlocutive self never possesses actuality, Crane cannot feel threatened by its presence; instead he returns to Whitman's work in order to bring into existence the poem awaiting just this desire for a renewed relation between separate but equal poets.

We can say then that Crane both remembers Whitman and imagines him. Now when he imagines Whitman's poetry, he turns Whitman's vision of the present into a power to act in the modern age. But when he remembers the Walt who has already "lived" Crane's reality, Crane implicitly converts his own present age into an act of memory. The present thus exists in two dimensions of consciousness—as a memory and as a possibility. Once we understand Crane's double process, we can also understand what Crane learned from Blake: imagination can undo the work of memory. Just as Blake equated memory with imitation and exposed Milton's epic form as a mere imitation of the figurative process of the imagination, so Crane understands the present age as a memory, hence a mere imitation—which is to say a repression—of its own possibility.

Through this revaluation of the modern age, Crane implicitly provides a stunning insight into the modernist complex that was our point of departure. By trying to grasp and *re*-present the present moment as present, the modern age lives the present moment as if the moment is already lost. The *wish* to live the moment as if it could be fully self-present converts it into a memory of a lost possession, for in denying the present's capacity to change, the wish reduces the moment to the fixed status of an already realized event; and at this juncture the dominant version of modernism as a wish to say things as they are betrays a deep aversion to what *can be other.* Representing things as they are means wishing to hold onto things as they have been; but Crane returns to Whitman and Blake not to recover the present as a self-present moment, that is, already to experience the present as if it possessed the presence of a past event, but to recover it as a possible present, what could be constitutionally and radically other than what has been.

Thus, in *The Bridge,* Crane revaluates proleptically even the most recent version of modernism, for he does not conceive of the modern poet as anxious over a precursor (as we have seen, the anxiety is itself a repression of the feared loss of the moment); instead he considers modernism an anxiety over its own freedom of will, an attempt to deny radical possibility by inventing the fiction of a moment possessed of a plenitude of being. Crane exposes the wish for a self-present moment as the blocking precursor, since this wish for total presence never lets the moment become possible. To effect a reversal, Crane replaces the Freudian unconscious with what could be called a prophetic unconscious—what Ernst Bloch calls an unconscious of the future, "a not yet consciousness, an ontological pull, . . . of a tidal influence erected upon us by that which lies out of sight."

More specifically, Crane attempts to forge this unconscious in *The Bridge* by revealing its presence throughout America's history. After beginning with the Blakean figure of Columbus, who, on the edge between worlds, hopes for a vision that can renew Europe, Crane places all American history within this moment as a repetition of the same desire for renewal. The oscillations in mood and tone in these scenes from American history stem from the degeneration of this desire into a compulsion to conquer time and space in "the strident rule of wings imperious," followed by the inevitable internalization of the will to conquer (once all the capes have been crossed), which results in the repetition compulsions of daily life ("performances, appointments, resumés"). But Crane cannot simply describe this transformation of Columbus' desire, for he sees the entire present age implicit in that desire. Repetition compulsion is desire turned against itself, and this desire to negate desire, like Columbus' wish for "one shore beyond desire," expresses a common urge to be free of desire. Unlike the compulsions merely to repeat the same desire, Columbus' profound longing results in a song of desire overcoming itself, a desire that is *beyond* any capacity to be satisfied and that delights in being *"one shore beyond."* And—to return to the critical dilemma in Crane's work—through this song, Columbus, instead of remaining caught within the bind of either a vision of a new world or a desire for such a vision, uses the dilemma to deepen his awareness, until he abides in the moment between the "either" (an actual new world) and the "or" (a mere desire for one), where he experiences *ever-renewed desire as the new world,* a "kingdom trembling in the naked heart."

Crane fits all American history within this moment. Just as Columbus came to his moment of the will's self-decision after he had satisfied the desire to conquer time and space, so Crane returns to that moment in American history after the technological conquest of time and space and confronts the voyager with the same ultimate task. In the section of *The Bridge* entitled "The Tunnel," the will of the traveler must reject all the evasions of itself implicit in twentieth-century routine and overcome itself through *despair over every illusion of its own satisfaction.* In Crane's remarkable reversal, twentieth-century reality becomes an image of the ocean that failed, once it had been crossed, to satisfy Columbus' will. In "The Tunnel," the traveler, moreover, heightens the intensity of the shared dissatisfaction (which is to say, the reality of the twentieth-century world) until this profound despair deepens into an awareness of the will overcoming its need to be satisfied. "The Hand of Fire" is the image for the will affirming in advance its capacity to succeed any representation intended to grasp it; and when the traveler realizes that the will is always in excess of any word intended to represent it, he knows that the will is a consciousness existing as a perpetual bridging, an ever-renewed passage onward. And when the consciousness itself exists as a bridge, what comes to consciousness is the knowledge that, if the past is constituted by this profound experience of longing, what has been never stops coming back.

Since each moment in *The Bridge* doubly repeats past and present, until the present moment becomes not a passing away but a pure passage, time itself only reenacts the will's process of choosing to let itself become rather than to hold on to itself. In Crane's poem, then, the primary trope is not Blake's "Imagination" or Whitman's voice but the will passing beyond itself. And when this passing occurs, the moment becomes impassioned with the delight of its own passing. Or, since we can never bring ourselves to speak of passion as a passing moment, perhaps it is more accurate to say that in passion we know life as a surpassing moment that we never tire of repeating.

V

In keeping with the spirit of this essay, we cannot very well end without suggesting what a poetry of pure possibility does indeed make possible. Since the implications inherent in these suggestions are vast enough to demand expanded treatment, I will limit them to suggestions, and possible ones at that.

Such a poetry, of course, makes a revaluation of any representational model of poetry, in however qualified a form, not only possible but necessary. A poetry of pure possibility neither imitates nor represents what is or has been. It is not anchored in any past perception and does not anticipate any specific future one; a free projection of the imagination, it preconstitutes, through a unique use of repetition, what might be. As we have seen, because possibilities can never be represented, they must continually be repeated before they can possess even a formal quality. Because repetition posits in advance the inadequacy of this merely formal quality, we have said that these possibilities repeat themselves before they can become themselves. But if repetition both precedes form and constitutes it, what results is neither an imitation or a re-presentation but what might be called an ongoing revision of what can get said only provisionally. This ongoing re-vision, however, suggests a sense not of diminished reality but of renewed possibility, for the re-vision is the activity of freedom itself.

If such a concept obviously violates all the proprieties and expectations of representational thinking, it also calls for a revaluation of the models validating it, including the self-reflexive ones; for in presupposing a double process whereby the poem first evokes a mimetic response and then, to assert a radical rhetoricity, denies it, this model does not abrogate mimesis but only obliquely affirms mimesis' authority by dramatizing mimesis' ability to renege on its promise to represent a world. But Blake, to use only one counterexample, negates all imitation in advance as the delusions of a satanic will seeking to take revenge on time passing by asserting the possessive power of a self-present subject. Blake conquers this possessive will by recovering an original power of the imagination. In Blake, nature ceases to be apart from man and becomes instead a latent power of man's imagination. While mimesis keeps this power latent, by keeping man dependent on already created nature, Blake's imagination re-creates nature out of the divine image. For Blake, however, this divine image is not a supernatural one but *the very experience of the relation between man and nature*. In Blake's poetry, this relation conflates two successive processes into simultaneity: God becoming as man and man becoming as God. But if man becomes as God, who already has become as man, man's becoming assumes the form of God's Second Coming, or the Last Judgment. Thus man's process of becoming as God, his use of the imagination, does not represent physical nature but returns nature to its status *before* the creation as the possible expression of a creator.

To effect this vision Blake engraves illumined images as the background for his printed words. The words characteristically assume the forms of proverbs and aphorisms recalling man to his power to be as God, while the images shine through these words and search into the image of the man who reads them, so that both the engraved image within the text and the image of the spectator without are brought into relation through the commanding power of the imaginative word. When we read Blake's illuminated books we seem to be seen through by the word we literally see, until the imaginative word absorbs both man and image into the radiant power that sees through all.

In the light of Blake's vision, a revaluation of the modernist dilemma also becomes possible. For by seeing words as expressions of an imaginative word that is itself, in origin, a repetition Blake does not bemoan the loss of present time through language; instead he exposes the felt loss of time as the satanic will to possess time in representations. He then replaces this will with the realization that present time is not the loss of what has been but the coming again of what is forever about to be. Blake affirms the word's power, not as representation of a world, but as *pure mediation* between man and world, for this mediation is itself time becoming present.

Once we understand the power of this word to let time become present as a coming again, we cannot conclude this discussion without noting that our "tradition" of poets is truly modern. For through the power of the word, it participates in a moment forever becoming present. The poets who partake of such a moment, however, neither repress nor imitate the poems of a precursor. If repression implies a disease of translation, it is fitting that a theory of literary history based on repression should appear at a time when the ability to translate a poem into a representable paraphrase has become problematic. But if this crisis of the model of representation has been repressed, we must understand a theory of the repressive complex inherent in poetic influence as itself a repression of the wish to hold onto a representational model of language. Now if we can imagine a poetry whose subject is the power of translation *before* the need for representation, we come close to an understanding of this tradition; for such poems are translations in the etymological sense of a carrying over, but a carrying over of nothing but the will to carry over. If these poems constitute, however, a crossing over of the will to cross over, they assert their status not as objective poems but as crossroads, intersections, or what we can call intertexts marking the point where the self-surpassing will returns. A poet who begins a work with the knowledge that it is in origin a translation does not assert its priority over a previous translation— does not even assert it as his or her own work. Like Whitman in "Song of Myself," such a poet incarnates a subject existing between poems already written and those about to be written; and, as we have seen, this intersubject speaks in the middle voice as the very subjectivity of the power to make poems. This intersubject cannot be limited to any particular poem: it speaks through all poems as the voice of their original repetition.

But if the intersubject turns each poem into a crossroads, it also becomes most apparent at the crossroads between poems. The entire process may become clearer if we consider Crane's relation to Blake; for Crane returned to Blake from the perspective of an age that no longer needed Blake's reminders of the deceitful will of nature. Through technology, modern man had asserted his will over nature, only to be left with his will turned against him. To redirect this process, Crane reduced Blake's entire mythic system (which was Blake's technology) into a single moment when Columbus, a repetition of one of Blake's mythic figures (Los), wills beyond any hope for fulfillment. In this moment, Blake's recognition, the language of perception, becomes invocation, the true language of the will. But the vocatives do not call forth images; rather, man's supreme technological image, the bridge, recalls the ever-renewed power of the will—and recalls it, not in Crane's voice (though Crane's voice got its true power as a repetition of Blake's) or in Blake's, but in a voice that has already repeated their voices and all others impassioned with the same power of the will. Perhaps I should not define this matter more precisely but should merely say that today it might be not only possible but even necessary to hear this voice.

ALLEN GROSSMAN

Hart Crane and Poetry:
A Consideration of Crane's
Intense Poetics

The sea raised up a campanile . . . The wind I heard
Of brine partaking, whirling spout in shower
Of column kiss — that breakers spouted, sheared
Back into bosom — me — her, into natal power . . .

—From "The Return"

Throughout the criticism of Hart Crane's poetry there runs, responsive to his own intensity, the sentiment of something very important and uncommon at issue. Winters, Tate, Blackmur among early critics, and more recently Joseph Riddell, Eric J. Sundquist, David Bleich, and John Irwin, the former in ethical and esthetic terms, the latter in various analytical languages, describe relationships between the catastrophe of Hart Crane's life and the nature of his work, different, I think, in degree and perhaps also in kind from such relationships in other authors. It is agreed, whatever else may be in question in the matter of Crane, that he was, undeniably, a poet of stature, and that the sources both of his unquestionable achievement and of his equally unquestionable aberration (whether the latter be considered as an imperfection of his work, or his stopping of that work in death) are

From *Critical Essays on Hart Crane*, edited by David R. Clark. Copyright © 1981 by Allen Grossman. G. K. Hall & Co.

inextricably bound up with the sources of his monumental authenticity as an artist. Crane was not merely a poet; he was a poet of unmistakable gifts who staked everything upon poetry, who had no other presence in the world, and whose art attests a perilous extremity of ambition unaccountable except on the hypothesis of a life at risk. Indeed, Crane's singularity and claim arise directly from the conjunction in him of unmistakable authenticity and equivocal success—as if there were discovered in his life a degree of proximity to the sources of art inconsistent with the life of art itself. In Crane we see, I think, not only a pathology working out its implications in the context of a gift (a case common enough) but also something of the boundaries of poetry as an instrument for effecting human purposes. In this essay I wish to consider whether the harrowing cooperation of the authentic powers that Hart Crane brought to his art with the enormous need that he addressed in it does not indicate (as Crane himself from time to time felt that it did) some boundary at once of poetry and human hope—whether, in short, what you cannot have or be, you also cannot in well-formed poems say.

The four line poem called "The Return," which this essay takes as text, was in effect a final communication, a suicide note. On one of the four manuscript pages relating to "The Return" Hart Crane's mother, Grace Hart Crane, searching like so many others for the "cause" of her son's death, notes (the annotation, now erased, is still sufficiently legible) that she found a version of this poem in his suitcase—on top, and asks whether it bears any "significance to his death." This poem, to which his mother appended her awesome question, gives in brief the full cycle of her son's myth and life, and, in so far as it functioned in the event as a message to his mother across the boundary of death and life, includes her in fact, as it included her in imagination, in the central action of his life. The mother's initials on the manuscript page acknowledge the receipt of the message, completing as a final transgression by mother and son of the boundaries of fiction and experience, the cycle of departure from and return to source which the poem takes as its mythic subject and which the poet acted out in the manner of his death. As would be appropriate for a final communication, the poem contains Crane's metrical signature, the rhymed quatrain that he used not only as a constituent of many of his characteristic poems but particularly as a closural structure. Hence, "The Return"—as the signature set to the work—was correctly placed by the editors of the Liveright Collected Poems (Waldo Frank, Grace Hart Crane, and Sam Loveman) at the end.

According to John Unterecker "The Return" was probably begun in the same creative period during which The Bridge was in large part written, beginning on the Isle of Pines in October of 1926. If this were the case, it would belong among the poems Crane thought to group under the common title, *The Hurricane*, including "O Carib Isle," "The Island Quarry," "The Royal Palm," "The Idiot," and "Eternity." (To these poems that he names should be added as part of the hurricane group "The Air Plant" and "The Hurricane"). But "The Return," not in fact mentioned in the letters, also shares its language and myth with Crane's latest works, an elegiac condensation of the history of his *agon*.

At the end of the prose poem "Havana Rose" (1932), for example, Crane assigns to the mantic doctor (the biologist Zinsser) a sentence that articulates the imaginary history of which "The Return" is an epitome, and that also became the program of Crane's death poem, "The Broken Tower."

> And during the wait over dinner at La Diana the Doctor had said—who was American, also—"You cannot heed the negative—so might go on to undeserved doom . . . must therefore loose yourself within a pattern's mastery that you can conceive, that you can yield to—by which also you win and gain mastery and happiness which is your own from birth.

The sense of this oracle is approximately the following: ending at the beginning in the inheritance of the birthright—the return to "natal power"—this journey (the archetype is the *nostos*, the "return"), which begins with the imprudence of refusing irony ("You cannot heed the negative") and passes through the loosing (or losing) of the self in "pattern's mastery," resolves in the end into the implicitly vortical shape (determined by the simultaneity of progressive and regressive vectors) of the hurricane marriage of discourse with origins ("mastery and happiness"). This marriage of discourse as mastery with source as happiness (the "kiss" of "The Return") defines the scene of authenticity to which Crane's poetry invites the reader—a scene primal, awesome, and ruinous like that to which "the bird of loudest lay" invites in the sovereign instance of "intense poetics" in English, the pseudo-Shakespearean "Phoenix and Turtle." I shall suggest in what follows that this marriage does indeed require a "pattern" for its sanctioning, a pattern that Crane never found because in a profound way he never sought it (though he thematized it as an act of deferral again and again) and to which the structures he does use are related as substitutes and postponements that keep open the space of hope by leaving undefined the region in which discourse is possible. Poetry as discourse was for Crane, as for us all, an instance (and therefore a principle and history) of persons in relationship. Obscurity of discourse in his poetry was for him a postponement and equivocation of the decision as to what relationships are permitted and therefore possible—an equivocation that we as readers enact when we dwell in the bewilderment of his style, and that we erase (but do not resolve) when we compel a "meaning." This is one function of the rhetoric that I have called Crane's "intense poetics."

Modern poetry, as apart from Crane's "slain numbers" we understand it, exhibits the lesser authenticity and greater poetic success of a true experimental art, one that defines the singularity of its motive in terms of a determinate set of outcomes encoded as structure. As such it was devised to set at a distance what Yeats in *his* marriage poem called, with reference to the dead Lionel Johnson, "A measureless consummation that he dreamed." Crane's intense poetics (by contrast) were defiled, unsanctioned, having the novelty of wild exploit rather than invention or experimentation and, inevitably, the strange authority, as I shall show at some length, of the imaginary themes of art rather than its actual imaginative forms. My concern, in brief, is to emphasize the non-experimental (and anti-modernist) characteristics of Crane's enterprise, to suggest that in the absence of the invention of new structures Crane's poetry tends to hallucinate or thematize structures (building, bridge, tower) and to develop a rhetoric of condensation, his well-known iconic "obscurity." In effect, Crane takes authenticity not as a sanction but as a subject, evolving a "difficult poetry" (a poetry without an intratextual interpreter, which therefore postpones meaning) of which the mode is the Longinian high or grand style, a style with inherent affinities to an earliness that preempts growth and leaves only metamorphosis as a strategy for change. This style, as I shall show, is the manner of utterance not of the imaginative singer of our poetry but of the imaginary subject (not of "Wordsworth" but of the solitary reaper, not of "Keats" but of the nightingale) and as such is inherently "obscure," obscure in a sense that can be stated. Finally, I wish to deal with Crane's central motive, the intense hierogamic kiss of absolute acknowledgement and the sense of immense comedic hopefulness he brought to poetry as both an inference from the nature of his art and as a discovery of its boundaries.

I

It is no longer in any way remarkable to suggest that, considered in the context of the poetic practice of his contemporary modernism, Hart Crane was not an experimental poet. At about the time of Crane's birth Yeats, to take the salient case, decisively redefined the idealist poetic enterprise that he had brought to high finish (but not to completion) in *The Wind Among The Reeds* (1899), and in so doing passed judgment on the poetic task that Crane was compelled to labor at in the next generation. Yeats' ironic distancing (as in "Adam's Curse" [1901]) of his own death-bound early ambition (not now the *impossible* task, but only that task "most difficult" among the class of tasks *not impossible*) made Yeats as a poetic speaker the audience and interpreter, in effect, of his own early motive, and announced that ironization of questioning that Eliot identified for his generation in the allusive poetics of "The Love Song of J. Alfred Prufrock" as the mark of high modern structural innovation in poetry. The voices at risk internal to Eliot's *The Waste Land* could no more have spoken the poem that quotes them than could Joyce's Stephen Daedalus have written *The Portrait of the Artist as a Young Man*. Crane, by contrast, spoke from the point of view not of the Daedalian survivor but of the Icarian over-reacher, spoke not as the survivor in retrospect but as the mariner in course of the unsurvivable voyage. Yeats feared ("To the Rose upon the Rood of Time") that he would come to speak a "tongue men do not know," and so he changed the rules of the game; Crane really spoke that obscure tongue, refusing to change the rules. To have done so would have meant for him betrayal (modernism was in moral terms the treasonous friendship of which he obsessively complained) of the task set him by his great passion for consummatory validation, the obligation entailed by the great hope that brought him to poetry. Whether or not Crane's enterprise constituted a misreading of the medium which he practiced, whether what he wanted was within the gift of art, is, as I have already suggested, one of the issues that the career of Hart Crane brings to mind.

Modernist experimentalism was precipitated by the discovery that certain central promises of poetry (as well as of the other arts) were impossible of attainment, shadowed by that "abridgement of hope" to which Paul Fussell has recently drawn attention. If poetry were to go on it must change toward the ironic thematization of central aspects of its traditional function as a reconciling, honor-conferring, and perpetualizing medium. Crane, who sometimes mimicked or repeated but only very selectively participated in the high modern innovation, refused to change the rules of the game (the "pattern's mastery") because he viewed those rules as the implicit fulfillment, the pre-text as it were, of the success he had not ceased to expect ("mastery and happiness which is your own from birth"). As a consequence we find him *pressed against* the logic of grammar (his well-known "logic of metaphor" is still the metaphorization of meta-phor as logic), and against the resistant abstract "cable strands" of metricality that sustained the iconic and internally centered structures he imagined as responding to the purposes in view of which poetry justified the labor of its making. The result was that he achieved an agonistic discovery of the boundaries of the traditional art he practiced, rather than any redefinition of the structures of that art such as implied, in the case of Eliot or Williams or Stevens, a new avenue of practice. Crane's achieved work, his success, is an intense version of what he found; and his singular rhetoric is constituted by the compelled strategies of that intensity, the consequence of his unwillingness to relinquish what in his reading of the role and means of the poet he felt to be poetry's promises. No other poet, to my knowledge, tried with such relentless integrity to get so much out of the poetic means at hand as did Crane; and that is, as I see it, the beginning of an understanding of his claim on our attention.

II

The poems of Crane most marked by his characteristic manner belong to that rough class of poems called "difficult" to which also belong such diverse cases as "The Phoenix and Turtle," Blake's "The Mental Travel-ler," certain of Yeats' early poems, Roethke's "Lost Son," and some of the poems (to take a recent instance) of John Ashbery. "Difficult poems" are poems that lack an intra-textual interpreter. As a class of limiting cases, they call attention to the extent to which the poems of tradition are themselves "readings" and administrations of already vanished (or phe-nomenally impossible) states of affairs. Crane's disposition to construct difficult poems in this sense, poems that leave undefined the relationship of their authenticity to any finite consequence or meaning, thus keeping open and unconstrained the reach of their discourse (they might mean everything, import the accessibility, the permissibility, of all relationships, *validate* the truth of the boundlessness of desire) delegated to the reader the role of the exegetical participant. Hence the reading of Crane's poems, as difficult poems, situates the reader internal to the poem, and assigns him the task of completing rather than deriving significances. (Hence also the critical tendency to find Crane's poetry incomplete, or imperfectly articulated by its symbols.) Crane himself attempted to com-pensate for this feature of his poetry by making interpretations of his own structures. When he wrote for Harriet Monroe the famous exegesis of his Melville poem, he was doing the business of the culture that his poem omitted, seeking to provide not so much an access to the poem as a means of escaping from it. By analogy with Eliot's practice in the "Preludes" ("Every street *lamp* that I pass *beats* like a fatalistic *drum*" [italics Crane's]),

Crane implies that the "logic of metaphor" is provided by the inference of a middle term, the inference of a person in whom disparate terms of experience are integrated, a person whose ideal reconciling powers can exist *only* as an inference. This sensibility justified the logic of metaphor by disappearing, by vacating just that space in which as registration of personal presence (as lyric speaker in the traditional sense) the person as mind creates the interpretable world by accounting for the relationship of things in it. Crane's poems summon and await their reader much as the solitary reaper in Wordsworth awaits the exegetical *deixis* of the journeyer who says, "Behold her. . . ."

Another consequence of Crane's practice of the "difficult" poem was his own production of "exegetical" poems (poems about other poets) as a counter-effort to be the outsider describer, the Daedalian survivor of enterprises like his own, or inversely as an effort to find his counterplayer and interpreter, the one who will be both inside and outside his own enterprise. *The Bridge* in its latter half—Part IV (Whitman), VI (Dickinson), VII (Poe)—searches the tradition for an hermeneutic friend who might "close" the enterprise by stabilizing its meanings, but who must be a memorializer who can remember an event without betraying its authenticity. In the end, however, he finds even "Shakespeare" validated by indistinguishability from the hurricane authenticity of his subject, "pilot, —tempest, too!" In fact, Crane becomes in his poems about poets not an exegete or elegist (or like the modern Yeats a definer of possible life by contrast to impossible example, or like Keats on Lear a man interpreted by his master) but a trans-historical concelebrant at the same altar on which he himself experiences "transmemberment." Crane's poets are boundary demons like himself whose fidelity to authenticity (the "natal power" of "The Return") is measured by their unbornness, whose myths have no outside. When in his poems Crane does contemplate his own interpretation, he produces images of the textualization of the self as an agony of circumscription, or in his own word "conscription"—a mutilation, as we see in his terrifying uses of the word "engrave," or the word "counted."

Crane's quasi-sonnet, "To Emily Dickinson" (1927), closer in its language to Amy Lowell's sonnet on Keats than to the language of Dickinson herself, specifies Dickinson's subject as that "Eternity" which was in the hurricane poem so called the name he gave to the white horse ("Like a vast phantom maned by all that memoried night/Of screaming rain—Eternity!") that stands forth epiphanically as the fact corresponding to the song of the "sweet, dead Silencer." Silence and whiteness (the whiteness of Crane's masterpiece *White Buildings* whose "Legend" is "As silent as a mirror is believed/Realities plunge in silence by . . .") are the specifying features, the paradoxically obliterative marks, of that state of affairs, the truth and the fact, which his "difficult" poems solicit as desire and postpone as text—the world unqualified by the treacheries of mean-ing. As I shall have occasion to suggest later in this essay, Crane's language and subjects are always (like Dickinson as presented in the language of Lowell) out of place, defiled, because as discourse they have not yet undone the exile which separates them from source—"Unwhispering as a mirror/Is believed."

To Emily Dickinson

You who desired so much—in vain to ask—
Yet fed your hunger like an endless task,
Dared dignify the labor, bless the quest—
Achieved that stillness ultimately best,

Being, of all, least sought for: Emily, hear!
O sweet, dead Silencer, most suddenly clear
When singing that Eternity possessed
And plundered momently in every breast;

—Truly no flower yet withers in your hand,
The harvest you descried and understand
Needs more than wit to gather, love to bind,
Some reconcilement of remotest mind—

Leaves Ormus rubyless, and Ophir chill.
Else tears heap all within one clay-cold hill.

Crane's exegetical poems tend to be hagiographic in character—the lives of witnesses who, because their truth is beyond interpretation ("more than wit to gather, love to bind"), die in an act which like the Crane poem validates the truth of vast inference ("reconcilement of remotest mind") and pre-empts the lesser reconciliations of interpretation. The poem as a sign and the poet elegized by the poem tend to be equally silent, equally Silencers. Yeats' hagiographic poems in the same period function, as I have suggested, to delegate away from the text, from the actual poem, the agonistic predicament of the dead and silenced subject. This Crane does not do. Instead, he reports "to" his "Dickinson" his *rediscovery in her* of the terms of his own enterprise ("The harvest you descried and understand"). In Crane's intense poetics discourse functions as a repetition or condensation—the scene itself once again of the event referred to—rather than in the ordinary sense a mimesis or fictional displacement (or delegation) of a state of affairs. Structure in poetry is in the ordinary case an interpretation of meaning, or a repetition of meaning in another code. The irrelevance in Crane of structure to meaning calls attention to the "difficulty" of his poems, their status as instances, rather than accounts, of unsurvivable exploits. As in "The Phoenix and Turtle": "Death is now the Phoenix' nest."

The heroism of Crane's "Dickinson" is his own, and consists in persistence, like his own, in the "endless task" of responding faithfully to *all* the implications of "hunger." This activity drains the world of its terms (as the death of Shakespeare's birds took Beauty and Truth out of phenomenal existence), leaving "Ormus rubyless, and Ophir chill." If it does not do so there is only vacancy—"Else tears heap all within one clay-cold hill"—the vacancy which finds sentiment without an object. If it does do so, the one word which has vortically taken in all other words as the condition of its nominalization, leaves behind silence and a trace—the "difficult poem," manifest only in so far as it fails of perfect accord with its imaginary subject. Hence, Crane's poetic hagiography is a continuation rather than, as in Yeats' case or in Robinson's or Auden's, an interruption and ironization of the elegists intentions. "Eternity" is the moment of language's "clarity"—a clarity different from discursive intelligibility— obtained by the singer as "Silencer" whose life is the trace of an action, or a word, become true at the point of disappearance in death. All Crane's hero-poets—Dickinson, Melville, Poe, Shakespeare—repeat his posture as an agonist at the boundaries of possibility ("junctions elegiac") struggling with a medium (language and its artistic forms) that decays at the point of fulfillment of its promises, decays into the authority of its own signified—"O sweet, dead Silencer, most suddenly clear." Like the whiteness of the "white buildings" the silence so often evoked in Crane is the inferential plenitude toward which his actual poems are the pre-texts, and in view of which his refusal of significant form is a postponement. In difficult poems there is no intratextual interpreter, and in Crane this absence opens a space in which the poem is not yet present and will never be.

III

Crane's relationship to the forms he used was entirely ambivalent. On the one hand they were the necessary mechanisms of presence, and on the other deforming "gates of life." Like the terrifying (black and swollen) portals of emergence in his elegiac autobiographies, poetic structures gave access to reality, and also withheld it; and the same was true for the poetic languages of tradition which he could not re-invent and could not do without. Crane precipitated upon basically nineteenth century forms and diction-systems (not fundamentally different from those of Keats, Patmore, and Swinburne) a passion for consummation which crowded the small and unforgiving space of appearance (the term, the trope, the line, the stanza) with his verbal *bricolage*, the broken pieces of the vast gestures and uncompromising sentiments he would not give up and could not make fit whole in the secular window of his means. This crowding of the frame came to constitute a trope peculiar to himself—not the modernist "ambiguity," which hierarchizes, or ironically totalizes a plurality of meanings—but a singularly naive rhetoric of shadowed wholeness (the impossible simultaneity of all the implications of desire) that struggles merely to include all meanings in the one space of appearance. In short, Crane's structures do not, except in trivial cases, take the shape of his subject because there is no metrical order of desire in all its outcomes; and yet there is no shape of presence except the metrical frame, and its syntagmatic correlative the grammatical sentence.

Crane's crowding of the frame produces his characteristic intense version of traditional usage, a rhetoric of *condensation* which manifests itself both on the horizontal axis of figuration (a matter which he was at pain to justify in his explanatory essays) and also in the vertical axis of narrative. As rhetoric, the intense poetics of condensation has the effect of precipitating "difficulty" by eliding the person who perceives (one remembers Crane's remarks to Harriet Monroe about, "The dice of drowned men's bones": "These being the bones of dead men who never completed their voyage, it seems legitimate to refer to them as the only surviving evidence of certain messages undelivered, mute evidence of certain things, experiences that the dead mariners might have had to deliver"); as narrative, the poetics of condensation elides the human world by collapsing consequence into source, consummating the dominance of authenticity over structure. The true person of inference is the proportionless whole broken by the finite scalar frame of appearance of which metrical structure is the sign ("the broken world," "broken eyes," "Dawn's broken arch," "broken intervals"). The point of the manifestation of the person marks the moment of the pre-emption of consummation, hence (as I have said) the idealization of silence and whiteness as the ultimate refusal to appear, as the escape from all speech and the turning away of all light. In the moment of its release the eye is led, not along the wavering path of sentiment (the right side of the mountain in "The Island Quarry") but straight into the stone, putting an end to the monumental carving.

Crane's preferred type of fundamental narrative (of which *The Bridge*, and "The Island Quarry" are as much instances as "The Return") is the *nostos*, the tracing of "the visionary company of love" back to the primal scene or source condition where it is an unbroken unity—"Back into bosom—me—her, into natal power. . . ." The effect of the rhetoric of condensation is to assign more and more of the contest of desire to fewer and fewer terms, until all that truly is is finally condensed upon a single word. This is the rhetorical architectonic of Crane's vortex or spout. As there is finally only one word (as will be seen in the reading of "The Return" at the end of this essay), so there is also only one moment—the present. Crane's modernist contemporaries such as Yeats and Eliot tended to use the word "modern" in an ironic sense (the common usage until Whitman) as a term specifying the emptiness of *this* moment in history. Consistent with Crane's de-ironization of terms, the modern as present time has for him apocalyptic fullness. It is the moment of sudden actualization, perfect in proportion as it is like the inferential, totalizing, imaginary single word: nothing and all.

The scenario of "The Return" is restated (once again in terminal position) in the last sentence of the concluding paragraph of "General Aims and Theories":

> New conditions of life germinate new forms of spiritual articulation. And while I feel that my work includes a more consistent extension of traditional literary elements than many contemporary poets are capable of appraising, I realize that I am utilizing the gifts of the past as instruments principally; and that the voice of the present, if it is to be known, must be caught at the risk of speaking in idioms and circumlocutions sometimes shocking to the scholar and historians of logic. Language has built towers and bridges, but itself is inevitably as fluid as always.

Crane's shock to logic (its scholars and *historians*) is the situation of discourse at the point of the extinguishing of continuity in timeless presentness, where event is not recapitulated diachronically but becomes as language what language is in itself, "inevitably as fluid as always." Language as "natal power" receives back the towers and bridges of language as mediation (scholars' language and historians' language) in a consummation that is the intersection of sign and signified—the end of the quest at the moment of beginning. This poetics, which treats language in terms of its fluidity in which lies *per impossible* the synchronicity of all its meanings, becomes associated in Crane's mind with the "present" and the "new."

Crane means by "the present" the place of the liberation of the will, technology being one of the symbols of that liberation, conferring speed which rivals time and the capacity to execute the wishes of dream; Crane means by "new" the competence ("This competence" as in "The Wine Menagerie") to journey across that particular space, fundamental to all issues about space in Crane (and Whitman) which separates persons, as "other" minds, one from the other. Indeed, Crane situates in the present the consummatory energies which Yeats came to situate in the past. And Crane's technologizations of the past ("utilizing the gifts of the past as instruments principally") aligns the powers of the past with the will in the present, abolishing the historicity of tradition, but also condensing upon the present all the daimonic intensities of authentic earliness. For Crane, past and present, one mind and the other, meet not in myth but in fact. "New" as a cultural term carries from the time of the Gospels implications of subjectivity, the covenant reestablished within. In Crane's usage it implies ("New thresholds, new anatomies!") the transgression of the rule of subjectivity which is of course the immiscibility of minds; as also in Crane's usage technology implies, not the triumph of structure, but its dissolution. In Crane's intense poetics the world has no outside, and language is seen (for example in "Voyages II") as from the inside, in its energies and earliness which have, like the inside of the body, no social form.

It was, of course, the high modern habit to incorporate the past as an ironic measurement of an historically irreversible decline. Ambivalently conceived, the past was for Yeats ghosts on the wind, hostile to life and necessary to life. In the same way that Crane's imaginary poetics constructed states of reference identical to the reality he sought (short-circuiting the constraining social logic of mediation), so also in the name of the poetics of the "new" he undertook to write *as* his predecessor, ignoring the equally constraining and prudential history of styles, as if he had no body and no unexchangeable place in time. Crane's pentameter verse, for example, has in this sense a character precisely contradictory to the blank verse that opens the second part of *The Waste Land*. Eliot's poetry is devised as a system that measures its distance, as an ironic matrix of systems, from all other systems while at the same time bringing them antiphrastically to mind. Crane's by contrast functions to abolish the historicity of models, accomplishing his purposes and values, as he remarks in "General Aims and Theories," "as well . . . with the vocabulary and blank verse of the Elizabethans as with the calligraphic tricks and slang used so brilliantly at times by an impressionist like Cummings." The nature of Crane's stylistic anachronism can be seen by noting its similarity to the speeches of Melville's Ahab and Starbuck as lineated by Matthiessen in *The American Renaissance*. Of these speeches Matthiessen says:

> The danger of such unconsciously compelled verse is always evident. As it wavers and breaks down again into ejaculatory prose, it seems never to have belonged to the speaker, to have been at best a ventriloquist's trick.

But it is precisely the posture of speaking from the impossible point of view of the irrecoverably early and therefore imaginary past which constitutes for Crane the defiance of irony and distance upon which he founds his truth. Ahab was doomed to the vortex that swallowed up the Pequod. Crane interpreted and transvalued that vortex as "the vortex of our grave," the eye of perfected response.

In "General Aims and Theories" (once again) Crane notes: "I have been called an 'absolutist' in poetry. . . ." He contrasts the sense in which he accepts this description with his understanding and repudiation of "impressionism." The impressionist, he says, "is really not interested in the *causes* (metaphysical) of his materials, their emotional derivations or their utmost spiritual consequences. A kind of retinal registration is enough. . . ." This distinction accords with Crane's practice. Crane is a poet of metaphysical cause, emotional derivation, and "utmost spiritual consequences" in the sense that his poetry abolishes mediations and absolutizes relationships. In the language of "The Return" the thematization of that abolishment is the hierophantic hurricane "kiss" which has no social or, in any ordinary sense, perceptual correlative. Crane's kiss of total response ("Kisses are,—/The only worth all granting.") is a social term which has no social meaning, as his poems segregate the language of social transaction (he is after all from first to last a love poet) into a strange region of elite discourse, the "absolute" region not of retrospect or anticipation but exploit. In this region he does indeed reach a boundary of discourse, an absolute that has no "poetic precedent," a "capture" (not a registration) of presence. Crane's "So I found 'Helen' sitting in a street car" (Apollonius of Tyana's displacement of Helen of Troy) constructs the impossibility of meeting Helen, or anybody else, by investing the present with the past in such a way that the subject matter of the poem is not the juncture between two terms but the impossible multiplied presence of both terms simultaneously. As soon as the present—the space of meaning— becomes thus actualized, it becomes phenomenologically remote. Crane invests the present not with the intelligibility, but with the unreachability, of the past, and the past with the urgency of the present, thus burdening his hope (the enrichment of present time) with the unobtainability of memory and the unexchangeability of particular experience. Crane's logic of metaphor, just because it bypasses the social logics of inference which repeat prudentially the logic of history and language, destroys the very space of presentness and appearance which it is devised to obtain. By collapsing origin and consequence (between which all historical and psychological life is situated, and perhaps all poetic life as well) Crane founded his poetic enterprise on an (imaginary) mode of discourse prior to the structures of discourse as mediation ("Language has built towers and bridges, but itself is inevitably as fluid as always").

Connate with this intention is Crane's de-ironized use of the past (his instrumentalization of the history of styles, his treatment of the history of styles as an array of undisqualified possibilities). This is the poetics not of an imaginative state of affairs on which actual states of affairs can be modelled, but of an imaginary state of affairs which is normally in the history of poetry (and very distinctly in the modern period) seen from a measured distance. But Crane always treated his poetic models in a sense, in Matthiessen's term, ventriloquistically. His poetry is "literary" in a way that Eliot's, for example, is not. He was the captive, the "sexton slave," of the historicity of his models (whether modern, Victorian, or Elizabethan). Hence his models, of structure and style, were bitter friends indeed, an enemy element, at the most intimate point of self-presence. In so far as they became his, he had destroyed their proprium. In so far as he became theirs his identity was in question. His search for nurturance in primordial lineage encountered, in the result, only more colonists and claimants, so that his poems present us with a speaker without a voice, ambivalent toward the terms of presence, the structures of his art.

IV

It has not been sufficiently realized that Crane is not a mystic but a realist for whom the fact of structure (metrical and grammatical), as the condition of presence, stands as the unalterable fact of "the world." Mystic language in Crane serves in place of the language of desire severely conceived, for which there is no other language in the dialects of poetry. Crane's major poems put poetry in question, in so far as they are experiments that seek to discover whether there is anything a man can say (whether there is any poem) consistent with unconceded human hope. This is the cultural question that lies inside the intensity of Crane's poetics; and it is this issue that is at stake when we decide whether there is, or is not, a good poem by Crane among those (such as "For the Marriage of Faustus and Helen," or "Voyages," or "The Broken Tower") that are marked by the "absolute," the unrelinquishing intensities of his concern.

Precisely because Crane devised, in the modernist sense of the word, no "new" structures (nothing like Yeats' segmented integrations in "Among School Children," or Eliot's matrices of spatialized time as in *The*

Waste Land, or Williams' metrically open line-frames as in "On the road to the contagious hospital"), he tended in his poetry to hallucinate mechanisms, and structures, to repeat the problem of form as image as a way of searching for, voyaging toward, trying, and postponing a structural means of access to the space he sought, where all the powers and justly desired outcomes of sentiment would be simultaneously at home. These "orphic machines"—the bridge, the tower, the airplane, the carillon, the hurdy-gurdy, the phonograph, the camera—function like poetic forms in that they produce experience and are burdened and deformed by desire. They are images of mind, and like mind (as other mind) portend knowledge:

> I saw the frontiers gleaming of his mind;
> or are there frontiers—running sands sometimes
> running sands—somewhere—sands running . . .
> Or they may start some white machine that sings.
> Then you may laugh and dance the axletree—
> steel—silver—kick the traces—and know—

"The white machine that sings" is one of Crane's many imaginal experiments toward a structure that can mediate source (like the severed head of Orpheus). In the above passage that structure (or mechanism) is indistinguishable from other mind itself, both the goal of the quest for love and its means—conceived as the frontier of subjectivity, "new" because transgressed.

Traditional poetry (the poetry of insight rather than intensity) views inactual ideal states from the point of view of the achieved structures of the actual text which constitute, in so far as they are successful, stable mediations, interpretable interpretations, and therefore concessions to possibility. Crane by contrast wrote in the impossible ethos or intense position of the inactual ideal state (at the "frontier" of mind considered as borderless) and, inversely, *thematized* possible structures. Hence, the inevitability of the central and equivocal poem, *The Bridge*—a speculation, based on Roebling's Victorian system, toward the possibility of "the curveship" (privilege and solving shape) that does mediate relationship absolutely. But technology for Crane (he is particularly concerned with the then new technologies of flight and electronic communication) became a parody and promise of transgressive psychological enablement, as were in the bad end of his life sexuality, drink, and poetry. Technology substituted for the novelty (the "new" state of relationship) which poetic structure could not finally concede him, and constituted experiment beyond the prudence of art. In a like manner, Crane attempted to construct ("hallucinate" would again be the appropriate term) genealogies, also myths or machines of access to origins correlative to the other high modern administrations of history and archetype toward the provision of the sufficient terms of lyric presence. But for Crane these genealogies were always colored by consciousness, not of their nurturant fictionality as in Yeats, nor of their confident historicity as in Eliot or Pound (Crane's quotations were pressed out to the epigraphic margin), but of their impossibility. Crane, seeking identity rather than reference, ventriloquism rather than quotation or indirect discourse, registered in the many postures of extreme mutilation his poetry contains ("Blamed, bleeding hands") the real difference between wishing and having. It is not merely the case of the "Lie to us,—dance us back the tribal morn!" of "The Dance"—the anxious realism of "Lie" being the trace of an intra-textual consciousness of the artistic equivocality of that poem, which has been so often noticed—; but also of the admired early poem in the "wavering" line of "tears and sleep," "My Grandmother's Love Letters," where the effort is to assess the possibility of rescuing the present by voyaging to the source of the melting text of love.

> There are no stars to-night
> But those of memory.
> Yet how much room for memory there is
> In the loose girdle of soft rain.
>
> There is even room enough
> For the letters of my mother's mother,
> Elizabeth,
> That have been pressed so long
> Into a corner of the roof
> That they are brown and soft,
> And liable to melt as snow.
>
> Over the greatness of such space
> Steps must be gentle.
> It is all hung by an invisible white hair.
> It trembles as birch limbs webbing the air.
>
> And I ask myself:
>
> "Are your fingers long enough to play
> Old keys that are but echoes:
> Is the silence strong enough
> To carry back the music to its source
> And back to you again
> As though to her?"
>
> Yet I would lead my grandmother by the hand
> Through much of what she would not understand;
> And so I stumble. And the rain continues on the roof
> With such a sound of gently pitying laughter.

Like "The Return" this poem is a dream of rescue. For Crane rescue is the goal of the labour of the poem, paradoxical heroism of the doomed mariner. The almost unbearable condition of presence to the world, which the actual poems of Crane repeat as "difficulty," is the state of affairs from which he undertakes to save himself and his undistinguishable counterplayer ("me—her"). The effort to "keep" what in the intense poetics of lettered consciousness has been "pressed so long"—the effort to work out in poems the conditions of rescue from the murderous poetics of presence to the world—raises questions about the adequacy of all mechanisms of access to that source prior to art from which the "love letters" come. The rescue—from art not to it—involves reference to a condition prior to the exile in language, prior to the mother (for poetry in Crane is not the conscious self-confirming and liberating father tongue, but the incestuously unconscious and implicating mother tongue). It is to that "natal power"—the power of the "mother's mother"—that this poem undertakes to reach, the "orphic machine" being the phantasmal instrument ("Old keys that are but echoes") which requires a strength from silence (the whiteness of speech, its truth and its transcendence) that proves unobtainable. This doomed orphic journey of rescue (Elizabeth is, of course, the mother of John whose severed head, like Orpheus', is found toward the end of "The Wine Menagerie") is enabled by a rare moment of spatial openness ("the world dimensional"), a moment of personal subjectivity that implies a confidence about identity that is the furthest reach of Crane's imagination. It emerges again only in Crane's death poem "The Broken Tower" as "The commodious, tall decorum of that sky." Crane is the native of condensed, borderless, non-spatial, imaginary states of affairs, for whom the task of imagination is to produce the conditions of ordinary life—the labor of the hindered realist. The presence not of the mother but of the mother's mother awakens the sentiment of possible life and confident self-identification.

"My Grandmother's Love Letters" is a private elegy in the style of Patmore, Arnold, and Henley. But unlike the 19th century author for whom the wavering right hand margin implies the absence of theological assurance of transcendental reference, Crane expresses by the same metrical feature momentary release from an overwhelming objective prohibition ("stars"). Arnold's "folds of a bright girdle furled" becomes the "loose girdle of soft rain" (not yet the "screaming rain" of "Eternity"); and in the presence of a person (as in "Praise for an Urn") Crane's speaker becomes a person, in uncondensed dimensional space, whose body is the condition of the obtaining of his truth. But in this poem we also see the primordial discovery for Crane that the dimensional and undeformed body cannot

execute the task of rescue, and therefore the reconstruction of the inevitability of a condensed poetics in which the hand is deformed, becomes
"long"—not the instrument of the contingent and exilic "hand in hand"
of the real fallen world of "wandering steps and slow" but of the impossible Edenic fusion of absolute relationship, of speed. Only in the absence
of the stars can Crane be a self, and only in the absence of the self can he
be a poet.

The deformation of the hand is required to obtain access to source,
and Orpheus-like carry power of rescue back into the world of consequence ("And back to you again/As though to her," where "her" is not
now the grandmother but the mother). The effort at love through music
exceeds the deformation possible to the hand; and the rescue of the
grandmother is subsumed by the irony. Hereafter, the gentle poetics of
irony, the region where there is room enough for an intratextual interpreter ("And I ask myself"), is replaced by the hurricane poetics of
condensation which overburdens all structures and especially the structure
of the most inevitable of Orphic machines, the natural body. In "My
Grandmother's Love Letters," "Praise for an Urn," and "Chaplinesque,"
human space ("lucid space," as in "Praise for an Urn") appears and
disappears. The sphinx of intense poetics takes up its station on the
threshold, and the prayer to the sphinx as muse is for access to feeling:

> (Let sphinxes from the ripe
> Borage of death have cleared my tongue
> Once and again; vermin and rod
> No longer bind. Some sentient cloud
> Of tears flocks through the tendoned loam:
> Betrayed stones slowly speak.)

Crane's most "difficult" poems are, as I have pointed out, often
preempted autobiographies ("Legend," "The Repose of Rivers," "Passage"
are examples). In "Passage," in particular, the argument with the laurel
ends at the breaking of personal memory on the point of literate record.
"What fountains did I hear? what icy speeches?/Memory, committed to the
page, had broke." The enormous task of absolute relationship (the rescue
of the personal world from mediation) brought Crane to poetry; but under
the burden of that task poetry as textual fact ("committed to the page"),
poetry as the case of presence of that ideal sort considered as an actual
state of affairs, destroyed through a demonization of mind ("My memory I
left in a ravine,—") such access to sentiment and personal growth as
would have promised a gratifying life in the world. As utterance obliter-
ated by its style Crane's poetry stands as a repetition of a countenance

erased by its art of presence. The fate of the "hand" in Crane summarizes the outcome of the search for access to the world of persons, for the hand is the instrument of the secular bond and also the allegorical sign of the body as inscriber. The question in "My Grandmother's Love Letters" addressed to the self ("Are your fingers long enough to play/Old keys that are but echoes . . . ?") contains inside it the issue as to whether there is any way of saying as an undeformed natural speaker what Crane's motive to art demands. As the response of a realist to an impossible demand Crane's poetic phenomenology of hands—"troubled hands," "reliquary hands," "snowy hands," "lover's hands"—confesses the incommensurability with human form of his labor at human validation.

In Crane, the story about structure—bridge, tower, tree, hand—follows as image rather than precedes as available creative knowledge the moment of the poem's construction. His thematized structures are less the outcome than the unfinished business of his invention. Poetic structure, whether the phantom modernism of *The Bridge* or the nineteenth century French formality of "The Broken Tower," was unaccommodated to his meaning because no structure, the function of which is to bear meaning into the world of appearance, is free from the finitizations that are the sufficient condition of appearing at all. Like the hand and bridge and tower, language itself, under the weight of his concern, was deformed and became another hallucinated system wrenched from recognition (and therefore deprived of its power to confer recognition) by the poetics of intensity.

"Language has built towers and bridges, but itself is inevitably as fluid as always." The whole cycle of Crane's myth is the story about the dissolution of forms. The fundamental form of which all the other modes of structure are versions—erected, deformed, and finally dissolved—is language as the vehicle of acknowledgement.

> The sea raised up a campanile . . . The wind I heard
> Of brine partaking, whirling spout in shower
> Of column kiss—that breakers spouted, sheared
> Back into bosom—me—her, into natal power . . .

These lines are a "fragment" only because fragments are all that can appear; but they are also a "whole" poem in that they record their own disappearance antiphrastically. In "The Return" we find Crane's story about language and desire ("mastery and happiness," "towers and bridges") disentangling itself from exile, and resolved into the fundamental genealogy, the "natal power" which in any determinate manifestation it can only imply. As we have said, Crane's account of desire is "mystic" merely because it is extreme; and his account of structure and above all of language as a finite system under stress is realistic, referenced toward the question of possibility by its display of undisguised deformity. At the end of "My Grandmother's Love Letters" the speaker, in the ambiance now of the mockery of the rain, leads his grandmother "Through much of what she would not understand. . . ." The sense of mockery and unintelligibility responds to the terms of a solution to the problem of the source of love incompatible with the human use to which that solution is to be put. The consciousness of a hope inconsistent with any outcome of desire invades even Crane's most lucid poem of sentiment. Under the burden of hope the structure of relationship itself dissolves. What is the nature of that hope?

Unlike the cultural vortices of the Eliot/Pound/Lewis axis, Crane's "whirling spout" represented the all-consuming experience of acknowledgement which seemed to him the one proper subject of poetry and the sustaining condition of life. His dream of rescue was a story about the restoration of relationship between persons. He had no other subject. The resort to poetry for the execution of this subject was an inference from the fact that poetry is founded on, and justified by, solutions to the questions of persons in relationship (across the distance of otherness to one another, and across the distance of death). Whatever the accident of biography that pitched Crane toward the poetic art, he addressed poetry in terms of the great imaginary promises to which the tradition of the imagination points: honor and immortality. His originality consisted in supposing that the promises of poetry and its actual life in the world could be indistinguishable.

For Crane acknowledgement was a crisis, both of mind and of representation, in which existence was altogether at risk. This crisis presented itself whenever Crane encountered the paradoxicality of the unqualified relationship he desired—a relationship that draws into itself, vortically, the totality of experience, admitting no secondary subject, no space of digression, no otherness. The high modern poetry of Crane's contemporaries aspired to a putative universality of reference ("Let us go then, you and I. . . .", "Something there is that doesn't love a wall. . . .") Crane's poetry aspired to a totality of existence ("—And yet this great wink of eternity. . . ."). In this inherently obscure (because inward referenced) vortex all relationships are condensed into one relationship, all words into one word, all moments into one moment. This single "flower" is not merely an occasion of experience but the occasion that replaces all other occasions of experience, and in view of which all other relationships are judged. This vortical relationship has the name of all other relationships, as in Yeats the vortex or gyre is the shape preliminary to the subsumption of all shapes. In the vortex exile ends. And, in the sense in which it is not survived, so ends also the inherent paradoxicality of story. The vortex has no outside, as in "The Return" there is no station of the speaker except the creative source itself in which the "me" and the "her" are one in the perfected acknowledgement of co-presence at origin. As Crane's hope is an inference from the promises of poetry (honor and immortality) so the image of his hope is an inference from the mechanisms of lyric individuation that requires a recapitulation of the self from the point of view of origin. In this sense the seriousness of the lyric person (Crane's intensity) is always incestuous, and therefore, like Crane's style, touched with abhorrence and disfigurement, portending an autonomy which is not "elite" (as Crane's poetry is sometimes called) but inimical to civility in the largest possible sense. The rescue contemplated, however, is not incest but the nurturing of the "me" and the "her" at a common bosom, the "natal power" of both.

As an allegory of discourse the vortex has no interpreter; it is the most difficult of all poems. The "whirling spout" or tower-column (like the bridge and indeed all Crane's thematized structures, white machines) is the momentary suspension of language in the human world before its descent (return) into the fundamental fluidity ("fluid as always") which is language's estate when it is, as it were, for itself. From this we understand the *nature* of a language (I shall deal with its tradition in the next section of this essay) iconic of source, inherently obscure—such as Yeats points to but does not enact as exploit in the famous interrogation, "How can we know the dancer from the dance?" "Consummation" is an alien subject in English as the anomaly of "The Phoenix and Turtle" reminds us. The intense poetics of consummation as Crane practiced them are correspondingly alien and uncommon, defining the boundaries of poetry as a means for modeling or anticipating experience. In so far as poetic structure, and the decorum of speech, are the form and principle of the entrance into appearance of the poetic subject matter, Crane's motive has, in proportion as it is perfected, no intelligible saying or human sentence. The motive of authenticity (as Yeats learned and Eliot preached) is not a poetic motive at all.

Crane's poetry, then, is an exposition of the fate of structures— the body of man, man's language, man in language (the poet), and the things of man's making—when brought into service of the unconceded comedy of human enhancement ("Let us unbind our throats of fear and pity") of which the central act is fundamental acknowledgement— the "kiss."

V

The style of this enterprise is the "high" style, or more precisely (as I shall explain) the *imaginary style* of which Crane's anachronistic high styles are modal signs. Beyond any embodiment in actual poems the motive of poetry is, in the tradition, a constant allusion. On this allusion or idealization Crane (by an inversion) has attempted to model the fact of his text. Both Winters, early on, and, more recently, Joseph Riddel remark that what Emerson proposed the poet should do Crane really does. The matter can, I think, be stated more generally. The nature and function of "poetry" (as eternal, divine, regenerative, honoring, etc.) are generalized in poetry's apologies, not from the fact of any text in history, but from the imaginary, inactual, or true poem which the actual poem carries inside it and alludes to ("Let there be. . . ."; "Sing, goddess, . . ."; "Behold her. . . .") as, for example, the song of a solitary reaper is carried inside Wordsworth's actual poem, "The Solitary Reaper." Wordsworth's actual poem, to pursue the example, is infected as a pseudo-ballad by the oral nature of the imaginary and true ballad inside it, but is itself precisely the finite, intelligible, ironized shadow of the infinite, unintelligible ("Can no one tell me what she sings?") substance of which, as the real poem that comes to hand, it is also the trace of access.

Crane's practice reverses the relationship between the actual, and the virtual or imaginary poem in the tradition. In effect, he puts poetry in question by making a severe moral interpretation (a literal interpretation) of its promises. He attempts to identify the actual poem with the nature of the imaginary or virtual poem, and to array the former (the actual poem) with the latter's putative features, so that the poem he writes has the nature of the poem (the siren song, or the voice of the nightingale) to which the poet of tradition, and particularly the Romantic tradition, alludes. The lyric speaker in the poem of tradition is the intratextual interpreter of the virtual poem, who both recalls it and postpones it as a state of affairs (as in Dryden's "Alexander's Feast" or Yeats' "After Long Silence": "That we descant and yet again descant/Upon the supreme theme of Art and Song"). Crane's version as "difficult poem" of the virtual song—the supreme theme—in which (by the inversion) the natural speaker is only an allusion has therefore no intra-textual interpreter. In the tradition, it is not a model of possible states of affairs but rather the apocalyptic moment of the "untuning of the sky." Taken as a model of a possible state of affairs the virtual poem is, in a sense, a hurricane.

The state of affairs in literature which finds an actual work which has inside it an inactual utterance of another sort is a perennial trope of poetic structure. Novels as fictional *books* tend to have real libraries inside them, whereas poems as fictional *speaking* tend to have inside them the source of utterance or speaking itself, whether as lady or bird or god, wind or tower. Poetry, therefore, tends to be closer to the natural, or (as Adrienne Rich has remarked) the psychological unconscious, than fiction; and the imaginary poem is the voice of the authenticity of language rather than its reference, the signless or silent voice of the thing signified. In poetic practice, the closer the actual poem comes to the virtual poem the "higher" the style. The virtual poem is the trace of "natal power" and the high style is inevitably involved with earliness. "Genesis" and the Homeric exploits of Poseidon are juxtaposed in Longinus as instances of the grand or sublime in literature. Crane's Columbus like Freneau's (and like Melville's Ahab) is a high-style speaker because his transaction is with earliness and founding. The Bible (especially the Gospels) is the archetypal work of one kind that gives an account of works of another kind, the work of God. The voice of Wordsworth's "leech-gatherer" (the account of which is modelled on the biblical accounts of the voice of God—the sound of many waters) resonates as the high style ("lofty utterance"), but when taken inward becomes "like a stream/Scarce heard; nor word from word could I divide. . . ." This untranslatable voice of Wordsworth's daimon is the central "obscure" language of our civilization. It is primordial (Whitman's "hum of the valved voice" is another example) and prior to exile; it is weighted with what Owen Barfield calls "archaism" and manifests the iconic obscurity of existence prior to its meanings. In it time and space do not exist, and its name, if it has one, is unity. In this authenticity Crane robed his discourse, making his styles repeat the implications of the imaginary poem that constructs only its own source.

The high style was, of course, the enemy gesture for the central poets of modernism. Yeats survived it as an early self, Pound shattered it as structure and reconstituted it as myth, Stevens mocked it as "magnificent measure." Crane's speaker does not survive his early self, is himself shattered, and makes the playing of "Old keys that are but echoes" the activity effective for redemption. But it all hangs by a thread. The sound of mocking laughter is everywhere in Crane and turned against the speaker, not delegated away. The imaginary enterprise, dragged into the real world under the auspices of intense poetics, is absurd, hypertrophic, a solecism. The high style, as the sign in the modern world of the virtual poem, is by its nature out of place; and, like the divinity which attends it, out of place it is also defiling. The reader who functions in Crane's intense poetics as the survivor self, and who must complete the diadic trope of enclosure (providing the real discourse in which the imaginary can have manifest existence) is repelled or embarrassed because he is called upon not to interpret the difficult poem but to finish it. This act of supplementation is the correlative for reading of the specific difference that difficulty makes in the poem. Stylistic solecism (language out of place) is the literary equivalent of defilement (the ritual consequence of the transgression of boundaries), as philosophical idealism is its conceptual equivalent. Crane's style requires of his uneasy readers tolerance of proximity to undefended authenticity, and the ability to endure the absurdity of imaginary states of language without ironizing them by a meaning or dismissing them by a judgment. What the imaginary style invites is acknowledgment of the man in the defilement of his authenticity, most authoritative in effect when his "failure" is greatest.

A principal event of Crane's later creative period was the hurricane on the Isle of Pines in 1926. That hurricane (with which, as we have noted, "The Return" is associated) had the character of a transgression of the boundary between experience and art because Crane felt himself to have, by his birth as it were, a Longinian disposition toward "hurricane poetics."

> I write damned little because I am interested in recording certain sensations, very rigidly chosen, with an eye for what according to my taste and sum of prejudices seems suitable to—or intense enough—for verse. . . . One should be somewhat satisfied if one's work comes to approximate a true record of such moments of "illumination" as are occassionally possible. A sharpening of reality accessible to the poet, to no such degree possible through other mediums.

A little earlier on the same brilliant, but also truculently self-justificatory letter, he remarks in response apparently to an accusation by Winters of philosophical (and moral) opportunism:

> You seem to think that experience is some commodity—that can be sought! One can respond only to certain circumstances; just what the barriers are, and where the boundaries cross can never be completely known. . . . I can't help if you think me aimless and irresponsible. But try and see if you get such logical answers always from Nature as you seem to think you will! My "alert blindness" was a stupid ambiguity to use in any definition—but it seems to me you go in for just about as much "blind alertness" with some of your expectations.
>
> If you knew how little of a metaphysician I am in the scholastic sense of the term. . . . It's all an accident so far as my style goes. It happens that the first poem I ever wrote was too dense to be understood, and I now find I can trust most critics to tell me that all my subsequent efforts have been equally futile.

Crane's conception of poetry by contrast to prose as singularly adapted to the registration of "intense" sensations, and his disposition, an "accident" that befell him at the very beginning of his experience of composition, toward a style "too dense to be understood" are (as we can now see) vitally related. Obviously, the disruptive boundary between "intense" experience and ordinary experience defines for Crane (as for Longinus) not only the difference between poetry and prose, but also the difference between his own kind of poetry and other kinds. The segregation to poetry of ideal or philosophical subjects and to prose the account of social fact was a late nineteenth century decision reflected, for example, in the work of Crane's autodidact predecessor Stephen Crane, and in the work of the Symbolist contemporaries of the young Yeats. It persists in contradiction to the modernist program in the popular conception of poetry to this day. Crane's anti-modernist difference consisted in the employment of the high subject to put the adequacy of poetic structures in question on the ground of their own promises. The "heroic pathos" (Riddel's phrase) of Crane's poetry results from the sense conveyed of an enterprise conducted (and not randomly) beyond the limits of its possible outcomes, with that tolerance of flaws that Longinus predicted for the artist of sublime occasions whose motives "often go beyond the boundaries by which we are circumscribed."

As Crane notes, his preference for intense subjects began with the beginning of his poetic career (note, for example the two quatrains called "The Hive" [1917]). It persisted down to the palinodial death-poem, in signature quatrains, of 1932, "The Broken Tower." Our elegiac four lines, "The Return," is an exposition—"suddenly clear"—of that preference for intensity, the return (not versing, but re-versing) of structure into authenticity. In this context, we have observed the relationship between Crane's "difficulty" and the imaginary or virtual poem of tradition, and between the imaginary poem and the high style. The anachronism (disjunctive earliness) of the high style ("Infinite consanguinity it bears") implies the urgent relevance of the question of origins to every moment of consciousness, making the business of bornness and validation the unfinished and pre-emptive business of mind both in love and art. Crane's subject was the establishment not of culture, but of existence itself, the reconstruction of the primal scene with the intention of undoing the dismemberment of birth by the "transmemberment" of song that traces "the visionary company of love" back to the hurricane kiss of beginning (which might be any moment of experience)—and then to begin again. There will be a "new threshold" (a new birth) and a "new anatomy" (a new body). The only moment "intense enough—for verse" is the moment simultaneously of destruction and creation that requires a "new" language, not the cultural instauration of Pounds' pseudo-apocalyptic "Make it new," but the re-speaking of the traditional imaginary language of creation, poetry prior to its poem, mind prior to the difference of other minds. There can be no other meaningful occasion of verse. Eliot's speaker is posthumous of civilization; Crane's is prior to the measured consanguinities of civiliza-tion. Crane's poetic procedure is not the ironization of styles, but a dismantling of styles, the decreative analysis and exhaustion of poetic means through the overburdening of fundamental concern. The hierogamic kiss of primary acknowledgement discountenances all states of language except the "natal power" of the mother tongue beyond imagining.

The high style is intrinsically early because it is referenced back toward the earliest instance of the art (the epics of origin and foundation, such as Virgil's with which Crane compares *The Bridge*), and toward the point of the emergence of discourse from mystery (the oracle and sacerdo-tal riddle—"Remember, Falcon-Ace,/Thou hast there in thy wrist a San-skrit charge/To conjugate infinity's dim marge—/Anew . . . !"). It is always also the limit of a prohibition, being not merely discourse which is by implication totalistic and at the incestuous boundary of origin (the bottom of the sea), but being of course also by its nature a repetition of the already accomplished, the prior poetic act that Crane did not ironize by quotation. Crane's identic repetition of styles, like his figural compres-sions and his synesthesias, re-expresses preemption of difference, of devel-opment, his intransigent refusal to be born in *this* form. The primal scene in Crane—"white, pervasive Paradigm"—has no structure. Therefore, structure was for him an alien element, keeping him *in representation* but always *outside* his motive. In *The Waste Land* Eliot developed a structure in which nothing can be out of place. In Crane's anachronistic and disfunctional rhetorical pastiches ("prayer of pariah and the lover's cry") nothing can be in place, for nothing that is still in discourse can be at home. From this situation (a mind without a realm) he was required to make thematic a principle of representation (abstract, meta-discursive) in which the anxiety of energies out of their proper place might be held or covenanted absolutely; but it is primordial, a word not yet constrained by reference. Crane was a poet of first creation, continually soliciting genesis, the highest style of all.

> The imaged Word, it is, that holds
> Hushed willows anchored in its glow.
> It is the unbetrayable reply
> Whose accent no farewell can know.

When Crane speaks of the "accident so far as my style goes" he is talking about a psychological formation (whatever its biographical basis) which compelled him to put culture in question more severely than it was put in question by his contemporary moderns. What was at issue for Crane, as I have said, was personal existence itself. "The Return" was the history and principle of his world.

VI

The Return

The sea raised up a campanile . . . The wind I heard
Of brine partaking, whirling spout in shower
Of column kiss—that breakers spouted, sheared
Back into bosom—me—her, into natal power . . .

Interpretation of Crane's poems tends to specify the terms which are constituent of his world by procedures more internal to the linguistic facts of his text, and at the same time more abstract, than is the case with less "difficult" poetry. This occurs, as we now see, for several reasons: first, because the reader is presented not with the traditional finite and internally interpreted structure which bounds and mediates an infinite allusion (language in its liquidity), but with in effect an infinite structure (unbounded, liquid) in which finite structures, like the campanile, rise, are burdened, and fall. The reader must supplement the poem, endure its undefended and illogical energies, rather than "gather its sense." The reader is ambiguously internal to the poem, a part of its project. Secondly, the surface of the poem is designed to exhaust the finite procedures which the reader brings to it. All poetry is in some sense uninterpretable; but the "difficult" poem is *situated* on the virtual uninterpretability of the poetic text, the "infinite consanguinity" of its elements. In a context signifying states prior to difference that functions by a rhetoric that elides the separated individuality, the making of difference (which cannot be avoided) will have no end. The sense of Crane's text (the response it anticipates) must lie in the acknowledgement of its authenticity. Such a response will be mediated by a theory of its "difficulty" which does not erase or neutralize the complexity and peril of the terms of presence at the extremity of demand. Crane anticipates not a meaning but an answer, a candid glance, a kiss.

"The Return" is a message from death, uttered like many of Emily Dickinson's poems from the imaginary station ("death"), with the authority of authenticity itself—"natal power." The past tense in which it is cast negotiates a difference, therefore, not merely temporal. As a poem in the imaginary mode "The Return" is an exposition (in the condensed rhetoric of intense poetics) of the *nostos* morpheme /re/, which has inside it the rescue of the world as the story of the success of desire ("kiss"). The condensation of more and more meaning upon less and less language (the "crowding of the frame"), until all is found in nothing or silence is arrested in Crane's most characteristic practice at the level of the morpheme, the almost atomic trace of the imaginary (or divine) "unfractioned idiom." The morpheme (in this case /re/) stands as an instance of the one word of which all other words are images, the Word within the word or "imaged Word." The assonance of all words with this word is not a question of sound alone, but of sound making sense (the remotest "reconcilement" will be of mind); and there is by implication no end to the reduction. "Criticism" cannot complete the analysis, because the reductions criticism can make are mere signs of the non-finite reduction of all to one which is the "meaning," thematized in the poem by an action ("Back into bosom—me—her, into natal power . . .") which ends in an elision of process (". . ."). Inside the /re/ is the "me" which becomes inverted (inversion or reversal is for Crane the process of decreation, the vortical rotation) in the "heard," as "brine" and "partake" are in "shower," and as "breakers" is in "sheared." And, finally, as "me" is in "her," and both in "power." At the oceanic bottom of the rhetoric of condensation the morphemic element manifests, as I have suggested, the "infinite consanguinity" (Ezekiel's sound of many waters, Wordsworth's "stream/ scarce heard; nor word from word could I divide") which is momentarily betrayed ("plundered momently") by the fact of mortal language (the actual poem) and recovered in the elision of the "return," the ambivalent rescue of silence which takes the actual poem inside it.

In Crane mind takes world inside it, and gives back a transient image ("a moment on the wind") in which the mind is in the world as a campanile, an orphic machine, the fragile disappearing difference of the speaking person. The "campanile" is a structure and a word out of place, raised up and then cancelled, made futureless. The hurricane wind (a parody, as R. W. B. Lewis notes, of the Romantic "corresponding breeze") enters as the assault of eternity (passionate hope) on the structures that manifest it, and which as in "The Broken Tower" it will overburden and break. The "I," as the tower that will be broken, is introduced postpositive to (inside) the wind. The hierogamic sacrament of "brine" as salt wine of the sea ("partaking" as participation and dismemberment) is heard (overheard as the primal scene is overheard) under the eternal auspices of the "ing" participle which introduces chiastically the atemporal present-ness of the grammatically multistable "kiss" (a grammatologically emphatic form of the existence copulative "is"—also noun as verb in present tense, verb as static arrest of noun). This participatory sacrament becomes the marriage deep in the language as it now unfolds—the /her/ of "heard" ("I heard") passing through the /she heard/ of "sheared" into "me—her," while "partaking" passes by way of "shower" and "breakers" back into "natal power" ("natal" being iconic of decreative reversal, /na/ becoming /al/).

Chiastic doubling as in the second line of "The Return" ("Of brine partaking, whirling spout in shower") constructs a disjunctive figure in terms of the "ing" suffix so that "partaking" as present-making participle is bound back toward "wind," but "whirling" has its principal grammatical bond prospective toward "spout," creating an empty space in which the consummatory kiss transpires ambiguously inside and outside of grammatical time. This kiss is the boundary of discourse; and here ensue the "breakers," the sense of shore as limit and therefore breaking from which the "me" and "her" are swept ("sheared," implying "she heard" as at the beginning of the first line "I heard") into the rescue of "natal power." The "kiss" is the point of obscurity (the primal scene that is both overheard, as Mill says poetry must be, and transgressively participated in by the speaker), where the inside and outside of discourse are confused, and definition equivocated. This kiss, the moment in which the speaker is begotten and consummated, projects the relationship between the "difficult" poem and the reader in trouble with respect to "interpretation" because he is situated transgressively both within and without the text. The analysis of Crane's language of desire as it imitates and, at the same time approaches and thematizes the oceanic nature of its reference, situates the reader, as I have said, internal to his text. Its rhetorical formality manifests boundlessness, and its structures are at once intrinsic to its meaning and utterly (philosophically) alien to them. They are the structure of what has no structure, no "earthly shore."

Hence, Crane did not experiment with "open form" in any significant poem. The meter of the "The Return" (the four line stanza of Rimbaud's "Le Bateau ivre," Tate's "The Mediterranean," and Masefield's "The River"—the first and fourth line being the French Alexandrine and the second and third English pentameter) is an instance of his "hand," his desituate formality. He refused to devise a structure that dissimulated the resistance of reality to desire. This sense of form is expressed by Valéry in terms appropriate to Crane:

> As for the arbitrary nature of these rules it is in itself no greater than that of the rules of language, vocabulary, of syntax. . . . The exigencies of a strict prosody are the artifices which confer upon the natural language the properties of resistance, of matter that is alien to our spirit and, as it were, deaf to our desires. . . .

Crane's insistence on the historicity of syntax, forms, and styles (which produces that sense of grammatical coherence and referential obscurity that Winters noted early on) is the measure of what I have called his "realism," an inability to concede any aspect of desire ("happiness") or of the facts which are deaf to our desires ("pattern's mastery"). The homelessness of the whole spirit in the "broken world" of art thus pro- duced (in the absence of modernist concession to the weak mystification of open-form speculation toward merely secular infinities, or the greater "treachery" of the modernist ironization of hope) makes of Crane a passionate ghost, a "returner" or *revenant.* "Cathay" is the empty space of the dwellinglessness of a mind that finds no rest in any structure faithfully conceived, of the poet who is not in his poems as Hopkins is, or Lawrence or Thomas. Crane's unsatisfied spirit is still abroad ("LOST AT SEA") because never at home in the texts which manifested it. This uncanniness of Crane, the sentiment to which the equivocation of boundaries gives rise, is found in Keats' *revenant* fragment, his return of the hand:

> This living hand, now warm and capable
> Of earnest grasping, would, if it were cold
> And in the icy silence of the tomb,
> So haunt thy days and chill thy dreaming nights
> That thou wouldst wish thine own heart dry of blood
> So in my veins red life might stream again,
> And thou be conscience-calm'd—see here it is—
> I hold it towards you.

Critics of Crane have been disposed, as I said at the beginning, to assume relationships of cause and effect between his philosophic and (I would add) stylistic decisions, and his suicide. Blackmur put it this way:

> Crane had, in short, the wrong masters for his chosen fulfillment, or he used some of the right masters in the wrong way: leeching upon them, as a poet must, but taking the wrong nourishment, taking from them not what was hardest and most substantial—what made them great poets— but taking rather what was easiest, taking what was peculiar and idiosyn- cratic. That is what kills so many of Crane's poems, what must have made them impervious, once they were discharged, even to himself. It is perhaps, too, what killed Crane the man—because in a profound sense, to those who use it, poetry is the only means of putting a tolerable order

upon the emotions. Crane's predicament—that his means defeated his ends—was not unusual, but his case was extreme.

This is incorrect. Crane's means that were defeated by his ends were poetry's means, and the ends were poetry's ends, the "hardest and most substantial." Riddel is closer when he observes:

> For his own part, Emerson wrote poems which almost literally were dedicated to defining what this poet must *be*, not to rendering what this poet does *see*. They are essentially verse essays in poetics, poems which explore the role of the poet but never dare to assume that role.

Crane did assume that role. He devised the forbidden language not of the familiar meta-poetic imagination, but of the virtual poem in its difficulty and strangeness. Blackmur's remarks, and the tendency of Riddel's otherwise acute analysis of Crane's "poetics of failure," assume either (Blackmur's case) that the poet must constrain desire to the criteria of civility ("a tolerable order") whatever the truth may be of the demand of sentiment or (Riddel's case) that the involvement of the poet as speaker and as the subject of his own elegy (the song of himself) in the problematics of presence is gratuitously (or pathologically) destructive to the man in history. But the psychological causes of Crane's suicide could not have been determined by, or healed, in the context of his art. Crane did not misinterpret the nature of poetry or misunderstand its means. He put them to the test in the form in which he found them on the basis of a demand neither gratuitous nor ill, as the expectation of loving acknowledgement and the correlative certitude of self-presence is an expectation neither gratuitious nor ill.

What is at stake in Crane, as my comments are intended to suggest, is the Columbus discovery of a limit of discourse that is also a limit of experience—a discovery only possible if, like Columbus, the voyager supposes there is really something there (a passage through *per impossible*) where the culture assumes just the end of the world. This discovery can only be made if the goal of poetry, as Crane profoundly demonstrated, is not the "poem" but an investigation (not finally a text but an exploit) of the relationship between the means of presence, of which poetry as it comes to pass is a case, and the high hypothesis of human hope that the poem keeps in mind and of which the pathology that put Crane's life at risk made him aware. What Crane discovered is that presence is not its own accomplishment, and that the imaginative culture that keeps alive inside it the seed of its imaginary motive and validity was not, in the world (family and nation) in which he lived, whole. This discovery could only have been made by a radical fidelity to poetry's ends and a relentless disposition to postpone versions of its means, the ironic structures of well-made and decorous poems, which would have conceded those ends. The political and ethical systems in the poetry of Pound, Eliot, Yeats, and Frost are not on the whole admirable. Crane by contrast did not accept premature hierarchizations or relinquishments in order to sustain the structure and protect the "intelligibility" of his art.

The great *nostos* archetype ("return" as rescue through reestablishment of fundamental relationship) of which Crane's *The Bridge*, his "Voyages," and his "The Return" are displacements takes, in the history of literature, two forms: one is the return to the remembered place (like Odysseus' return to Ithaka); the other is the return to the unremembered place of origins (like Socrates' return to the Idea, or Shelley's "Die,/If thou wouldst be with that which thou dost seek!" or the Columbus landfall of *The Bridge*). The return to the remembered place through the good use of time leads to an enhancement of the mortal self, involving an internalization by the voyager of his own past and then its revalidation in the external world (recovery of Ithaka and remarriage with Penelope). The return to the unremembered place is by contrast sacrificial, requiring and justifying the destruction of time and the self at home in it. Both are comedic systems, but the latter is accompanied as in Crane's versions by an inability to delegate away from the self (whether to the god as in the Mass, or to the dead hero-friend as in the elegy) the immense losses attendant on a self-realization so absolute, a growth so vast. The return to the unremembered place is the archetype of Dante's *Paradiso*. The "shower," penultimate in our "The Return," but which concludes Crane's death poem "The Broken Tower" ("The commodious, tall decorum of that sky/Unseals her earth, and lifts love in its shower"), repeats the image at *Paradiso* XIV, where the consolation of the resurrection of the body is argued:

> Qual si lamenta perchè qui si moia,
> per viver colassù, non vide quive
> lo refrigerio dell' eterna ploia.

> Whoso lamenteth that we here must die to live
> up yonder seeth not here the refreshment of
> the eternal shower.

The eternal showers ("eterna ploia") restore the body whole. In Crane, however, symbolic restitution does not compensate mortal loss, and his poetry everywhere remembers the dismemberment inherent in transformation. Crane has no language, as the mere poet he was, to effect the purposes of self-validation in this high sense, and he had no permission to relinquish the enterprise. Yeats and Eliot dealt with this predicament in culturally atavistic ways, through affiliation with the vanishing institutions of Church, aristocracy, national (and other) mysticisms. Crane's "failure" is evidence of his fidelity to the secular means at hand.

Throughout Crane's poetry there is an effort to imagine time, to devise return from the unremembered to the remembered place—to make the imagination work in terms of the structure of possibility given:

> Bind us in time, O Seasons clear, and awe.
> O minstrel galleons of Carib fire,
> Bequeath us to no earthly shore until
> Is answered in the vortex of our grave
> The seal's wide spindrift gaze toward Paradise.

Crane's palinodial effort, to return from the imaginary authenticity that was his station, and, as a use of the power with which that authenticity invested him, to make of inevitable death ("our grave") a morally adequate response to paradisal expectation, is the final indication of his cherishing of the real secular state of affairs. The scene of answering (the glance, the adequate return, of which the linguistically embedded sign was the decreative rhetoric of reversal, as in the skewed sequence of the last two lines of "Voyages II" cited above) was obsessive in Crane and defining of him. The bridge was the answerer as hurricane wind-flower ("O Answerer of all,—Anemone,—"). By contrast to the scene of answering in the tradition, however, in which the God seeks answer of man's harmonies, Crane spoke on behalf of the central authenticity of his humanity as the "divine" child in search of a mortal response—a structure—that would render intelligible his "melodious noise," unseal his earth. We see his enterprise as in the reversal of a mirror in Milton's "At a Solemn Music":

> That we on Earth with undiscording voice
> May rightly answer that melodious noise;
> As once we did, till disproportion'd sin
> Jarr'd against nature's chime, and with harsh din
> Broke the fair music that all creatures made
> To their great Lord, whose love their motion sway'd
> In perfect Diapason. . . .

"Diapason" comes down to Crane ("Take this sea, whose diapason knells/On scrolls of silver snowy sentences" ["Voyages II"]) from Milton through Dryden's "Alexander's Feast" as the full sound of reality in accord with desire, the "new" creation. This sound was for him (as for Milton) a music, a high style of speaking, man's reconciliation with source as the other person by whom we are made human. In the vital palinode or retraction of his death poem ("The Broken Tower") Crane redefines his notion of a mortal structure capable of reciprocating his hope. The Babel-tower of the primal scene which "Broke the fair music" ("The steep encroachments of my blood left me/No answer") itself breaks down and there arises ("lift" is Crane's term for the return of things to their proper place) a new space described in the classical Augustan language of scalar reconciliation ("commodious," "decorum"). The terms of this unsealing contain the terms of "The Return" and go beyond them to the representation of a personhood, commensurate with Crane's sentiment of human destiny, capable of making answer to death in a smile, a kiss, or a music—capable of reading the difficult poems of impenitent seriousness. At the end of his last poem the genesis event occurs and the hurricane abates, becoming the nurturant rain that brings up ("lifts") the green world:

> The commodious, tall decorum of that sky
> Unseals her earth, and lifts love in its shower.

The death Crane imagined was not the death he died.

LEE EDELMAN

"Voyages"

Echoing the Whitman of "As I Ebb'd with the Ocean of Life," Crane images the sea, in "Voyages I," as a reductive medium washing against the shore. In the following poems, however, he retreats further into its depths, echoing the Whitman of "Out of the Cradle Endlessly Rocking" as he evokes its erotic texture. Initiating that vision of eros—which for Crane means a profound meditation on the rhetoricity of desire—Crane exclaims in "Voyages II":

> —And yet this great wink of eternity,
> Of rimless floods, unfettered leewardings,
> Samite sheeted and processioned where
> Her undinal vast belly moonward bends,
> Laughing the wrapt inflections of our love.

"The bottom of the sea is cruel," Crane declares, "—And yet" the sea is a "great wink of eternity," a realm of erotic figurations both "rimless" and "unfettered" as the imagination strikes free of all bounds. The sea may reduce those who dare to "cross" its "line," but the negativity of death gives way to a transformative rebirth in a vision of Eros and Thanatos joined to one another. Vision becomes preeminent in "Voyages II" as space takes precedence over time and figure gains ascendancy over syntax. Now that Crane, as "brother-thief of time" has re-written poetic history in "Faustus and Helen" even the temporal succession of words in a sentence takes on figurative significance. In keeping with this subordination of historical—and therefore poetically constraining—time, to figurative—and therefore poetically productive—space, "Voyages II" abandons normative syntax to proclaim the triumph of imagination over reality. Thus the broken "—And yet" with which "Voyages II" begins, disjoins itself from the essentially disjunctive interpretation of the sea in "Voyages I."

Retreating from the shore, Crane turns his gaze instead to the sea itself, its "rimless floods" representing the defeat of time through the conversion of history into limitless space. The paternal fetters of temporal continuity, lamented in Section I of "Faustus and Helen," are exchanged for the "unfettered" maternal realm of endless spatial expanse. The repetition of images from earlier poems helps to focus the meaning of this spatialization. The sea represents "eternity" by means of a "wink," an image that may not immediately suggest the sublimity of extension. But that wink recalls the "flickering . . . prefigurations" of Helen's eyes, flickerings that were then refigured as the gap, the "hiatus/ That winks above" the "body of the world" as it weeps for the celestial muse from which it is severed. Rather than ironizing the sea, the image of the "wink" evokes Crane's Helen, suggesting that the celestial and the oceanic muses serve as mirror images of one another, winking above and below the dividing "line" of the earth's surface. In this manner the distance between the sea's surface and its bottom doubles the gap between the earth and the sky, doubling at the same time the potential space to be negotiated by poetic desire.

Appropriately enough, given the specular nature of the muses of the sea and the sky, the sea's "undinal vast belly . . . bends" toward the heavens, reenacting the bending that serves as Crane's figural reading of chiastic exchange. As the moth in "Legend" bent to the flame and the poet, as Faustus, bent toward Helen, so now the "undinal" belly of the sea "bends" "moonward," toward the body that governs its tides. This bend or convergence signifies the fatal complicity and the mirror-like doubling of these two ambiguous muses. For the sea bends "moonward" toward the planetary body that bespoke Crane's reductive enterprise of "whitening" in "For the Marriage of Faustus and Helen."

That the productive, image-spawning sea should bend toward the reductive, image-breaking moon, emphasizes anew that in Crane's dialectic creation and destruction are Blakean counterparts. In poetic practice he seems to know what he lacked an adequate meta-language to describe: that every movement toward the stability of chiasmus carries a trace of the break that figures the violence of anacoluthon. He recognizes that language—in spite of all efforts to deploy it in stable, "indestructible" figurations—must always be undone, reduced once again by the force of its own negativity. He acknowledges, therefore, the danger posed by the goddess-like muse of the sea, just as it was posed by Helen across the

winking of an anacoluthon-like "hiatus." Although he envisions the sea
in terms that evoke substantiality and reciprocity; though he reifies its
textuality by describing it as "samite sheeted" (an image that recalls
Tennyson's sword-wielding Lady in the Lake), and by praising its ability to
encompass the "inflections" (in its root sense, the "bendings") of the
lovers, Crane knows that her transitive laughter remains uncomfortably
indeterminate. Whether the oceanic muse, in "laughing the wrapt inflections of our love," intends her laughter as derisive or celebratory, the poet
can hope to survive poetically only by becoming "wrapt" in his own verbal
"inflections," only by engaging in an act of union with his specular
double, the Narcissus-like image of himself that is "imminent in his
dream."

    Embarking on this voyage of erotic figuration, Crane addresses this
lover, this other self:

> Take this Sea, whose diapason knells
> On scrolls of silver snowy sentences,
> The sceptred terror of whose session rends
> As her demeanors motion well or ill,
> All but the pieties of lovers' hands.

In view of the similar call to action in Section II of "Faustus and Helen,"
Crane's imperative—"Take this Sea"—betrays considerable bravado. In
the earlier poem, referring to Helen, the poet suggested to his "ominous"
companion, "Let us take her on the incandescent wax." Now, joined by a
new companion, he even more recklessly defies the prescriptive code of
sexual conduct, challenging his lover to join him in a violation of this
regal, and menacingly "sceptered" sea. He urges the very Oedipal transgression that he cautioned against in "Voyages I." Sherman Paul observes
that "in an early version of the poem the poet says that 'She/ is our bed'
and 'enlist(s) us/ to her body endlessly' "; and he comments: "this is a
forbidden act for the poet who has established the maternal character of
the sea. Yet with this challenge Crane asserts his ability to defy the
disjunctive "sentences," the "rends" that are rendered by this arbitrary
muse, "the sceptred terror of whose session rends/ . . . / All but the pieties
of lovers' hands." Resolute in their love, Crane and his companion can
withstand these ruthless severing waves. Having immersed themselves in
the medium of disjunction, and having introjected its radical power by so
doing, they are able to escape the sea's reductions by reducing the sea
instead. Crane refigures it, therefore, as a text of "snowy sentences," a
"white" or reductive text. Translating sound into visual substance, he
reifies the sea's "diapason" as the "sentences" inscribed in the "scrolls" of

the curving waves. And by figuring the sea as such a text, by *interpreting* it in this fashion, he both appropriates its power and neutralizes the figure-making authority of its "sentences" by asserting his own poetic authority to read and refigure the sea. Thus if the ocean "rends," like anacoluthon, all continuities save "the pieties of lovers' hands," those hands are exempted because the products of their "pieties" are poetries rife with a figural energy that aspires to the balance of chiastic exchange, and that is imaged in the lovers' linked hands.

To figure the sea as such a text, however, Crane adopts the strategy of Faustus in Section I of "Faustus and Helen." Wherever he discovers a hiatus he must fill it with a flower—a flower of language—in the substitutive process of poetic desire. For the gap of negativity that figures desire has the potential to figure death unless the poet can forestall such death by filling the gap, by answering reduction with an act of substitution. Thus the following stanza responds to the "terror" of the ocean's "snowy sentences" by unleashing the rhetorical power of a tropological efflorescence:

> And onward, as bells off San Salvador
> Salute the crocus lustres of the stars,
> In these poinsettia meadows of her tides,—
> Adagios of islands, O my Prodigal,
> Complete the dark confessions her veins spell.

Though these bells call to mind the "bells and voices" that "atone/ The abating shadows of our conscript dust" in Section III of "Faustus and Helen," the stanza's two figural centerpieces are the sea's "poinsettia meadows" and the "crocus lustres of the stars." These complementary fields of flowers point to Crane's attempt to fill the "hiatus," the space of desire, opened by each of his two winking muses. But his primary energy in these acts of substitution is directed toward his efforts to master the sea. Thus he reads it now as defendant, not judge; the "sceptered" authority of the ocean as magistrate is subordinated to the guilt, the "dark confessions," her "veins spell." These "veins" hark back to the "arteries" that figured the reductive, "whitened" materiality of rhetoric in Section I of "Faustus and Helen." Similarly, the "veins" of this "snowy" sea spell a "dark confession" to the extent that their whiteness marks an emptying of tropological "colors" that bespeaks, simultaneously, the darkening of "opacity" of rhetoric. The sea is changed from a body of water to a literary corpus, a text; and this change results from the poet's refusal to surrender to the "spell" of the muse. Instead, he refigures the sea by turning that spell into an act of spelling. Refusing to be reduced by the musical presence of the sea's "diapason" and "bells." Crane transforms those sounds into "sentences" in a "snowy" or reductive text of absence.

Even the famous image of "adagios of islands" contributes to this movement from sound to sight, from music to visual notation. In the midst of "General Aims and Theories," Crane, discussing his "logic of metaphor," offers a significant gloss on this overdetermined figure: "the reference is to the motion of a boat through islands clustered thickly, the rhythm of the motion, etc. And it seems a much more direct and creative statement than any logical employment of words such as 'coasting slowly through the islands,' besides ushering in a whole world of music." While "adagios" may imply a "world of music," that world has already been "ushered in" by the earlier figures of sound. But these "adagios," insofar as they are understood as slow movements of a work in sonata form, suggest the slow tempo—the sluggish "motion"—enacted by the music itself. This transformation of tempo into motion suggests a spatialization of time, and this "rhythm of motion," as Crane phrases it in his letter, leads away from the auditory aspect of "adagios" to imply, instead, the sense of the word as it is understood in the realm of dance. As John Irwin observes, "another of the possible meanings of 'adagio' is 'a slow ballet dance requiring skillful balancing,' quite frequently a *pas de deux*." Crane's image, then, leads from music to dance, from the aural to the visual, from time to space. And in a similar way the "adagios of islands" leads from a sense of "adagios" as a description *of* the islands, to a sense of those "adagios" as activities enagaged in *by* the islands. In this latter reading the poetic figure itself describes the dance of figures, particularly as those figures enact rhythmic motions, like the *pas de deux*, of balance and reversal. In this sense of figurative rearrangement and construction, the "adagios," as figures of chiastic reversal, are able to "complete" the "dark" or disjunctive confessions of the sea.

As the sea confesses its violent "sentences," the poet asks his lover to engage in markings of his own:

> Mark how her turning shoulders wind the hours,
> And hasten while her penniless rich palms
> Pass superscription of bent foam and wave,—
> Hasten, while they are true,—sleep, death, desire,
> Close round one instant in one floating flower.

The oceanic muse "wind[s] the hours" like a Fate relentlessly measuring out time. But Crane projects this activity in spatial terms to "complete" or counterbalance destiny. He evokes the sea as the very matrix of time, the origin of hours that are wound by the perpetual "turning" of the waves.

This "turning" calls to mind the poet's own need for continuous troping or substitution, and it is significant, therefore, that Crane figures the sea's movement as a passing from palm to palm of the "superscription of bent foam and wave." Needless to say, this bending is more fully under the poet's control than was the "moonward" bend of the opening stanza; for the superscription borne by the sea represents the legend or exergue that identifies the image as one that the poet has coined. Reducing the "penniless" sea to an imaginatively enabling—almost Stevensian—poverty, Crane and his companion, as they "mark" it, make the sea itself something "rich" and strange. They strike their own poetic coin from it and engrave their "superscription of bent foam and wave"—and the bending of that wave marks once more his aspiration toward stability and self-enclosure.

At this point of gathering strength, the loss or lack on which Crane's poetry turns coalesces for a moment in one eloquent figure: "sleep, death, desire,/ Close round one instant in one floating flower." Recognizing that the truth of poetry is always, as Jacques Derrida would say, "under erasure," that "the superscription of bent foam and wave" is only "true" in the instant of its positing, Crane recalls Shelley's description in "Alastor" of another visionary's voyage:

> The boat fled
> With unrelaxing speed.—"Vision and Love!"
> The Poet cried aloud, "I have beheld
> The path of thy departure. Sleep and death
> Shall not divide us long!"

Following Shelley's example, Crane claims his triumph over the forces of division and undoing by submitting to that division and transforming its negativity into the unity of a stable, enclosing figure. Interestingly enough, elsewhere in "Alastor" Shelley identifies "sleep" and "death" as reciprocal voids through which the phantom of desire must be pursued; he associates "sleep" with the celestial "hues of heaven" while linking "death" to the ocean's "blue vaults." Waking from a dream to seek the realization of his desire, the Poet in "Alastor" looks upon "the empty scene as vacantly/ As ocean's moon looks on the moon in heaven." This image of a mirrored absence, a doubled space of vacancy, gives way to speculations on the deeper relationship between sea and sky, between death and sleep:

> Does the dark gate of death
> Conduct to thy mysterious paradise,
> O Sleep? Does the bright arch of rainbow clouds,
> And pendent mountains seen in the calm lake,
> Lead only to a black and watery depth,

> While death's blue vaults, with loathliest vapors hung,
> Where every shade which the foul grave exhales
> Hides its dead eye from the detested day,
> Conducts, O Sleep, to thy delightful realms?

Crane too perceives the common absence or lack that constitutes the point at which death intersects sleep, for he knows that sleep is burdened with dreams in which the image of desire is always only "imminent." His emphasis on "desire" thus completes and fulfills the Shelleyean pairing of "sleep and death," because Crane knows that absence is the space of desire, the "hiatus" in which poetry both finds discontinuity and refuses it by planting flowers of language in the void. Though "sleep, death, desire" may be enclosed, then, in a single figure "one floating flower," that flower, like all the "flowers" of Crane's language, is itself determined by the pull of those forces; it serves as a substitutive offering by which the poet both fills and refigures the space of desire so as to forestall poetic death.

This movement toward figural enclosure becomes a means of defying the disseminative force of temporality:

> Bind us in time, O Seasons clear, and awe.
> O minstrel galleons of Carib fire,
> Bequeath us to no earthly shore until
> Is answered in the vortex of our grave
> The seal's wide spindrift gaze toward paradise.

The poet asks that he and his lover be bound "in time," and with a characteristic Cranean pun, these sons of the maternal sea are bound together in the very word "Seasons." The relationship between these sea-sons and the seasons of time's cycle remains purposely ambiguous, however. Crane wishes here not only to be bound in due time, before it is too late, to his specular double; he wants also, through his union with that Narcissus-like image, to be bound into the fabric of time itself which he endows with the materiality of a text. As the notion of "seasons" points to a cyclical—and thus a conservative and spatial—concept of time that contrasts with the linearity of an historical continuum, so the structure of this first line portrays the triumph of space over temporal progression. The placement of the phrase "and awe" at the end of the sentence poses the problem of determining its relationship to the preceding syntax. On the most fundamental level, the question to be answered is whether "awe" is a noun or a verb here. Taking "awe" as a verb one could rephrase the line so as to read: "O Seasons clear, bind us in time and awe us"; while taking it as a noun permits two possible readings: either, "O Seasons clear, bind us and bind awe in time," or, "O Seasons clear, bind us in time and in awe." The rhetorical figure that creates this confusion is anastrophe, by which meaning is "turned back" toward an earlier syntactical structure. Its effect, in this instance, is to frustrate interpretation by defying the linear progression of syntax: defying, that is, the progressive unfolding of meaning through time. In its structure, then, this sentence bends in upon itself with "O Seasons clear" serving as the point of intersection for several possible formulations, so that "Bind us in time, O Seasons clear," is matched by either: "O Seasons clear, bind us in awe," or "O Seasons clear, awe us," or "O Seasons clear, bind awe."

In this way, Crane and his lover "turn back" the meaning of the sea, reversing the disjunctive impulse of its muse in a figure of unity and "binding." Unlike the "dice of drowned men's bones" that Melville, in "At Melville's Tomb," "saw bequeath/ An embassy" until they "beat on the dusty shore and were obscured," Crane and his companion refuse to submit to the "obscurity" of that "dusty shore" until they themselves have become an inheritance, a poetic bequest to others:

> Bequeath us to no earthly shore until
> Is answered in the vortex of our grave
> The seal's wide spindrift gaze toward paradise.

The violent spray or "spindrift" attending the seal's "gaze toward paradise," must be "answered" or completed chiastically by the violence of the "vortex." The lofty or celestial response to temporality must be balanced by the profundity of an oceanic counter-response. This vortex, this circular and self-engulfing structure, is not only the "grave" in which the poet and his lover are turned, but it is the very locus of poetic turning or troping itself. Like the enclosing action of the "floating flower" in the previous stanza of the poem, it draws everything to its turning rhetorical center to cast it forth transformed. The productive negativity of "the vortex of our grave" thus "answers" "spindrift" with a spinning rift that represents a node of poetical strength.

Thus the poem's final emblem depicts an exchange, a movement of response and counter-response, between the downward pull of the whirling "vortex" and the upward "spindrift gaze." Loss and gain are interwoven, reduction and vision conjoined. As the Shelleyean intersection of sleep and death posed a reversal in which the greater reduction augured the greater transformation, so Crane's poetic vision refigures disjunction as an "answer," a reply or an enfolding. At the end of "Voyages II," then, if he figures his death in the whirling vortex, it is because he knows that such a vortex is the "calyx of death's bounty," is itself a flower of language, a trope through which he attains to the center of all troping in the constant activity of turning. Through this figure of death Crane turns death aside, refigures it in the enclosure of his "one floating flower." For the "calyx of death's bounty," in "At Melville's Tomb," is imaged as "giving back/ A scattered chapter, livid hieroglyph." This "giving back," this poetic return, is Crane's willful answer to death, his recuperation of discontinuity in what Nietzsche would recognize as a lie against time.

II

Crane's "Voyages" sequence recapitulates the cyclical rhythm of his poetry, the endless movement of his imagination within a spiral of creations and destroyings. In his allegory of rhetoric, anacoluthon yields to chiasmus which breaks down once more into anacoluthon. And the cycle continues until Crane allows it to resolve itself into an overarching and daringly connective catachresis. If the first four stanzas of "Legend" enact the pre-catachrestic process in miniature, the six poems that constitute "Voyages" work it out on a larger scale. The sequence begins with a "skull & cross-bones insignia" that depicts a transgressive crossing even as it warns against transgression. With "Voyages II," it withdraws into the sea where emblems of balance and antithesis are ceaselessly created and destroyed, drowned and reborn in an ocean that perfectly embodies Crane's cyclical poetics. Thus, if "Voyages II" ends with a figuration of the poet dragged down in the whirling vortex, "Voyages III" must initiate a resurfacing and a retrieval before it submits to its own downward pull:

> Infinite consanguinity it bears—
> This tendered theme of you that light
> Retrieves from sea plains where the sky
> Resigns a breast that every wave enthrones;
> While ribboned water lanes I wind
> Are laved and scattered with no stroke
> Wide from your side, whereto this hour
> The sea lifts, also, reliquary hands.

However cruel the engulfing maternal ocean may be, the poet denies her ability to disjoin him from his lover. For the theme that is "tendered" by this poetry is explicitly a theme of tenderness, of erotic exchange that "bears" or gives birth to "infinite consanguinity." If the ocean, according to "Voyages II," enjoys the privilege of "eternity," Crane, by seeing his imaginative order—his poetic line of descent—

extending to infinity, endows his love, and thus himself, with an immortality equal to the sea's.

This "tendered theme," then, "bears" emblems of "infinite" unfolding that find expression in Crane's elaborate images of intertwining:

> This tendered theme of you that light
> Retrieves from sea plains where the sky
> Resigns a breast that every wave enthrones.

The figural path traced by Crane in these lines moves from the heavens, the arena of "light," down to the "sea plains," then back up to the sky before coming to rest in the waves of the sea. The verbs that conduct this passage—"retrieves," "resigns," and "enthrones"—describe the imagination's shuttle between the specular extremes of sea and sky in a series of actions that indicates an enormous energy of exchange and reversal, and that suggest, as well, a figural economy that bears upon the production of "theme." Each wave here "enthrones" a "breast" that the sky has resigned or given up to the sea plains, and in return the sky's "light" retrieves a "tendered theme" from the "lanes" or the lines of the sea. The result of this exchange, this scattering and recuperation, is an oceanic birth, like that of Aphrodite, the goddess who presides over the "Voyages" sequence and informs its figural eros.

Here, though, Crane envisions that birth of an "infinite consanguinity" from the "theme" of tenderness that is tendered by the interpenetration of the sea and the sky. In the image of a sky that "resigns a breast that every wave enthrones," he suggests that the "consanguinity" that his "theme" of eros "bears" pertains to a distinctly literary eroticism and fecundity. For "resign" here implies not only an act of submission or giving up, but also a gesture of reappropriation by means of a poetic act of re-signing. This re-signing or refiguring, as in "Voyages II," betokens the ability to survive poetic breakings. Thus in the previous poem the poet resigned himself to the "sceptered terror" of the sea in order to internalize its reductive force and thereby re-sign the sea itself. Only through this process can he hope to be "enthroned," and, by claiming the "sceptered" authority of the sea, to introject its "unfettered" expansiveness in order to bear "infinite consanguinity." In this way reduction is answered by expansion, death is answered by eros, and the "dark confessions" that the sea's "veins spell" in "snowy sentences" are answered by the "theme" that Crane associates with the "blood" of "consanguinity."

The strength of this counter-response and this refiguring can be seen in the activities that the poet now arrogates to himself:

> . . . ribboned water lanes I wind
> Are laved and scattered, with no stroke
> Wide from your side, whereto this hour
> The sea lifts, also, reliquary hands.

The maternal ocean, in "Voyages II," could "wind the hours" with her "turning shoulders," but now it is the poet who actively turns through "ribboned water lanes" that he, not the ocean, is able to "wind." Not only does he engage in "scatterings" of his own here, but he also appropriates the ability to "lave," a richly evocative Whitmanian term that applies, in "Out of the Cradle Endlessly Rocking," to the erotic activity of the sea. By joining them to such lavings, the poet underscores the productive aspect of his figural "scatterings," emphasizing anew that he sees his rhetorical enterprise as an activity of desire. In this sea of textuality that tenders his "theme," he performs "no stroke"—of pen or of arm—"Wide from [the] side" of lover; they second each other like mirror reflections, implying a balance and mutuality even in the midst of dispersion.

Interestingly enough, the sea now appears to suspend its incursions and to give them its blessing. In homage, or perhaps in imitation, "the sea lifts, also, reliquary hands." As such images as the "pieties of lovers' hands" make clear, linked hands represent, throughout Crane's work, a sexual union, an erotic gesture of interchange and convergence. By lifting its own hands in response to the lovers', the sea, for the time being, seems no longer an agency of arbitrary undoing and division. But the hands that it lifts are characterized as "reliquary," suggesting not only saintliness, but the act of severing and violation through which hands are disembodied and thus become objects of spiritual reverence. Though the line conveys, to some extent, a gesture of erotic welcoming—like Whitman's allusion, in "Out of the Cradle Endlessly Rocking," to the "white arms out in the breakers tirelessly tossing,"—it evokes, as well, the sea's potential cruelty that can eventuate in violent dismemberment. Such dismemberment, with its implicit sexual connotations, points toward the punishment for Oedipal transgression, menacingly implying a radical loss that the poet may be made to suffer.

It is under these circumstances that the poet and his lover dare to achieve their erotic consummation:

> And so, admitted through black swollen gates
> That must arrest all distance otherwise,—
> Past whirling pillars and lithe pediments,
> Light wrestling there incessantly with light,
> Star kissing star through wave on wave unto
> Your body rocking!

In accordance with Crane's concept of an "infinite consanguinity" born of his gestures of re-signing or refiguring, the coupling of poet and lover engenders a host of other couplings that produce a virtual symphony of specular reciprocity: "light wrestling there incessantly with light,/ Star kissing star through wave on wave unto/ Your body rocking!" As the human bodies rock together matched images of one another, other bodies—both celestial and oceanic—join in pairings of their own. Again, a passage from "Alastor" serves as the subtext of Crane's powerfully emblematic figurations. Shelley writes of

> . . . the fearful war
> Of wave ruining on wave, and blast on blast
> Descending, and black flood on whirlpool driven
> With dark obliterating course.

For Shelley as for Crane, this turbulence, "obliterating" as it may seem, heralds a positive movement in his poetic quest or voyage. In "Alastor" these pairings lead toward the vortex, in Crane's poem they take place within and beneath it, after the poet and his lover have been "admitted through black swollen gates." Crane figures himself with his companion in the "hiatus," the "black" void of a space both celestial and oceanic, a space of desire that "must arrest all distance otherwise," where they intimately entwine amid the pairings of light, stars, and waves.

This image of consummation calls forth the image of consumption, but the appearance of death does not signal poetic failure on Crane's part, but rather the necessary dialectical counterweight to his celebratory figures of eros. Thanatos inevitably rises to complete antithetically this erotic vision. But the image of Thanatos itself becomes profoundly antithetical:

> . . . and where death, if shed,
> Presumes no carnage, but this single change,—
> Upon the steep floor flung from dawn to dawn
> The silken skilled transmemberment of song.

To "shed" death, to cast off the ghostly status that has attended the poet from his first appearance beneath the surf in "Voyages I"; surely this must be a token of literary success. But the word "shed" is tainted with grimmer implications, with suggestions of "bloodshed" that cast a shadow of doubt on the nature of this "shedding" of death. The poet observes that this "shedding" "presumes no carnage"; but "carnage" again points in opposite directions at once. Though he may wish to indicate that this reversal of death—if that, in fact, is what it is—does not involve an assumption of flesh, the more immediate connotation of "carnage" evokes extensive and bloody slaughter. In the process of offering reassurance that no "carnage" is presumed, Crane manages to color his figure with its bloody implications. Rather than achieving a reversal of death, he effects an uneasy truce. The uncertainty of this middle ground, with its simultaneous resignation to and victory over death, resonates most tellingly in the poem's neologism: "transmemberment."

In the letter to Waldo Frank where Crane wrote of the love affair that prompted him this sequence, he characterized that experience as one of "transformation" and "transubstantiation." The term he employs in the poem itself, though, is far richer than either of these. "Transmemberment" conflates "transformation" and "dismemberment," yoking together the movements of chiasmus and anacoluthon, the preparatory stages of Crane's rhetorical project. Yet the term invokes another essential word as well, one that figures prominently in that rhetorical enterprise of reduction and reconstruction. Between "dismember" and "transmember" lies Crane's pivotal term: "remember." This liminal word encompasses both the destructive, "whitening" aspect of memory (as in "I can remember much forgetfulness"), and its movement toward reconstructive, emblematic designs (as in "Repose of Rivers" where the poet declares: "Finally, in that memory all things nurse"). The "single change" announced in the lines, "Upon the steep floor flung from dawn to dawn/ The silken skilled transmemberment of song," returns the poem to the state of flux where death performs its part in the dialectic of transformation, but Oedipal dismemberment is evaded, postponed, or refigured as the "transmemberment of song." By remembering to forget death—to "shed" it—the poet attains to the chiastic "transmemberment" that generates both "infinite consanguinity" and "song"; but he suffers the continuous violence, upon the sea's "steep floor," of being "flung from dawn to dawn."

In the compensatory economy by which the poet here approaches imaginative stability, by which, that is, he "retrieves" poetic "transmemberment" from reductive dismemberment, "Voyages III" recalls Whitman's poem of self-scattering and retrieval through song, "When Lilacs Last in the Dooryard Bloom'd," with its "retrievements out of the night,/ The song, the wondrous chant of the gray-brown bird." Whitman's poem, like Crane's, compensates for figurative dismemberment with images of conjunction, and it ends like "Voyages III," with an assertion of "transmemberment": "Lilac and star and bird twined with the chant of my soul." In Crane's celebratory poem of "consanguinity," though he must suffer to be "flung from dawn to dawn" upon the sea's cruel bottom, that punishment assures him a perpetual earliness, an inscription in the "virginal" and "cool" domain of "dawn." With this knowledge he makes his final request: "Permit me voyage, love, into your hands . . ."

Pivoting symmetrically around the word "love," this line aspires syntactically to a conclusive stability and balance. "Voyage" and "hands" here are both tropes of eros generated by "love" itself. Each half of the phrase points inward so that they meet, and cross, at "love." But even at this consummate juncture of crossing and reciprocity an unsettling element obtrudes itself. For the line trails off into ellipsis, betokening disjunction. Though the line would like to bend in on itself in the perfect enclosure of "love," the final punctuation leads onward to inevitable dissolution. Punctuation, in this case, proves prophetic both for the lovers and for Crane's poetics.

III

Although Crane, throughout his poetry, pushes syntax toward figure, creating what can be seen as figures of syntax. "Voyages IV" finds him straining against syntax without elevating that effort to the status of a figure. In strenuous wrenchings of what is, at best, a complex and hypotactic style, the poem seems intent on subverting not only syntactical continuity but also the authority achieved by his previous figures of breaking and bending. The poet seems poised between the formalism of design—the balanced enclosure that governs chiasmus—and a new descent into the fragmenting of form—the project of anacoluthon. In the first stanza his language twists in on itself without achieving chiastic stability, and it hangs suspended in terms of syntax without registering anacoluthon:

> Whose counted smile of hours and days, suppose
> I know as spectrum of the sea and pledge
> Vastly now parting gulf on gulf of wings
> Whose circles bridge, I know (from palms to the severe
> Chilled albatross's white immutability)
> No stream of greater love advancing now
> Than, singing, this mortality alone
> Through clay aflow immortally to you.

From the first here Crane engages in emphatic declaration to cover the uncertainty of his self-reflections. But the element of doubt cannot be obscured by the insistence of his claims. His use, for instance, of the possessive "whose"—"Whose counted smile of hours and days," "Whose circles bridge"—seems almost to announce a question rather than to introduce a subordinate clause. And his attitude is palpably tentative, even hypothetical ("suppose/ I know") as he links phrase to phrase in these lines. Though he posits a "love" that is both "singing" and "advancing now," his own song, eager as it is to move beyond its cycles of negativity and recuperation, seems to lack assurance as to how it should advance. It circles in upon itself with no clear resolution, lingering almost on the borderline between his two favored figures of syntax. Both are subjected to a reductive anatomy as he attempts to break down their figural significance so as to break through the repetitive process that he desperately wishes to deny.

Throughout this poem he tries to discover some form of connection that need not succumb to the insistent force of disjunction. He wants to assert a love he can "count" on an erotic "smile" that will "bridge" the implicit negativity of "mortality," allowing his figural "singing" to flow forth "immortally." Though his imagination tries to deny violation by "madly" calling up images of "meeting" and "mingling," what he struggles against is his knowledge of inescapable division, his knowledge of the "widening" "gulf" that in time must "lead" his lover's eyes to "blue latitudes and levels." He wants to "claim" that even this "parting" can be conducted "inviolably," as a type of connection, but he fears he can know only the persistence of ruptures opening "gulf on gulf."

The poem is thus divided between what it knows and what it claims. Crane here will neither admit the defeat of the formal balance he aspires to, nor will he recommence the struggle to overcome his rhetorical reductions. Apparently unwilling to "spend out himself again," he tries to reclaim the "foreknown" emblem of "transmemberment" from the previous poem, and in the fourth stanza of "Voyages IV" he alludes to and echoes that verbal signature:

> In signature of the incarnate word
> The harbor shoulders to resign in mingling
> Mutual blood, transpiring as foreknown
> And widening noon within your breast for gathering
> All bright insinuations that my years have caught
> For islands where must lead inviolably
> Blue latitudes and levels of your eyes.

In his attempt to re-sign this signature, Crane betrays his own resignation of the rigorously dialectical process, settling instead for a mere rehearsal of his earlier achievement. Willfully, and almost wearily, he recalls the consummation of "Voyages III," evoking both "transmemberment" and "consanguinity" in his figure of "mingling/ Mutual blood." No longer content with the "gulf" of desire, he acknowledges unhappily, in the second stanza, that the "region" of poetry remains always to "wreathe again" with new figures, new flowers of rhetoric. And in the fourth stanza he views the activity of poetic substitution as a process of repetition with everything "transpiring as foreknown," with stability giving way to disjunction, and mutuality to division and loss. Thus the emblem of chiastic crossing—an emblem that he attempts to "insinuate" as a process of "gathering" what his own "years have caught" into his lover's "breast" —cannot endure "inviolably," but must yield to the "fatal tides." The "widening noon" into which he would step the legend of these "bright insinuations" lacks a "bright logic" that would allow him to "bridge" the poetic "gulf" of negativity.

In fact, intimations of negativity and reduction permeate "Voyages IV." Where the "transmemberment of the previous poem "presume(d) no carnage," the "word" here is "incarnate" and thus emphatically material. The very re-signing of its "signature" in "mingling/ Mutual blood" recalls the "barter" of "Faustus and Helen" whereby poetry was reduced to the materiality of rhetoric. Now the limiting bounds of a harbor begin to obtrude on the oceanic domain, introducing the possibility of an end to Crane's poetic and erotic voyaging—a possibility implicit in the "chancel port" and the pun of "portending eyes." This tension between Crane's assertions of imaginative inviolability and the reductive implications of his figures themselves becomes palpable in the poem's third line: "Vastly now parting gulf on gulf of wings." The phrasing here echoes obliquely the formula by which the previous poem depicted erotic crossing and mutuality: "star kissing star through wave on wave." But that echo carries the poignancy of what Freud called *verneinung* or negation, for it tries to drown out the distinctly disjunctive import of the figure itself. Here the formula is used to image "parting," not consummation, the opening of a "gulf" or rift, not the joinings of specular intercourse. The emblematic design of verbal coupling is put in the service of negativity, as if the poet would evade the inevitable cycles of breaking and bending by combining them both in a gesture of denial, a gesture that looks forward to some synthesis beyond these alternatives of thesis and antithesis. Thus in "Voyages IV" he begins to propose a catachrestic extension of language.

Yet his movements toward such a rhetorical extension lack confidence or authority. They betray an anxiety that acknowledges his persistent implication in a poetics of negativity. Forcing "fragrance" to take on the aspect of a verb, he begins the second stanza with a catachrestic pronouncement: "All fragrance irrefragibly." But the uncertain status of "irrefragibly"—is it a neologism or merely a misspelling of "irrefragably"? —undermines the strength of that verbal abuse. The wrenchings of paradox ("this mortality alone/ Through clay aflow immortally to you," "Madly meeting logically in this hour") and pun ("Portending eyes and lips and making told/ The chancel port and portion of our June") register Crane's efforts to accomplish the extension that can lead him beyond his cyclical alternations of formal design and material reduction, of chiastic stability and anacoluthon-like undoings. But though he longs to be "advancing," to "bridge" the "parting gulf," the need for rhetorical undoing or anatomy is still too strongly felt.

If he cannot yet move beyond those cycles, he is capable of analyzing them, and he reflects throughout "Voyages IV" on the syntax and figures of the earlier poems. Just as he mingled the design of chiasmus with the image of rift and disruption, so too he reinterprets his previous figures as he reflects on his poetic practice. Harking back to the sea's "poinsettia meadows," the "crocus lustres of the stars," and the "one floating flower" of "Voyages III" in which "sleep, death, desire/ Close round" in a single "instant," the poet now wonders:

> Shall they not stem and close in our own steps
> Bright staves of flowers and quills to-day as I
> Must first be lost in fatal tides to tell?

It occurs to Crane that these apotropaic flowers of language may themselves have plunged him in "fatal tides," that his emblems of enclosure and reciprocity may have been as dangerous, in their own way, as the "sceptered terror" against which he called them forth. The death that was "shed" or forgotten by the reflexivity and balance of inversion, is death, Crane remembers, by drowning—like Narcissus—in pursuit of one's own mirror-image. It is death, as Melville would recognize, through solipsistic self-enclosure. Unlike the forgetfulness in "Faustus and Helen" that left him "lost yet poised in traffic," Crane's poetry here lacks poise or assurance as he envisions an effort of endless reduction that he must first be "lost in fatal tides to tell." His flowers take on, with this fearful perception, a distinctly ominous aspect. Their stems, as verbs, "stem" creative activity. Though figured in the "bright staves" of the ocean's "lanes" or verses, these "flowers" cannot stave off the "fatal tides" that claim the poet. Even their quills, which might have evoked, in another context, the poet's own tools of inscription, suggest here the thorns of his tropological flowers turned against their creator, transformed into pricks against which he futilely kicks. No longer do "sleep, death, desire,/ Close round one instant in one floating flower"; the very stability of that enclosure has

turned into an image of engulfment or disjunction as the rhetorical flowers
he has planted "stem and close in [his] own steps." As he struggles against
the necessity of endless poetic substitution, as the oceanic space of desire
becomes the space of "fatal tides," as he nostalgically longs for the
comforts of metaphor, the matchings of language "meeting logically,"
Crane reacts against the inevitable withering of all his rhetorical "flowers"
in the very moment they are offered up. He sees himself literally drowning
in the turning "tides" of trope, and weary of his "relentless caper," he
seeks solid ground for his figural "steps."

This movement away from erotic celebration and toward an analysis of his figural practice coincides with his introduction into the poem of
verbs of quantification. When he wonders if he "must first be lost in fatal
tides to tell" the "bright staves of flowers and quills," he refers as much to
enumeration as to reportage, suggesting both an accounting *for* and an
accounting *of* his images. This element of quantification appears both in
the poem's second stanza, where Crane writes of "making told/ The
chancel port and portion of our June" and in the very first line, "Whose
counted smile of hours and days." In each case this enumerative impulse
points to Crane's calculated refiguring of his poetic figures, his restless
attempt to combine them in order to achieve a different sum.

The "counted smile," in this context, serves a crucial tropological
function. It figures, in a sense, a geometrical figure, for Crane knows this
"smile" as "spectrum" and "pledge," as an arc of promise congruent with
the curve of the covenantal rainbow. It figures his hope that by going
through chiasmus and anacoluthon he can arrive at a point beyond either
one. Thus as he envisions the "gulf of wings" giving way to the perfect
enclosure of "circles," so those circles must in turn be imaged as extending
into the sweeping arc of a "bridge." Such an outward movement finds its
analogue in the "advancing" stream of love that bespeaks Crane's desire
for a rhetorical advance in his enterprise of "singing." Unable though he
may be to complete, in this poem, that catachrestic extension beyond his
figures of syntax, Crane struggles to transform those breakings and bendings into the arc of a new rhetorical covenant. The "smile" as "spectrum"
is a token of that covenant, and it offers a "pledge" of erotic presence that
recalls the flickerings of Helen's eyes, "half-riant before the jerky window
frame." In doing so it promises an escape from the solipsism threatening to
"close in" the poet's "steps."

Does Crane's restlessness for that catachrestic extension suggest
that he has exhausted the possibilities of memory and emblem? Recognizing their solipsistic complicity, he seems impatient to move beyond his
own spiraling movements further and further inward, impatient to move

beyond his dialectic of creations and destroyings and beyond his earlier meditations on poetic negativity. In "Voyages IV" he finds himself in a state of self-enclosure so complete that despite his longing to "bridge" that negativity with the arc of a "smile" he can only analyze and refigure the cost of his own poetic process.

His problem can be focused in the figure of the "severe/ Chilled albatross's white immutability." The image is introduced as part of Crane's effort to characterize the unparalleled strength of his love—a love than which none greater can be found from tropic to pole, from "palms to the severe/ Chilled albatross's white immutability." But the linguistic excess of this image, the imbalance created by its imaginative engagement with the albatross at the expense of the "palms," makes the figure an index of Crane's anxiety about the scope, and the "colors," of his poetic "spectrum." In poems such as "For the Marriage of Faustus and Helen," Crane's insistence on whiteness betrayed an urge toward reductive absolutism, an urge to push rhetoric to its "virginal" origins in the material stuff of figure itself. Here, however, this sense of rhetorical materiality takes on the more unpleasant aspect of "chilled" and icy "immutability." This unchanging whiteness evokes the landscape Crane depicted in "North Labrador," where a virginal world with "no memories" lay silently in its own enclosure, "hugged by plaster-grey arches of sky." In such a "cold-hushed" realm there is "no birth, no death, no time nor sun" to "answer" the "leaning ice" as it "flings itself silently/ Into eternity." That solipsistic and icy "immutability" images the effect of emblematic enclosure upon the reductive "whitening" of memory. Where memory triumphs over time, collapsing lateness into earliness, emblem consolidates that victory, asserting the primacy of space or of rhetorical design, over temporal process and flux. But this suppression of temporality has potentially "fatal" consequences for the poet. It can lead to the silence of solipsism, to the claustrophobia of self-enclosure, trapping him in the "cold-hushed" fortress of his own rhetorical cycles. The association of Coleridge's "albatross" with this "chilled . . . white immutability," adds to the sense of isolation by evoking the inhibiting self-consciousness of the Ancient Mariner, the self-consciousness that forever sets him apart and condemns him to repeat the same tale.

Meditating on that self-enclosure, Crane complains that the tropological flowers of his language "stem and close in our own steps." Though Crane and his lover are still at sea, aflow on a "stream . . . of love," this use of "steps" instead of "strokes" has a logic of its own. "Legend" concluded with an image of "stepping" that signified the triumph over cyclical process that Crane, in this poem, is struggling to achieve through his figural "advancing" or extension toward the arcs of a rainbow, a "smile," and a "bridge." In "Legend" Crane's "steps" both allegorized and enacted catachrestic extensions by figuring catachresis as a "Relentless caper for all those who step/ The legend of their youth into the noon." Now, at the end of a fitful and uncertain segment of his "Voyages," Crane once again tries to step his poem across the "fatal tides" of loss, across the "widening" gulf that echoes the "too wide . . . breast" of the sea itself.

The final couplet attempts to negotiate that gap:

> In this expectant, still exclaim receive
> The secret oar and petals of all love.

But what Crane, all too properly, is "expectant" of here is the inevitable incursion of discontinuity. He knows full well that separation must undo the "mingling" mutuality of his relationship with his lover. In their violent scatterings of language, therefore, these lines achieve not so much the outward extension or rhetorical advance of catachresis, as the uncertainty that points once more to the negativity of language. Although the words are wrenched from their ordinary contexts, their rearrangements yield provocative disarray instead of new configurations of meaning. As R. W. B. Lewis notes, "something is obviously wrong with either the grammar or the punctuation of those lines . . . One can move words around experimentally; but they are curiously inert and heavy counters." Lewis goes on to suggest that "still" functions as a noun here, but it is impossible to say whether it might not equally well be an adjective, an adverb, or even a verb. "In this expectant" can be read as a subordinate clause as easily as "expectant" can be joined to "still" in modifying "exclaim." The sentence appears to treat "exclaim" as a noun that signifies "exclamation," but its contiguity with "receive" pulls "exclaim" back in the direction of an imperative verb. "Exclaim receive" may constitute a compound predicate or, conceivably, "receive/ The secret oar and petals of all love" may be what the lover is requested to "exclaim." In short, the chaos resulting from these verbal dislocations is as significant as is the impulse toward catachrestic extension. Thus the rhetorical advance that Crane would "claim" and "exclaim" is "x"-ed or crossed out by the rhetoric it is couched in.

Yet if this movement toward catachresis reinscribes discontinuity, the poem's last line offers a modest hope of constructing a figural "bridge." The erotic and rhetorical flowers of "all love," reduced here to synecdochic "petals," are now joined by the "secret oar," which suggests both a sexual and a literary weapon against the disjunctive force of the sea. It intimates poetic survival in the midst of these "fatal tides" by hinting at the extension or outward prop upon which catachresis will depend. Indeed, if the poet and his lover can both "receive/ The secret oar," they can make it a bridge to lead them beyond reduction and reconstruction.

IV

The penultimate section of the "Voyages" sequence marks the return of negativity with a vengeance. Far from effecting an extension, "Voyages V" envisions a critical moment of breaking as the "secret oar" of the previous poem turns into an instrument far less benign:

> Meticulous, past midnight in clear rime,
> Infrangible and lonely, smooth as though cast
> Together in one merciless white blade—
> The bay estuaries fleck the hard sky limits.

Sky and sea are "cast/ Together" here once again, but not in the undulating reciprocity seen earlier. The "chilled" whiteness mentioned in "Voyages IV" has gained its full ascendancy and previous images of softness and pliancy—suggested by the "samite sheeted sea," the "crocus lustres of the stars," and the "one floating flower"—give way to "hard sky limits" joining the water's surface in "one merciless white blade." The poem has turned from the "unfettered" and "rimless" world of the mother, to the world of "limits" associated with the father. And that paternal realm wields a "merciless white blade" with which to punish the Oedipal transgressor. Even the sea suffers reduction and circumscription; it narrows here into "bay estuaries" iced over with white or reductive "rime," "as if too brittle or too clear to touch." With the reappearance of the shore, and the introduction of this "brittle" quality, the poem returns to the world of "Voyages I," where the sea's margin was imaged with "crumbling fragments of baked weed." But the "brilliant" daylight of the earlier poem has yielded to an hour "past midnight," and the warmth of the previous vision has been supplanted by an ominous chill.

Though the immutability of this "merciless" whiteness has its origins in "Voyages IV," the difference between this poem and its predecessor can be gauged by comparing the use of "irrefragibly" there with the use of "infrangible" here. In the earlier poem, Crane tries to deny that the tide is turning against his reconstructive efforts. With willful desperation he proclaims that the "fragrance" of his rhetorical flowers persists "irrefragibly." Though possibly a misspelling, as suggested earlier, "irrefragibly" may intentionally conflate "irrefragable" and "irrefrangible," as the poet proposes a verbal construct—like "tremorous" in "Legend"—

that will assure both the irrefutability and the inviolable integrity of his poetic achievement. In "Voyages V," though, "infrangible" describes the inviolability not of his poetics, but of the external forces of reduction. These "bay estuaries" are "infrangible" because they have been joined to the "hard sky limits" in an icy seam that answers the "undinal" bending of sea toward sky with a "hard" and masculine welding.

Does anything escape this "merciless white blade" of rhetorical reduction, this "white immutability," which, as Melville suggested in "The Whiteness of the Whale," "by its indefiniteness . . . shadows forth the heartless voids and immensities of the universe, and thus stabs us from behind with the thought of annihilation?" Certainly "sleep"—which was associated with "death" in "Voyages II" as an activity of "desire"—cannot withstand its divisiveness here:

> The cables of our sleep so swiftly filed,
> Already hang, shred ends from remembered stars.
> One frozen trackless smile . . .

"The cables of our sleep" suggests simultaneously the telegraphic inscriptions of desire in dreams and a reification of our dream or desire for metaphysical connection or support. In either case these "cables" hang severed from "remembered stars," implying the dialectical relationship of a reductive or negative act of memory and the re- or trans- membering figured as "star kissing star" in "Voyages II." "Swiftly" and "already" emphasize the unexpected rapidity of this inevitable flux, as the "merciless white blade" divides dream from actuality, the poet's self from the image of himself that is "imminent in his dream." The pairing of specular doubles that even the ocean's "sceptred terror" failed to rend, cannot survive the "hard limits" imposed by this unchanging masculine shore. Crane attempts, therefore, to refigure the divisive edge of this horizon in the same way that he refigured the sea in "Voyages II" and death in "Voyages III." He struggles to assert the superiority of his own figural constructions over the brutal absolutism of the "one merciless white blade," by willfully interpreting it as "one frozen trackless smile." This "smile," of course, refers back to the "counted smile" of "Voyages IV," which figured Crane's desire to resolve his creations and destroyings into the arc of a "spectrum" that would "pledge" the connective extension of a "bridge." This same rhetorical aspiration informs "one frozen trackless smile"; but even this "smile" can only recapitulate the solitude and frigidity of this whitened world. Trailing off into an ellipsis that signals syntactical incompletion, it succumbs to the whiteness out of which it is formed, a whiteness that Crane attempts to evade as it turns its agencies, here, against him.

This sense of reduction pervades "Voyages V," as earlier figures of negativity return to undo the most significant emblem of erotic exchange that the poet has dared to propose. The moonlight that Crane, in "For the Marriage of Faustus and Helen," took as his guiding light and his paradigmatic image of rhetorical reduction, directs its whitening energies, now, at the poet and his lover themselves. It assumes a power of negation that Crane no longer can control:

> What words
> Can strangle this deaf moonlight? For we
> Are overtaken. Now no cry, no sword
> Can fasten or deflect this tidal wedge,
> Slow tyranny of moonlight, moonlight loved
> And changed . . .

In the beginning Crane did, indeed, love moonlight, taking it as a figure of memory's power to whiten and thereby make possible creative revision. But the "slow tyranny" of its reductions governs the movements of the sea in which Crane has sought emblems of chiastic construction with which to consolidate memory's triumph over time. Inevitably, the reductive moonlight draws the tide once more to the shore, subjecting Crane's oceanic "transmemberments" to inevitable division, sundering all constructions with "one merciless white blade."

No longer content with a whitening that exposes the rhetoricity of every text and reveals all aspirations to pathos as illusions generated by poetic substitution, Crane cries out for the "cry" of pathos; he yearns for the presence of voice that would undo the persistent emptying of meaning by moonlight. But that agency of reduction—itself viewed reductively as a "tidal wedge"—is "deaf" to the fictions of pathos that it exposes as nothing *but* fictions. Caught in the white glare of moonlight and rime, the poet and his lover "are overtaken" by disjunction—a situation depicted graphically by the space that separates "For we" from its predicate at the beginning of the next stanza: "Are overtaken." The "fatal tides" of rhetoric have turned against the poet and no "words" of his can silence or "strangle" the reductive voice of the moon—a moon that is "deaf" to every "cry" that would "deflect" its negativity.

Inevitably, then, this moonlight falls between the poet and his lover:

> "There's
> Nothing like this in the world," you say.
> Knowing I cannot touch your hand and look
> Too, into that godless cleft of sky
> Where nothing turns but dead sands flashing.

Unlike Crane, the lover sees beauty in this agency of reduction; he can face the nothingness signified by that "godless cleft of sky" because he interprets the falling moonlight as an emblem of metaphysical connection, a restringing of the severed cables hanging shredded in stanza two. Lacking Crane's poetic insight into the significance that attaches to this "wedge" of light, he can look into the moonlit space and exclaim, "There's/ Nothing like this in the world," denying thereby the negativity of moonlight and celebrating what he takes to be the unworldly, transcendent beauty it affords. But if the lover's assertion suggests an exclamation, it suggests a simple denial as well, a willful claim that there *is*, in fact, nothing in the world like the "cleft" of nothingness into which he stares. In this way the lover adopts the strategy of negation that Crane himself made use of in "Voyages IV."

But contrary to his lover, Crane fully understands the "meticulous"—in its root sense of "fearful"—truth: that the moonlight itself is a "merciless white blade," and that it, too, figures the "hiatus," the "cleft," the nothingness that undoes all couplings. Therefore he cannot touch his lover's hand, recapitulating the earlier "pieties" of interchange and reciprocity, while "look[ing]/ Too, into that godless cleft of sky" that must sever so intimate a bond. Although he bewails the reductive of moonlight, Crane recognizes all too well the power of its radical materialism; he knows that it is the governing agency not only of the sea, but of poetry as well. The starlit sky itself becomes, through the force of this whitening perspective, a void, an abyss filled with "nothing" but the fatally reductive tropes or "turns" of stars that Crane figures as "dead sands flashing." That nothing else "turns" here signals Crane's reaction against the need to fill poetic space—the "cleft of sky"—with flowers that always "stem and close in our own step." It provokes a nostalgia for presence whose underside is a bitterness at the instability of all his poetic constructions. In a radical internalization of lunar negativity, he demystifies the celestial, sun-like stars that evoked erotic reciprocity in the image of "star kissing star." Now they are seen as mere physical substance and described as "dead sands flashing." These glittering celestial "sands" evoke the brilliant shore of "Voyages I" and in the process enact an exchange between the earth and the sky that reinterprets crossing not as the intertwining of erotic doubles, but as the fatal crossing of skull and bones—a crossing that acknowledges, as Crane asserts, that these flashing sands are "dead."

This betrayal of eros and this reinterpretation of the rhetorical figure that designates its pairings, shocks the poet who never "dreamed" that his union could be undone. By the same token, he never imagined that the very emblem of erotic coupling could be appropriated to serve as a figure of reduction turned against the poet himself:

> "—And never to quite understand!" No,
> In all the argosy of your bright hair I dreamed
> Nothing so flagless as this piracy.

The theft that claims "the argosy" of the beloved's "bright hair," constitutes an act of "piracy" for Crane. That piracy refers to the violent interruption of the lovers' shared voyage, a parting of the ways that asserts a negativity like that of anacoluthon, the scheme that breaks syntactical coherence so that it becomes impossible to "quite understand" the unity of an utterance. But in describing this act of violation, Crane calls attention to something that is missing. The "piracy" that claims this sexual "argosy" comes "flagless," without its wonted insignia. And that insignia, of course, is the skull and crossbones, the "Jolly Roger" of piracy. By emphasizing the absence of that distinctive flag, Crane produces an oscillation that places the poem under the sign of chiasmus even while displacing the chiastic emblem that governs it. That oscillation can be glossed as his awareness of the dialectical relationship between breaking and bending, between the chiastic "X" as an image of death (the warning of the skull and crossbones) and the erotic promise of its enclosure and exchange (the sexual slang of "Jolly Roger"). The poet seems to realize, in a sense, that he has been double-crossed by the emblem of crossing as it cancels or crosses-out the sense of reciprocity and reasserts once more a "fatal" discontinuity.

In the final stanza of the poem Crane registers his understanding of this duplicity:

> But now
> Draw in your head, alone and too tall here.
> Your eyes already in the slant of drifting foam;
> Your breath already sealed by the ghosts I do not know;
> Draw in your breath and sleep the long way home.

Despite the physical proximity indicated in these lines by Crane's address to a companion who is situated "here," the poet realizes the irreducible distance that has come between them. He understands the solipsistic loneliness that no mutuality or balance can withstand. Each remains "alone" and the dividing gap again obtrudes itself as the lover seems, suddenly, "too tall," that is, too remote, too far away. With "foam" and "ghosts" the reductive whiteness reclaims the poet's companion, but Crane is exempted from the disjunctive "drifting" and scattering presaged here. Projecting those images upon his lover—whose "breath" is "sealed," precluding expression, while his "eyes" are "already in the slant of drifting foam"—Crane commends him to a "sleep" in which the image of desire will once again only be "imminent," now that the "cables" of union hang severed from stars that are only "dead sands."

V

A beginning as well as an end, "Voyages VI" departs in a number of ways from the previous sections of the poem. The most immediately noticeable change occurs on the level of structure or form. Although there have been traces of formal organization earlier in the sequence—stanzaic regularity in "Voyages II," a persistent base meter of iambic pentameter, and even a hint of rhyme in the musical couplet "Upon the steep floor flung from dawn to dawn/ The silken skilled transmemberment of song"—"Voyages VI" is the most consistently formal section of the poem. Interestingly, though, while this section of "Voyages" accedes to rhyming quatrains and metrical regularity, its meter is diminished from the normative blank verse of the earlier poems to a less expansive iambic tetrameter. This paradoxical concurrence of loss and gain, of diminution and transformation, becomes the informing motif of "Voyages VI." Thus the achievement of structural regularity coincides with the disappearance of the poet's specular double, with the disappearance of his balancing counterpart in the imaginative design of reciprocal exchange. It coincides, also, with a movement toward almost reckless self-assertion, despite—or perhaps because of—the limitations constraining the poet in this section.

This formal regularity, then, argues no weakening of the poet's quest for a revisionary poetics. Rather, it recalls the moment in "Legend" when Crane, in the final stanza of that poem, abandoned the *vers libre* of the earlier stanzas and opened himself to the iambic pentameter he had previously suppressed. Far from implying poetic conservatism, this gesture effected a transumption of tradition, a self-conscious appropriation of the high literary style of Anglo-American poetry. The image corresponding to that appropriation in "Legend" was one of a "perfect cry" that produced a "constant harmony" able to triumph over "silence" at last. Having gone through the cycle of creations and destroyings "twice and twice," "again . . . and yet again," until the "bright logic" was "won," Crane finally could perform the task essential to all who would revise poetic tradition: the task he described in "General Aims and Theories" as one of offering the reader "a single, new *word*." That undertaking, with its implicit suggestion of catachresis, informed Crane's embrace of formal music at the end of "Legend," an embrace that made possible the final catachresis of his "Relentless caper for all those who step/ The legend of their youth into the noon." Similarly, in "Voyages VI," Crane's move toward formal regularity augurs a final transformation or shift of perspective in the flux of his "sea change" as he gestures toward the catachrestic word that might compensate for his losses in this poem.

The sense of poetic shift is announced thematically in the "shift" the poet notices at the outset of "Voyages VI":

> Where icy and bright dungeons lift
> Of swimmers their lost morning eyes,
> And ocean rivers, churning, shift
> Green borders under stranger skies.

This stanza begins by trying to define a place, and the terms by which it does so produce a number of reverberations. The lines suggest a continuity with the previous sections by recalling, in these "icy dungeons," the "chilled" and "frozen" qualities of "Voyages IV" and "V." Similarly, the turbulent vortex of sections II and III survives in the "churning" of these "ocean rivers," a locution that itself evokes "the stream of . . . love" in "Voyages IV." But the poet's lover, whose eyes, at the end of "Voyages V," were "already in the slant of drifting foam," makes no appearance here; instead, his absence is obliquely imaged in the "lost morning eyes" of the "swimmers"—eyes that the watery "dungeons" "lift" not only in the sense of "raising," but also in the colloquial sense of "stealing" or "making off with." For those "lost morning eyes" unmistakably suggest a lost innocence or earliness; and since "eyes" and "morning" both are lost, the possibility of transumptive vision seems to be cancelled by a blindness that figures lost poetic strength. Crane's repudiation of eros, his refusal to acknowledge the love that disjunction has undone, obtrudes itself in the tokens of limitation and loss that fill the poem.

These figures of constraint, significantly, often occur in antithetical formulations. The "dungeons" that imprison these "swimmers" beneath the "ocean rivers," engage in the contradictory activity of "lifting"; and those "dungeons," deep at the bottom of the sea, are neither dark nor gloomy, but "bright." The effort to recuperate loss here recalls the transformations of Shakespearean "sea change"; and when the currents "lift/ Of swimmers their lost morning eyes," Crane reinterprets, at a later time and "under stranger skies," Shakespeare's own "rich and strange" figuration: "Those are pearls that were his eyes."

Ariel's song, of course, laments the putative death at sea of Ferdinand's father, the King of Naples. But Crane's blind swimmer, his "morning eyes" now "lost" suffers the blindness that is the punishment for the son who engages in Oedipal rivalry with the father. The poet's blindness, then, with its inevitable Freudian suggestion of castration, figures the dismemberment (by the father's "merciless white blade") that attends transgression. At the same time, however, it carries traces here of a willful self-laceration, of a denial and a dismissal of eros through the casting out, the projection, of sexuality. But if Crane seems to sever himself from eros, it is a loss that he accepts in hopes of a greater gain. In his effort to "shift" the significance of the Shakespearean trope of "sea change," in his attempt to refigure it as his own "under stranger skies," he desires to make the figure itself more "strange," and thus, as Stevens would have it, more true. For only that which is "rich and strange" can lay claim to imaginative originality. No longer trusting the "indestructibility" of erotic enclosure, Crane indicates a desire to "shift" his rhetoric from the inversions of specularity to the "strangeness" of catachresis. That trope of extension is figured here in the movements of Crane's "ocean rivers"—an image that recalls his earlier need to believe that his "stream of . . . love" was "advancing" in "Voyages IV."

Just as the covenant at the end of "Legend" was heralded by music, so the movement here toward catachresis is indicated by Crane's description of these "ocean rivers" that "shift" as

> Steadily as a shell secretes
> Its beating leagues of monotone,
> Or as many waters trough the sun's
> Red kelson past the cape's wet stone.

As usual, Crane invests his imagery of the sea with nuances that acknowledge its figural status. These "leagues of monotone" identify not only units of measure—thus invoking the "beating" of metrical "measure"—but they also connote "leagues" as in pacts or covenants. In this way the "leagues of monotone" point to the revisionary company of poets who "beat" the past into the "monotone" of a late, interpretive echo. In league with such poets, Crane claims the power associated with the shell: the power to capture the sound of the sea and to figure or "secrete" it as music.

This power, significantly, coincides with a daring speech act that allows Crane to assert that "many waters trough the sun's/ Red kelson past the cape's wet stone." The poet here figures the sun as a ship—substituting for, and superseding, the lost "argosy" of the lover's "bright hair"—whose "kelson" the "many waters" "trough." The image in mimetic terms, appears to describe sunset as the sinking of that ship, as a fiery Turneresque descent into the waiting "trough" of the sea. Sherman Paul elaborates on this "natural" interpretation by speaking of it as "the setting sun of death, of a Gotter dammerung." Yet this naturalistic reading of the image fails to account for the linguistic mediation that characterizes it as a trope. When Crane writes that the "many waters trough the sun's/ Red kelson," he forces the noun "trough" to function as verb, misusing it to make it denote the action of making a "trough" for the sun. This "strange" use of language allows the figure to suggest the sun's momentary balance on the surface of the water while some extension of it—its "kelson"—projects into the sea, forming a figurative link between ocean and the flaming ship of the sun. That link is effected by an act of "troughing" that denotes at once an act of parting and of enclosing—the water closes around the sun's "kelson" while it opens to engulf the sun itself. By means of its extension, therefore, the sun is both in the water and out of it at once, and in this way it parallels the verbal extension that Crane forces upon the noun "trough"—an extension of meaning that falls within the domain of catachresis.

. . . Catachresis appears quite often—and this is certainly true for Crane—in figurations that pertain to the sun. Jacques Derrida, in "White Mythology," discusses Aristotle's "treatment of the Sun" in the *Poetics*. He finds that the sun's emission of light—an activity that Aristotle acknowledges "has no name"—can only be named by substituting "the proper name of something" else. Such a process, Derrida observes, "refers us back to the problem of the proper name," which is to say, to the question of catachresis, a definition of which Derrida quotes from Fontanier:

> *Catachresis, in general, consists in this, that a sign already assigned to a first idea should be assigned also to a new idea which has no other sign at all, or no longer has a sign as its proper expression.* It includes, therefore, any Trope whose usage is forced or necessary, any Trope which results in a purely *extended* sense.

Since it is "more than essential: it produces essence, being and appearing", Derrida notes that "it is difficult to know what is proper to the sun." Though the source of illumination and the prerequisite for sight, the sun is nevertheless impossible to see: "One may not look upon it on pain of blindness and death." Both the source of all metaphor and a metaphor itself, subject to displacement and eclipse, the sun is both absent and present, absolutely hidden at the same time it is hidden in absolutely everything. To name it properly, therefore, is impossible. As Wallace

Stevens asserts in "Notes Toward a Supreme Fiction," "the sun must bear no name." Any attempt to utter its unspeakable name must take place through the catachrestic borrowing of the name of something else.

In "Voyages VI," then, after figuring the sun's position through the catachresis of the second stanza, Crane goes on to consider the power and freedom associated with this figural naming—a naming that is always a form of misnaming, and therefore a form of blindness:

> O rivers mingling toward the sky
> And harbor of the phoenix' breast—
> My eyes pressed black against the prow,
> —Thy derelict and blinded guest
>
> Waiting, afire, what name, unspoke,
> I cannot claim: let thy waves rear
> More savage than the death of kings,
> Some splintered garland for the seer.

Though abandoned now and "derelict" Crane designates himself as the "guest" of the "ocean rivers": not as a guilty trespasser but as one chosen and invited. By describing himself as "blinded," however, he places himself in the company of the swimmers who have "lost" their "morning eyes." No longer can he claim the virginal earliness of one who works "from dawn to dawn" the "silken skilled transmemberment of song"; for the hour is now late and the sun is setting, though still bright enough to blind. The image of the "phoenix' breast" may strive to intimate the possibility of renewal, but that renewal from "dawn to dawn" is attributed here to the sun and not the poet.

Figuring the sun as a ship in the second stanza of the poem, Crane directed his attention, from his watery "dungeon," to its fiery "red kelson." Now he images his loss as blindness when he writes of his "eyes pressed black against the prow," for that prow bears the full weight of a synecdoche for the blinding ship of the sun. Confronting directly that image of power, Crane points toward the dismemberment imposed upon those "brazen" or presumptuous enough to transgress against anteriority. At the same time, however, this figure, in which the poet seems to "blacken" his own eyes, points toward a willful gesture of self-blinding, an act of denial in which the poet refuses to see—that is, to acknowledge—the luminosity of the sun. Instead, he internalizes its attributes by presenting himself in the posture of one who is "waiting," as he puts it, "afire."

In this auto-elegiac gesture, the poet compensates for loss by denying it, introjecting tropes of power and willfully projecting those of death. The highly qualified and tentative line that begins the fourth stanza finds him "waiting," explicitly, for a "name, unspoke," a name that he acknowledges he "cannot claim." What he "cannot claim" here is the extension that he attempted to "claim" and "exclaim" in "Voyages IV." That "name, unspoke" suggests a catachrestic designation of the sun by which the poet could figure himself and thereby appropriate the power of that star that sinks, as Milton noted in "Lycidas,"

> . . . in the ocean bed,
> And yet anon repairs his drooping head,
> And tricks his beams, and with new-spangled ore,
> Flames in the forehead of the morning sky.

Though Crane fears that this "name, unspoke" may be one that he "cannot claim," he refuses to allow that his "waiting" may be futile, for he knows, with Whitman, "how quick the sunrise would kill me,/ If I could not now and always send sun-rise out of me" (*Song of Myself*). Arrogating to himself, therefore, a solar incandescence he demands of the ocean "churning" around him:

> . . . let thy waves rear
> More savage than the death of kings,
> Some splintered garland for the seer.

The sea itself, with its rearing waves, becomes a chariot for Crane, recalling the Miltonic image of the sun as a solar car. "Afire" in this chariot, Crane appropriates the imaginative powers of the past in a daring gesture that clearly evokes the "savage" encounter with paternal authority when Oedipus, at the crossroads, confronted Laius in his chariot. The usurpation of power implicit in the "death" of that king informs the Shakespearean context from which Crane takes this phrase; for it is King Richard, in *Richard II*, who cries out against the rebelliousness of Bolingbroke: "For God's sake let us sit upon the ground/ And tell sad stories of the death of kings" (III, ii).

Crane, in his attempt to undo his diminution, calls forth a power even "more savage" than such figures of transgressive revision as the Oedipal and Shakespearean images of the "death of kings." He undertakes, in a sense, to refigure the very figurations of transgression; and that refiguration entails the shift to a "more savage" poetics, a poetics that will gain the poet a "splintered garland" and make him a "seer" in his "blindness."

While that "splintered garland" echoes Shelley's revision of Milton in "Adonais"—"Their garlands sere, their magic mantles rent"—it serves also to encapsulate imagistically the rhetorical movements of Crane's poetry. In its circular enclosure the garland suggests the autonomy of chiasmus, while in the fracture that leaves it "splintered" it points toward disjunctive anacoluthon. The strung petals that form this garland can be "splintered" only if that word takes on an extended meaning—a meaning neither wholly literal, since flowers cannot splinter, nor wholly figurative, since the "splinters" or thorns of flowers participate in the literality of the "garland." What Crane has strung on his garland, then, are the tropological flowers of his rhetoric, which he invokes as both compensation and reward for his assertion of imaginative autonomy. Indeed, the full extent of that gesture reveals itself only when the "splintered garland" is understood not merely, as R. W. B. Lewis asserts, as "the conventional symbol of poetic genius and achievement," but simultaneously as a garland of splinters, which is to say, a crown of thorns. By this image Crane reclaims, supremely, the figuration of the phoenix for himself. The theological allusion reinforces his practice of poetic renewal achieved by means of splintering, breaking, or violation.

Just as he would be crowned in a fashion that evokes not the "death of kings," but the death of the King of Kings, so Crane would also claim for himself the status of a seer. And what he foresees is, precisely, a new covenant with poetry, a poetics that will be "more savage" not merely, as Lewis suggests, in its "poetic theme," but also in its rhetorical practice. The "more savage" his poetics, the "stranger" his poetry; and the "stranger" his poetry is, the more original it will be. Only by thus revising the Oedipal figurations of transgression can Crane hope to salvage his poetic enterprise and earn the "name, unspoke," that places the poet at the center of presence, like the sun. But to attain such a poetic eminence, to effect this new covenant with literary history, Crane must negotiate between his desire for the security of chiastic designs and his ability to introduce a negativity so powerful that no construction can bridge its gap. His inability to conduct a safe passage between these dangers becomes evident in the following stanzas, as he calls forth the poetic promised land that his new covenant would make possible:

> Beyond siroccos harvesting
> The solstice thunders, crept away,
> Like a cliff swinging or a sail
> Flung into April's inmost day—
>
> Creation's blithe and petalled word
> To the lounged goddess when she rose
> Conceding dialogue with eyes
> That smile unsearchable repose—

> Still fervid covenant, Belle Isle,
> —Unfolded, floating dais before
> Which rainbows twine continual hair—
> Belle Isle, white echo of the oar!

The syntactical dislocations of these lines show clearly that anacoluthon has not been supplanted. The poet has yet to go "beyond" it, and his poetry here seems to be "swinging" between catachrestic bridgings and violent breakings. Convoluted as it is—and convolution in Crane's poetry serves always as a token of evasion, of an attempt to escape rhetorical constraint—the syntax of these lines can be reconstructed to disclose a discursive logic. R. W. B. Lewis proposes the outline of such a reading when he writes, "I take 'creation's word' to be the subject of 'crept away' ". This persuasive suggestion must lead, however, not to the cele-bratory interpretation of "Voyages VI" that Lewis goes on to offer, but to a recognition that the poet, despite his evasions and denials, can no longer "claim" the "petalled word."

That "word," of course, "blithe and petalled," makes explicit the connection in Crane's poetry between creative originality and flowers of language or tropes. The mastery of figuration, the ability to reinterpret literality and anterior figures alike, provides the poet his only protection against the necessity of reduction. In "Voyages II" Crane wielded that authority to translate the sea into a text that bore his own "superscrip-tion"; in "Voyages III" he made use of it to "shed" the "death" of dismemberment for the "silken skilled transmemberment of song." Here, though, he implies a loss of that ability to master figuration—a loss that his "savage" and evasive syntax desperately attempts to conceal. The catachrestic aspirations of "Like a cliff swinging or a sail/ Flung into April's inmost day" are defeated by the void into which they are cast. These catachrestic ploys fail because figuration, as Crane knows, inhabits the realm of the "lounged goddess." Whether that goddess, rising from her creative, and procreative bed, is Aphrodite, as Sherman Paul suggests, or Eos, as Lewis and others argue, tropological energy is inextricably bound up with the agencies of eros. Crane, in his willful blindness, his strategy of negation, would evade the knowledge that with the loss of eros he has lost the energy of figuration as well.

But if blindness figures castration—and thus the most radical dis-junction from eros—what Crane has willfully sought to blind himself to is, precisely, the fact that he has already *been blinded*. The "petalled word" has "crept away" to the erotic "lounged goddess" enabling her to be figured as "conceding dialogue with eyes" and leaving the poet bereft of "creation's . . . word," bereft of "dialogue," bereft of eros, and thus blinded or left without "eyes."

Though the catachrestic arc—which the poet hoped to prefigure in the "splintered garland" that would signify a new poetic covenant—appears once again in the "spectrum" of the "smile," that smile "reposes" no longer with the poet but with the erotically potent goddess. The image of the goddess "conceding dialogue with eyes" may seem, at first, problematic. In what sense does she concede dialogue? Surely the phrase implies, primarily, that "dialogue," the "response to counterresponse" characteristic of chiasmus, derives from the "lounged goddess herself, and represents a gift, a concession of rhetorical energy. The poet cannot radiate, solipsistically, his own poetic power, but must receive it as the creative endowment of eros. This recognition of his poetic limitation constitutes, on Crane's part, a deep concession—a concession to which he dare not admit. So he reverses the formulation and projects that gesture of concession onto the goddess herself in an effort to maintain the fiction of his own rhetorical autonomy. If the goddess, then, controls "creation's . . . word," she "concedes" or grants "dialogue" only by means of a concession that implies the acknowledgement of defeat. But Crane knows that when the goddess concedes "dialogue with eyes/ That smile unsearchable repose" she can afford to concede "dialogue" because she points beyond "dialogue" to the "smile" or "pledge" of catachrestic extension.

Crane, in consequence, can only persist in denying that the new covenant remains "beyond" him, even though the language in which he couches that denial indicates a return to the cycles of reduction and enclosure:

> Still fervid covenant, Belle Isle,
> —Unfolding floating dais before
> Which rainbows twine continual hair—
> Belle Isle, white echo of the oar!

Crane conjures here "Belle Isle," a geographic embodiment of the "covenant" that, despite his imprisonment in "icy dungeons," remains, he would assert, "still fervid." But the stanza itself embodies a lexical chiasmus in which the "still fervid covenant" that describes Belle Isle in the first line is parallel to, and exchanges position with, the fourth line's "white echo of the oar":

Still fervid covenant _____ Belle Isle

Belle Isle _____ white echo of the oar

The "covenant" that Crane effects, then, merely reinscribes chiasmus and anacoluthon into the poem in a gesture of retrenchment. For not only does the stanza as a whole hang suspended syntactically from the previous structures of meaning, but through its chiastic reversal the stanza redefines "covenant" in terms of Crane's persistent image of "whitening." Though it echoes the conclusion of "Voyages IV"—"The secret oar and petals of all love"—"white echo of the oar" manifests itself as an "echo" that is "white." The sexual freighting of the earlier figure undergoes reduction here, for this "white echo" exposes the rhetorical substructure that under-lies even figures of erotic connection. Draining the pathos from the earlier figure, this "white echo of the oar" defines Crane's "still fervid covenant" as "still" constrained by a powerful negativity.

Significantly, just as the first and fourth lines enact a lexical reversal with respect to each other, so, too, do they participate as units that enclose the conceptual chiasmus of the stanza as a whole. For while the outer lines name Belle Isle through appositives, the inner lines de-scribe its actual appearance as envisioned by the poet as prophet or "seer." These lines, moreover, identify the willfulness of Crane's claim to Belle Isle by demonstrating precisely how far he remains from his goal of attaining it. Where the chiastic scheme of Crane's stanza encloses and enfolds, Belle Isle itself consists of an "unfolding floating dais." Where Crane's appositives define the "covenant" as a "white echo of the oar"—as a covenant drained simultaneously of eros and color both—the true "covenant" is signalled by arching "rainbows" that "twine continual hair," a sexual image that calls to mind the lost "argosy" of the lover's "bright hair." The true covenant, then, entails erotic extension beyond the bendings of inversion or the breakings of reduction.

Crane can only claim here what lies beyond his reach. In his diminished state where "creation's blithe and petalled word" has "crept away" to the goddess of the eros he has lost, Crane cannot engage in the catachrestic movement that he will invoke, in the final section of *The Bridge*, as: "Unspeakable Thou Bridge to Thee, O Love." Because that "unspeakable" word remains "unspoke," the poet cannot go beyond mere "waiting." Unable to undertake the "unfolding" of the catachrestic word, he can only strive, at the conclusion of "Voyages," to hold on to whatever stability he can:

> The imaged Word it is, that holds
> Hushed willows anchored in its glow.
> It is the unbetrayable reply
> Whose accent no farewell can know.

In the guise of advancing boldly toward Belle Isle here, Crane is looking anxiously backward, unable to bid farewell to the chiastic phase of his poetic process. The "imaged Word" connotes the reciprocity of image and text in a Renaissance emblem, an enclosed and stable field of meaning in which both extremes bend inward. Upsetting the balance of that gesture, however, Crane, in this final stanza holds fast the "image" and hushes the "Word," as if "Love," if not unspeakable, were too painful to be spoken.

Like any of Crane's spatializing figures, this "image" seeks to stabilize and thus to "anchor." It "holds/ Hushed willows anchored in its glow" by enclosing them in a muffling light like that of the "moonlight" in "Voyages V"—a light no "word" could "strangle." Instead of the "perfect cry" that Crane proposed at the conclusion of "Legend," he offers in this final stanza a disconcerting "image" of silence. The "glow" or aura that anchors these willows virtually holds them captive. Insofar as they are "hushed" they seem to be suppressed, rebuked, or silenced. In "Repose of Rivers" such willows were transformed into a natural Aeolian harp as their swaying motion "carried a slow sound./ A sarabande the wind mowed on the mead." But in "Voyages VI" he seems to fear that such musical mowing will cut too deep, that it could only manifest itself as a dismemberment of song. Fearful of risking further loss, he subordinates sound to sight, giving up the aural presence of the "Word"—which has, at any rate, "crept away"—before he loses the "image" as well. Indeed, it is the "image" itself that both hushes and anchors this "Word"; it is the "glow" of the visual that interferes with the resonance of sound. The "Word" of this emblem can no longer balance the image it accompanies; and if an emblem is a sort of speaking picture, this stanza presents a picture that it will not let speak, lest the word it utters be a word of "farewell."

What Crane offers in this reading of Belle Isle, therefore, is a "reading" in the most reductive sense. His "Belle Isle" is properly described as a "white echo" because it is sound or resonance that Crane whitens or reduces here as he strives to "anchor" his poetry in an awareness of its own textuality. The "Word" in this stanza, despite the capitalization that aspires to invoke an Eliotic transcendence—is emphatically a literal, even a literary, word. Indeed, in the image of the "imaged Word," Crane figures his own rhetoricity. Making a virtue of necessity, he transforms erotic loss into a trope of poetic gain by reclaiming the power of negativity to expose the nature of poetic desire. In "Voyages IV" the poet complained as he saw his tropological flowers "stem and close in [his] own steps." Now he knows that the only way to avoid betrayal by figural language, the only way to assure that the "accent" of his poetic feet will know "no farewell," is to propose a "covenant" of figural self-consciousness:

a covenant in which his language acknowledges the limitations and illusions of poetic language. He thus embraces negativity in the hope of using it as an "anchor," a means of stability. If he has lost erotic "dialogue" he can assert the fictionality of poetic voicing and find in his rhetorical accents the one "unbetrayable reply." It alone is "unbetrayable," it alone can know "no farewell," because it alone acknowledges the absence on which poetic figuration is based. Thus the "Voyages" sequence ends with a reassertion of critical self-consciousness as Crane reads "Belle Isle," his trope of covenant, as *merely* an "imaged Word" or trope. He knows it is less an imaginative place than the place of textual imaginings and he undertakes to anchor himself in that textual space of silence and desire. The pathos of this conclusion, then, lies in Crane's need to drain figural language of pathos in order to evade the pathos of temporality and "farewell." "Voyages" thus ends with his reduction of pathos to the synchronic workings of figure, but that reduction intends his poetic survival through a strategy alert to the diachronic dimension of any figural practice. That engagement of history is central to the establishment of a "covenant" and that covenant with poetic history remains to be figured in *The Bridge*.

Chronology

1899	Harold Hart Crane, born July 21 in Garrettsville, Ohio, only child of Clarence A. Crane, a candy manufacturer, and Grace Hart.
1908	Family moves to Cleveland, Ohio.
1916	Publication of first poem, "C 33," on the fate of Oscar Wilde. Moves to New York City.
1918	Returns to Cleveland; works as newspaper reporter.
1919	Sojourn to New York City; works for *The Little Review*. Goes to Akron, Ohio, to work for his father. First homosexual relationship.
1920–21	Resides in Cleveland, and then in Washington, D.C. Is estranged from Clarence Crane.
1922	Works in advertising in Cleveland.
1923	Composition of "For the Marriage of Faustus and Helen" completed. Returns to New York City; genesis of *The Bridge*. Works in advertising.
1924	Moves to Brooklyn Heights.
1925	Finishes composition of "Voyages." Receives grant from Otto Kahn.
1926	Sojourn on Isle of Pines, where crucial portions of *The Bridge* are written. Publication of *White Buildings*, his first book.
1927	Sojourn in California.
1928	Receives legacy, and is estranged from Grace Hart Crane. Goes to France.
1929	Returns to New York City; completes *The Bridge*.
1930	Publication of *The Bridge*.
1931	Reconciliation with father in Ohio. Goes to Mexico on Guggenheim Fellowship to write epic on Montezuma. Death of Clarence Crane. Relationship with Peggy Baird.
1932	Finishes "The Broken Tower." Sails from Vera Cruz on the S. S. *Orizaba*, intending to return to New York City. Apparent suicide on April 26; the body was not recovered.
1933	Publication of *Collected Poems*, including *Key West: An Island Sheaf*.

Contributors

HAROLD BLOOM, Sterling Professor of the Humanities at Yale University, is the author of *The Anxiety of Influence, Poetry and Repression* and many other volumes of literary criticism. His forthcoming study, *Freud: Transference and Authority*, attempts a full-scale reading of all of Freud's major writings. He is the general editor of *The Chelsea House Library of Literary Criticism*.

R. P. BLACKMUR was Professor of English at Princeton University. His books include a study of Henry Adams and a complete edition of his own poems.

MARIUS BEWLEY was Professor of English at Rutgers University. His works include *The Complex Fate* and *The Eccentric Design*.

HARVEY GROSS is Professor of English at New York University. He is the author of *Sound and Form in Modern Poetry*.

ALAN TRACHTENBERG is Professor of American Studies at Yale and the author of *Brooklyn Bridge: Fact and Symbol*.

THOMAS A. VOGLER is Professor of English at the University of California, Santa Cruz, and the author of *Preludes to Vision*.

JOSEPH RIDDEL is Professor of English at the University of California, Los Angeles. His books include critical studies of Wallace Stevens and W. C. Williams.

R. W. B. LEWIS is Professor of English at Yale. His works include *The American Adam, Trials of the Word* and studies of Edith Wharton and of Hart Crane.

SHERMAN PAUL is Professor of English at the University of Iowa. He is the author of studies of Emerson, Thoreau, Charles Olson and Edmund Wilson.

JOHN T. IRWIN is Chairman of the Writing Seminars at Johns Hopkins University. Under the name of John Bricuth, he is the author of *The Heisenberg Variations*, a volume of poems. His other works include *American Hieroglyphics* and a study of Faulkner.

DONALD PEASE teaches at Dartmouth College, and has published many essays on modern poetry and poetics.

ALLEN GROSSMAN is a distinguished poet and the author of a study of W. B. Yeats. He teaches at Brandeis University.

LEE EDELMAN teaches at Tufts University and is the author of a forthcoming book on Hart Crane.

Bibliography

Andreach, Robert J. *Studies in Structure, The Stages of the Spiritual Life in Four Modern Authors*. New York: Fordham University Press, 1964.

Antoninus, Brother (William Everson). "Our Modern Sensibility." *Commonweal* 77 (Oct. 26, 1962): 111–12.

Butterfield, R. W. *The Broken Arc: A Study of Hart Crane*. Edinburgh: Oliver and Boyd, 1969.

Combs, Robert Long. *Vision of the Voyage: Hart Crane and the Psychology of Romanticism*. Memphis: Memphis State University Press, 1978.

Hanley, Alfred. *Hart Crane's Holy Vision: "White Buildings."* Pittsburgh, Pa.: Duquesne University Press, 1981.

Hazo, Samuel John. *Hart Crane, An Introduction and Interpretation*. New York: Barnes and Noble, 1963.

————. *Smithereened Apart: A Critique of Hart Crane*. Athens: Ohio University Press, 1977.

Hinton, Norman D., and Rodgers, Lise. "Hart Crane's 'The Moth that God Made Blind'." *Papers on Language and Literature* 16 (Summer 1980): 87–95.

Horton, Philip. *Hart Crane, The Life of an American Poet*. New York: Viking, 1957.

Irwin, John T. "Naming Names: Hart Crane's "Logic of Metaphor."" *The Southern Review* 11 (Spring 1975): 284–99.

Lewis, R. W. B. *The Poetry of Hart Crane: A Critical Study*. Westport, Conn.: Greenwood Press, 1978.

Liebowitz, Herbert A. *Hart Crane, An Introduction to the Poetry*. New York: Columbia University Press, 1968.

Lyon, Melvin E. *The Centrality of Hart Crane's "The Broken Tower."* Lincoln: University of Nebraska Press, 1972.

Monroe, Harriet. "A Discussion with Hart Crane." *Poetry* 29 (Oct. 1926): 34–41.

Parkinson, Thomas Francis. *Hart Crane and Yvor Winters: Their Correspondence*. Berkeley: University of California Press, 1978.

Paul, Sherman. *Hart's Bridge*. Urbana: University of Illinois Press, 1972.

Perry, Robert Louis. *The Shared Vision of Waldo Frank and Hart Crane*. Lincoln: University of Nebraska Press, 1966.

Spears, Monroe K. *Hart Crane*. Minneapolis: University of Minnesota Press, 1965.

Strier, Richard. "The Poetics of Surrender: An Exposition and Critique of New Critical Poets." *Critical Inquiry* 2 (Autumn 1975): 171–89.

Sugg, Richard P. *Hart Crane's "The Bridge": A Study of Its Life*. University: University of Alabama Press, 1976.

Trachtenberg, Alan, ed. *Hart Crane: A Collection of Critical Essays*. Englewood Cliffs, N.J.: Prentice-Hall, 1982.

Unterecker, John Eugene. *Voyager, A Life of Hart Crane*. New York: Farrar Straus and Giroux, 1969.

Uroff, Margaret Dickie. *Hart Crane, the Patterns of His Poetry*. Urbana: University of Illinois Press, 1974.

Voelcker, Hunce. *The Hart Crane Voyages*. New York: Brownstone Press, 1967.

Vogler, Thomas A. *Preludes to Vision, the Epic Venture of Blake, Wordsworth, Keats and Hart Crane*. Berkeley: University of California Press, 1971.

Weber, Brom. *Hart Crane, A Biographical and Critical Study*. New York: Bodley Press, 1948.

Winters, Yvor. "The Significance of 'The Bridge' by Hart Crane." In *In Defense of Reason*. Denver: Alan Swallow (New Directions), 1943.

Acknowledgments

Index